The
Unwritten History
of
𝔅raddock's 𝔉ield
(Pennsylvania)

PREPARED BY THE HISTORY COMMITTEE
UNDER THE EDITORSHIP OF GEO. H. LAMB, A. M.
FOR
THE CELEBRATION
OF
THE GOLDEN JUBILEE OF BRADDOCK
THE SILVER JUBILEE OF RANKIN
AND
THE ONE-HUNDRED-SEVENTY-FIFTH ANNIVERSARY OF THE
FIRST WHITE SETTLEMENT WEST OF
THE ALLEGHANIES
1917

George H. Lamb

HERITAGE BOOKS
2007

HERITAGE BOOKS
AN IMPRINT OF HERITAGE BOOKS, INC.

Books, CDs, and more—Worldwide

For our listing of thousands of titles see our website
at
www.HeritageBooks.com

A Facsimile Reprint
Published 2007 by
HERITAGE BOOKS, INC.
Publishing Division
65 East Main Street
Westminster, Maryland 21157-5026

Copyright © 1917 George H. Lamb

— Publisher's Notice —
In reprints such as this, it is often not possible to remove blemishes from the original. We feel the contents of this book warrant its reissue despite these blemishes and hope you will agree and read it with pleasure.

International Standard Book Number: 978-0-7884-1237-X

PREFACE.

Early in January, 1917, a meeting of the business men of Braddock was called to discuss the project of celebrating the fiftieth anniversary of the incorporation of the borough, which event occurred June 8, 1867. It soon developed that this year was also the twenty-fifth anniversary of the incorporation of Rankin borough. It was then suggested that as the first white settlement west of the Alleghanies was made on ground now within the borough limits of North Braddock on or about 1742, the celebration should include the one-hundred-seventy-fifth anniversary of this settlement. Accordingly it was resolved to hold a celebration in commemoration of "The Golden Jubilee of Braddock, the Silver Jubilee of Rankin, and the one-hundred-seventy-fifth anniversary of the First White Settlement West of the Alleghanies".

The celebration was at once placed in the hands of an Executive Committee, consisting of Chas. E. Dinkey, Chairman; A. P. Roderus, H. B. Miller, Dr. F. K. Whitfield, J. Knox Milligan, H. R. Hunter, L. F. Holtzman, Esq., Wm. J. Dixon, Leo. A. Katz, E. D. Nugent, F. G. Bishoff, W. H. Sullivan, W. J. McBeth.

The Finance Committee consisted of Chas. E. Dinkey, Chairman; A. P. Roderus, L. A. Katz, L. F. Holtzman, A. M. Scott, Chas. J. Carr. Other committees with their chairman in each instance were:—

Program, F. F. Slick,
Invitation, Geo. C. Watt,
Printing and Advertising, W. A. Kulp
Music, Thos. E. O'Connor
Decorations, Leo A. Katz
Parades, Wm. J. Dixon
Museum, John G. Kelly
Memorial Services, John F. Lewis
Children's Festival, Prof. F. C. Steltz
Pageant, Prof. W. E. Albig
Concessions, Geo. W. Kutscher
Information Bureau, Dr. F. K. Whitfield
Mardi Gras, Jas. L. Quinn

Firemen, E. N. Patterson
Airship Exhibition, E. H. Broden
Pioneer's Camp Fire, H. C. Shallenberger
Banquet, W. H. Sullivan
History, Geo. H. Lamb
Hospital Corps, Dr. A. W. Schooley
Awards, Hon. M. Clyde Kelly
Railroads and Transportation, Chas. B. Guttridge
Reception, H. J. Learn
Municipal Affairs, J. J. Keller
Pageant Costuming, Mrs. J. W. Hanna
Fire Works, W. H. Sharah
Sports, Thayer M. Torreyson

All the committees were well organized, and the finance committee had its work nearly completed by the middle of April. The history committee likewise had its work well in hand. At a meeting of the executive committee, together with the chairmen of some of the committees that had been doing the preliminary work for the celebration, it was resolved to postpone the celebration for one year, because the United States had been drawn into the world war. At the same meeting it was deemed best that the History committee should continue their work of preparing the Unwritten History of Braddock's Field, and should proceed to erect four historic tablets as planned.

The story of Monongahela and Braddock of Old has been told many, many times. The new Braddock has been so busy doing the big things that no one has had time to pause in the onward rush to tell of it.

This modest volume, written in commemoration of fifty years of Braddock history and twenty-five years of Rankin history, and to connect up the modern with the ancient, even back to the first white settlement on the ground a century and three quarters ago, deals chiefly with the recent life achievements of this community. The number of old residents who have helped in its compilation, and have contributed from their memory and experience to the information gathered is too numerous to receive personal mention here, but their assistance has been invaluable and will merit and receive the thanks of many who are to come after them.

A member of the history committee has been assigned to each chapter and each is responsible for what appears under his name.

The editor of this work desires to acknowledge the very valuable assistance of his associate editors, Mr. W. J. Aiken and Mr. Hugh P. Meese.

GEO. H. LAMB,
Editor-in-chief.

Braddock, Pa.
July, 1917.

TABLE OF CONTENTS.

Subject	Writer	Page
Introduction	Geo. H. Lamb	7
Early History and Pioneer Settlers of Braddock's Field	Miss Dillie Steinmetz	11
Braddock and the Coal Industry	S. R. McClure, Esq.	25
Transportation on the Monongahela	W. Espey Albig	31
The Municipalities	J. E. Little, Esq.	40
Port Perry and Turtle Creek	Wm. S. Heath	49
The Railroads	Albert Diethrich	65
Braddock Electric Railways	D. Newton Greer	73
Camp Copeland and the Civil War	Mrs. Jennie S. Lapsley	78
A Survey of Industrial Braddock and Brief History of the Edgar Thomson Steel Works	Hugh P. Meese	82
The Making of the Local American	Wm. J. Aiken, Esq.	150
The Post Office	Chas. L. Cummings	158
Braddock Newspapers and their Makers	Frederick W. Oakley	166
Churches	Rev. James Vernon Wright	180
Schools	Geo. W. Gilmore	195
Financial Institutions	E. M. Sharah	208
The Carnegie Free Library	Geo. H. Lamb	220
The Braddock General Hospital	W. T. Morgan, M. D.	230
Medical History of Braddock	S. Roy Mills, M. D.	245
Fraternal Societies	Reuben D. Abbiss, Jr.	250
Fires and Firefighters	Harry H. Kelly	274
Woman's Activities	Mrs. Samuel Hamilton	280
The Evolution of Local Business	Charles Rose	298
Conclusion	Geo. H. Lamb	311
Index		317

BRADDOCK OF LONG AGO.

INTRODUCTION.

BY GEO. H. LAMB.

Braddock's Field is one of the very important localities in American history. There are few places and few incidents that may be termed pivotal, perhaps not more than seven in the whole range of United States history. To illustrate: The settlement at Jamestown and the landing of the Pilgrims on Plymouth Rock were both pivotal, because each was the representative of a phase of civilization that was destined to wield a mighty influence for centuries, finally terminating in civil war. On the other hand, the settlement of any and all other colonies was not pivotal, because no one was representative of a distinct idea separate from the others and big enough to color all subsequent history.

Each of the pivotal events is associated with a definite place, and merely to indicate the location is to call up in memory the mighty force exerted by the incident that occurred there. Chronologically these events associated with their localities are:—Jamestown, Plymouth Rock, Braddock's Field, Lexington, Independence Hall, Saratoga, Gettysburg.

Some students of history may choose to add one or two events to this list, though it is doubtful if any other place can substantiate its claim. But no one will deny the word pivotal to each of the places named.

For present purposes interest is centered on the third of the localities mentioned, Braddock's Field. If authority were needed to demonstrate the merits of this place to such recognition it is right at hand. Parkman quotes Voltaire as saying, "Such was the complication of political interests, that a cannon-shot fired in America could give the signal that set Europe in a blaze." Parkman adds this comment. "Not quite. It was not a cannon-shot, but a volley from the hunting-pieces of a few back-woodsmen, commanded by a Virginia youth, George Washington."

Thus Voltaire makes the Battle of the Monongahela a pivotal point not of American history alone, but of world history. While Parkman sees in the battle not merely the war which ensued between France and England, known in America as the French and Indian war, but looking beyond this mighty struggle, he sees the independence of the English colonies and the upspringing of a mighty nation.

And Parkman gets the right perspective. For on that memorable July 9, 1755, the colonists made two discoveries that were destined to play a strong part in the shaping of future events. One was, that the colonial militia were not inferior in any sense, on their own ground, to the trained British soldiery. The other was that on that day they discovered their native born leader; and from that hour, George Washington was a marked man—a man of destiny, and the colonists knew it.

But the territory formerly known as Braddock's Field, now comprised in the boroughs of Braddock, North Braddock, and Rankin, has other claims to historic eminence, besides the Battle of the Monongahela, commonly called Braddock's Defeat. Here, on the banks of the Monongahela just below the mouth of Turtle Creek, stood John Frazier's cabin. Whether we consider the statement of Governor Dinwiddie, which fixes the date of the building of this cabin at 1742 or earlier, or accept a later date as some records seem to indicate, the fact is incontestible that Frazier was the first white settler anywhere in this region, west of the Alleghanies. The French made settlements at about this time on the shores of the lakes as far west as Detroit and Michilimackinac, but John Frazier was the first white man to build a cabin in the Monongahela valley.

Braddock's Field again came into prominence at the time of the Whiskey Insurrection. On Friday, August 1, 1794, there were gathered on this field men from the four western counties of Pennsylvania to the number of eight thousand. These were the men who believed that the new internal revenue tax on whiskey was aimed at their chief industry and amounted to confiscation of their property. After a demonstration of their strength in and by this assembly they returned quietly to their homes and later yielded peaceably to the government's demands.

Again, in 1825, when the Marquis de La Fayette, who had assisted the colonists in gaining their Independence, made his return visit to this country as the "Guest of the Nation," after an absence of nearly a half century, he was entertained here for one night, May 28, 1825, in the home of Mr. George Wallace. This house, later used for a young ladies' seminary, is in a good state of preservation and bids fair to stand for another century. It is now occupied by Mrs. Allen Kirkpatrick, a daughter of Mr. Geo. H. Bell, who acquired it from the Wallaces nearly eighty years ago.

During the dark days of the Rebellion, Braddock's Field was again brought into public notice by the location here of Camp Copeland, a recruiting and training station for new enlistments.

The exact location of the Battle of Monongahela has been a matter of some controversy. The site of Frazier's cabin is definitely known. The spot where Braddock's army crossed the Monongahela is likewise clear beyond the shadow of a doubt. But the controversy has raged over the question of how far up the hill side the army advanced. The

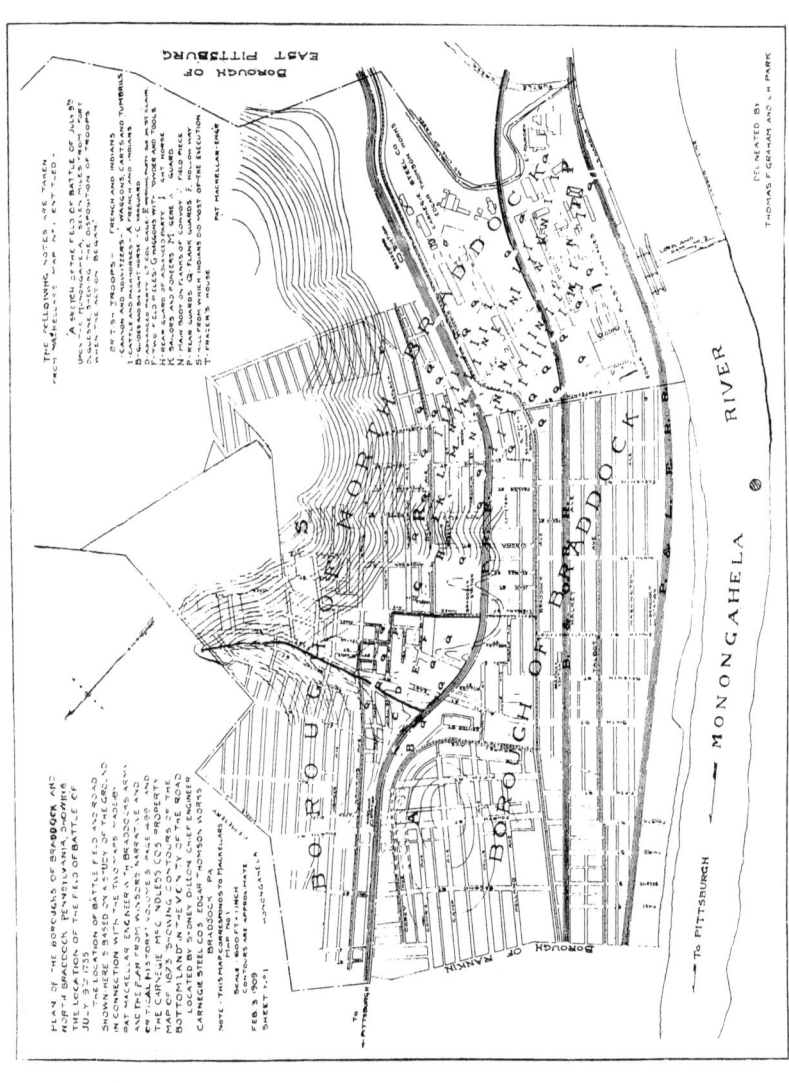

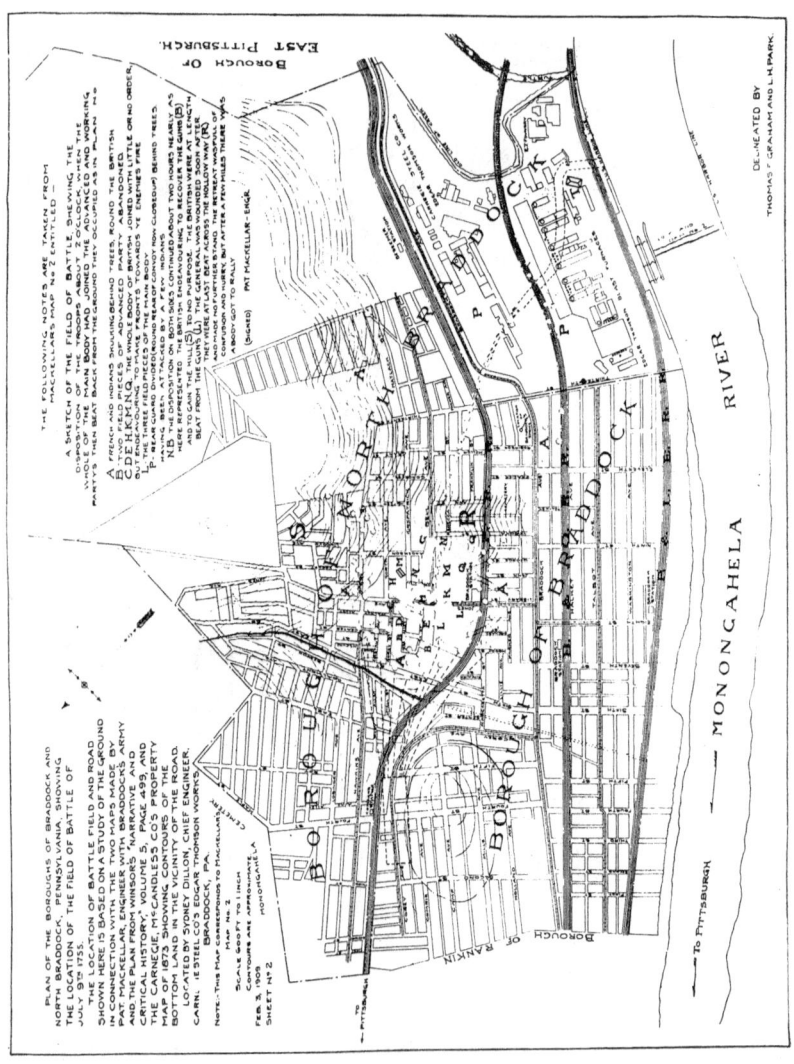

best information on the subject is to be had from two maps, or plans of the battle, made by Patrick MacKellar subsequent to the battle.

Patrick MacKellar was the engineer with Braddock's expedition. It was his business to go ahead with the axemen and lay out the route. After the battle, he was asked by General Shirley to prepare a map of the ground. He prepared two sketches, submitting them to the surviving officers of the expedition, by whom they were approved. Map No. 1, is entitled, "A sketch of the field of battle of July 9th, upon the Monongahela, seven miles from Fort Duquesne, shewing the disposition of troops when action began". The title of Map No. 2, is, "A sketch of the field of battle shewing the disposition of troops about 2 o'clock, when the whole of the mainbody had joined the advanced and working parties then beat (en) back from the ground they occupied as in plan No. 1."

Although these maps were known and used by Parkman and others, no serious attempt was ever made to reconcile them with the ground as it exists to-day until the year 1909. In that year, Mr. Sidney Dillon, then chief draftsman of the Edgar Thomson Works of the United States Steel Corporation, now chief engineer of the Carnegie Steel Company, stimulated by some special researches made by Prof. John K. Lacock, of Havard University and Prof. Henry Temple, of Washington & Jefferson College, made a composite topographic chart, laying the MacKellar maps on the maps of the present boroughs of Braddock and North Braddock. Mr. Dillon also had access to the Carnegie McCandless Company's topographic outlines which showed contours of the bottom lands as they existed before ground was broken for the erection of the great steel mills and furnaces which cover much of the site.

Mr. Dillon's maps are regarded as authoritative. They carry the action somewhat farther up the hill, and a little to the west of the position the old residents were accustomed to regard as the main theater of battle. But there is nothing in recorded history inconsistent with the Dillon location; while contours, time, and recorded references in journals and letters of the period harmonize remarkably well, even to minute detail with these maps. Especially is this true of Washington's statement that the advance line had proceeded "about six hundred perches" beyond the river when attacked. The location of Braddock's spring, where the General was given a drink as he was being carried back from the fight adds weight to the argument.

Braddock community has a modern history to be proud of, as well as colonial. Here, within the borough limits of North Braddock, are located the Edgar Thomson Steel Works, among the greatest of their kind. These works were the first of the great Carnegie works, and have always been regarded as the foundation of the Carnegie fortunes. In Rankin are the McClintick-Marshall mills which recently demonstrated to the world their importance by making and installing all the locks in the Panama canal. Not less than seventeen huge blast furnaces and many open hearth furnaces, and many plants of less importance, but which in some localities would be deemed colossal, are found here. The Braddock library is the "oldest Carnegie Library in America", and the Carnegie Club, operated under the same management, has been and is a pioneer in welfare work for mill men, and a community center for every kind of philanthropic movement. Braddock banks have no equal in communities of this size. The mercantile interests are cared for by hundreds of stores, some of them large enough and doing a business sufficient to merit the title metropolitan. The several boroughs are well churched and well schooled. There are five main trunk line railroads and six distinct trolley lines, while the Monongahela river which touches all three boroughs of the community center carries a freightage greater than that of New York City, much of which originates here.

The chapters of this book take up and elaborate these matters in detail. As its title implies, the purpose of the history committee is not so much to review what has hitherto been written, but to condense and preserve the events of recent times, bringing local history up to date.

EARLY HISTORY AND PIONEER SETTLERS OF BRADDOCK'S FIELD.

BY MISS DILLIE STEINMETZ.

In the early part of the eighteenth century the region along the Monongahela River near the junction of Turtle Creek was inhabited by Queen Alliquippa and her tribe, the Delawares. Her royal wigwam was located a short distance above the junction and here she ruled, with her tribe in complete and satisfied subjection to her authority. In 1742 John Frazier, his wife and family, came to this wilderness from the country near Philadelphia. Frazier, perceiving the junction of Turtle Creek with the river, thought it a suitable place to build a cabin, and accordingly Alliquippa not only gave him permission to build, but also gave him a grant of several hundred acres of land. From historical and traditional stories concerning Frazier, there is no doubt of the fact that he was the first white settler west of the Alleghany Mountains. The site of this cabin has long since been obliterated by the great industrial plant, the Edgar Thomson Steel Works. Governor Dinwiddie, of Virginia, in his report at the Council and House of Burgesses of Virginia under date of Feb. 14, 1754 refers to this cabin as mentioned by Washington in his report of his mission to the French constructing forts on the Ohio. Governor Dinwiddie states that Frazier had lived here upwards of twelve years. Also, Christopher Gist in his Journal says that he and Washington stayed there the night of Thursday, November 22, 1753, and again Sunday, December 30, and Monday, Dec. 31, 1753.

Washington had made a trip to Fort Le Boeuf in the winter of 1753-54 and reported that the French were contemplating building other forts. Accordingly Governor Dinwiddie was convinced that inaction on his part would lose to the English the whole of the Ohio Valley. A council was held at Alexandria, Va., on April 4, 1755, which decided to send an expedition against the French at Fort Duquesne, which was at the point where the Allegheny and Monongahela Rivers form the Ohio. General Edward Braddock who was commissioned General-in-Chief of His Majesty's forces in America, and who had arrived at Alexandria, Va., Feb. 20, 1755, was to lead the expedition, assisted by Virginia provincials under George Washington. After a long, tedious and laborious march, Braddock's troops arrived at the spot, where the town of Braddock now stands, on July 9, 1755. They were marching along towards Fort Duquesne when a heavy, sharp fire of musketry was poured in upon them from an unseen foe. The troops became panic stricken, and when Braddock was mortally

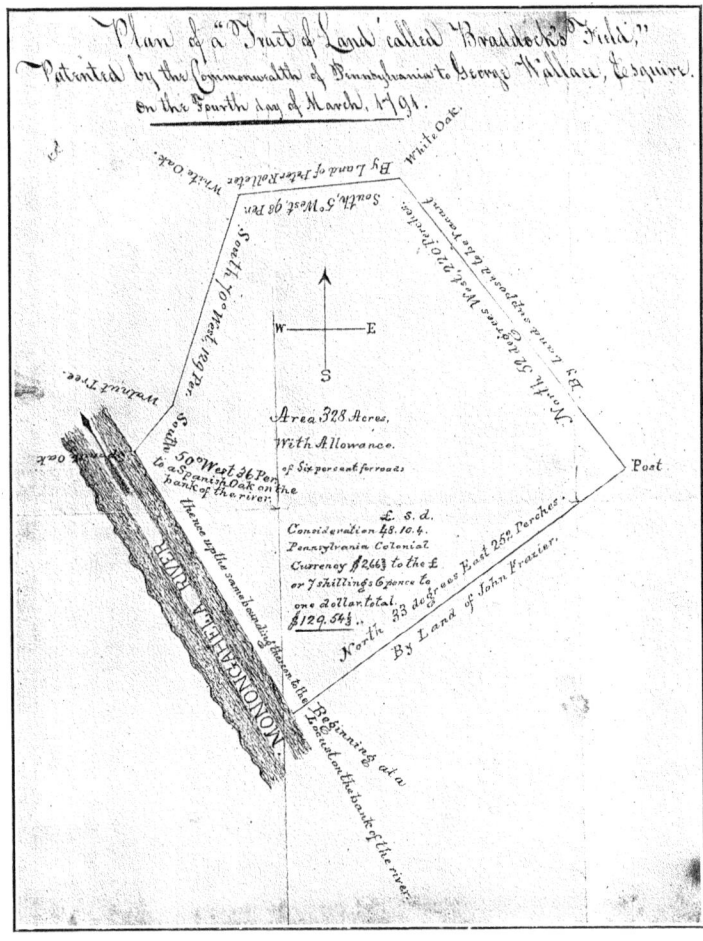

PICTURE OF PLAN GRANTED TO WALLACE.

wounded, Washington and his men covered the retreat, and carried the wounded general to a camp near the present city of Uniontown, where he died July 13, 1755. This conflict is known in history as Braddock's Defeat, and the territory where it occurred is Braddock's Field. In this conflict George Washington and his provincials were schooled in the arts of war which gave them the confidence in their prowess, that enabled them later successfully to throw off the yoke of oppression and establish a nation which is now attracting the admiration and wonder of the world.

Another time this territory figures in the history of the country was in what is known as the Whiskey Rebellion. The Scotch-Irish farmers west of the Alleghanies lacking a ready market for their surplus grain, found that they could dispose of their corn and rye, by distilling it into whiskey. In 1791, Congress, to increase the revenue, put a tax on the product, and the people refused to pay it, saying it was oppressive. The authorities decided the tax must be paid, if force had to be used, and on August 1, 1794, the insurgents met on Braddock's Field, thousands of them, distillers and their sympathizers, all ready for any act of violence. Governor Mifflin being unable to quell the rebellion, President Washington declared the national government would. He called for troops from Pennsylvania and adjoining States and soon an army, fifteen thousand strong, was marching for the mountain barrier as Braddock and Forbes had marched years before. A show of force was enough and the insurgents yielded and there was no further trouble in collecting the tax.

George Wallace, Esq., of Pittsburgh purchased a tract of 328 acres of land from Peter Rowletter, Rowletter having gotten it from Captain Edmondstone, who signed the grant in the name of King George of England, Edmondstone at that time being commandant at Fort Pitt. The records show he was the last British commandant of Fort Pitt. This tract of land called Braddock's Field was patented by the commonwealth of Pennsylvania to Wallace on the Fourth of March, 1791.

In 1804 Wallace built a country home on this grant which was known as the mansion and was occupied by Mr. Wallace and his wife. Mr. Wallace died and by the conditions of his will, at the death of his wife, the farm known as Braddock's Field was to go to his nephew, George Wallace. This said George Wallace became involved to the United States Bank, now the Bank of Pittsburgh, and the property was sold at sheriff's sale and purchased by the bank.

The farm and the Mansion were bought in 1846 by James W. Buchanan and George H. Bell, and the records show, "the said Buchanan by Articles of Agreement, between him and the said Geo. H. Bell, dated July 29, 1850, declared that he held the same for the use of himself and the said Bell, each being entitled to the undivided half thereof." The records further show that the part of Braddock's Field south of Braddock Street or the plank road was to be sold and any surplus, after meeting all balances, was to be equally divided. Of the part north of said line Bell should have the land eastwardly of the Wilkinsburg Road, or the present Jones Avenue, and Buchanan the part westwardly of said road.

George Bell, his wife, Margaret, and his family took up a residence in the Mansion about 1848, when it was relinquished by the Wallace family, and it has since remained in this family, being occupied at the present time by George Bell's daughter, Mrs. Allen Kirpatrick, a most amiable woman, and her daughter, Mrs. David F. Collingwood and family. This house is historically noted, for in it, Judge Wallace entertained, on his final visit to the United States in 1825, the loyal and true friend of the colonists, the Marquis De Lafayette.

The southerly portion of the purchase was sold in different sized plots some as large as thirty acres. John Robinson bought a plot near the present Thirteenth Street on the northern side of the plank road on which he erected a large brick house in 1851-'52, known as the "Robinson House," which was occupied by the family and was a noted hostelry during the Civil War. Other pioneers who located on this tract were Jacob Williams, Major Furlong and Matthew Lawler. Across the plank road located such sterling citizens as George Hunter; David Bradford; Neil McIntyre; Thomas Cook; Edward Sweeney; John Crum; the Boyd sisters, Jane and Mary, and Samuel McCutcheon. In this same district just east of the present Eleventh St. on the plank road, located a colony of Germans, all having come from Alsace-Lorraine, composed of the Holtzman; Winkenbaugh; Schweinberg and Walters families. Mr. Holtzman came to Braddock's Field in 1852. Later he married and on Oct. 4, 1856, the first child in the family was born, Lewis F., at the present living on Holland Avenue. He has spent his life in the town of his birth, holding many positions of trust, having been Justice of the Peace for more than a quarter of a century. He is a broad minded, liberal man taking a deep interest in everything that relates to the welfare of the community.

Mr. and Mrs. John Walters came to Braddock's Field about 1854. Mrs. Walters was known as "Granny Walters" to thousands of people of Braddock and the vicinity, and especially to the children, who knew her for her pleasing disposition and kind words. Two early settlers of worth who located near the others were Edward McCrady and wife, nee Rebecca Hamilton, known to the people of the new settlement as "Mother McCrady" for her kindness and hospitality. Their sons are the largest contracting firm in the district, known as McCrady Bros. A piece of ground on Talbot Avenue and Eleventh Street was bought by Wilkins Township, for the

VIEWS OF THE MANSION.

first school which was erected on the famous field, in 1858. From this school emanated many boys and girls who have become men and women of influence and power in the world. Adjoining the school property settled a man of gigantic stature and a unique character, W. W. McDowell, who with his two maiden sisters, Eliza and Mary, came from Green Springs, located across the Monongahela River, which was the center of activity in those days due to the coal mines developed there.

A pioneer riverman, Captain Wilson Packer, who had towed coal boats down the river for years, and whose tow boats later rendered the United States government valuable aid at the battles of Pittsburgh Landing, Memphis, and Vicksburg, built himself a fine home, on the east side of Eleventh Street along the river, in 1853. Here the family resided until the death of the parents many years later.

In the early fifties, Matthew Henning, a man whose influence for good was far reaching and invaluable in the establishing of a new community, and William Redman, a man of remarkable judgment and very retiring disposition, both of the firm of Henning & Redman, who operated the coal works at Green Springs, bought a large tract of land extending from Eleventh Street to Redman's Lane, the present Ninth Street, and from the plank road to the river. Later they divided the land at the present Tenth Street, Mr. Henning taking the eastern section and Mr. Redman the western. In the fall of 1853 Mr. Henning with his refined Christian wife moved into the new home on Eleventh Street near the river, just opposite the Packer home, where they lived until their deaths having reared a large family of intelligent, useful children.

Mr. Redman lived in a home on Ninth Street near the river, where he with his wife, who before her marriage was Ann Fawcett, raised a large family, many of whom are still among the leading citizens of Braddock. This lady will always be remembered by the people of the borough and vicinity as bright, intelligent, kind "Grandma Redman". She was only recently called to her reward at the venerable age of eighty-nine years. A member of this family, Charles, born in the Redman Homestead, June 27, 1854, is the oldest living native citizen of Braddock.

Some of the earliest settlers on this tract of land which had been converted into

CHARLES REDMAN.

THE UNWRITTEN HISTORY OF BRADDOCK'S FIELD. 17

WM. REDMAN.

MRS. ANN REDMAN.

an orchard were Zachariah Brown, his brother Allan, and sister Mrs. Dietrich, who moved to the Fields from Turtle Creek in 1857, and still reside here; Samuel Hart, a Civil War Veteran, who was always ready to tell of his service for Uncle Sam in the true spirit of loyalty. His wife and he lived to be very old people and were highly respected citizens. A neighbor of Mr. Hart was Thomas Strathern, whose name is a precious memory to many Braddock people. He lived to a great age leaving behind a large family of the second and third generations to revere his memory.

In 1852 Martin Dowling and wife and family of fifteen came to the field from Green Springs and located on Braddock Avenue, near Tenth Street. Two of his daughters, Mrs. Katherine Eaton and Mrs. Eliza Holleran are still living in the same square where their father located. Mrs.

MATTHEW HENNING.

MRS. MATTHEW HENNING.

ISAAC MILLS, SR.

MRS. ELIZABETH MILLS.

Eaton is in her seventy-ninth year and remembers clearly and speaks accurately of the early period. She says, "When we moved to Braddock's Field in '52 there were only a few houses as there were only a few people in the territory. The houses I remember were the Wallace House, the Robinson House, which had just been completed; the Billy Smith Cottage, a brick dwelling which still stands on Braddock Avenue near Thirteenth Street; the William Redman home on Ninth Street; the John Hughes home on the southeastern corner of Ninth Street and Talbot Avenue; the Thomas Fawcett home on the northeastern corner of said streets, he being Mrs. Ann Redman's father; a cottage close to the river near the Redman home, which was one of the Wallace farm houses, and was occupied by a family named Wagner; the Mills home, a small house near Eighth

JAMES McCLEARY.

MRS. JAMES McCLEARY.

THE UNWRITTEN HISTORY OF BRADDOCK'S FIELD.   19

Street on Braddock Avenue occupied by John House, who operated the brick yard, located near the site of the present water works, which was started by a man named Price in 1846; the house on Oak Street known as the Todd house, was one of the Wallace farm houses; the little fort-like house at the head of Eighth Street, where the State Bank now stands, was the lodge of the gate keeper on the Wallace farm. My father built a small four roomed house opposite the site of the St. Thomas Church. The fields were all used as farm land and the land toward Port Perry where the Edgar Thomson Steel Works now stands was a hickory grove where the children went nutting."

A man who added financial and social influence to the community was Dr. J. D. Schooley, who had for years almost the exclusive medical practice of the district. His homestead stood on Braddock Avenue just east of Ninth Street. His son Dr. A. W. Schooley succeeded his father and has had the esteem and confidence of the people of Braddock for years. Dr. Linn and Dr. Maggini were prominent physicians in the early history of Braddock. A man of strong character and decision of purpose who came to this section in the days of the stage coach and who later by thrift and economy had large holdings was John Sherwin. James Petty was also one of the oldest citizens. He was one of the first of the "forty-niners" to drive a mule team from St. Joe to Sacramento. He was an ardent Republican and manifested great interest in the politics of the section. Edward Oskin and his sons and grand sons have fixed the stamp of enterprise and thrift on the borough. James Berkey, David Antis, Charles Kelly, John Giles, Hugh and John Soles and Jacob Weber, the first shoemaker of the borough, were reliable energetic pioneers. Samuel Rothauff, who located on Talbot Avenue at the foot of Tenth Street and raised a large family whose descendants are residents of the present borough, was one of the first settlers. The father-in-law of one of his grandsons, Mr. James Hanlon, is the oldest living resident of the borough at the present time, being ninety-one years old, May 4, 1917. Peter Seewald and Conrad Speidel were substantial citizens and keen business men. A man of wonderful energy and strict integrity was Hope Hand, who came from Port Perry

JAMES HANLON.

in '63 and became one of the borough's reliable citizens.

The tract from Ninth Street to Eighth Street, and from Braddock Avenue to the river was bought by Reese and Berger. This was later occupied by such men as McVey and Walker, who started one of the first manufacturing plants in Braddock, the foundry, in 1865, which was active until about two years ago, when it was destroyed by fire; James Horton, a man of force of character; William McAdams, a man with a keen sense of right and duty and a very retiring disposition, who is still living at the advanced age of eighty-three years; T. W. Sharp, a faithful and zealous citizen, known to his fellow men as "Honest Tom"; James McCleary, who came to Braddock's Field in 1855, a sincere, conscientious man, who enjoyed the respect and confidence of all classes, and when the borough was incorporated had the honor of being its first "Squire". His only son William, familiarly known as "Duke" was born here and has spent all his life here being one of our progressive citizens. H. M. Lytle was a successful business man showing an active interest in things that related to the betterment of conditions. John Ebner, who came to Braddock in 1866 direct from Germany, was one of our first butchers and was a reliable dealer. These sterling characters had the interests of the district at heart and when it became a borough gave of their time and energy to establish it on a firm foundation.

The portion from Eighth Street to Seventh Street and from the present Pennsylvania Railroad to the river was bought by Col. Parker, who built a colonial mansion, which was a land mark for half a century or more and was razed in 1912 to give place to the new government building, which is a very artistic, substantial structure and an ornament to the district.

The plot from Seventh Street to Sixth Street and from the Pennsylvania Railroad to the river was bought by Lang and Miller. Later it was occupied by William Sarver, a stalwart man, who came here when the battle field was a farm, and helped to till the soil. He raised a large family. One son, William, who was born here Jan. 1, 1856, still lives in the borough, having lived here all his life. A settler who is a man remarkable for his vitality and progressiveness at the age of eighty-seven is Joseph Walton, who lives here with his wife a few years his junior, having come from Butler County. In a log cabin near Sixth Street on Braddock Avenue, Peter Baughman and his wife, Elizabeth, located in the early fifties and were known to people of the community as "Father and Mother Baughman."

In 1804 Steven Mills came with his family from Morristown, N. J., in the Conestoga Wagon, and located on the Troy Plantation, at what is now City Farm Station, on the Baltimore and Ohio Railroad, building a log cabin, a few hundred yards west of the present site of Carrie Blast Furnace Plant, which stood there until about eighteen years ago. While living here Mr. Mills negotiated for the purchase of the "Petersburg Plantation," the boundaries of which were approximately a line starting at the Monongahela River at a point near the present foot of Sixth Street and Corey Avenue, thence to Coalmont Street, North Braddock, thence across the hill to Hannatown and thence down through Tassey Hollow south to the river. Before the consummation of the purchase Steven Mills died, and his oldest son, Isaac, completed the deal and obtained a title to the property from the Bank of the United States later the Bank of Pittsburgh. After the purchase of this farm, Isaac Mills married Elizabeth, the daughter of Col. John Snodgrass, in 1833, and resided in a log cabin on the brow of the hill, between the present Fourth and Fifth Streets, overlooking the river. They lived in this house until 1847, when Isaac Mills Sr. began the erection of a new home near the site of the old one, which was completed in 1850, and which was the Mills Homestead until 1906, when it was purchased by the Braddock General Hospital Association, and is now the central one of a group of buildings known as the Braddock General Hospital. Isaac Mills, Sr. and his esteemed wife took an active interest in the development of Braddock and vicinity. They were interested in the industrial, religious and civic life of the community. This man was one of the sturdy pioneers who were responsible for the laying out of the town of Braddock, and the incorporation of the borough and he was honored by being its first burgess. He was a man of great physical strength, a public spirited citizen, and a man true to his convictions. His interest in the affairs of the town and the welfare of its people continued throughout his very active life to the time of his death in 1879. His large family of children have taken an active part in the borough which their parents helped to create. Isaac, Jr. filled the office of burgess, Charles was the founder of the Braddock Daily News; and Eliza was one of the instructors in the first schools of the district.

Other enterprising early residents whose achievements have added greatly to the material prosprity, social, political and moral influence of the community are: Captain Thos. Lapsley, who served in the struggle for the preservation of the Union, and his loyal wife; Jordon Fritzius, Sr., a man of strong convictions and courageous spirit; Washington McClure, one of the old timers from Green Springs, who was a good humored citizen and an old time riverman. Jonathan Shallenberger and his devoted wife were esteemed citizens; Henry his brother, is at present cashier of the State Bank of Braddock. William Gettys Holland and wife and family came to Braddock's Field in 1852 from Ohio. His son, Robert M., who married Jonathan Shallenberger's daughter, held many positions of trust in the borough, and was a man of keen judgment. William, another son, was an honest business man of the district. Mrs. Sarah Holland McCune, his daughter, has always taken an active part in the growth and contributed to the advancement of the municipality. She attended school, before there was a public school building, when it was held in the basement of the Disciple Church at the head of Eleventh Street on Braddock Avenue. She completed her education in the two roomed school built on the present site of the Carnegie School. Later she taught in the schools for many years, and many of the citizens hold as a treasure the influence of such a character as Mrs. S. E. McCune. She is still living and is a very young woman in looks and speech although in her seventy-eighth year. She came to Braddock's Field the same year Mrs. Eaton did and remembers the district at the time to be much as it has been described in this article. James A. Russell, an energetic and sagacious business man, was the leading undertaker and embalmer of the district for many years. John G. Dowler and his sons, Eli and Thomas, who came to Braddock in 1861, engaging in the lumber business, were substantial citizens and wise business men. C. C. Fawcett was a very influential and progressive citizen of Braddock for years, but a few years ago he went back to the original Fawcett farm near McKeesport to live at ease. Margaret Bell, who was a teacher in the first schools of the locality, and by her teaching and influence did much to mold the character of the later citizens, endeared herself to all the early settlers. Walter Collins and his wife have lived here many years noting the remarkable changes in the surroundings. Philip Sharah, a man far advanced in years has lived here the greater part of his life and has always been pleased to note the progress. Alexander Dempster, was a most capable and efficient business man and by his sagacity did much to promote the welfare of the district. Daniel McCain, a bridge builder by trade, came to Braddock about 1865, and reared a large, refined, cultured family who have contributed to the advancement of the section. John Benn was a large property holder and a man of power. William Fritzius, Thomas Cosgrove and Owen Sheekey were

THE UNWRITTEN HISTORY OF BRADDOCK'S FIELD.   23

progressive men who were always interested in the welfare of their fellow citizens. Mrs. B. L. Wood and her family located on a tract of land on Braddock Avenue extending east from Second Street and they became reliable citizens always ready to co-operate in any movement for advancement. Mrs. Boli came with her family from Port Perry and located on upper Second Street, where she still lives and is a very active, intelligent woman although in her eighty-eighth year. Thomas Addenbrook, a man who has always had the welfare of the community at heart, has been instrumental in bringing about many reforms that have been for the uplift of the people of the vicinity, and has for his wife the eldest daughter of Matthew Henning. She is no less interested, in the good of the people of Braddock, than her husband.

The plot east of the Wilkinsburg Road held by George Bell was later occupied by his sons-in-law Joseph Anderson and Allen Kirkpatrick, highly respected citizens. On the west side of the road J. B. Corey bought a part of the ground, held by James Buchanan, in 1865, coming from Port Perry. Here he, in his eighty-fifth year, and his venerable wife, in her eighty-third year, and his daughter Mrs. Weimer and her family live in a neat cozy house, just north of the Pennsylvania Railroad. He is a man of keenest intellect, wonderful energy, enduring perseverance, and temperate habits, and though he has passed so many mile stones these attributes are still an index to his daily record. It is interesting to note in this connection that Mr. Corey's granddaughter, Miss Elizabeth L. R. Weimer, is at present the very energetic President of the Braddock Red Cross, which is establishing an enviable record.

Many influential people located in this district and contributed a great deal in energy and suggestion to the growth and welfare of the community. Of such we mention James Stewart and George Bayard who came to Braddock's Field in 1827 and 1836 respectively, and resided here for many years witnessing many changes; John Harrison, a pioneer resident, who lived here long before the timber was cleared away; John and Alexander McCaulley, who were in and around Braddock and saw it transformed from a wilderness to a thriving city; John Kolb, Sr., who came direct from Vienna to Braddock, in 1847, with, it has been told, only twenty-five cents in his pockets when he arrived, but by thrift and economy was able to accumulate considerable and was a highly respected citizen. Mr. Kolb's two sons, Emery and Ellsworth Kolb, Braddock boys, have recently won distinction by their explorations and moving pictures of the Colorado canyon. Mrs. Barkley, known as "Black Bab", who had been a slave of Judge Wallace, and to whom he had given a tract of three acres off the west side of the Braddock Farm; but neglecting to acquire the legal papers for the dower, she eventually lost it, but continued to live in the little log house with her husband and family until her death; John Baldridge, a Westmoreland County boy, who was identified with some of the leading enterprises of the community; David Elliot, who inherited his grandfather, David Soles's, farm, and to a degree inherited his grandsire's frugality and thrift; Benjamin Braznell, a sturdy English coal miner, one of Braddock's most enterprising citizens; Rev. Lauck, who in 1865 was one of Braddock's largest property holders, and who laid out in town lots a large part of what is now North Braddock; Major R. E. Stewart, a major in the civil war, who was one of the leading attorneys of the Allegheny County bar and an upright citizen.; Philip Marks, who was a pioneer settler and a man of keen judgment and strict integrity; Abe Best, who came from Westmoreland County and served as burgess and constable in North Braddock for many years, and who is at the present time night sergeant. He is eighty years old and is said to be the oldest person in active service in the district.

On the adjoining farms to Braddock's Field farm, were the McKinneys, to the northeast; Col. William Miller on a farm to the southeast; on the south, across the river, on the hillside overlooking the Braddock Farm, the "Irish Gentleman," a noble man, Thomas J. Kenney; on the west, to the south John Adams owned a farm; descendants of Adams were later citizens of Braddock; to the west the property of Thomas Rankin, for whom Rankin Borough was named; to the north west the farms of Col. W. G. Hawkins and Robert Milligan; to the north overlooking the famous Braddock Farm that of David Soles and adjoining this the McKelvy and Kelly Farms.

GEO. H. BELL.

MRS. GEORGE H. BELL.

BRADDOCK AND THE COAL INDUSTRY.

BY S. R. McCLURE, ESQ.

The mining of coal, while for a time a chief industry of Braddock, shows at the present time little evidence of having been a principal factor in the upbuilding of the community. As compared with the large mines of the present day, the mines at Braddock were small. This was necessarily the case from the fact that the land is cut up into comparatively small sections by deep ravines, and each hill was mined by itself. The history of Braddock is somewhat related to the mines about Port Perry, but is principally concerned with the mines in the two hills included in the Borough of North Braddock, these two hills being separated by the Sixth Street ravine, or, as it is called in North Braddock, East Sixth Street.

Historians have written of Braddock in the early days before the advent of the white man among these hills, of Queen Aliquippa and other legendary characters, of Washington's visit to this district while on his famous journey from Virginia to Fort Duquesne and Lake Erie, of his stopping at Frazier's Cabin and his visit to the mythical Tonnaluka's Cave, and of the later day when Braddock's Field was marked by a few farm houses and well kept farms, while Port Perry was a thrifty village, and much more has been said of Braddock and the steel trade and the place of Braddock in the beginning of Carnegie's operations in the building of the most wonderful system of iron works the world has ever known. But little has been said of that intermediate period which marks the beginning of the coal mining industry at Braddock; the days when a visitor to Braddock might see nothing of the now familiar sights, but in the early morning hours the coal miners, with their lamps on their caps, wending their way to the pits on the hillsides.

The old coal miners of the Braddock district included many industrious, thrifty and prosperous men. Conspicuous among these are the late Benjamin S. Braznell (owner of the Braznell Block), who, beginning in the Braddock district as a coal digger, became an operator, at one time a member of the firm of A. A. Corey & Company, and later engaged in larger operations in Fayette County, Pennsylvania, and Alexander Dempster (owner of the Dempster Block), well known in this district as a coal and real estate operator. A catalogue of the successful coal miners of the

Braddock District would be a long list and would include the names of many of our respected citizens.

J. B. COREY.

The earliest coal mining in the district was in the hill east and north of Port Perry, on a tract of land then known as the Miller farm, long owned by Colonel W. L. Miller. These mines were opened about 1835 to 1840. It was here that J. B. Corey, later one of the principal operators in the Braddock district, got his first experience in coal mines and from there he began his career as a coal shipper. This was before the time of railroads in this district and the coal was floated down the river in what were called "joe boats". These boats were fifty to sixty feet in length and about sixteen feet in width and were loaded two or three feet deep with one to three thousand bushels of coal. By 1840 the boats were increased in size to seventy-five feet in length and by 1850 they had grown to one hundred seventy feet in length by twenty-five feet in width and were loaded seven feet deep and a pair of the boats would contain as much as seventy thousand bushels of coal. These boats were floated to all points down the Ohio and Mississippi Rivers, much of the coal going to New Orleans. The business was hazardous, boats being often wrecked, the market being sometimes overstocked, and the sale of the coal at a profitable price being uncertain.

At the time of the secession of the southern states, Mr. Corey was connected with a firm which included Judge Thomas Mellon. The firm had made heavy shipments of coal to New Orleans. The coal of the northern men was at that time confiscated with the result that this company was apparently ruined, having lost all its invested capital and it would require Fifty Thousand Dollars additional to pay its debts. The New Orleans agent of the firm, however, was pressed into the Rebel service and directed to look after the coal. He managed to so place the coal that when orders were issued for a boat of the confiscated coal, the coal of other companies was taken out to fill the order. This continued until Commodore Farragut and General Butler came with the Union forces and drove out the Rebel Army and not only was the coal saved, but coal had greatly advanced in price so that the firm instead of being Fifty Thousand Dollars in debt was Two Hundred Thousand Dollars to the good.

The first coal operations in Braddock are difficult to define. From the time of the earliest settlers there were various pits, as they were called, opened into the edge of the coal veins for the purpose of getting fuel for the settlers. Early in the history of the district, George Bell and J. W. Buchanan, who bought a large tract of land covering the eastern portions of Braddock and North Braddock, undertoook coal mining but made little progress. Mr. Bell attempted to open a pit in the Upper Sixth Street ravine, but a dispute arose between him and Isaac Mills (the owner of the large Mills farm, which included the westerly part of Braddock and North Braddock) as to the location of the boundary line between their farms. This dispute lasted many years in the courts and ultimately the administrators of the estates of both these men sold the right to mine the coal to J. B. Corey & Company, who operated in the hill west of Sixth Street.

The earliest operations were in the hill on the east side of the Sixth Street ravine. It is said that the pits first opened were those below the Braddock Cemetery. Thomas Fauset, an early land owner in this district, hauled coal from the mine to the river and floated it to Pittsburgh, about 1843. There were tracks constructed down the Sixth Street hollow for the operators on both sides of the ravine. In getting the coal out of the mines on the east side of the ravine dogs were used for a time. The use of dogs in mines is well known to Welsh coal miners, but apparently few people of the present day know of their use in this valley, though the old men who are familiar with the coal mines of this district remember their use in various places throughout the valley. The miner wore over his shoulder, straps made in form somewhat after the manner of shoulder braces, with a hook at the back. From this a chain was attached to the small mine car and as the miner pulled his loaded car out of the mine, the dog, trained to harness, pulled by his side, or if the miner had two dogs, one pulled at each side. The dogs used in the mines were large strong dogs and were the property of the miners who used them in their work. The dogs fought among themselves, as dogs will do, and were somewhat feared by other residents of the community, but generally they were good workers and loyal to their masters. Later, mules were purchased by the operators to move the cars in the mine and these in turn were supplanted by steam power. Joseph Taylor, grandfather of John Taylor, of Jones Avenue, is remembered as one of the earliest mine superintendents of this district.

The Robinson pit was opened at a point below the present location of the Pennsylvania Railroad at Thirteenth Street by John Robinson, more famous on account of the Robinson House, the old hotel of stage-coach days, which stood until a few years ago just above Braddock Avenue near Thirteenth Street. The Robinson pit employed only a few men. The cars were lowered by gravity to a point near the present location of the Baltimore & Ohio Railroad, from which point the men pushed them down to the river and loaded the coal on flats.

There were other small pits in the east hill. Alexander Dempster for awhile conducted a mine for the local trade. The McCauley pit for the local trade was opened about the present location of Kellar & Milliken's brick works, under that part of the hill once known as Hillside Park. Another pit, known as the McKinney pit, was opened west of that, under the old earthwork forts which were constructed during the Civil War.

The principal mine in this hill, however, was at the head of Robinson Street. It was first opened as a country pit, was operated at one time by John Giles, at another by Cheney & Baldwin, and was later operated extensively by General Felix Negley. When the Civil War broke out, General Negley left the mine to join the army and it was operated by a company in which Judge Thomas Mellon was interested. For use of the miners the operators erected about a dozen houses, the group being referred to collectively in the old days as "The Patch". These houses were constructed two stories high in front, with a one story kitchen at the rear.

BENJAMIN BRAZNELL.

About half of these houses were situated above the present location of Bessemer Station. One of them is still standing above Bell Avenue. The rest of them were located about Thirteenth Street. When these miners' houses were built, there were only about a dozen other houses in all within the present limits of North Braddock Borough. The daily output of the mine in its best days was two to three thousand bushels and was shipped to Pittsburgh by railroad; the Pennsylvania Railroad, a single track line having been constructed about 1850 from Pittsburgh as far east as Brinton. A track from the coal mine was constructed from the pit mouth down the hill along the present location of Robinson Street.

Little was done in the hill west of Sixth Street until 1865, when J. B. Corey organized a company and bought out the rights of both parties involved in the disputed property line which had long been the subject of litigation between Isaac Mills and George Bell. The company included John Baldridge, who for many years took an active part in its management and upon the dissolution of the company bought much of the land which the company had owned. This company, about 1865, opened three pits near the present location of Coalmont Street. A track was constructed down Sixth Street Hollow, and during the eighteen years through which the mining continued, coal was taken out of about two hundred fifty acres, including a large part of the Mills and Soles farms. When the market was good, from one hundred to one hundred fifty miners were employed and the output of the mine was from five thousand to eight thousand bushels daily. Mr. Corey prides himself on being the author of a sliding scale agreement under which the company made its contract with the miners in its employ and through the use of which strike troubles were greatly reduced. The work in this hill was completed by a new company organized by A. A. Corey and known as A. A. Corey & Co.

Dickson, Stewart & Company, who are known as coal operators in this valley, constructed the lime kilns on top of the east hill overlooking the Sixth Street ravine and had some coal mines about Swissvale, operated extensively under Oak Hill, near Turtle Creek, and opened the mines which were later owned and operated by the New York and Cleveland Gas Coal Company about Turtle Creek and east and north of Braddock. The Duquesne mines, commonly called Mucklerat, north of Hannatown, were long operated by the New York and Cleveland Gas Coal Company, until labor troubles became so continuous and so violent that the company was compelled to close the mine and abandon it. After it had been closed for some years, it was reopened by Mr. J. B. Corey, who entered into contract with the miners of that district under the sliding scale agreement that had been used by his company in North Braddock and the mine was then operated for several years without serious trouble.

There has continued a little mining of coal in the hills of North Braddock, taking out remnants of coal here and there, and cleaning out the old mines, until the present time. The coal miners of the early days and their children, however, as the coal mines in this district were worked out, took up other lines of business or employment and the history of coal mining in Braddock was practically ended with the closing of the Corey mine about 1883.

TRANSPORTATION ON THE MONONGAHELA.

BY W. ESPEY ALBIG.

Although the traffic on the Monongahela River from Brownsville to the Ohio had advanced from the canoe of the Indian and the Kentucky boat of the emigrant of Revolutionary times, to a water borne traffic of no mean size in passengers and miscellaneous freight, and to more than a million bushels of coal annually before the Monongahela waterway was improved by the installation of locks and dams late in 1841, yet no records remain of the constantly increasing stream of commerce passing over this route between the east and west. Here and there remains a fragment from a traveler, a ship builder or a merchant giving a glimpse of the river activity of the later years of the 18th century and the early ones of the 19th century.

The Ohio Company recognized the importance of this waterway, and early in 1754 Captain Trent on his way to the forks of the Ohio by Nemacolin's and the Redstone trails built "The Hangard" at the mouth of Redstone Creek. From April 17th, when he surrendered his works to the French and retreated in canoes up the Monongahela, this avenue became more and more important until the steam railways supplanted the slower traffic by water.

The easy navigation of this stream led that man of keen insight, General Washington, into error, when, under date of May 27th, 1754, he writes: "This morning Mr. Gist arrived from his place, where a detachment of fifty men (French) was seen yesterday......I immediately detached seventy-five men in pursuit of them, who I hope will overtake them before they get to Redstone, where their canoes lie."

These men, however, had come by Nemacolin's Trail; but the force of 500 French and 400 Indians which followed close upon the heels of Washington after his defeat of Jumonville, and captured him at Fort Necessity, came up the Monongahela from Fort Duquesne in piraguas.

The expedition of General Braddock in 1755, disastrous though it was, opened up the way from the East to the fertile lands of the Ohio Valley. Under date of May 24th, 1766, George Groghan, Deputy Indian Agent, writes from Fort Pitt: "As soon as the peace was made last year (By Colonel Bouquet) contrary to our engagements to them (the Indians) a number of our people came over the Great Mountain and settled at Redstone Creek, and upon the Monongahela, before they (the Indians) had given the country to the King, their Father."

A letter written from Winchester, Virginia, under date of April 30th, 1765, says: "The frontier inhabitants of this colony and Maryland are removing fast over the Alleghany Mountains in order to settle and live there."

This migration was augmented by Pennsylvanians, following the act passed in 1780, which provided for the gradual abolition of slavery. About this time, too, it became generally known that the Monongahela Valley was Pennsylvania territory rather than of Virginia. Kentucky was an inviting district and her charms were made patent to all. So general became migration to Kentucky that the name "Kentucky Boat" was applied to the flat used in transportation on the Monongahela at that time. Boat yards for the constructing of all manner of river craft were opened at Brownsville where the overland route from Cumberland and the east first reached communication with the western waters, and at Elizabethtown (now Elizabeth) fourteen miles from the mouth of the Monongahela River.

In 1784 a petition was presented at the September term of the Fayette County Court for a road from "Redstone Old Fort along the river side to the grist—and sawmill at the mouth of Little Redstone and to Collo. Edward Cook's," since, "the intercourse along the river is so considerable, by reason of the number of boats for passengers, which are almost constantly building in different parts along the River side." The petition was granted.

The Pennsylvania Journal, of Philadelphia, in its issue of February 13th, 1788, carried the statement that "Boats of every dimension may be had at Elizabethtown, in the course of next spring and summer...... where provisions of all kinds may be had at a very cheap rate, particularly flour, there being no less than six grist mills in the circumference of three or four miles." In its issue of August 20th in the same year the Pennsylvania Journal carried an advertisement that at "Elizabeth, town on the Monongahela" the proprietor (Stephen Bayard) "has erected a boatyard......, where timber is plenty, and four of the best Boat Builders from Philadelphia are constantly employed."

Captain John May, who gave his name to the settlement at the mouth of Limestone Creek, Kentucky, and who in 1790 was killed by the Indians while descending the Ohio, under the date of May 5th, 1788, writes in his diary: "This day was raised here (at Elizabethtown) a large shed for building boats. Almost all the Kentucky boats from the east pass this place: near two hundred have passed this spring."

The hardships entailed by this migration were enormous. During the severe winters when the Monongahela was ice bound the road leading through Brownsville to the river was lined on both sides with emigrant wagons whose occupants with difficulty prevented themselves from perishing from the cold.

The Indian ravages on the boats on the Ohio and on the settlers in the Kentucky country occurred with terrifying frequency. Possibly fifteen hundred people perished through these attacks in the seven years following the close of the Revolutionary War. Finally the boats going down from Pittsburgh formed in brigades. Denny's Military Journal, of April 19th, 1790, gives an account of one such flotilla containing sixteen "Kentucky Boats," and two keel boats. The flat boats were lashed together three abreast and kept in one line. The women and children along with the animals were placed in the middle boats, while the outside ones were defended and worked by the men. These boats were guarded on either flank by the keels. In this case the Indians did not attack, but the unwieldy craft were almost wrecked in a furious storm of wind and rain. Despite these drawbacks, however, by 1790 the Kentucky country had a population of approximately seventy-four thousand people, many of whom had come down the Monongahela.

With the opening by France of the West Indies to trade and the right of deposit secured at New Orleans from Spain, the western trade, enormously expanded, bid fair to be controlled by Pennsylvania. Pittsburgh at the mouth of the Monongahela had a commanding part of that traffic. Except for three or four months in the dry season this town was crowded with emigrants for the western country. Boat building was the chief industry of the place. Log canoes, pirogues, skiffs, bateaux, arks, Kentucky broad horns, New Orleans boats, barges, and keel boats with masts and sails—all were waiting the emigrant. The people of the Tennessee and Kentucky country brought all their supplies from Philadelphia and from Baltimore, now almost an equal commercial rival of her northern neighbor, and shipped their produce to New Orleans.

On March 31st, 1836, the "Monongahela Navigation Company" was authorized by Act of Assembly. It was to make a slack water navigation from Pittsburgh to the Virginia State line, and as much farther as Virginia would allow it to go. The capital was to be $300,000, in shares of fifty. The locks were to be four and one-half feet high. The charter was issued in 1837. The state subscribed $25,000, and later in 1840, $100,000 on condition "That all descending crafts owned by citizens of Pennsylvania, not calculated or intended to return, from any point between Millsborough and the Virginia State line, shall pass free of toll thru any lock or dam of the lower division of said improvement, until the company shall put the first dam above Brownsville in the second division under contract, and complete the same......"

The ill-starred United States Bank, now an institution of Pennsylvania, was required to subscribe for $100,000 of stock. The total subscriptions amounted to $308,100. From Pittsburgh to Brownsville was found to be fifty-five and one-half miles, and the ascent thirty-three and one-half feet; forty-one feet—a total of ninety and one-half miles, and ascent of seventy-four and one-half feet, requiring seventeen dams. Higher dams were then authorized, making four necessary below Brownsville, and three above to the State line.

Before these dams could be completed the credit of the state, which had been strained to the breaking point during the '20's and '30's for internal improvements, broke; the United States Bank collapsed, leaving unfilled its obligation of $50,000 to the Company; many of the private stockholders refused payment; the State's subscription of $100,000, being in bonds was collected at a loss; Baltimore capitalists refused aid; and, crowning all, a break developed in Dam No. 1 in 1843, which made expensive repair necessary. The whole project became a "mortification to its friends and projectors, and a nuisance to the navigation." The Legislature, however, in order to improve the financial condition of the state, directed, by Act of July 27th, 1842, repeated by Act of April 8th, 1843, sales of all its corporation stocks, including the $125,000 in this Company. This stock was bought in for $7,187.50 by a group of men—who with effective energy had on November 13th, 1844, the entire improvement repaired and completed for use to Brownsville, where connection was made with the National Road, which in turn connected at Cumberland, seventy-five miles distant, with the Baltimore and Ohio Railroad from Baltimore. Pittsburgh at last was brought within thirty hours of the Atlantic Seaboard.

Long before the Monongahela River had been improved, however, and the steamboat had driven the keel boat and the flat boat from the western waters, the feeble frontier settlements of the Monongahela Valley were preparing to utilize the commercial possibilities of the southwest. In 1800 certain farmers near Elizabeth built a schooner of two hundred and fifty tons burden, launched it in the spring of 1801, christening it the "Monongahela Farmer." Her cargo taken on at Elizabeth and Pittsburgh, consisted, among other things, of 721 barrels of flour, 500 barrels of whiskey, 4,000 deer skins, 2,000 bear skins, large quantities of hemp and flax, and firearms, ammunition and provision for the crew, which consisted of eight men. The vessel was not rigged for sailing at this time. In the instructions to the master, Mr. Jno. Walker, he is directed to "proceed without unnecessary delay to the City of New Orleans......Should the markets for flour be low at New Orleans and the vessel appear to sell to disadvantage you in that case have it in your power to sell a part of the cargo, to purchase rigging, fit out the vessel and employ hands to sail her to any of the Islands you in your Judgment and to the Best information May think best, and then make sale of the vessel and cargo."

This boat left Pittsburgh on a June rise, was attacked by the Indians, lost one man by drowning, was detained by reason of low water for three months at the Falls of the Ohio (Louisville), and for some weeks on a bar, now called Walker's bar, above Hurricane Island, reached New Orleans and with her cargo was sold profitably, although the flour was soured by being stored in the damp hold. The master contracted yellow fever, but recovered, and returned home after an absence of fourteen months; and, during the following year (1803), superintended the construction of the brig Ann Jane, 450 tons burden, loaded her with flour and whiskey, and sailed her with profit to New York by way of the rivers, the Gulf of Mexico and the Atlantic Ocean.

Thus the commerce of the Monongahela flourished until the Enterprise, 45 tons, the fourth steamboat produced on western water, was built at Brownsville in 1814. The era of steam had begun.

The Monongahela products were becoming well known. Its flour "is celebrated in foreign markets, for its superiority, and it generally sells for one dollar more per barrel in New Orleans than any other flour taken from this country to that market. The best and greatest quantity of rye whiskey is made on this river. Peach and apple brandy, cider and cider-royal are also made in great abundance."

The slack water equipment multiplied commerce enormously. It was estimated that during 1837 the loss occasioned to coal alone by the ice was at least $40,000. In October of 1838 there was approximately 750,000 bushels of coal laden on boats which had been waiting three months for a shipping stage of water.

Under date of January 1st, 1840, Thomas McFadden, wharf master of Pittsburgh, gives a statement of the number of arrivals and departures of steamboats employed regularly in the Monongahela trade: "In addition to which a number of steamboats have occasionally gone to Brownsville, &c., and a large number of flat-boats, loaded with coal, have descended the river without stopping at this port."

Steamers.	Tons.	Voyages.	
Liberty	83	21	
Franklin	34	65	
Pike	35	34	
Shannon	77	43	Tons.
Ploughman	38	58	14,196
Royal	68	29	
Excel	41	13	
Exact	61	3	

Traveler, Ranger, D. Crockett, running constantly and employed in towing flats, rafts, &c.

      686 keels and flats loaded with produce............9,482
      1,048 flats loaded with coal, brick, &c, tonnage unknown.
      Total tons 23,678

During 1845 toll was received to the amount of over $15,000 from freights and rafts, etc.; above $8,000 for passengers of whom almost twenty-three thousand were through passengers; and above $5,000 for coal, amounting to more than four and one-half millions of bushels.

This favorable showing was increased during the next year to above $20,000 for freights; to above $12,000 for passengers; of whom almost 35,000 were through passengers to or from the east; to above $10,000 for coal, amounting to more than seven and one-half millions of bushels.

Commerce continued to increase. Classified freights continued until the tolls in 1852, when the Pennsylvania Railroad reached Pittsburgh, and the B. & O. reached Wheeling, amounted to more than $30,000 annually. Coal tonnage grew steadily greater until in 1855 it reached the amazing total of almost 1,000,000 tons, and fifteen years later to twice that amount, this latter rapid increase being due in part to the building in 1856 of two locks above Brownsville, which carried the slack water navigation to within seven miles of the Virginia line. Through passenger traffic reached its climax in 1848 with a total for the year of almost forty-eight thousand souls.

To this latter traffic and classified freight the National Road contributed largely. For from the time it was thrown open to the public in the year 1818 until 1852 it was the one great highway, over which passed the bulk of trade and travel, and the mails between the East and the West. As many as twenty four-horse coaches have been counted in line at once. During the eight years before the coming of the railroads more than two hundred thousand passengers traveled over the road by way of the Monongahela; also another one hundred thousand traveled between Brownsville and Pittsburgh, and over four hundred and fifty thousand traveled part of the way between these two places. William Henry Harrison as President-elect of the United States, used this route, and his body was returned by the same route. It looked like the leading avenue of a great city rather than a road through rural districts. One man in 1848 counted 133 six-horse teams passing along the road in one day, and took no notice of as many more teams of one, two, three, four, and five horses. "It looked as if the whole earth was on the road; wagons, stages, horses, cattle, hogs, sheep, and turkeys without number." In the year 1822 six commission houses in Wheeling received approximately five thousand loads of merchandise, and paid nearly $400,000 for its transportation. About two-fifths of this passenger and freight traffic after 1844, when the slack water improvements reached Brownsville, was directed through the Monongahela.

Of the classified freight in the commerce of the Monongahela, salt occupied a large place, as immense quantities were brought from the salt works in New York. Whiskey, butter, lard, cheese, flour, oats, sand, apples, hoop poles, nails, tobacco, wool, feathers, bacon, pork, staves, brick, ginseng, and beeswax were staple articles of commerce. Pittsburgh continued to be the distributing point. The Monongahela proved to be a valuable feeder to the State canals. Of the 80,000 barrels of flour, which came down it in 1851, more than nine-tenths were reshipped eastward by the Pennsylvania canal; and other items in like manner.

Braddock's contribution to the commerce on the Monongahela began early. On June 12, 1839, Messrs. Corey and Adams, of Braddock, began quarrying stone above McKeesport for the construction of Lock and Dam Number Two, which was to have been placed at Braddock's lower riffle, but by reason of changing the height of the dams to eight feet Lock Number Two was eventually located at the head of Braddock's riffles above the mouth of Turtle Creek. This Lock was completed by Corey and Adams and opened for navigation on October 18, 1841. The tolls for the succeeding two months of that year amounted to $1,000 per month. In 1845 the tolls at this Lock amounted to almost $3,500, while in 1870 they made the amazing total of almost $82,000. In 1893, despite the growing competition of the railroads, the tolls exceeded $53,000.

The operation of the Edgar Thomson Plant of the Carnegie Steel Company increased the importance of the Monongahela's commerce to a marked extent, although the greatest tonnage was that of coal shipped to the southern markets. In the years 1844 to 1872 a little less than 400 millions of bushels was shipped from Pool Number Two. A better idea can be had of this great amount when it is remembered that in one acre of coal there is about one hundred thousand bushels.

One of the best remembered events connected with the history of the Locks in the Braddock district was the breakup of the ice pack in February, 1867. The engineer of the Navigation Company describes it as making a noise like distant thunder, and striking the dam with such force as to shake the lock walls and rattle the windows in the houses in the village of Port Perry.

Of all the workers on Lock Two, the name of one stands out clear—Michael Hart. He had been employed in its construction, and was continued as a lock tender for more than twenty-five years afterwards. He was regarded as the most active and speedy lock-tender on the River at that time. The boatmen had a maxim, "We will have a quick passage through the lock, old Mike is on watch".

It is not to be thought that the improvement of navigation in the Monongahela was secured by the harmonious co-operation of the Valley, or that its practical operation was materially helped by the shippers. "It is a remarkable fact," says the engineer, Sylvanus Lothrop, in his report to the President of the Company, January 4th, 1847, "that with so many unanswerable arguments to recommend it to, and enforce it upon, the public attention, no work in the country has ever encountered greater obstacles than this. Instead of being, as it ought to have been, fostered by our citizens, and hailed by the inhabitants of the Monongahela Valley as a blessing to themselves, it met with nothing but the most chilling regards from the one, and with either the most violent prejudice, or the most determined hostility from the other." Protests were made against the toll charges, and in 1848 the Valley was aflame with the cry that the locks should be cut down to a height of four and one-half feet so that in times of freshet the boats might float, unhindered by locks, to the Ohio. Much difficulty was encountered in securing rapidity of movement through the locks. Rival coal crews fought, in the face of definite regulations, for

THE UNWRITTEN HISTORY OF BRADDOCK'S FIELD.   39

precedence in passing through the locks. The Company early established rules, in vain. The State legislature (1851) passed special legislation to facilitate passage, and later (1864) made the penalties more severe, yet many times the locks for hours at a time were idle while the fighting crews blocked the entrance, and the prosperity-carrying Ohio "rise" receded below the boating stage.

When the Monongahela River was about to be bridged at Smithfield street in Pittsburg, it was seriously proposed that the bridge be built so low that the boats could not pass under, thus necessitating the transfer of freights, and a profitable business for longshoremen.

Out of such strife and from such humble beginnings arose the mighty traffic which now yearly sweeps down the Monongahela through locks, augmented in number and increased in size, and now owned and operated without charge to the traffic, by the United States Government. No longer does the Ohio wait upon the "rise" of her tributary from the south, but rather is the waiting reversed, until such time as the United States shall have done her "perfect work" for "the beautiful river."

THE MUNICIPALITIES.

BY J. E. LITTLE, ESQ.

The Borough of Braddock, Pa., was incorporated by the Court of Quarter Sessions of Allegheny County on the 8th day of June, 1867. The first set of officers elected comprises the names of men nearly all of whom have been prominent in local affairs for many years. The first set of officers were:—

    Burgess, Isaac Mills, Sr.

    Council, George Fritz, William Redman, Joseph McCune, William McAdams, John Harrison.

    Judge of Elections, Isaac Mills, Jr.

    Inspectors, W. S. Packer, Jesse McCune.

    Assessor, W. A. Holland.

    Auditor, James A. Russell.

    Justices of the Peace, Jas. McCleery, J. Gibson.

    Constable, Washington McClure.

The names of the men who have served the borough as burgess since its incorporation, with the length of term of each are:—

*Isaac Mills, Sr.	1867, 1868, 1869
*James Petty	1870
*George Fritzius	1871
*Samuel Motheral	1872, 1873
*Thomas J. Dowler	1874, 1875, 1876
*M. G. Corey	1877
†J. G. Dowler*	1877
*Peter Sewald	1878
*Thomas W. Sharp	1879
*John M. Frederick	1880, 1881
*Jesse P. McCune	1882
*Wm. Sherwin	1883, 1884
*Isaac Mills, Jr.	1885
*Thomas W. Sharp	1886, 1887, 1888
H. C. Shallenberger	1889, 1890
Jas. A. Russell	1891
Thos. G. Aten	1892
H. C. Shallenberger	1893, 1894, 1895, 1896
Peter F. Emmert	1897, 1898, 1899
*John Brennan	1900, 1901, 1902
*James Purcell	1903, 1904, 1905
J. E. Little	1906, 1907, 1908
*John Brennan	1909, 1910, 1911, 1912, 1913
Finley K. Whitfield	1914, 1915, 1916, 1917.

*Deceased.   †Finished term of M. G. Corey.

The borough authority in 1917 is vested in the following:—
Burgess, Dr. Finley K. Whitfield.
Borough Clerk, William P. Conway.
Superintendent of Public Works, W. H. Williams.

DR. F. K. WHITFIELD,
Burgess of Braddock.

H. B. MILLER,
Burgess, North Braddock.

A. P. RODERUS,
Burgess of Rankin.

L. F. HOLTZMAN, ESQ.
President of Braddock Council.

Health Officer, Jas. E. Wills.
Borough Solicitor, George Weil, Esq.
Council, L. F. Holtzman, Esq., President; W. S. Lowman, Wm. J. Dixon, E. D. Nugent, T. L. Howard, Jas. L. Alexander, Jas. A. Morgan, E. B. Schafer, Michael Verosky, D. M. Kier, J. W. Milligan, John Shields.
Chief of Police, Jas J. McCarthy.
Chief of Fire Department, Thos. K. Martin.

List of Burgesses of Rankin Borough from the time of its incorporation in 1892 to the present:

George A. Sloan, appointed .... June, 1892-March, 1893
Thos. M. Cain, elected .... 1 year, March, 1893-March, 1894
Fogel G. Bishoff, elected .... 3 years, March, 1894-March, 1897
Thos. B. Brown, elected .... 3 years, March, 1897-March, 1900
Lowrey H. Bishoff, elected .... 3 years, March, 1900-March, 1903
John S. Donnellan, elected .... 3 years, March, 1903-March, 1906
Peter J. Traynor, elected .... 3 years, March, 1906-March, 1909
J. Knox Milligan, elected .... 4 years, March, 1909-Jan'y, 1914
Albert P. Roderus, elected .... 4 years, Jan'y, 1914-Jan'y, 1918

The officers and Council of Rankin for 1917 are:—

Burgess, A. P. Roderus.

Borough Clerk, A. J. Argall.

Borough Engineer, U. G. Duvall.

Health Officer, Reynolds Johns.

Borough Solicitor, Jos. F. Mayhugh, Esq.

Council, J. Knox Milligan, President; C. B. Guttridge, Thos. Kane, W. C. Watkins, W. H. Johns, T. B. Brown, George Miller.

Chief of Police, Emil Mura.

Chief of Fire Department, Samuel Johns.

Burgesses of Borough of North Braddock from the time of its incorporation as a borough in 1897 to date:

Henry L. Anderson, May 24, 1897. Died, March 22, 1899.

F. K. Leighton, appointed by court and sworn in April 1, 1899. Re-elected for full term, March 4th, 1901.

A. T. Reid, March 4th, 1903.

George B. Whitfield, March 5th, 1906.

James A. McWilliams, March 2nd, 1909. Died, May 7th, 1910.

John F. McCune, appointed by court and sworn in June 6th, 1910, and served until July 7th, 1911.

William V. Hyland, President of Council, served as Acting Burgess until the appointment of A. L. Best, November 13th, 1911.

A. L. Best, served until January, 1914.

H. B. Miller, January 5th, 1914 to date.

The borough authority for the year 1917 is vested in the following:—

Burgess, H. Blair Miller.

Borough Clerk, John O. Jones (also acts as Health Officer).

THE UNWRITTEN HISTORY OF BRADDOCK'S FIELD. 43

Street Commissioner, Sheridan Newton.
Borough Engineer, George Seifers.
Borough Solicitor, Jos. F. Mayhugh, Esq.
Council, Harvey R. Hunter, President; John Phillips, Morgan Harrity, Robert S. Sadler, Dr. B. M. Bartilson, C. R. Baldridge, John Krohe, Wm. R. Aites, A. Heverly.
Chief of police, I. N. Hummell.

The three boroughs represent a large concentration of wealth in small space. It is said that one reason for the Pittsburgh desire for expansion, is the vast amount of taxable property that would be added to the city by the absorption of these and some forty other boroughs. These three boroughs have a combined valuation of nearly thirty-two million dollars, according to the 1917 duplicate, excluding the assessment on occupations, divided as follows:—

Braddock, $11,668,460.00.
North Braddock, $13,284,980.00.
Rankin, $7,074,280.00.

The number of persons (or corporations) owning real estate is:—
Braddock, 2,058.
North Braddock, 2,362.
Rankin, 622.

One person in eight owns real estate.

These figures seem to call for a word of explanation. It may be wondered why North Braddock has more assessables and greater valuation than Braddock. The answer is the same that in the final analysis is the active cause of every condition in all municipalities, that is, the physical geography of the locality. Braddock occupies the level ground between the foot hills and the river. It has the stores, the banks, the offices, in fact, is the business center, in addition to a number of industrial plants. And it is from these sources that it derives the greater part of its taxable values. North Braddock occupies the hill sides, with their summits and valleys. It is the residence section. This accounts for the number of taxables. This explanation would seem to give Braddock the wealth and North Braddock the population. So it would but for the further fact that the entire Edgar Thomson steel plant which represents about half of the valuation and pays a corresponding proportion of the tax of the upper borough, is situated entirely within the corporate limits of North Braddock.

Similar causes give to Rankin, one of the wealthiest boroughs in proportion to area to be found anywhere, its vast wealth as compared with the number of taxables. Here are located the enormous Carrie furnaces, the Rankin Wire mill, and the McClintick-Marshall plants, as well as other works of less magnitude.

All the wealth and prosperity of the community rests on the steel industry. In times of great business activity every person wanting work can easily find employment in these mills. And it has been well said that steel is the foundation of all industries. Persons who have lived here all their lives have little idea of the comparative prosperity of this region. True, times of depression have been seen and will come again. Many believe it would be well to make a systematic and persistent community effort to secure a greater diversity of industries. York, Pa., by the last census about the size of Braddock, has three times as many corporations. If half of our population depended on the textile manufactures, for instance, depression in steel would not prostrate our business life as it did in the panic of 1907.

From the foregoing, it is easily deduced that the three boroughs are one in everything except the matter of local government. This multiplicity of administrative function has been the occasion at times of more or less friction between the several sections of the community. Particularly was this manifest in the matter of railroad crossings, when, for several years the abatement of the death traps was delayed pending united action of the separate councils. The subject of sewers is another source of controversy that is perennial. North Braddock can get an outlet for her sewers only by constructing them through Braddock borough, and who is going to meet the expense? This question has been discussed for a generation, and while it is being debated, the storms of every season cause damage that would go far towards paying for the sewers.

Duplication of activity is also seen in three sets of borough buildings, three equipments of fire-fighting apparatus, and three sets of borough officers.

Physically, each and all of the boroughs may be said to be well equipped. Every street and nearly every alley in Braddock is paved. The same is true of Rankin, and North Braddock is almost as well provided. Certain sections of all three boroughs have had for years, rigid building restrictions, no frame structures being permitted in the crowded localities.

None of the boroughs has an excessive bonded debt, and the tax-rate is not particularly burdensome in any. What bonded debts there are have been contracted in payment of valuable properties, the buildings now being worth much more than the value of the outstanding bonds. In the case of Braddock, the water works alone could be sold for enough to reduce the bonded indebtedness to an insignificant amount.

Immediately prior to the Civil War, the Pittsburgh and Connellsville Railroad, which had been built from Connellsville to Port Perry, was extended through the Borough of Braddock to Pittsburgh. The right of way was given, therefor, by Isaac Mills, extending from Sixth Street to the West End of the Borough line. The railroad took possession of Halket Street from Ninth Street to Thirteenth Street, without authority from anyone. Halket at that time was the principal street of the town. For some years Ninth Street was the principal business street. Eventually business located on Braddock Avenue. The business center of the town, like the course of Empire, has moved steadily westward, along Braddock Avenue.

Since the early seventies (when the steel works were constructed), the town has steadily grown, both in population and in wealth. Most of the working forces were brought here by Captain W. R. Jones. They were young men, away from home, without family ties, and many of them recently discharged from the army, in whom, the four years in the war, had bred a spirit impatient of restraint.

With this element, and every other house on Braddock Avenue a saloon, running full blast twenty-four hours in the day, Braddock had much the aspect of a Western Mining Camp. Women seldom went on Braddock Avenue on Saturday nights. Street fighting seemed to be a favorite and universal diversion. The Borough minutes show that J. Alex Speedy was elected Chief of Police in 1880. It was also his duty to "fill, clean, and light the street lamps". He was a brave, courageous man. He attempted to stop street fighting on Braddock Avenue, and he, more than any ten men, vindicated the right of the municipality, to have the Borough free from street fighting. With fist or mace, he subdued the disorderly, and was a good rough and tumble fighter.

In the early days council met at the residences of the various members and occasionally in the school house. For many years the Burgess presided at the meetings of council.

Subsequently a municipal building was erected opposite the site of the present municipal building. One of the municipal officers chosen at the first election, was James A. Russell, Borough Auditor. So far as I know he is the only surviving member of the first set of officers elected.

In 1885 the Water Works were erected. W. H. Williams, the first engineer of the Water Works, is now the Superintendent of Public Works. The first sewers were constructed on Eighth and Ninth Streets. At the time of the incorporation of the Borough, Braddock Avenue was a plank road and was first paved with cobblestones in 1883. At that time (in 1883) L. F. Holtzman was a member of council. He has served almost continuously since in that body.

In addition to serving as member of council for many years, a great part of the time acting as president of that body, Mr. Holtzman has, during an almost coincident period, held the office of Justice of the Peace. In this capacity he has distinguished himself for his good judgment and fairness. It is so common as almost to amount to a scandal, that in many petty courts, judgment is almost invariably rendered in favor of the plaintiff, the thought seeming to lie back of the decision, that this course produces business. Not so with Squire Holtzman. He listens to a case patiently and renders judgment according to law and evidence. Indeed, in many instances he induces parties to settle the matter in dispute out of court. Again, he will, by writing a letter to the offender, secure an abatement of the evil complained of before it reaches the critical stage.

In North Braddock for many years was a man, the counterpart of Mr. Holtzman in many respects, in the person of Mr. Fred W. Edwards, or "Freddie", or "Little Fred", as he was affectionately called. Justice of the Peace and Councilman, he early became identified with county politics, serving several terms in various county offices, and recognized throughout the state as one of the forceful political leaders. Overwork in the interests of his friends cut him off in the midst of his usefulness.

Rankin, too, has had its own record of local politics. Indeed it has been said that "Rankin has more politics to the square foot than Chicago has". In Rankin's case it seems, to an outsider, to be for the pure joy of battle; for, while the courts have frequently been called upon to decide who was the duly elected councilman, or school director, or constable, no such criminal scandals and criminal prosecutions as have disgraced many cities and counties and even states, have ever been brought out in connection with Rankin elections. Men who have been active in Rankin affairs for many years for the pure love of the game are J. Knox Milligan, C. B. Guttridge, Gideon H. Jaquay, Esq., Chas. J. Carr, Esq., Jerry Lutz, A. P. Roderus, Ignatz Horr, Esq., J. S. Donnellan, Esq. The Colored Republican Club and the Italian McKinley Club, each of which votes as a unit in local affairs, add considerably to the complications at election time.

In all these boroughs, party politics is entirely overlooked, the question of alignment depending on the local problem that demands present consideration. The amusing part of it, to an onlooker, is, that the local leaders do not work together for any number of successive campaigns, and the men who are standing side by side this year may be in opposite camps at the next election.

A political factor that should be mentioned in this connection is Hon. Melville Clyde Kelly, though his activities have been State and National, rather than local. First elected to the state legislature at the age of 26 as the champion of local option, he put up a magnificent fight in that body for a losing cause. Not only did Mr. Kelly take the side of local option, but he was always found working by voice and vote, in season and out, for every legislative enactment that he believed to be right, regardless of what interests might be favored or injured; and the powers that be always found in him a force that had to be reckoned with.

The next election found Mr. Kelly contending with Hon. John Dalzell for the seat in the National Congress, which the latter had held for twenty-six years, where he was known as the champion of high tariff. Mr. Kelly was elected and to congress he carried the same fearless principles he had exhibited at Harrisburg. When the Sixty-fourth Congress was chosen, Mr. Kelly was elected to stay at home. That seemed to make no difference to him, and like the good loser that he was, by voice and pen he kept on delivering sledge hammer blows against evils and corruption wherever manifest.

In the campaign of 1916 Mr. Kelly was again candidate for congress against Hon. Wm. H. Coleman, who had defeated him in 1914. This time Mr. Kelly was elected and he is now serving his district and his Nation in the momentous events that are working out in these strenuous times of conflict.

Courtesy of JOHN J. TREVASKIS.

PORT PERRY AND TURTLE CREEK.

BY WM. S. HEATH.

INTRODUCTORY

At first glance, the reader will wonder why the history of Port Perry and Turtle Creek should be incorporated in this work, and why it in any way would be associated with the Fiftieth Anniversary of Braddock; but in the perusal of the same, one will find that a history of Braddock would be incomplete unless this chapter were included, as both Port Perry and Turtle Creek are closely allied with, and associated in, the making of Braddock; so many of the former citizens of Port Perry now being Braddock residents.

It is a strange coincidence that Mr. George H. Lamb, Chairman of the Historical Committee, would select the undersigned for this important task, I only having been a resident of this vicinity since 1898, and it naturally would seem to be the proper course to select a resident of each of these places to write the facts, or near facts, concerning their history. Yet, the selection of myself to do this work, seems not inappropriate for the following reasons:

I was born in the Monongahela Valley, this county, as was also my father, Samuel J. Heath, my grand-father, Captain Samuel Heath, and my great grand-father, Robert Heath, who was the son of Samuel Heath, who acquired two tracts of lands from the Commonwealth of Pennsylvania called "Battletown" and "The Dart". These papers I have in my possession. My great grand-father's brother, Samuel Heath, Jr., was born in Old Fort Pitt, (where the Indians had chased his father's family), on August 1st, 1773, and on the day he was twenty-one years of age, August 1st, 1794, he was with the crowd who mustered in Braddock's Field in the Whiskey Insurrection. My great great grand-fathers farm, (a portion of which we yet own), was near Monongahela City and Mingo Creek and Church, the very center of the Whiskey Rebellion.

I am indebted for much of my information in compiling these chapters, to the History of Allegheny County, as published by A. Warner & Company in 1889, and the Memoir and Recollections of J. B. Corey, our much esteemed fellow citizen, and to many kind friends, who have been unstinted in their efforts to aid me.

PORT PERRY.

Versailles Township was one of the original seven townships into which the County of Allegheny was divided and it extended from the mouth of Turtle Creek along the Northerly side of the Monongahela River up to the mouth of the Youghiogheny River and thence up the Youghiogheny River to Crawford's Run; Thence by the line of the County to the mouth of Brush Creek; thence down Turtle Creek to the mouth. The immediate cause of the division of Versailles Township was the growth of the two villages of Port Perry and Coultersville, at the opposite extremes of its territory, and in September 1869 by decree of Court, the Townships of North and South Versailles were erected out of Versailles Township. Later, viz: July 3, 1875, by decree of Court, the second precinct of South Versailles was erected into the Township of Versailles.

Port Perry is situated at the mouth of Turtle Creek in North Versailles Township on the Monongahela River. It was originally known as Pieriestown, so called after a man named Pieries who owned the land there, and laid out the first plan of lots. Colonel Miller afterwards bought the Pieries holdings and the Fritchman farm and laid out a new plan of the same place. The name was, in 1850, changed to Port Perry. I note (J. B. Corey's Memoir) that in 1840 there were eight families in the village of Pieriestown. One history states that while it is a comparatively old town, its appearance has not improved with age and truly as has been well said by George H. Lamb, Librarian at Braddock, Pa., Port Perry is a victim of prosperity. Towns usually improve with age, but Port Perry as a town has been practically obliterated by the growth of great industries as the years have gone by. In J. B. Corey's Memoir we find that his father brought his family to Port Perry on the occasion of having secured, in company with his brother, the contract to erect the lock and dam known as No. 2, for the Monongahela Navigation Company, J. K. Moorehead being president of the Company. The work on the dam was started in the year 1840. J. B. Corey was then about eight years old. At the present time he is nearly eleven times that age and in comparatively good health. I saw him on the streets of Braddock as this was being written, greeting old and new acquaintances with a vim that was surprising in one of his great age.

The location of the Town at the mouth of Turtle Creek and on the Monongahela River seems to be the natural one, and in the year 1840 Port Perry was a town composed of eight families, as above stated, and the

THE UNWRITTEN HISTORY OF BRADDOCK'S FIELD.   51

site of the present town of Braddock was covered with its original forest; and while Braddock to-day looks down upon Port Perry with irony, yet the demolition of Port Perry helped to make Braddock and vicinity.

Of the business carried on in Port Perry prior to 1840, not much can be learned but that of mining coal. One of the first coal mines was located at Port Perry, the coal being floated down the river in flat boats. Coal mines along the river began to flourish after the building of No. 2 lock and dam, and navigation was brisk, when the river was navigable. The Monongahela river was first navigated by steam in 1825, and then only when the river was high. A boat store was located in Port Perry, where they used to furnish supplies to the boats and it became a favorite Post Office for the rivermen to get their mail. Some of the packets that used to navigate the river here, were the Luzerne, Colonel Bayard, Elector, Chieftain, Elisha Bennett, Fayette, Albert Gallatin, W. J. Snowden, Elizabeth, Germania, Geneva, James G. Blaine and James F. Woodward, the fastest of all these being the Elizabeth. They were all side wheel steamers except the Snowden and it was a stern wheel boat and was too large to operate in the swift currents of high water. The boat Tom Schriver operated between Pittsburgh and West Newton on the Youghiogheny River. Transportation by way of these boats was heavy both in passengers and freight and many of the early citizens of Port Perry followed the river in one capacity or another.

A Post Office was established in Port Perry in 1850 and this was the occasion of the change in the name from Pieriestown to Port Perry. The first Postmaster was John McCloskey appointed by President Polk. He served until 1861 when John Craig, brother-in-law of George T. Miller was appointed by President Lincoln. Craig died in 1864 and John Russell, brother of James A. Russell of Braddock, was appointed to take his place. He served until 1868, and was followed by Jackson Young 1868-1885 when J. K. Wood was appointed Postmaster by Grover Cleveland. J. L. Porter was appointed by President Harrison in 1889. He served until the inauguration of President Cleveland for his second term; Mrs. C. McCue was then appointed and served until President McKinley was inaugurated in 1897 when Samuel Davidson was named Postmaster, who served until January 1902 when P. Stucki was appointed Postmaster by President Roosevelt. At his decease his daughter Mrs. M. C. Toner was made Postmistress April 20th, 1903, and is still serving her country in that capacity. P. Stucki, the father of Mrs. M. C. Toner emigrated from Switzerland to the United States in 1857 settling in Port Perry, and it is stated that for forty-one continuous years their home was never vacant at night.

The first church in Port Perry—the Methodist Episcopal, to the best information obtainable, was built about the year 1848, and seems to have had its beginning from a Sabbath School that was started by Mrs. Corey, the mother of J. B. Corey. It seems that Mrs. Corey builded better than she knew for many citizens have told me that the little brick church was the scene of all their entertainments and gatherings and helped to make Port Perry for them the garden spot of the world. The Pittsburgh and Connellsville Railroad which passes through Port Perry was opened in 1857 and at that time the road only extended to Port Perry and the trains went up around to Brinton and thence to Pittsburgh over the tracks of the Pennsylvania Railroad. The line of the Pittsburgh and Connellsville Railroad was extended from Port Perry to Pittsburgh in 1861 and was built by William J. Morrison. This road is now owned and operated by the Baltimore and Ohio Railroad Company. The Pittsburgh, McKeesport and Youghiogheny Railroad now operated by the Pittsburgh and Lake Erie Railroad was opened in 1883. The main line of the Pennsylvania Railroad is connected with the Monongahela division of the same road by a bridge across the river at Port Perry. It passes over the town from the mouth of the tunnel. This tunnel has now been done away with. The Union Railroad also by a bridge connects the Edgar Thomson Steel Works with the Duquesne and Homestead Steel Works. It is claimed and no doubt it is true that the heaviest tonnage in the world passes through Port Perry, and the encroachments of the railroads with their tracks and yards have all but annihilated the town. James A. Russell who came to Braddock in 1862 says that at that time, Port Perry was larger than Braddock, and people went from Braddock to Port Perry, to buy their groceries, etc. The McCloskey Coal Works were then located in the upper end of Port Perry and the same were operated by John McCloskey who was the father of Mrs. Timothy E. Kenney of Holland Avenue, Braddock, Pa. Col. Wm. L. Miller was the big man of Port Perry and owned the store which supplied the steamboats, and was called the boat store. George T. Miller operated the saw-mill, and at the time of the Civil War 1861-1865 Miller made about two million gun stocks at this mill. He also had extensive boat yards and used the saw-mill for that purpose, and also for reducing logs into building material. About fifty per cent of all coal boats on the Monongahela River were built in these docks. Car shops for building Railroad cars were in operation for some few years, also a pump shop for making wood pumps, for use on coal boats did a good business. A cooper shop producing barrels had an extensive trade as well as did the stone quarries on the hill side near the town. Abraham Moore, father-in-law of Thomas George, opened the first quarry for the purpose of filling in the first dam with stone.

John King operated a blacksmith shop. The lock master at No. 2 dam and locks always resided in the town of Port Perry. The first lock master was John Derrickson, who served from 1849 to 1856. The next lock master was Captain B. L. Wood, 1856 until his death in 1872, when he was succeeded by his son Charles W. Wood. During the administration of the latter the locks and dams were sold to the United States Government. C. W. Wood was succeeded by Edward Finnin a brother of John T. Finnin, note-teller in the First National Bank of Braddock, Pa. He in turn was succeeded by James A. Sweeney, and he by the present lock master Robert McGreevey. The first physicians, were Doctor Snodgrass and Doctor Oliver.

Mr. A. P. Aiken who resides in Mills Ave., Braddock, Pa. states that in the early sixties the population of Port Perry was about thirty-five hundred people. It will require a little thought on our part at the present time to believe this possible, but Mr. Aiken's word is as good as his bond and the facts of his statement were by me confirmed, from other old residents. Mr. Aiken also states that there were thirteen saloons which did a flourishing business in the town. That the mud at the upper end of the town was black, at the lower end yellow, and at Hamburg a little settlement near the border of Port Perry it was red; the color of the mud on a man's shoes denoting where he got his whiskey.

Walter R. Collins, an old resident of Port Perry, now residing in Braddock and a member of the Grand Army of The Republic, moved to Port Perry in 1867, it being the time that about fifty feet in the center of the old dam had broken out. He was employed in rebuilding the dam, under Squire Richard Harrison. They completed the work that summer and then he opened a bakery business in Port Perry, he therefore being the first baker in this community. Madge Struble was ticket agent for the Baltimore and Ohio Railroad, and as an assistant she had Wilson Marks, a man well known to many in this district. She afterwards married Wilson Marks. Mr. Marks's father Philip was employed as watchman at the old Port Perry trestle. One of Mr. Collins's friends who resided in Port Perry was Thomas J. Lewis afterwards Justice of the Peace in Braddock, and the father of Frank E. Lewis, employed in newspaper work in Braddock. The Lewis home in Port Perry was sold to the Pennsylvania Railroad Company while they were putting the tunnel through Miller's hill in order to connect with their main line in Brinton. The assistant engineer or superintendent of this work was Charles M. Schwab now of the Bethlehem Steel Company. A coping stone on the face of the tunnel slipped and crushed to death, the foreman, a Mr. Miller. His widow is still living in Braddock. Mr. Collins's father-in-law, Gilbert Stephens, and his brother Richard Stephens, were boat builders of Elizabeth, Pa. and built the boat and rowed it conveying General La Fayette from Elizabeth to Braddock, May 28th, 1825. This is the occasion on which General La Fayette stopped at the Kirkpatrick Mansion at the corner of Bell and Jones Avenues, North Braddock, Pa. Samuel L. Heath a son of Samuel Heath who was born in Fort Pitt, August 1st, 1773 was a member of the "Jefferson Guards" and helped to receive LaFayette and shook hands with him on the occasion of his visit to this part of our country.

Captain B. L. Wood, the father of Chas. W. Wood and Wm. P. Wood of Pittsburgh, and Mrs. Ada R. Preusse of 308 Holland Ave., Braddock, was superintendent of Lock No. 2, and we note a clipping from a Pittsburgh, Pa. newspaper dated Monday, August 20, 1888 at which time it seems that the Monongahela Navigation Company had refused to open the locks on Sunday for the proposed Sunday Excursion of August 19, 1888, of the County Democracy, in honor of Congressional Guests, which recalled an incident occurring at Port Perry Locks, some years ago, when the late B. L. Wood was superintendent. The rule then as in 1888 was, that the locks should be kept closed on Sunday, except for the passage of mail-boats or during a coal boat rise. Captain Wood it seems enforced the rule at lock No. 2 to the letter, and his inflexibility was so well known to captains and others employed on boats plying the river that while they might succeed in passing through Lock No. 1 at Soho, they always managed to tie up at No. 2. On the occasion referred to, the Captain of a tow boat with a tow of empty barges made a boast when passing through No. 1, that he would get through Port Perry all right. He was known as a man of determined manner, and as he had one equally determined to deal with, the Navigation officials told him it was of no use to make the attempt. The boat reached the lock early on Sunday morning and as the office was closed the captain sent word to the Superintendent that he had a tow of empties and desired to go through. A reply was sent that the lock would not be open until twelve o'clock Sunday night. The boat Captain was not to be rebuffed, and he sent word to the Superintendent that he would like to see him. When the Superintendent appeared the Captain said in his blandest manner; "Captain I have an emergency trip to-day and would like to get up the river." "You know the rule in force here." said Captain Wood. "You know too that it is one that I never violate; I cannot make any exception in your case and will not." "All right then." said the steam boat Captain, whose anger was at fever heat, "I'll make things pleasant for you during the day, if I am compelled to stay." The steam boat Captain then secured his tow of barges and ran his boat into the open lock chamber, preparatory to opening up hostilities. He directed the engineer to keep a full supply of steam and then attempted to hold another conference but failed. The Superintendent's house was located just across the street, and when the second effort failed the tow boat Captain pulled the steam whistle wide open and gave a few premonitory blasts, as a sample of the plan of warfare he had mapped out. As it was not heeded, his whistle was again turned on and then from nine o'clock Sunday morning until between twelve and one o'clock on Monday morning there was not a moment's cessation. The shrieks were varied with all the ingenuity that the steam boat man could devise, to increase the annoyance. One second there would be an ear splitting shriek, at another time a wail would be sounded that seemed to emanate from the lost ones in the lower regions. As hour after hour passed there was not the slightest show of annoyance on the part of the Superintendent, while the steam boat man raved up and down the wall anathematizing the Navigation Company and the Superintendent in particular. He sent a messenger to the city to get an order but the messenger returned with the information that the direction of the Superintendent must be obeyed. The novel contest attracted people from Braddock and vicinity and throughout the day crowds were going to and from the scene. The noise was simply terrible but the Sunday rule was not violated, and the steam-boatman swore that he had never met such a stubborn man. Some residents of Port Perry threatened to prosecute the boat Captain but the next day he looked so crestfallen that the threats were not carried into execution. We presume that there are residents in this vicinity who will recall the day.

Henry C. Shallenberger, president of the State Bank of Braddock, operated a store for W. H. Brown & Sons for about ten years, and the last year that he was there, sold about $50,000 worth of groceries, etc. He received as his salary $125 a month, and was sent by the Browns to a point above Brownsville to manage a store at that place. Mr. Shallenberger, however, after being a year at Brownsville, resigned his position, accepting a position in the First National Bank of Braddock at $70 per month, having told Mr. Harry Brown that it was worth $250 a month to have to live at the place above Brownsville.

An incident is recalled in the career of W. J. Dixon, who was born in Port Perry and is now one of the Honorable Councilmen of Braddock. During his first campaign for office they twitted him of not being a citizen, he having been born across the water. The Pennsylvania Water Company maintained a pumping station for quite a number of years with Mr. M. B. Scott as the man in charge. Mr. Scott has served in this capacity for about twenty-six years. The pumping station has been sold to the Pittsburgh & Lake Erie Railroad and they now are demolishing the same. It will soon be but a memory. Mr. Thomas George, who went to Port Perry in 1852 is still living there and is now nearly eighty-seven years of age. He is hale and hearty and his memory is keen, and his recollections of the early citizens of Port Perry are interesting and some times very amusing. Mr. George states that everybody that came to Port Perry went out rich and I immediately commenced to look for a house to rent but could not find one. Mr. George has three children living, Mrs. Elizabeth Kerr, Miles George and Mr. John George, now living at 535 Talbot Avenue, Braddock, Pa. Other well known citizens who have been connected with the history of Port Perry are the following: Jacob Mangus, who was the Captain of the steamboat, Enterprise; Thos. Moore, John Jenkner, Patrick McGreevy, George Brenneman, John Shields, now Councilman in Braddock, Patrick McLaughlin, Daniel Simms and John Simms, Sledge McMichaels, Charles Loughrey, Samuel Hart, Patrick Purcell, who was the father of the late James Purcell, a former Burgess of Braddock, Elisha Pancoast, a renowned gun maker, George Nimon, David F. Cooper, Phillip Sharah, now of San Jose, Cal., the father of William H. and Edward M. Sharah, Samuel C. Wilkinson, A. P. Aiken, Dr. Maggini, father of B. A. and Robert Maggini, and also Timothy Gallagher, who came to Port Perry, August 18, 1854, and whose daughter Mary, now the wife of Ezra Davis, lives on Hawkins Avenue, North Braddock, Pa., William Finnin, J. N. Elrod, whose widow still lives in Port Perry, William M. King, who died June 18, 1917, Patrick Cain, Matthew Melvin, whose widow Sarah, is about seventy years of age and still living there; William Fritzius, (the father of George B. Fritzius), George Fritzius, and Jordan Fritzius the father of Oliver B. Fritzius, of Homestead, Pa., and Adaline Corey, the mother of Ellis Corey, the Steel man; James Dickson, the father of William Dickson and one of the first men from Port Perry to answer President Lincoln's call for troops in 1861; James Alexander, Peter Kidd, William Franey, and M. J. Ward, proprietor of the Old Jefferson House for years, John Noey, John Loew, who was pit boss for the McCloskey Coal Co., and father of Mrs. Joseph Striebich, John A. Loew and Mrs. Joseph L. Mayer; William H. Bishoff, the father of Fogal G. and Lowery H. Bishoff, Squire Joseph McCloskey, who is a distant relative of John Mc Closkey the coal man. Squire McCloskey says that he well remembers the steamboats unloading freight at Port Perry, which among other things consisted of large hogsheads of sugar and molasses, which came direct from New Orleans. He also remembers very well the day the steamboat did the whistling in the lock as spoken of earlier in this narrative. I also note the fact that William Mayhugh, who resides in Forward Township and is the father of Joseph F. Mayhugh, the attorney at law of North Braddock, Pa., formerly lived in Ohio, and shipped lumber from Long Bottom, Meigs County, Ohio, to the McCloskey Coal Works at Port Perry.

Port Perry, does not have a saloon within its border at the present time, nor has it had one for the past two years, although it is stated that in the early days, there were quite a few saloons in and about Port Perry, and the whiskey drunk was full proof of their existence. In politics the town was Democratic, and in jest it has been said that the tally sheets were made out before the polls were closed. However, while the town has been much maligned, and the butt of many a rude jest, yet some of our staunchest citizens first saw the light of day in this place.

> Oh! Port Perry thou ancient one
> By the Riverside so bright,
> All thy great acts basely undone
> By Jacob taking Esau's right.

TURTLE CREEK.

In the first session of the Court of Quarter Sessions of Allegheny County, on December 16th, 1788, Justice George Wallace presiding, the County of Allegheny was divided into seven Townships, the most important of which was Pitt Township, and included within its confines part of the present Borough of Turtle Creek.

Pittsburgh became a City in 1816, and five years later, 1821, Pitt Township was in part decreased by the forming of Wilkins Township, taking up to Brush Creek, now called Thompson Run. The part of Turtle Creek lying on the Easterly side of Thompson Run was included in Plum Township, whcih was one of those irregularly organized Townships on the Eastern border of the County. An attempt to create Patton Township out of a portion of Plum Township was made in April 1807. In 1808 a counter petition was filed representing that the Township was only eight or ten miles long and from three to five miles in breadth. At an election held, it was reported that a division at that time was improper and unnecessary, and for nearly forty years thereafter the question was not agitated. At the March Term 1847, a petition was referred to the customary number of viewers who failed to give the matter any consideration. A second petition was filed at the June Term, representing the Township as being thirteen miles long and six miles wide, that there was not that identity of interest which should exist among the people of the same Township, and praying the Court to appoint a second commission for its division. August 26, 1848, R. E. McGowen, N. Patterson and G. W. Hawkins, were appointed for that service. A favorable report was filed November 4, 1848, and on March 4th, 1849, by a decree of court Plum Township was divided. The Southerly part of Plum Township received the name of Patton Township. History states that this part of the County was popularly known at an early period by no other name than Turtle Creek, and that its settlement occured at a comparatively early date. Between 1765 and 1785 the following were settlers in Patton Township: William McElroy, William and Robert Johnson, Christopher Striker, Joseph McClintock, who was the grand-father of John C. McClintock now living in Turtle Creek, Robert Beatty, whose descendents are still living in Patton Township, Robert Clugston and William Clugston, the Clugston Post Office being named after this family; also Sarah C. Clugston is of this same family of Clugstons, and was the wife of John C. McClintock above named. The first family is supposed to have been Mrs. Martha Myers who got one of the old patents for a tract of land called "The Widow's Dower".

In Washington's Journal of his tour of November 23, 1770, the following appears: "After settling with the Indians and the people that attended me down the river and defraying sundry expenses accruing at Pittsburg, I set off on my return home, and after dining at the Widow Mier's on Turtle Creek, reached Mr. John Stephenson in the night." This tract of land called "The Widow's Dower" took in a portion of the premises now owned by A. O. Tinstman, at present occupied by C. P. M. Tinstman and John M. Larimer. The First U. P. Church of Turtle Creek is also on a portion of the tract. The Widow Myer's house where General Washington stopped, was located at the corner of Sycamore Street and Monroeville Road on the John M. Larimer lot.

The Widow Myer's Hotel, or Tavern, as it was called in those days, was the first stage stop out of Pittsburgh. These stops were located along the road from Pittsburgh to Philadelphia at various places, presumably at about fifteen mile stations. It was customary to change the teams consisting of from four to six horses at these stations. These stages would make from four to six miles an hour, including stops. This was a little better than what the old pedestrians used to make. (The writer has heard his mother's uncle, who was in the cattle business in the early days and bought up cattle through the Western part of Pennsylvania, the Northern part of West Virginia and the Eastern part of Ohio, state that on numerous occasions they would, while looking for cattle, walk a mile in fifteen minutes, or four miles an hour. They would keep this pace up for four, five and six hours at a time.) The time consumed in journeying from Pittsburgh to Philadelphia, or vice-versa was naturally much greater than at the present, with railroad trains running from sixty to seventy miles an hour, and automobiles making the trip from Pittsburgh to Philadelphia in twelve hours.

Turtle Creek Borough is situated on the opposite side of the Creek from the Station of that name on the Pennsylvania Railroad. Turtle Creek was the terminus of a Coal Road leading up Thompson Run and this Coal Road, called the Allegheny River Railroad, now belongs to the Westinghouse interests and connects their industries with the Union Railroad. The Town itself came into existence after the construction of the Greensburg Turnpike. This was also the first Post Office in this section of the County. The Borough of Turtle Creek was incorporated in 1892 and the first meeting of Council was held September 12, 1892, the first Burgess being W. H. Semmens, the present State Senator, who was also a member and president of the first Council. The first Secretary was John A. Clugston, with the following members of Council: Charles R. Church, Peter Double, Dr. W. L. Hunter, W. J. Smith and R. G. Zischkau. The present Burgess is R. G. Reid; the present Borough Secretary is Joseph J. Schmidt, and the present members of council are W. H. Kenyon, president; A. P. McMullen, W. C. Jones, J. D. Henderson, J. M. Skelton, S. J. Black, E. A. Dias, Thos. Cole and Philip Jones. The First School Board of Turtle Creek was organized on September 16, 1892. The directors were P. W. Boli, president; John T. C. Bowman, secretary; J. C. Hunter, J. C. Miller, J. C. Mates and Harry Church. The present members of the School Board are S. M. Cunningham, president; E. R. Smith, secretary; Robert R. Patterson, M. D., H. M. Cunningham and Charles R. Trevaskis. The Principal is Prof. W. A. Rodgers. They employ thirty regular Teachers and four Special Teachers. The enrollment at this time is eleven hundred fifty-seven (1,157) pupils.

In the year 1898, the School Boards of the Boroughs of Wilmerding, Turtle Creek and East Pittsburgh organized the Union High School, having previously been instrumental in having passed in the State Legislature a special law authorizing separate districts to establish and maintain joint high schools. The School therefore was organized and started in October 1898, with an enrollment of thirty-three (33) pupils.

The first class graduated was the Class of 1901, with an enrollment of 18 pupils. In all 440 pupils have been graduated from the school to date.

During the present year, 402 different pupils have attended the school. The 1917 graduating class consisted of 42 members. This is a recognized first-class, high school maintaining two courses of study, the regular academic preparatory course and the commercial course, each of four years. The school is supported on a pro rata basis according to the number of pupils attending from each respective district. At present the enrollment includes pupils from the districts of Wilmerding, Turtle Creek and East Pittsburgh, Wall, Patton, Wilkins, Braddock, Penn, Plum, North Versailles, Trafford, Chalfant, Franklin, Westmoreland, Export Boro, and two special pupils. The school has grown so rapidly that it is compelled to work on a double schedule until the completion of the new $200,000.00 building now under construction. The faculty consists of fourteen instructors at the present including the manual training and domestic science and arts departments. The principal of the school for several years and at present is Herman W. Goodwin. The school is doing a work hardly to be over-estimated, and a notable feature is the large proportion of boys to girls going through the school to graduation. The present graduating class consists of 24 boys and 18 girls.

Among the churches are the United Presbyterian Church, organized in June 1820, by Rev. Joseph Brown. The present pastor is Rev. Frank G. Findley, with a membership of about 250; the Presbyterian Church was organized in 1867 by Rev. Dr. Wightman, with a membership of about 50. The present pastor is Rev. Grant E. Fisher, with a membership of about 450. The McMasters Methodist Episcopal Church was organized February 1872, with Rev. Dr. Slease as the first minister. The present pastor is Rev. Dr. W. C. Weaver, the membership is about 600; St. Coleman's Roman Catholic Church was organized September 1882. The first pastor was Rev. Thos. Neville. The present pastor is Rt. Rev. Monsignor W. A. Cunningham and his assistants are Rev. J. P. Shields and Rev. N. J. Vitale. They have about 550 families, representing about 3,000 members. Other churches are the First Baptist Church, present Pastor, C. W. Townsend; the Christian Church; Lutheran Church; Alpha Reformed Church and the First Methodist Protestant Church, being a split of the McMaster M. E. Church.

The population of the Borough of Turtle Creek at this time is 7,000. A large portion of the present works of the Westinghouse Electric & Manufacturing Company and the Westinghouse Machine Company are located within the limits of this Borough and most of the citizens are engaged in some capacity or other at this great plant, which at the present time employs about 25,000 people.

The Union Railroad is one of the interests of the United States Steel Corporation and runs through a portion of this town and makes connection with the Bessemer and Lake Erie Railroad.

The Banks are the First National Bank and Turtle Creek Savings & Trust Company.

The first coal shipped by rail to Pittsburgh was mined and shipped by Dickson and Stewart, from their mine called "Oak Hill Mines" located opposite the present site of the East Pittsburgh Station on the Pennsylvania Railroad. The coal was known as the finest and best gas coal in this region, and was purchased by the Philadelphia Gas Company, and was used in making artificial gas, which was in extensive use before the discovery of natural gas. Oil and gas interests are sinking quite a number of gas wells in this vicinity, but as yet have not struck the center of the gas.

The Hon. J. C. Haymaker, at present one of Judges of the Common

Pleas Court of Allegheny County, was born in Patton Township on the Simpson Farm, his mother's father's place. The farm is at present owned by Judge Haymaker. The Judge's father and mother, with their family also lived in Turtle Creek. It seems that his Honor, Judge Haymaker, loves the chase; and many are the tales told of the fun they used to have in chasing "Sly Reynard" around the hills. Squire J. C. McClintock, Stewart Tillbroke and Judge Haymaker all had fox hounds and coon-dogs and hunted over "Riche's Hill" and what is still known as the "Shades of Death". It seems their favorite mode of hunting was to take a position on the point of Riche's Hill at which location they could hear the dogs nearly all the night. Squire McClintock says they spent many a happy night at this great sport, and as an example of their prowess, Squire McClintock had fifty-six (56) coon hides tacked on both sides of his barn, the "catch" in one fall.

Duncan Hamilton, (whose daughter, Mrs. Harry Alters, lives at Monroeville) ran the old grist mill which was located on the west side of the residence of S. A Rath. There was also an old distillery located on what is now known as Sycamore Street. The stone out of this old distillery is now located in the building in the rear of Ross' Fruit Store, the date being 1755. Hugh Maxwell, an early settler in Patton Township who later resided in Turtle Creek for thirty-five or forty years, died last winter.

The Borough of Turtle Creek made rapid progress after the erection of the Works belonging to the Westinghouse Interests along the North side of the Creek in the Boroughs of East Pittsburgh and Turtle Creek. Its principal street is Penn Avenue, and is traversed by a Street Car line running from Pittsburgh, via Wilkinsburg, Ardmore, East Pittsburgh, through Turtle Creek to Trafford City. By other lines the borough has direct connection with the entire Monongahela Valley. There are also macadamized roads extending out into the Township, seven roads centering in this Town. The Greensburg Pike, now called Penn Avenue in the Borough of Turtle Creek, is a portion of the Great Lincoln Highway.

Wm. A. Bryans, who came to Turtle Creek about 1870 and has been indentified with the progress of the Borough, has in his possession three almanacs called the Pittsburgh Magazine Almanac for the years 1821, 1822 and 1823. It is time well spent to call at the Squire's Office and look over these books. He also has a page from a Squire's Docket, and we note in this docket the name of Mr. Wm. McElroy, who is the McElroy spoken of earlier in this recital.

Among those identified with the progress of Turtle Creek and ever striving for its success we find the Hon. W. H. Semmens, formerly member of the Pennsylvania State Legislature and now State Senator from that Senatorial District; Dr. W. L. Hunter, Joseph Hezlepp, John Black, Thomas McMasters, Capt. Jobe, Anthony Lewis, James Gilmore, Sr., father of the members of the Gilmore Drug Company, (Jas. Gilmore, Jr., one of the sons lives on a farm on the Greensburg Pike and still attends the United Presbyterian Church in Turtle Creek), Chas. Naylor, John Larimer, A. O. Tinstman and C. P. M. Tinstman, John C. McClintock and sons, Charles and Garfield, and daughters Flora and Sadie P., Samuel C. Wilkinson, John T. Trevaskis and his brother A. L. Trevaskis. Mrs. Gale Hunter Slick, wife of F. F. Slick, who resides at the corner of Jones and Bell Avenues, North Braddock, and her sister, Mrs. Leonora Markle Anderson, who resides in New York City, are daughters of Dr. W. L. Hunter, now deceased.

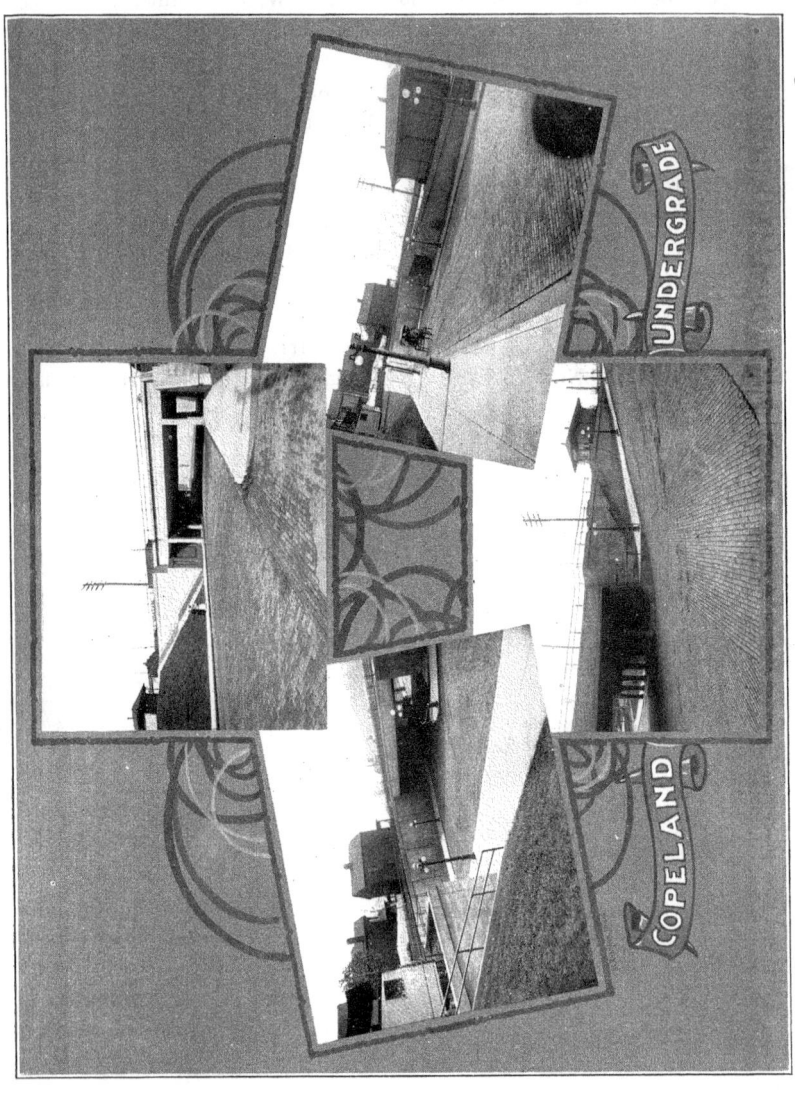

THE RAILROADS.
BY ALBERT DIETHRICH.

The transportation facilities of a community are very large factors in its growth, prosperity, and culture: and lack of such facilities results in a corresponding lack of progress. There are large sections of the United States, today, which are in a very backward state of development, largely on account of their inadequate means of communication with the rest of the world.

The history of Braddock shows the value to a community, of a situation in which ample transportation facilities are available.

One of the events in which this city took a very conspicuous part, the Whiskey Insurrection, was brought about by the lack of facilities for carrying the products of this region, of which Pittsburgh is the center, to market. The principal product was grain, and there was no means of transporting such a bulky commodity east in paying quantities, on account of the mountains, and the western route, down the river, was practically closed because a large part of the course of the Mississippi River was in control of France, not very friendly to the United States at that time. Consequently, the farmers of this section found that the easiest way to obtain the value of their corn and other grain was to convert it into whiskey, in which state a man could carry in a small container what represented a much greater bulk of grain, and receive for it a larger sum than for the corresponding amount of grain. Hence, when the Government put a tax on this whiskey, which took away the profit, the people of Western Pennsylvania arose in revolt, and Braddock's Field was the scene of the mobilization of the insurrectionary forces.

In its later history, however, Braddock has been very highly favored in its transportation facilities, and owes most of its prosperity and importance to that fact. Even if the railroads had not been developed as they were, the city was situated in a favorable location for traffic on the rivers, and canals, which in the event of the non-development of railroads, would naturally have become the chief routes of travel.

The means of transportation were very limited in the early times, and improvements did not begin till about 1805. The river was the line of communication westward, and eastward the only methods in use were by pack-horse, or by carrying on foot, which required nine or ten days for the trip from Pittsburgh to Philadelphia.

At first there were two routes to the east, the old Braddock Trail to Cumberland and Baltimore, and the route through Bedford, Chambersburg, and Harrisburg, to Philadelphia. On these roads the freight was first carried by pack-horses, but this was soon superseded by four or six horse wagons, of the type later known as "Prairie schooners", which carried a trough for feeding the horses, and in which the drivers lived while on the road. This wagon traffic lasted until 1829, when the Pennsylvania Canal was opened.

In 1805, a stage line was started, between Pittsburgh and Philadelphia, the trip requiring three days.

But freighting by wagon soon proved inadequate for the growing needs of the country, and attention was turned to canals. About 1829 the Pennsylvania Canal, connecting Pittsburgh and Philadelphia, was constructed by the state. The canal boats were built in sections, and carried over the mountains on inclined railways, which were later used, temporarily, to connect the eastern and western sections of the Pennsylvania Railroad.

But the canal was badly managed, and had not proved a successful venture financially, having failed to pay even the interest on its debt.

Just about this time, between 1813 and 1829, steam as a motive power was being developed in England, and in 1830 Stevenson succeeded in attaining a speed of thirty miles an hour with his engine. The first railroad in this country was built in 1826, but for some reason, development was not very rapid.

The Baltimore and Ohio, the first steam road in America, was also the first to attempt to enter the Monongahela and Ohio Valleys. It came as far as Cumberland in 1842, and tried to reach the Ohio through Western Pennsylvania. But the people of Philadelphia, thinking that the trade of this section, if carried on a road having its terminus in Baltimore, would be diverted to that city, placed obstacles in the way of the granting of the right of way to the Baltimore and Ohio, and thus, through sectional jealousy and lack of foresight, the road was driven to adopt the route through West Virginia, to Wheeling.

Finally, the object was accomplished by strategy. A bill for the incorporation of the Pittsburgh and Connellsville Railroad was tacked on to an omnibus bill, and passed by the Legislature while the Philadelphians were off their guard, and as this road was really a part of the Baltimore & Ohio system, its incorporation gave the latter road the opening it desired into the Pittsburgh district.

Progress on the construction of this road was so slow, however, that many of the stockholders grew impatient at the delay and invested in the Pennsylvania and Ohio, which later became the Pittsburgh, Fort Wayne and Chicago Railroad.

At this time the Philadelphia people determined to organize a road of their own, and the Pennsylvania Railroad was chartered in 1846, with a capital of $10,000,000.00, and construction was begun in 1848.

In 1852, the road was opened, though at first the inclines of the canal were used in crossing the mountains, and it was not till 1854 that the road was completed so that trains could run through on its own tracks.

The Pittsburgh end was constructed as far as Brinton, where it was delayed for some time at the point where the plank road between Braddock and Turtle Creek had to be crossed, as the crossing of a previous right of way was a more difficult matter at that time than now. This connection was made in 1852.

In 1857 the Pennsylvania Railroad bought the main line of the Pennsylvania canal, paying $7,500,000.00 for it, thus obtaining a monopoly for the railroads, of the traffic east and west.

The canals had been badly managed, and graft and engineering difficulties made them unprofitable, as over $30,000,000.00 had been expended on them and they had failed to pay the interest on their debts. Also, at this time, popular opinion was so strongly in favor of the railroads, that the value of the "Miserable ditches" was not appreciated, and the canal was sold. It has since been realized that, if the main canal between Philadelphia and Pittsburgh had been maintained and brought to a point of high efficiency, it would have tended to regulate freight charges, and prevent discrimination.

The Pittsburgh and Connellsville, or Baltimore and Ohio Railroad, was built from Connellsville as far as Port Perry, now Bessemer, in 1856, and connected by a short junction line with the Pennsylvania at Brinton, and from there Baltimore and Ohio trains ran to Pittsburgh on the tracks of the Pennsylvania. In 1860 the contract was awarded for the completion of the road to Pittsburgh, and this section was finished, so that trains could run through to Pittsburgh in 1861.

The first freight locomotive on the Baltimore & Ohio at this point was of what was known as the "Camel back" type, and is said to have been very noisy while in operation. Other engines in use in the early times were designated by names, as the "Harmer Denny", and the "George

OLD CAMEL BACK LOCOMOTIVE.

PRESENT SYSTEM TRAVEL.

Washington". Another, the Number 5, was continually getting off the track.

Some of our most famous men of affairs received their early training on these primitive railroads. J. Edgar Thomson, after whom the Edgar Thomson Steel works are named, was the first Chief Engineer, and later President, of the Pennsylvania; and Andrew Carnegie was once Superintendent of the same road.

Things were done in a much more simple manner in those days than at present. An incident which happened on one occasion shows the absence of red tape in the management at that time. While Andrew Carnegie was Superintendent, Mr. J. B. Corey, a coal operator, who still lives in Braddock, went to Mr. Carnegie and asked for some coal cars. Carnegie said "All right, they will be out there before you will". Mr. Corey said that would be impossible, as he intended going out on the next trip of the one passenger train which ran between Pittsburgh and Braddock at that time, and which was lying in the station ready to start. Then Mr. Carnegie ordered that the coal train be coupled on ahead of the passenger train, which was done, much to the displeasure of the conductor, John Routh, a famous character in the early days of railroading on the Pennsylvania, and the coal cars really reached Braddock before Mr. Corey did.

As another instance of the lax methods of the early days may be cited the means of acquiring the right of way. When the Baltimore & Ohio Railroad wanted to go through Braddock, they just laid their tracks down on Halket Avenue, one of the main streets, running the entire length of the town, without asking permission of any one, and no one seemed to object. At that time there was a good wagon road along the right bank of the Monongahela, clear to McKeesport. This road looked good to the Baltimore & Ohio, and they appropriated it also. At first only one track was laid. Later it was double-tracked, and finally the four tracks occupied all the space between the foot-hills and the river. The township then went into court and got an order compelling the railroad to build a wagon road along the hill side. In compliance with this order the railroad scratched the hill side a little, but six months after the wagon road was completed a goat couldn't walk over it without danger of falling off. After years of litigation the matter was finally adjusted, only recently, by the railroad's paying into the township treasury a definite sum.

From these comparatively simple beginnings the Pennsylvania and Baltimore and Ohio Railroads have developed to the great institutions which they are today.

In 1883, the Pittsburgh, McKeesport and Youghiogheny Railroad, a subsidiary of the Pittsburgh and Lake Erie Lines, was constructed through Braddock, during the excavation for which a number of Indian skeletons and implements were dug up. This railroad, as originally planned, was to have run along the south shore of the Monongahela River, but, in order to obtain some of the business of the Edgar Thomson Steel works, the plan was changed, and the road crossed the river and ran along the right bank of the river. Besides this, the Pittsburgh, Virginia and Charleston Railroad, of the Pennsylvania System, runs on the opposite side of the river, and connects with the main line of the Pennsylvania through the tunnel at Port Perry; and the Bessemer and Lake Erie, and Union lines also touch this district at the same point. The Western Maryland also has connections here, using the tracks of the Pittsburgh and Lake Erie Lines. Braddock thus has a direct outlet over five of the greatest railroads of the country; the Pennsylvania system, the Baltimore & Ohio, the Pittsburgh and Lake Erie, (a part of the New York Central), the Bessemer & Lake Erie, and the Western Maryland.

The Bessemer and Lake Erie was built in 1898, by the Carnegie Steel interests, because of discrimination in freight rates against this district by the old systems.

These roads have made many improvements since the original tracks were laid. Both the Pennsylvania and the Baltimore and Ohio railroads have developed from single track to four track roads. About 1880 the Pennsylvania widened its line to four tracks, and the present Braddock depot was built in 1884, to replace the old one which had been in use since about 1865. Later, improvements were made on the line through Braddock which are probably as extensive as any to be found in the same length of track at any point on the road. The grade crossing at Fourth Street was eliminated, the present Copeland station and underground passageway, or tunnel, was constructed; bridges were built at Thirteenth Street and Second Street; a roadway under the tracks was constructed at Sixth Street, and the bridge and passageway at Library Street were entirely made new. Since the completion of these improvements, in 1913, there have been almost no accidents on the tracks of the Pennsylvania Railroad in Braddock.

In 1907, the Baltimore and Ohio began operations on the widening of their right of way through the Borough of Braddock, and bought all the property between Wood Way and its own tracks between Seventh and Eleventh Streets; increased the number of its tracks from two to four; replaced the Passenger Station at Ninth Street by the present one at Eighth Street; built the new Freight Station at Eighth Street, and paid a sum of money into the Borough treasury.

All these roads handle an enormous traffic, both in passengers and freight, to and from Braddock, and are factors of immeasurable strength in the manufacturing and commercial importance of the community, and the favorable situation of the city in this respect is a guarantee of the continuance of its importance and prosperity.

THE FIRST STREET CAR OF BRADDOCK—OPERATED ON BRADDOCK AND TURTLE CREEK ROAD, SATURDAY, JULY 25, 1891.—HENRY FOYE, MOTORMAN.

MODERN STREET CAR AS USED IN 1917.
MIDDLE SCENE—HENRY McNANY, GIVING THE KIDDIES A FREE RIDE JULY 4, 1908.

BRADDOCK ELECTRIC RAILWAYS.

BY D. NEWTON GREER.

The electric motor is one of the marvelous inventions of the nineteenth century. The railway system had not long been introduced when the first proposition to employ electric locomotive traction was made. As early as 1835 experiments in this direction were made by Thomas Davenport, who constructed a model electric car operated on a circular track by means of batteries.

In 1850, Professor Page of the Smithsonian Institution of Washington, D. C., employed the current from one hundred large Grove cells to operate an electric locomotive which developed sixteen horse-power, and ran at the rate of nineteen miles an hour on the Baltimore and Ohio Railroad; but it was quite impracticable for it was far too expensive. The discovery of a cheap and easy means of electric traction was later developed. The first practical overhead trolley line was built in Kansas City in 1884, in which double overhead conductors were used with a trolley wheel riding on top of the wire. In 1885 Mr. Daft constructed a third rail line in Baltimore, and Mr. Depoele installed an overhead trolley at Toronto, Canada.

The next step made in the development of the electric railway in the U. S., and the one which did most to stimulate capitalists and inventors to the action which has produced the marvelous perfection in electric railway transportation which we witness today, was the contract made by the Union Passenger Railroad Company of Richmond, Va., with F. J. Sprague to equip its thirteen-mile system of street railways for electric traction.

On January 1, 1888, there were thirteen electric railways with forty-eight miles of track in operation in the United States and Canada. These followed a period of consolidated interests among electric railway builders, and the modern era of electric railway development was opened. Since 1888, or in twenty-nine years, electric railways have grown wonderfully until now the valuation of electric railways in the United States is approximately one billion dollars.

THE BRADDOCK AND TURTLE CREEK RAILWAY COMPANY.

Street Railway service for Braddock began on Saturday, July 25, 1891, when the Braddock and Turtle Creek Street Railway Company brought three old horse-cars from New York City and converted them into electric cars. These cars were put in commission on Braddock Avenue and ran from the Baltimore and Ohio Station at Rankin to Thirteenth Street, Braddock. The novelty of the Electric cars at that time is shown by the fact that the receipts of that short line on that first Saturday amounted to Sixty-five dollars, in consequence of 1,300 persons having taken advantage of this new mode of travel.

Early in 1892 the line was extended to the McKinney homestead near Bessemer, on the East, and as far as Keating station on the West.

The late William Yost, Esq., was President, and George E. T. Stamets, lately deceased, Superintendent, of the company opening this line. Other stockholders were Joseph Wolf, the late Fred Edwards, Mrs. Mary Matlack. Henry Foye, present Lieutenant of Police, was motorman, and Charles Johnson, conductor, on the first of the three cars sent out. In 1892 Mr. Foye was appointed assistant superintendent. Henry McNany of 201 Main Street, North Braddock, was motorman on one of the three cars mentioned and has acted in that capacity somewhere on the line ever since. His present run is between Rankin and Keating. In an accompanying illustration a very commendable trait of character of Mr. McNany is exhibited. It was his custom on the Fourth of July to invite the children along his route to participate in a free trolley party, and he had no trouble in getting a crowd.

Byron Pierce and Herman Steiner were conductors on this line, David Bradford, J. E. Griffith and Christ Forney were motormen.

Herbert Delafield was a conductor on one of these early cars and the youngest street-car conductor in the country at that time, being but sixteen years of age.

The second invoice of cars obtained for service on this line was the product of the Braddock Union Planing Company, now the Braddock Lumber Company.

One of the noteworthy results of the coming of the electric cars to Braddock was the doing away with the old-time cobble-stone paving.

THE SECOND AVENUE PASSENGER COMPANY.

In the year 1893, the Braddock and Turtle Creek Railway was taken over by the Second Avenue Passenger Company, and the line extended as far as Glenwood. The latter company continued the line to East Pittsburg in 1895, and to Wilmerding in 1896. Herbert Delafield, the young man already mentioned, was conductor on the first car that went through to Pittsburg from Wilmerding.

The Corey Avenue line was built by the Second Avenue Passenger Company and the franchise was granted August 2, 1887. The object of this branch was perhaps to divert the traffic from the proposed line of the Monongahela Company through North Braddock to East Pittsburg.

THE BRADDOCK ELECTRIC.

Beginning in 1893 the Braddock Electric, with A. L. Saylor of Pittsburgh, President, and Charles Ellis of Swissvale, Superintendent, operated a strictly local line. Starting at the South Side of Braddock Avenue, the track led down Thirteenth Street, to Talbot Avenue; along Talbot to Second Street; up Second to Mills Street; along Mills to Fourth Street; up Fourth and across Pennsylvania railroad tracks at Copeland

HERBERT DELAFIELD,

The first Conductor to run a car from Wilmerding through Braddock to Pittsburgh.

HENRY FOYE,

Motorman on first Street Car operated in Braddock.

Station to Hawkins Avenue, and along Hawkins east, as far as Dookers Hollow; also from Talbot Avenue up Eighth Street to Braddock Avenue, up Library Street and Jones Avenue to Bell Avenue.

An effort was made to complete the circuit of this line at Thirteenth Street by crossing the tracks of the Pennsylvania railroad and connecting with the line in North Braddock. But this was met with strong opposition at all times, and the opposition was so acrimonious and the through lines so advantageous that the Braddock Electric was forced out of business.

THE MONONGAHELA STREET RAILWAY COMPANY.

The Mellon Brothers, buying out the holdings of the Braddock Electric Company, began the development of street railway business upon a vastly larger scale, under the corporate name of The Monongahela Street

Railway Company. The contract with the borough was signed November 10, 1896.

L. Wheeler, now deceased, was superintendent of this division and served until the summer of 1898, when Frank McCoy, who had been superintendent of the Pittsburgh and Birmingham South Side lines, was elected, and served until the time of consolidation. During the incumbency of Mr. McCoy, the development of the street car service was amazingly rapid.

In the road-building series begun by this company, the first unit was completed July 5, 1897, when the first car operated between Braddock and Homestead over the West Braddock bridge.

This route had a decided advantage over the Second Avenue line, which took its serpentine course down the right bank of the Monongahela river to Highland Station, and there transferred its passengers across Brown's bridge to Homestead.

The Yellow Line, so called because of the color of its cars, operated its first cars from Thirteenth Street on Talbot Avenue over West Braddock bridge to Pittsburgh, December 4, 1898. Twelve cars were scheduled, and made the round trip in two hours. When it came to opening the road to Duquesne and McKeesport, the first thought of the Mellon Brothers was to go up Talbot Avenue to Thirteenth Street and there cross the river on a bridge to what is now Kennywood Park. This of course met no opposition in borough council for the company had paid $5,000 for the franchise. To the surprise of all concerned the company began the construction of a line along the hill on the south side of the river, leaving Braddock on the other side of the river from the main traffic between the two principal cities of the county.

Thus the line was opened and the initial car operated between Duquesne and Braddock over the West Braddock bridge, December 10, 1898.

Onward is the word that charms the willing powers of the ambitious, and the next line was opened to East Pittsburgh via Eighth Street across Braddock Avenue; up Library and Jones Avenue and out Bell Avenue, February 1, 1900. On the same date, the first car on the upper line from Wilkinsburg through North Braddock to East Pittsburgh, was operated.

Another unit was added to the numerous lines already in operation when the Blue line, or the Swissvale and Rankin, on January 10, 1901, sent out its first car from Thirteenth Street on Talbot Avenue connecting with Rankin at West Braddock Bridge by extending the bridge over the B. & O. tracks. This line was believed to be the shortest and consequently the quickest route to the city. The road from Wilmerding to Pitcairn was opened in 1902 and continued to Trafford in 1903.

So engrossed was the company in the thought and work of putting their lines into speedy operation, that the housing of the cars seemed to have been lost sight of. When the matter was forced upon them, temporary quarters were secured with the consolidated company in the Homewood barns until the completion of their own barn at Rankin in 1900.

When the lines were completed and about to open, Superintendent McCoy, with other officials, took representatives of the Pittsburgh and local press over the road in two special cars. Returning from this tour of inspection a banquet was given in the assembly rooms of the new car barn on Talbot Avenue, Rankin.

THE PITTSBURGH RAILWAYS COMPANY.

The Monongahela Street Railway Company in building their roads and operating their rolling stock had rendered a service to this community better than they knew.

The climax in the development of street railway service was reached when, on the first day of January, 1902, the Monongahela Street Railway Company, the Consolidated Traction Company and the United Traction were merged into the Pittsburgh Railways Company.

Mr. Fred. R. Wilhelm, who came here in April, 1899, as dispatcher, was made superintendent of the Monongahela Division No. 4 at the time of consolidation, and has been the efficient executive ever since.

The street car industry has worked to the development of Braddock as a residence section for working-men in the mills. A five cent fare will carry a man from Braddock to any of the important works of the Monongahela Valley, including Homestead, Munhall, Duquesne, across the river; the enormous furnaces and machine shops in Rankin; the immense Switch and Signal Company's works in Swissvale; the Westinghouse in East Pittsburg; and the entire Edgar Thomson Works in North Braddock. Or a five cent fare will carry a resident in any of the communities named to any of the Braddock industries. Thus through the instrumentality of the street car lines above described more than 40,000 men are carried daily from home to work and from the mills back home for a nickel fare.

The traffic on these lines is enormous, having increased from those three small cars and one mile of track in 1891 to one hundred large cars, 65 miles of track and serving approximately 100,000 people.

CAMP COPELAND AND THE CIVIL WAR.

BY MRS. JENNIE S. LAPSLEY

Braddock's Field was a small town in 1861 when the call came for men and means to help preserve this Union of ours. Small though she was, she was patriotic and gave of her best. Men were soon enlisting and hurrying to the front, at first in the three months' service and then for three years.

A fife and drum corp was formed and with martial music helped to keep up the courage both of those who left and of those who remained at home.

A familiar sight in those days was the red shirts of the Home Guard as they went back and forth to their drill grounds, which were where the Carnegie School now stands. Their guns were mostly home made, shaped out of a piece of wood; but what matter, they answered the purpose of the drill. As there was not much work to be had, the men had plenty of time on their hands and the drill was a daily occurrence. From this organization many went into the army.

The other day while talking with a dear old lady about the Civil war, she told me how she had climbed the hill to the Pennsylvania railroad and as the train, crowded with its cheering men went by, she had held up her baby boy that its father might see it again. The old lady, Mrs. Nathaniel Lowry, and her son, Mr. John S. Lowry, now one of the substantial and most highly respected citizens of Braddock, prominent in industrial, fraternal, civic and church work, are still living in Braddock, but the father fell at Fair Oaks. As she told the tale I thought of the many sad stories that have been related of those days, and feared that our nation may soon be again living through such scenes.

Some of those who enlisted from Braddock's Field were: George F. House, Samuel T. Guthrie, John P. Guthrie, William H. Furlong, James McCauley, George Petty, Thomas Kinney, David McCune, Isaac Mills, J. A. Young, William Smith, Charles Harrison, Daniel Oskin, Alexander Law. Zacharia Oskin, William Ford, William Sarver, Eli R. Dowler, John W. Adams, Charles Adams, Frank Dunbar, William Redman, Hiram Baughman, C. C. Lobingier, J. T. Getty, John Strathern, A. R. Adams, W. H. Morrow, James Strathern, Nathaniel Lowry, Alex. McCauly, Wm. McCombs, Wm. Sherwin, John Soles, David Perry, Thomas Hadden, George

Gibson, Lester Gibson, Augustus Schultz, Conrad Speidel, John McCracken, James A. Russel, Frank Russel, John Kolb, Jack James and two brothers, George Smith, David Bradford, Robert Forsythe, Samuel Hart, James Johnson, Patrick McGreevy.

This list is probably incomplete.

Of this number nine are still living—four of them in Braddock.

Captain William Smith, Charles Adams, John Strathern, Nathaniel Lowry, David Perry, and John McCracken never returned home.

According to a circular issued by the War Department, Washington, D. C., July 3, 1863, three rendezvous for drafted men were established in Pennsylvania. One was to be at Pittsburgh and the site selected was a portion of the Mill's farm near the Pennsylvania railroad at Braddock's Field.

These depots were for the purpose of receiving and conducting to their several regiments the men of the draft, who were assigned to fill them. The commandants of the rendezvous were informed of the number of drafted men to be sent to each regiment, and they prepared the detachments and sent them as soon as the requisite number could be made up.

Brig. Gen. Thomas L. Kane was appointed in charge of this camp, July 4, 1863. He was relieved July 18, 1863 by Brig. Gen. Joseph T. Copeland. Gen. Copeland had charge until March 26, 1864 when he was relieved by Col. M. D. Hardin.

At first the camp was composed of tents, but later, lumber was obtained and buildings were erected, the work being done by the men in the camp.

In the picture reproduced here, may be seen the hospital in the foreground close to the railroad. In the entreme left is the Commandants' house, and next to it are the officers' quarters. The other buildings are the barracks for the troops.

The original picture was obtained from Mr. Walter Collins, who had it taken in 1864, while he was located at Camp Copeland with his company under Capt. James L. McFeeters, who was for many years after the war a resident of Braddock.

This insert is a picture of Mr. Collins who served three years. He saw much service under Pope and Burnside being in the battles of second Bull Run and Fredericksburg; then was under Grant when Vicksburg fell. Later he spent about a year at Camp Copeland helping to drill the men and taking charge of squads that were sent out to fill up regiments. Mr. Collins is now living on Washington street in Braddock.

CAMP COPELAND.

WALTER COLLINS, One of the men who Instructed the Recruits at Camp Copeland.

This camp's location so close to the town kept the people constantly in touch with the soldiers. At times there were as many as six or seven thousand men in camp. It is said by those who lived in Braddock's Field at that time, that these men were generally orderly and well behaved, giving the people little occasion for complaint. They were rather fond of stopping at the different homes to chat with the people, and never were above accepting a pie or cake when offered them, though they were not always careful to return the plates.

Sometimes the citizens would clash with the authorities in camp. Mrs. Nathaniel Lowry tells the following story: Many of the fences having been taken down and used for firewood, the animals of the surrounding farms sometimes went astray. One day a prominent citizen lost a pig and, going to the camp, blamed the soldiers for taking it. An argument arose and later a soldier went to the man's home and asked his wife to send a dinner to the gentleman. They had placed him in the guard house, and they kept him there until four o'clock that afternoon.

The camp was called "Camp Copeland" in Honor of Gen. Copeland while he was in charge. When Col. Hardin took command he named it "Camp Reynolds" for Gen. Reynolds, who had fallen at Gettysburg. Later, however, the name first given was again taken and we now always speak of it as Camp Copeland.

During the year 1864 there was much sickness in the camp. Many of the men died and were buried in the Robinson graveyard, but their bodies were afterwards raised and transferred by the government to the Soldiers' plot in the Allegheny Cemetery. There was at least one case of small-pox at this time.

A sad accident happened at the Camp when one of the Mills boys, while handling a gun, was accidently shot. He died shortly afterwards.

Religious services were held at Camp on Sabbath afternoons and were attended by the townspeople.

Soon those that remember Camp Copeland will have passed beyond and it will be only a small matter of history. During the time of its existence, however, it was woven very closely into the life of the people of Braddock's Field.

An order April 29, 1865 closed the camp, but the name still remains, that portion of Braddock being still called Copeland as is the station on the Pennsylvania Railroad at that place.

A SURVEY OF INDUSTRIAL BRADDOCK AND BRIEF HISTORY OF THE EDGAR THOMSON STEEL WORKS.

BY HUGH P. MEESE.

FOREWORD.

A history is not evolved from some historian's inner consciousness. It is, on the contrary, the result of a vast amount of digging and refining, the value of the history depending upon the patience with which the historian has delved and the clarity and judgment of his presentation.

It will be readily apparent to the reasonable man that in the odd moments of six weeks lapse of time no very exhaustive history can be both assembled and written out.

Space having only been accorded me for one full history, I have assigned that honor, correctly I believe, to the Edgar Thomson plant, in which a vastly greater number of Braddock's citizens have been employed than in any other establishment, and which is also the most famous of her industries.

To the many friends and associates who gave me such kind assistance and advice in the scramble for facts and dates, I wish to extend my deepest thanks.   HUGH P. MEESE.

Swissvale, April 7, 1917.

EDGAR THOMSON OPEN HEARTH PLANT.

EDGAR THOMSON WORKS—VIEW FROM HILL ABOVE BESSEMER STATION.

SURVEY OF INDUSTRIAL BRADDOCK.

In 1850 the Monongahela at Braddock's Field rolled through a quiet scene of sylvan beauty. Thickly wooded hills shaded her peaceful waters on the south, while on the Braddock side long grassy swards dipped to the river's brim.

The low land along the river, now filled in with cinder, ash, and slag, and usurped by belching steel plants, was the home of the bullfrog and the meadowlark, while on a summer's night a thousand glow worms swung their lanterns in the swamp land and gave the first faint prophesy of the myriad electric arcs that later were to change night into day upon that ground. Not clouds of smoke, but flocks of white-winged pigeons hung beneath the clear, unsullied sky, and in quiet hickory groves the oriole swung his nest where now the operator's cage scurries back and forth on the Edgar Thomson cranes. The robin and the woodthrush called, and no steam siren split the air, nor was the busy tapping of the woodpecker yet transformed into the clamor of the pneumatic riveter. The rail-saw not yet challenged the nightly supremacy of the screech-owl and the bat, and no sudden clang of steel startled the sleeper's ear. Truly a golden age.

But not for Braddock was the lure of green fields and running waters. Hers was to be a life of action and achievement, hers was no Lotus land of dreams. Already the faint tapping of a hammer and musical song of a distant saw-mill come at intervals on the quiet air: her industrial history is beginning.

As in so brief a survey only a few of the more important industries can be mentioned, we will waive consideration of the countless little enterprises that Braddock must have mothered between the days of Frazier's cabin and the middle of the last century, and assume our story with the barrel and furniture factory of seventy years ago.

This barrel factory, which also made chairs and furniture of the rougher type, seems to have been founded shortly before 1850 by a Mr. Soles and others of Scotch descent, who originally hailed from Massachusetts. The exact date of its commencement is shrouded in obscurity, but we know that about 1850 John and Daniel Richardson purchased the business and started the Braddock Saw Mill and Boat Yard, located on the present site of the city's water plant. This firm, in turn, was later bought out by Lazear, Sollinger, and Patton, and was doing business as late as 1878, when the property was purchased by the Borough of Braddock as a site for the city's water plant.[1]

---

[1] The data on this subject is the result of investigations by Mr. C. S. Marks.

THE UNWRITTEN HISTORY OF BRADDOCK'S FIELD.   85

In 1861, shortly after the inauguration of the great Civil War, the McVay-Walker Foundry was built at Braddock, and during the rebellion made many supplies for the Federal Government. Later this firm did much of the small casting work for the Edgar Thomson plant, and has really been the mother of all Braddock's steel and iron industries. It is still doing business today at the age of 57 years, although during 1916 the firm suffered a disastrous fire. It is undoubtedly the oldest of Braddock's larger industries.

Among the numerous lumber companies that followed the early planing mill were the Grannis Brothers and the Dowler Lumber Company. The Dowler Lumber Company was established in 1866, according to Mr. Thos. J. Dowler, and went out of business in 1912.

1872 saw the commencement of the world-famous Edgar Thomson Steel Works, and likewise the start of the famous local plant of McCrady Brothers, who now do such an extensive business in hauling and in sand, coal, lime, stone, etc. James McCrady did much of the hauling work for the new plant, and McCrady Bros. have grown steadily ever since, until at the present time it has over 60 teams and 11 motor trucks, and is well known for reliability and promptness all over Allegheny County. The firm today consists of J. H. McCrady, J. H. McCrady, Jr., Ed. McCrady, W. F. McCrady, H. C. McCrady, J. F. Baldwin, and W. L. Bender.[1]

Late in 1875 the Edgar Thomson Steel Works (which are treated at length later in this article) got into operation, and no industrial developments of major importance appear in this district until 1882. In that year the famous "Duquesne Forge" to which reference is so frequently made by old inhabitants, was built at Rankin on the ground now occupied by the McClintic Marshall Construction Company.

The Duquesne Forge[2] was originally constructed on Duquesne Way, Pittsburgh, by Joseph Heigh, William Miller later becoming a partner in the firm, and the name being changed to "Miller's Forge." The Pittsburgh plant was torn down and rebuilt at Braddock in 1882 under the old name, "Duquesne Forge," Miller and Alexander McKim (now of Swissvale, Pa.) being partners in the enterprise. The river industry was of great importance in those days, and the forge made all sorts of boat and ship supplies, such as stanchions, shanks, shafts, chains, gears, etc., some of the forgings running as high as 100,000 pounds weight. The original firm had done work for Government torpedo boats during the Civil War, and

---

(1) Data on McCrady Bros. secured from the office of that firm.

(2) Data on the Duquesne Forge secured from Mr. Alexander McKim of Swissvale.

when the Spanish War broke out the Rankin firm made some 300 cannon for the Government, weighing on an average 25,000 pounds apiece. The firm employed about 200 men, and was one of the large industries of its day. In 1905 McClintic Marshall absorbed the property.

The success of the Lucy, Isabella, and Edgar Thomson Blast Furnaces was very alluring to other steel men in the early 80's, and in 1883 we find William Clark Sons and Company building the first of what is now known as the Carrie Furnaces[1] at Rankin, on 35 acres of ground purchased from John Adams. The first blast furnace produced about 100 tons of iron a day, under the supervision of Superintendent Martin H. Thompson. The original furnace was removed from Port Washington, Ohio, and blown in February 29, 1884. They are each 100 feet high, with 23-foot bosh and 15-foot hearth. Subsequent superintendents of the plant have been:

William Rotthof,
Harry Watt,
George K. Hamfeldt,
Jacob A. Mohr.

The Carrie Furnace Company erected a second furnace in 1900, and the Carnegie Steel Company, which later took control, has built the following additional furnaces:—

Two furnaces in 1900.
One furnace in 1903.
Two furnaces in 1907.

The acreage has been increased from 35 to 66 acres, and the production from 35,000 to 894,000 tons of pig iron annually.

The plant now employs about 1,000 men, and is under the supervision of Mr. A. A. Corey, Jr., General Superintendent of the Homestead Steel Works. It is, of course, a subsidiary of the United States Steel Corporation.

The present operating staff of the plant consists of the following officials:—

Jacob A. Mohr, Superintendent,
H. A. Berg, Assistant Superintendent,
T. E. Kenney, Pay Clerk,
Michael Ryan, General Operating Foreman,

---

(1) Data on the Carrie Furnaces secured from J. A. Mohr, Superintendent, and a book entitled "The Inside History of the Carnegie Steel Company."

Chas. L. Davis, Assistant Master Mechanic,
Wm. Jackson, Assistant Superintendent Electrical Department.

In May, 1884, the Braddock Tannery, operated by Owen Sheekey and James Callery, commenced operations in Rankin on the site of the present Wire Mill. It covers 17 acres and originally employed about 60 men, and in its best days did a business of from $150,000 to $200,000 annually. The plant, however, was burned out in 1886, and thereafter did business on a somewhat smaller scale, employing only about 35 men. A second disastrous fire occurred August 28, 1893, upon which the firm went out of business, selling out to the Braddock Wire Company. On the occasion of the first fire they had sold about 12 acres to the wire company, and they now sold the remainder of their ground to the same concern. Information on this subject was secured from the sons of Mr. Owen Sheekey, and from the Superintendent of the Rankin Wire Mill, Mr. E. H. Broden.

In 1885 the W. R. McCloy Glass Works were erected at Rankin Station, on a 5-acre tract of land fronting on the Union Siding of the P. McK. & Y. and B. & O. Railroads, and extending back to the Monongahela river, the property adjoining the ground of the Duquesne Forge on the south. Here one of the first tank furnaces ever built in the Pittsburgh district for making crystal blown glass was constructed. The product chiefly consisted of lantern globes, fruit and candy jars. In the year 1887 The Braddock Glass Company, Ltd. was organized and incorporated, and the capacity of the plant enlarged by the installation of one 10-pot furnace. This company employed about 150 men, and in addition to the former product, also turned out a complete line of lamp chimneys. In March, 1892, the plant was totally destroyed by fire, which is said to have originated from sparks emitted by a passing switching locomotive. The whole country was at that time entering a period of depression, and the works were consequently not rebuilt.[1]

In 1886 Col. Thomas Fitch and William Edenborn purchased 12 acres of land from the Sheekey Tannery and built the first Rankin Wire Mill,[2] known as the "Braddock Wire Company." The development of the plant has been as follows:—

1886—Rod Mill.
1888—Galvanizing Department.

---

[1] Data on the glass works secured from W. R. McCloy of Union Street, Lafayette, Indiana.
[2] Data on the Rankin Wire Mills secured from Mr. E. H. Broden, Manager.

1890—Nail Mill.
1891—Fence and barbed wire departments.
1891—Cooper shop.
1892—Warehouse.
1895—Rod mill rebuilt.
1898—Galvanizing department rebuilt.
1905—Nail mill rebuilt.
1907—Boiler house rebuilt and enlarged.
1907—Warehouse rebuilt.
1912—Galvanizing department rebuilt.
1913—Nail Mill rebuilt.

The following list shows the resident managers of the plant, and the dates on which they took office:—

Col. Thos. Fitch	1886	August Mann	1902
Mr. Porter	1889	Chas. W. Lutz	1906
J. W. Govier	1889	F. H. Nullmeyer	1907
Peter McIlvrie	1890	F. D. Haynes	1909
Geo. Nash	1898	J. G. Mustin	1910
Walter C. Stone	1901	H. S. White	1913
	E. H. Broden	1916	

The plant today produces rods, wire, wire nails, staples, galvanized wire, annealed wire, woven fence, barbed wire, and nail kegs, and employs about 1,250 men. In addition to Mr. G. W. Jewett, who is Manager of Wire Mills in the Pittsburgh District of the American Steel & Wire Company, the following men are now on the operating staff of the Rankin Works of the American Steel & Wire Company:—[1]

E. H. Broden, E. D. Thompson, J. T. Saunders, William Murphy, J. W. Kilburn, H. B. Trott, Thos. Chambers, John Tompos, M. E. Reyneke, John McAfee, Fred Hultgren, G. W. Jewett, Jr., P. Crane, R. E. Hurrell, C. S. Young, A. Faloona, P. Olson, W. M. Riedl, J. C. Jamison, A. J. Rylander, A. J. Day, Chas. Eddstrom, John Nelson, J. P. Caulfield, C. Hultgren, and P. McDonough.

The plant from 1896 to 1898 was run under the name of the "Consolidated Wire Company," and was one of the holdings which John W. Gates, a heavy stockholder in the Consolidated, was later able to sell to the Steel Corporation.

(1) A subsidiary of the U. S. Steel Corporation.

J. A. FARRELL,
President, United States Steel Corporation, Formerly a Braddock Steel Man.

D. G. KERR
Vice President U. S. Steel Corporation.
(Formerly Supt. Blast Fur., E. T. Works.)

A Braddock lumber firm which has withstood the test of years is the Braddock Lumber Company,[1] originally the Braddock Planing Mill Co., established in 1887 by Henry Miller and W. A. Davis at the B. & O. Railroad and Eighth Street. The plant later changed hands and became known as the Braddock Lumber Company, the present management taking charge in 1908. In 1916 all interests of the firm passed into the hands of the present manager, William McCollum, and his brother, Mark McCollum, who are now full owners of the establishment. The plant is one of the largest and best equipped planing mills in Western Pennsylvania, and has the largest retail lumber yard and most varied assortment of stock in this district, employing at full capacity about 35 men. Officers: William McCollum, President; Lillian McCollum, Vice President; Mark McCollum, Secretary and Treasurer.

The Braddock Wire Plant[2] was constructed by Col. Thos. W. Fitch in 1891 on 5½ acres purchased from Redman & Haney. While the original plant produced but 90 tons of rods in 24 hours, the works today put out 400 tons of rods in 24 hours and 340 tons of wire, and the plant has shown steady progress.

Col. Fitch was manager of the plant from 1891 until 1899, when it was taken over by the American Steel & Wire Company and Geo. W. Nash appointed superintendent May 1, 1899. The successive superintendents of the plant have been: —

William Farrell	Jan., 1900 to July, 1901
August Mann	July, 1901 to 1903
J. G. Mustin	1903 to 1906
F. H. Nullmeyer	1906 to 1907
H. S. White	1907 to 1912
E. H. Broden	1913 to 1916
F. B. Hill	1916 to date

The plant at present consists of one Garrett Rod Mill, one 216 block wire mill, 16 annealing furnaces, one cold drawing department, one power house, machine shop, carpenter, and other repair shops. Mr. A. Eyman is Assistant Superintendent of the Braddock plant.

Another Braddock firm that commenced operations about the same time is the Rankin plant of the Consolidated Expanded Metal Company, now operated by H. B. Chess, Jr., P. F. Chess, and others. The company

---

[1] Data on the Braddock Lumber Company obtained from Mr. William McCollum.

[2] Data on Braddock Works of the American Steel & Wire Company, U. S. Steel Corporation, secured from Mr. F. B. Hill, Manager.

has offices in New York, Chicago, Philadelphia and Pittsburgh, and produces metal lath and concrete reinforcement at the rate of about 14,000 yards of lath and 100,000 feet of reinforcement daily at Rankin.

The original plant was erected about 1890 by Harvey B. Chess and Walter Chess, who removed a steel plant they had on the South Side to Rankin. Originally a puddling furnace was installed and a few plates rolled, but this business was soon abandoned. The original plant was erected on part of the A. Hayes estate, and has steadily grown since its inception, until now it employs from 100 to 150 men in the Rankin plant alone.[1]

The original Price & Alman Lumber Company began business a little before the above firm began operations, Joseph Price starting a lumber business on Corey Avenue, Braddock, about 1887. In 1897 Samuel R. Alman entered the firm and the business was moved to its present location. The firm now employs about thirty men, runs a first class planing mill, and does an extensive general lumber business.[2]

Another Braddock lumber firm that has reached a ripe age is McBride Brothers, which started in 1892 on an acre of ground purchased from Chess Bros., and has continued to the present day putting out high grade planing mill products. From 1892 to 1913 the firm consisted of M. J. McBride and E. F. McBride, and from 1913 to date has consisted of H. E. McBride, W. J. McBride, and C. J. McBride. The equipment of the plant at this writing consists of individual motor drive for the usual planing mill machinery, such as moulder, rip saw, cut-off saw, shaper, drum sander, scroll saw, surfacer, joiner, etc.[3]

A brick company that is one of the landmarks of Braddock, its plant lying high up on the bluff overlooking the Edgar Thomson Works, is the Keller & Milliken firm. They began operations in April, 1894, at the foot of Eighth Street, Braddock, moving in 1899 to the present location in North Braddock. The firm at present consists of John J. Keller and Homer A. Milliken, carries about 25 men, and produces from three to four million high grade brick per year.[4]

Another firm which does business on quite a large scale is the Crown Wall Plaster Company,[5] built in 1897 on ground purchased from

---

(1) Data obtained froom P. F. Chess, Pittsburgh office, and from E. T. Redding, Manager of the Braddock plant.
(2) Data obtained from Joseph Price.
(3) Data secured from office of the company.
(4) Data obtained from Mr. John J. Keller.
(5) Data from Mr. Wesley B. Holmes, President of the firm.

E. R. Dowler. W. M. Holmes, original president of the company, died January 18, 1916, when Wesley B. Holmes was elected to that office. The present plant has a capacity of 100 tons of hard wall plaster per day, and runs a factory 25 x 200 feet. They do business on both a retail and carload basis.

A Braddock enterprise that is now almost twenty years old is the Braddock Manufacturing Company, originally known as the Braddock Machine and Manufacturing Company. The plant was constructed in 1898 and 1899. The first stockholders' meeting was held November 2, 1899, in the office of Attorney Joseph F. Mayhugh, at which the following members were present:—

Henry Stanyon,	James Sloss,
Jno. B. Miller,	R. V. Miller,
Henry Gauermann.	Jos. F. Mayhugh.

The meeting voted the incorporation of the Braddock Machine & Manufacturing Company with a capital of $3,000. John D. Miller was elected the first President and Henry Stanyon, Secretary and Treasurer, at the same meeting.

On December 21, 1899, the capital stock was increased to $200,000 and we are informed that John Hutzen, James A. Russell, S. D. Hamilton, W. A. Kulp, Dr. G. E. Bair, Dr. Meals, William Howatt, John Rinard and Benj. Braznell, were prominent stockholders of the enlarged company.

In January, 1902, W. E. Corey, A. R. Peacock, D. M. Clemson, Thomas Morrison, and Chas. E. Dinkey purchased practically all of the outstanding stock of this company, and again there was a reorganization. While the concern had previously been merely an iron foundry, the new directors took steps at once to enlarge its capacity, and changed it to a steel foundry with a 20-ton Open Hearth Furnace, and many additional improvements throughout the machine shop.

Succeeding presidents of the firm were:—
John D. Miller,
A. R. Peacock,
R. G. Morrison,

On August 22, 1916, the old management was in turn bought out by a new company of which W. E. Troutman is President, R. W. Tener, Secretary and Treasurer, and F. B. McConnell, Manager. The new management has added a 20-ton O. H. Furnace to the equipment, making two 20-ton furnaces in all, and has installed many other improvements throughout the plant. The plant consists of a machine shop, foundry, and office building, and employs from 250 to 300 men. The firm is now capitalized at $300,000, and is capable of doing a business of a million and a half dollars annually. It is is known as the Braddock Manufacturing Company, producing high grade machinery and steel castings.[1]

One of the minor industries of the preceding era of development was the Baker Chain Wagon Manufacturing Company, whose original plant was built at Rankin in 1899 on a 2-acre plot of ground, the first chief resident manager being David T. Robling, who held office until 1910. Another early plant, the Standard Chain Company, whose land adjoined the Baker Chain Company's, has since been bought out by the American Chain Company, Incorporated, the present manager being Mr. Noah L. McArthur. While the original plant produced only about 400 tons of wrought iron and steel chain per month, the American Chain Co., Inc., now puts out about 850 tons of chain, ship cables, shackles, and automobile forgings monthly. The plant is fully equipped with chain welding hammers, drop hammers, forging hammers, bull dozers, steam hammers, and testing machines of the most modern pattern. [2]

One of the largest plants of the district is the Rankin plant of the McClintic Marshall Construction Company,[3] employing in the neighborhood of a thousand men. No. 1 Shop was built in 1901, followed by Shop No. 2 in 1906. The Rankin plant occupies 20 acres of ground directly across the Monongahela river from the Homestead Steel Works.

The two shops are duplicates of each other. The stock yard is about 150 feet wide and 1,000 feet long, traversed by four electric traveling cranes of 10 and 20 tons capacity. A large stock of material is kept constantly on hand to facilitate deliveries, and the company, being the largest independent manufacturer and erector of bridges and buildings in the United States, is known all over the country.

Each main shop building is 280 feet wide by 600 feet long, equipped with 20 electric traveling cranes, ranging from 5 to 30 tons capacity, which handle the work from the time it enters the shop until it leaves by the railroad. The punching, milling, reaming, and shearing machinery, all electrically driven, is the best obtainable, and the equipment throughout is thoroughly modern in every respect. In the main shop girders up to 90 tons in weight can be loaded on cars.

---

(1) Data secured from J. E. Mitchell, secretary to Mr. Thomas Morrison, and from the office of the present firm.
(2) Data from Mr. Noah L. Arthur, Local Manager of the American Chain Co., Inc.
(3) Data obtained from G. L. Taylor, Assistant Chief Engineer, Oliver Building, Pittsburgh.

THE UNWRITTEN HISTORY OF BRADDOCK'S FIELD. 93

The Company's general offices are on the first floor of a three-story office building, while on the second and third stories are 110 draughtsmen. The Rankin officials of the plant are as follows:—E. W. Pittman, Manager; R. A. Pendergrass, Engineer; K. M. McHose, Assistant Manager; H. B. Charles, Purchasing Agent; E. J. Patterson, Assistant Treasurer; C. O. Miller, Auditor; E. A. Gibbs, Manager of Erection.

The Sterling Steel Foundry[1] is one of the newest of Braddock's enterprises, being constructed in 1901 by the Sterling Steel Foundry[2] on 2½ acres purchased from Samuel Dempster. While the original plant produced but 1,000 tons per month, it now puts out 1,500 tons monthly of high grade steel castings. The plant employs about 300 men, and has a present size of 400 x 250 feet. Mr. Geo. W. Smith is President, other executives being:—

Wm. Nease, Vice President,
H. G. Smith, Treasurer,
M. A. Quinn, Secretary.
G. J. Chandler, Sales Manager,
D. B. Webb, Superintendent,
R. T. Mullett, Assistant Manager.

The equipment of the present plant is as follows:—

Two 20-ton Open Hearth furnaces.
One 30-ton crane.
One 20-ton crane.
Three 10-ton cranes.
Three 5-ton cranes.

In a fuller history of the town, attention would have to be given to the work of the many contractors who have built the town, and such a review would give in detail the accomplishments of such men as George Hogg, F. F. Schellenberg, W. S. Husband, T. A. Gillespie, and of the Hodder Construction Company and the Melcher Bros. While space is entirely lacking to recite the histories of these firms, their accomplishments are always before our eyes; their work is itself a silent but impressive monument.

One of the latest industries of this thriving little city is The Pittsburgh Machine Tool Company, which erected its present plant in 1910

---

(1) Information obtained from M. A. Quinn, Secretary, and Geo. W. Smith, President.

(2) Uriah Tinker and Harry E. Wainwright.

on a plot of ground 100 x 200 feet purchased from the Dawes Manufacturing Company. The Company was capitalized at $250,000, having originally been located on the Pittsburgh North Side, and moved to the present location in May, 1911.

The plant contains a thoroughly modern and up to date equipment of machine tools, such as lathes, planers, shapers, milling machines, gear cutters, etc., and turns out engine lathes, 26 inch, to 48 inch swing, and Curtis Rotary Pumps to the value of about $300,000 annually. The company employs about 100 men. F. J. Curtis is President and Manager of the present organization, Frank Moore, Vice President, and E. L. Taggart, Secretary-Treasurer.

All in all, the industries of Braddock are such as would be the boast of many a prouder and more populous city. For every man, woman, and child within her gates she produces daily more than a thousand pounds of commercial metal. Her products encircle the globe, and lie in every land under every flag. On ships, on boats, on automobiles, aeroplanes, or trains—however you go and wherever you go, there will you find the workmanship of this busy little city.

Far indeed is the Braddock of today from the Braddock of 1850. Silent is the kingfisher and the bobolink, and gone are the green fields, the shady groves, and running brooks. For the spirit of Braddock is a virile spirit. Impatient and afire with energy, she shook off the soft Arcadian mantle that nature had thrown about her and descended into the dust and blood of the commercial arena, only to arise, nobler than before, with the standard of steel supremacy in her grimy hand.

Not without pain and privation, travail and unceasing effort has she scattered her trademark all over the earth. She knows no rest; her mills and furnaces never sleep, the city's natural life is a spasm of human effort, and the thunder of her forges marks her heart beats. All day the clang of steel assails the ear, and at night a hundred lurid flames set up the pillar of fire that is the core of Pittsburgh's steel district, itself the steel center of the world.

Not steel or iron has made industrial Braddock, but brains and energy. With these qualities she has endowed her sons,—these and sublime courage. For, like a Spartan mother, she is a stern teacher. Those that chain the fiery monster, liquid steel, work in the Valley of the Shadow, and learn to look unflinching into the mouth of hell. But such a school makes men—Jones, Schwab, Gayley, Morrison, Kennedy, Kerr, the Dinkey boys, Unger, Farrell, Knox,—of such caliber are her graduates.

To the stranger within her gates, her diadem appears at night in the crescent of a thousand blazing arcs that light her famous industries. But those near the heart of Mother Braddock know that she forgets her glory that is of electricity, steel or gold, and pointing to her sons, says, like Cornelia,[1] "These are my jewels."

---

[1] Daughter of Scipio Africanus the elder, and mother of the Gracchi.

EDGAR THOMSON STEEL WORKS.

In the decade following the Civil War came the greatest period of business development this country has ever had, and a variety of causes combined to focalize this prosperity on Western Pennsylvania, the coal and iron center of the country.

During that disastrous conflict the price of iron had leaped from $18 to $73.60 a ton, and within six years of the surrender at Appomatox, the railroad mileage of the country had doubled in a gigantic business reaction. At the same period came the development of the Connellsville coke region under H. C. Frick, the first stirring of the natural gas industry in this section, and the introduction in America of the cheap and efficient Bessemer process for making steel.[1] Iron rails in this period sold for as high as $100 a ton, and a ton of steel rails brought $175 in gold.[2]

These favoring conditions gave a great impetus to the iron and steel business of the Pittsburgh district, and it is not surprising to find that brilliant and successful Pittsburgh ironmaster, William Coleman,[3] greatly interested in the new Bessemer process. As early as 1867, in fact, we find him endeavoring to interest his associates in the manufacture of steel rails.

When Andrew Carnegie himself, in the summer of 1872, saw how easily and cheaply the new Bessemer rails were made in Europe, he rushed back to Pittsburgh filled with enthusiasm for a Bessemer rail plant of his own. An option was immediately secured on 107 acres of land at Braddock along the Monongahela river,[4] and late in 1872 work was commenced on a wharf to handle the river freight. On January 1, 1873, the deal was completed when William Coleman purchased, for himself and as-

---

(1) William Kelly, born August 11, 1812, Pittsburgh, Pa., died February 11, 1888, Louisville, Ky., father of John G. Kelly, President, Braddock National Bank, made Bessemer steel at Eddyville, Ky., as early as 1847. One of his early converters is still extant with the date "1857" painted thereon. Sir Henry Bessemer made Bessemer steel in 1855. Kelly used the process at a factory at Wyandotte, Michigan, in 1863. A. L. Holley, a world famous engineer and steel plant promoter, introduced Sir Henry Bessemer's process at Troy, N. Y., in 1865, and at this period came the greatest publicity and expansion of the process. The Bessemer process was further developed by Mushet, Holley, Captain Jones, Reese, Gilchrist, and Thomas.

(2) Iron Age—August 16, 1883.

(3) A successful iron rail manufacturer and real estate speculator. A pioneer in the Pittsburgh iron industry. Later became the father-in-law of Thomas Carnegie.

(4) Which land was right on the Baltimore & Ohio Railroad, quite near the Pennsylvania Railroad, and also on the Monongahela, thus having the best transportation facilities obtainable.

ANDREW CARNEGIE.

sociates, 61.7 acres of ground from Robert McKinney[1] and 45 acres from John McKinney,[2] at a total cost of $219,003.30. On this ground was built the world-famous Edgar Thomson Steel Works.

The firm for the operation of the proposed plant was regularly organized on January 13, 1873, the partners and various stock holdings being as follows:

Andrew Carnegie	$250,000
William Coleman	100,000
Andrew Kloman	50,000
Henry Phipps	50,000
David McCandless	50,000
Wm. P. Shinn	50,000
John Scott	50,000
David A. Stewart	50,000
Thomas Carnegie	50,000
CAPITAL STOCK	$700,000

This firm was known as Carnegie, McCandless & Company, and from motives of diplomacy they named the new plant after J. Edgar Thomson, President of the Pennsylvania Railroad at the time. A. L. Holley, one of the most prominent steel mill engineers in the world, was secured to design the new plant. Some of his original prints are still in existence in the Edgar Thomson drawing room. Phineas Barnes, who had just built the Joliet plant, was commissioned to superintend the erection, and accordingly may be called the first General Superintendent of the Edgar Thomson Works.

Early in 1873 the work on the wharf had been completed, under Chief Carpenter Ben Tuttle, and ground for the works proper was broken April 13, 1873, most of the grading and excavating being done under the supervision of Contractor Hughes and Messrs. Collins, Shoemaker, Syd Perry, and Thomas Cosgrove. The brickwork was originally let to a Mr.

---

(1) The present site of Furnaces "A", "B", "C", and "D", and the old Converting and Rail Mills.

(2) Site of the present blast furnaces "E", "F", "G", "H", "I", "J", and "K", and extending in a narrow strip along the west side of the Robert McKinney purchase to the Pennsylvania Railroad.

J. EDGAR THOMSON.

Miller from Bellevue, but at an early date this contract was cancelled and an employee, Thomas Addenbrook,[1] given full supervision.

The business boom of the country, however, suddenly collapsed in 1873,[2] and the new steel mill project seriously threatened to follow suit. In this emergency, however, they succeeded in floating a $200,000 issue of bonds, which tided them over the crisis, and construction operations, which had ceased altogether for about ten days, gradually resumed, although not with much impetus until 1874.

In this same year (1873) Morrell, President of the Cambria Iron Works, promoted Daniel N. Jones over the head of Captain William R. Jones, (who was really next in line for that honor) to the superintendency of that plant. "A prophet is not without honor *save* in his own country." Morrell had known Jones for years, and in his eyes he was still an irresponsible youth. Bitterly resenting this slight, Captain Jones resigned, and in August, 1873, came to Edgar Thomson as master mechanic, incidentally breaking up the entire Cambria organization, and bringing with him a nucleus of devoted fellow workers[3] who were experienced steel men, and made the new plant the success that it was.

Two early Braddock firms aided materially in the construction of the early plant: the McVay Walker Foundry (built 1862) made many of the smaller castings, and James McCrady did a great deal of the hauling.

On the completion of the plant, the contract of Phineas Barnes expired, and Captain William R. Jones was appointed General Superintendent.

The first blow was made at the Converting Works August 26, 1875,

---

(1) This genial, charitable, Christian gentleman was one of the true pioneers of the Edgar Thomson plant. He recently resigned after 40 years of service. He has, during all his life, been a devoted supporter of religious work, and is one of the most broad minded and tolerant men in that field today. In this work he kindly gave me every aid.

(2) A great outlay of capital had been used in re-building Chicago, burned down in 1871, also a great Boston fire occurred in 1872. Again, a quarrel between the farmers and the western railroads stopped the sale of railroad bonds and hurt the banks concerned in railroad building. Jay Cooke & Co., New York bankers, failed in September, 1873, and in that year there were 5,000 failures, and in 1874, 5,800.

(3) Among others: Thos. James, D. L. Miller, Noah Hutzen, Hiram Hutzen, Capt. Lapsly, Wm. Lapsly, John Noey, John Rinard, Jno. Little, F. L. Bridges, C. C. Teeter, Robt. Morris, John Frederick.

THOMAS ADDENBROOK.

and the first rail rolled, with impressive ceremonies, September 1, 1875.[1]

The plant of which Captain Jones was now to take charge is described by the old Allegheny Chronicle as follows:—

"A two-5-ton-converter plant and rail mill with nominal capacity of 225 tons daily. Cupola house 107 x 44 x 46 ft. high. Converter house 129 x 84 x 30 feet high. House for blowing engines 54 x 48 x 36 ft. high. Boiler house 178 x 40 x 18 ft. high. Producer house 90 x 46 x 26 feet high, artificial gas being used to heat the furnaces. The rail mill itself is 380 x 100 x 25 ft. high, with a wing (Blooming Mill) 100 x 35 x 17 ft. high. Office and shop building 200 x 60 x 18 ft. high, with a coal and iron building 40 x 20 x 10 ft. high. The producer house and rail mill have iron side columns with timber side framing, all others being entirely of brick."

For these little 5-ton converters A. L. Holley invented the removable converter bottom, vastly prolonging the converter's usefulness. The Blooming Mill was a 32-inch mill, run by Mackintosh-Hemphill engines. In the boiler house were 20 cylinder boilers with two large flues passing through the center about 25 feet long. The rail mill was a "three-high" 23-inch, hook-and-tong mill, operated by a 46 x 48″ engine. At the stands were six men, three on each side, who with hooks suspended from above, caught the rail when it passed through and lifted it to the next

---

(1) The Edgar Thomson plant was not, as is sometimes erroneously supposed, a pioneer steel plant in America. In 1875 the country had about a dozen Bessemer plants, producing almost 400,000 tons of Bessemer steel annually. Regarding the steel business in the Pittsburgh district, I quote the following from Mr. George Stevens Page, manager of the Park Works of the Crucible Steel Company of America:

"In 1813 Tupper & McKowan operated the first 'blister steel' furnace in Pittsburgh. It did not prove a success.

"In 1841 Patrick and James Dunn made 'blister steel' for J. H. Schoenberger. The business was unsuccessful, and was abandoned in a year or two. About the same time Tingle & Sugden began making cast steel on a small scale for their own use for files. Not a success.

"In 1845 Jones & Quigg began making 'blister steel' for springs and plows. About the same time Coleman, Hailman & Company started making 'blister steel' for the same purpose.

"From about 1844 most of the manufacturers of puddled iron made 'blister steel', but Jones & Quigg, and Coleman, Hailman & Company were the only two establishments that could then be classed as 'steel works.' Both these firms tried to make cast steel but failed to make a success of it.

"In 1848 Singer-Nimick & Company engaged in making 'blister steel' and in 1853 took up the manufacture of cast steel for saws and agricultural implements, and increased their plant to make the finer grades of tool steels.

"What was known as 'blister steel' was made from puddled iron by packing the iron bars between layers of charcoal in a retort furnace and heating up the retort for a week or more, the wrought iron absorbing the Carbon. This product might well have been called 'carbonized wrought iron.'

"The 'cast steel' referred to was steel melted in a crucible and cast into moulds as is done today, producing crucible steel ingots.

"From all appearances, Singer-Nimick & Company in 1853 were the first to succeed in making crucible cast steel in Pittsburgh, the attempts of other parties at earlier dates having been without success."

THE EDGAR THOMSON STEEL WORKS—1876.

104 THE UNWRITTEN HISTORY OF BRADDOCK'S FIELD.

pass (it was a positive roll train, horizontal construction). There were twelve to fourteen rail passes in all. The hot saws were operated by a 14 x 24" engine. There were four straightening presses, and four drill presses operated by a 12 x 20" engine. Two cold saws were operated by an 11 x 20" engine.

We must pause to note a change in the name of the concern, even before this plant commenced operation. The panic prompted the Pennsylvania legislature to pass an act in 1874 authorizing the formation of limited liability companies. In the failure of Andrew Kloman, a member of the original firm, his partners saw the dangers of the existing contract, and accordingly on October 12, 1874, the firm of Carnegie, McCandless & Company dissolved into the Edgar Thomson Steel Company, Limited, capital $1,000,000, which purchased the new plant for $631,250.43 and assumed a mortgage thereon of $201,000. From an old catalogue, whose date I have placed at 1877, we find the organization of this firm to have been as follows:—

MEMBERS.

A. Carnegie, of Carnegie, Bro. & Co., 57 Broadway, New York.
John Scott, President, A. V. R. R. Co., Pittsburgh, Pa.
D. McCandless, Vice Pres., Exchange Nat. Bank, Pittsburgh, Pa.
D. A. Stewart, Pres. Pgh. Loco. & Car Works, Pittsburgh, Pa.
Thos. M. Carnegie, Treas., Keystone Bridge Co., Pittsburgh, Pa.
H. Phipps, Jr., Treas., Lucy Furnace Co., Pittsburgh, Pa.
Wm. P. Shinn, V. P., A. V. R. R. Co., Pittsburgh, Pa.

MANAGERS.

D. McCandless, Chairman.
John Scott,   Thomas M. Carnegie,   D. A. Stewart,
Wm. P. Shinn, Secretary and Treasurer.

OPERATING OFFICERS.

Wm. P. Shinn, General Manager,
Capt. Wm. R. Jones, Gen'l Supt.   Capt. Thos. H. Lapsly, Supt. Rail Mill.

CAPTAIN JONES.

JULIAN KENNEDY.

THE UNWRITTEN HISTORY OF BRADDOCK'S FIELD.   107

ADMINISTRATION OF CAPTAIN WILLIAM R. JONES.[1]

Here must have been a remarkable man. After a lapse of almost 30 years his aging employees still glow with pleasure at the mention of his name, and the most calm and philosophic of them flush with resentment at the suggestion that he could have had a fault. The whole world, in fact, seems leagued together to give this man a title of nobility "which it will forever defend."

Frankly admitted on all sides is the fact that Jones had a fiery temper. Beyond that, the most cynical, the most philosophic of his men utterly refuse to say one word that is not complimentary to the dead lion, and the conscientious historian can do nothing but record eulogy on eulogy.

His remarkable hold on the hearts of men originated in his physical and moral courage. Physically he was absolutely fearless, and morally he had the courage to give expression to every good impulse of his soul; to give freely and generously on every impulse, undeterred by fear of untoward consequences or accusations of partiality; likewise, he had the courage to confess his error when he was wrong, to apologize to the humblest of his men when he thought he had erred, and under any circumstances, to do or say whatever he thought at the moment to be right.

He was a great lover of sports, and in encouraging them established a tradition for his office which has ever since obtained. On the old race track (now the Union R. R. yard) he and C. C. Teeter and others often had horse races, and the Captain was himself a stockholder in the old Pittsburgh Base Ball Club.

One of the greatest mechanical geniuses of his time,[2] and a born leader of men, he was a most fortunate head for the young plant to secure.

---

(1) Born in Luzerne Co., Pa., Feb. 23, 1839. At age of ten apprenticed to Crane Iron Co. at Catasauqua, Pa., foundry and machine shop. At 16 regular journeyman machinist. Next to William Millens Machine Shop, Jeanesville, Pa. In 1856 went to I. P. Morris & Company's Philadelphia shops as machinist. In the panic of 1857, farm hand and lumberman at Tyrone. In 1859, machinist at Cambria Iron Works, Johnstown, and in the same year went to Chattanooga, Tenn., assisting in erection of blast furnace, where he married Miss Harriet Lloyd. In 1861 machinist with Cambria Iron Co. In 1862 volunteered on Lincoln's call, enlisting as private in 133d Reg. P. V. Promoted to corporal. Captain of Company F, 194th Reg. P. V. Was in battles of Fredericksburg and Chancellorsville. In 1865 returned to Cambria as Assistant General Superintendent. Resigned August, 1873.

There was a quiet rivalry between Jones and Barnes for the Edgar Thomson Superintendency, but Jones secured the appointment.

(2) Patented device for operating ladles in Bessemer process; improvement in hose couplings; fastenings for Bessemer converters; washers for ingot moulds; hot beds for bending rails; machine for sawing metal bars; apparatus for compressing ingots while casting; ingot mould; cooling roll journals and shafts; feeding appliance for rolling mills; gas furnace for boilers; appliance for rolls; housing caps for rolls; and the famous Jones Mixer, an "apparatus and method for mixing molten Pig Metal."

On the operating staff of Captain Jones were the following men:—Engineers and Chief Draughtsmen: Jno. Stevenson, Jr., Simon C. Collin, Wm. I. Mann, P. T. Berg, and C. M. Schwab, C. E.; Blast Furnaces, Julian Kennedy,[1] J. Cremer, James Gayley; Furnace Master Mechanic, Rich. Stevens; Mill Master Mechanic, Thos. James; Electrician, Wm. R. Pierce; Superintendent Boilers, John Noey; Converting Works, John Rinard and H. W. Benn; Carpenter, Geo. Nimon; Transportation and Labor, F. L. Bridges and Thos. Cosgrove; Chief Clerk, C. C. Teeter; Roll Designer, Robert Morris; Rail Mills, Capt. Thos. H. Lapsly and John Hutzen; Finishing Department, John Frederick; Secretary, W. E. Gettys; Masonry, Thos. Addenbrook; Chief Chemists: A. J. Preusse, S. A. Ford, H. C. Torrance, Albert DeDeken.

During that September the young plant put out 1,119 tons of rails, at a cost of $57 per ton. The very first rails sold for $80 a ton, but the average price for the month netted $66.50 f. o. b.[2] works, making a profit for the firm of $10,630.50 at the very start. By the end of the year the rail profits amounted to $41,970. During 1876 they made $181,000 and in 1877, $190,379.

The profits of the young concern would have been even larger but for the steadily decreasing price brought by steel rails:—

1873	$120	per ton
1874	100	per ton
1875	70	per ton
1876	58	per ton
1877	45	per ton
1878	42	per ton

With such a falling market, the ingenuity of Jones was taxed to the utmost, and the economy of Shinn and Phipps exerted to the full. It was at this time, in fact, that Wm. P. Shinn, General Manager, introduced the exact cost keeping system, which, perfected by Phipps, has obtained ever since. Only by constant invention and improvement could Jones keep operating costs below the falling market prices, for you will note that the selling price of rails in 1877 was $12 below the cost of producing those rails in 1875. As early as 1877, therefore, we find Jones making marked improvements at the mill, one of which was an automatic roller table, operated by a single man, to displace the hook and tong men at the stands.

---

(1) Mr. Kennedy was at E. T. Works from 1879 to 1883.

(2) "Free on board cars at......"

The longest rail rolled in ordinary practice was 40 feet, although at the Centennial of 1876 the young plant had a 90-foot rail on exhibition.

We come now to the next great period of development at the plant. While blooms for the rail mill were secured sometimes from Cambria and occasionally even from England, most of the pig iron came from Lucy Furnaces. All of the Edgar Thomson firm were not interested in Lucy's welfare, and hence discussions arose as to the proper price Edgar Thomson should pay for pig iron. Furthermore, under the direction of Captain Jones, the plant was rapidly proving itself a most profitable venture, and the success of the Lucy project was very enticing. From these considerations it was therefore decided to erect a blast furnace plant at Edgar Thomson, and the campaign started in 1879 under the supervision of Mr. Julian Kennedy. Andrew Kloman, one of the original partners, had failed, and a small charcoal furnace which he had built at Escanaba was purchased for $16,000 or so and transported to Braddock, where it became the old 65 x 15 ft. Furnace "A."[1] This furnace was blown in January 4, 1880,[2] and on her first lining produced an average of 56 tons daily, with about 2,650 pounds coke to the ton of iron. Mr. Richard Stevens, who had come to the plant in March, 1875, was given the position of Master Mechanic at the new Furnace Department, and ably assisted in making it a success.

A second furnace, "B", was blown in April 2, 1880, and the third furnace of the group, the "C", November 6, 1880. Furnace "B" in her first year produced an average of 5,500 tons per month on 2,570 pounds

---

(1) The "A", "B", and "C" Furnaces were constructed (according to Mr. Addenbrook) from drawings and plans furnished by the Philadelphia branch of Chas. Cochran & Company, an English concern.

The "A", "B", and "C" engines were built by Mackintosh, Hemphill & Company, of Pittsburgh. Originally they had 32" steam cylinders, 84" air cylinders, and 48" stroke. The shaft was 12" in diameter and crank pins 6", and engines were built for a maximum pressure of 7 pounds. There was one engine room with six blowing engines, and one pump house with three Worthington 3,500,000-gallon duplex pumps.

(2) The first furnace was lit by Captain Jones' daughter, Cora, and this pretty custom has been generally followed ever since. For some inscrutable reason what sentiment there is in the steel business seems to converge on the grim and fairly silent blast furnace. The far more impressive converter is ignored. Many blast furnaces received affectionate titles, such as "Carrie," "Edith," "Lucy," "Isabella," "Mary," Alice," etc.

coke to the ton of iron, and the "C" Furnace produced similar results.[1]

Labor was cheap,[2] and improvements came rapidly, and by 1881 the new plant had cleared $2,690,157.57 and its prosperity remained unchecked. During that year the rapid growth of the steel industry justified further expansion, and on April 1st, Carnegie Bros. & Co., as the firm was now called,[3] purchased 26 acres from Wm. Martin and wife, covering part of the present Open Hearth site and the Union Railroad yard tracks. In that year a Blooming Mill was erected, being enlarged to 36" size, followed in 1882 by a new converting works. Plans were also drawn for a new General Office building, and in the spring of 1882 the Captain at last took a well earned vacation and went to Europe, an experience which we may imagine he enjoyed to the full.

The corner stone of the present general office building was laid May 27, 1882, and from the papers found therein we learn that even at that early date the Amalgamated Association, a labor union, was having trouble with the manufacturers, although it did not develop into anything serious for years later.

In England, Captain Jones, who was such a common, every-day, figure on Braddock streets, where he would stroll along eating peanuts (which often cost him 25 or 50c a package—"no change, thank you,")—in England, this man was greeted as a marvel and a genius. What he had accomplished in production had astonished the British manufacturers and revolutionized the steel industry. The profits of the Braddock plant had rolled up enormously, and already repaid in full the original investment:—

---

(1) "B & C" were 20 ft. diameter of bosh, 80 ft. high. They had eight stoves, six being 75 x 20 and two 75 x 21 ft.

(2) Boys, 50c daily; general laborers, $1.20 and $1.30; blacksmith, $2, helper, $1.40; machinist, $2.25, helper, $1.40; carpenter, $2.10; bricklayer, $1.30; heater, $100 monthly; roller, $120; spiegel melter, $85; vesselman, $90.

(3) David McCandless, first chairman of the Company, died in 1879, and Wm. P. Shinn, General Manager, expected to succeed him. Thos. M. Carnegie, however, was elected. Shinn was bitterly disappointed, and at this time became involved in legal tangles with the other partners, finally resigning from the company. Consequently, a new firm was organized April 1, 1881, Carnegie Bros. & Company, Ltd., capital $5,000,000, the stock being divided as follows:—

Andrew Carnegie	$2,737,977.05
Thos. M. Carnegie	878,096.58
Henry Phipps	878,096.58
Dav. A. Stewart	175,318.78
John Scott	175,318.78
Gardiner McCandless	105,191.00
J. W. Vandervort	50,000.00

Although frequently invited, Jones was never a stockholder. He once told the executive officers, "Oh, pay me a h—l of a salary and let it go at that." His request was generously met for he received $50,000 a year.

THE UNWRITTEN HISTORY OF BRADDOCK'S FIELD. 111

1875	$ 41,970
1876	181,007
1877	190,379
1878	250,000
1879	401,800
1880	1,625,000
5-1/3 Years	$2,690,156

Meanwhile the blast furnace development continued, Furnace "D" being blown in April 19, 1882,[1] "E" June 27, 1882,[2] "F" October 7, 1886, and "G", June 20, 1887.[3] On April 1, 1887, an addition to the plant was purchased from John McKinney, 21 acres in all, covering the site of the present No. 3 Mill and Splice Bar department.

Just as the early steel makers gave their lives to the development of the young plant, so did their families abandon their very homes to its encroaching progress. About where the electric shop now stands, two rows of ten houses each had been built in 1876 and across the old road was another row of houses where No. 3 Mill now is. Four fine brick houses were built in 1882 on the site of the present "J" and "K" furnaces, and at different times were occupied by Julian Kennedy, Richard Stevens, Thomas Cosgrove, C. M. Schwab, C. C. Teeter, Morgan Harris, Michael Killeen, and Thos. James. These houses now began to be too close to the smoke and dirt of the works for the comfort of the occupants, and row by row they went down, the last ones, at the Furnace Department, being destroyed in 1890. (Capt. Jones himself lived in the house now occupied by Mr. A. E. Maccoun).

In September, 1888, Jones' greatest invention, the "Jones Mixer," 125 tons capacity, was placed in operation. The iron from all the furnaces is poured into this mixer, and thus uniform iron is supplied to the converters. The patent on this mixer was successfully defended by the Steel Corporation in 1905, and the idea has been used in all the steel plants of the world.

---

(1) The "A, B & C" engines had proved inadequate, so the "D & E" engines were built, for a maximum air pressure of 12 pounds. They also became inadequate for the work required, so the steam cylinders were changed to 40" diameter. These engines were built by Robinson & Rea, of Pittsburgh. Here were six engines for two furnaces, 40 x 84 x 48" stroke, 12" shaft and 6" crank pins.

(2) The "D & E" furnaces were 23 ft. diameter of bosh and 80 ft. high. They had six stoves each 78½ x 21 ft. and one Whitwell stove 78 x 20 ft. Cast houses were 54 x 180 ft.

(3) The "F & G" were 22 ft. diameter of bosh and 80 ft. high. They had seven stoves, 78½ x 21 ft. Cast houses 55 x 160 ft. Five 40 x 84 x 60" stroke blowing engines.

The plant up to this time had been under the control of labor organizations. The Amalgamated Association broke up in 1884, only to be succeeded by the Knights of Labor. The plant had been run on an eight-hour basis, and when the company attempted to inaugurate a twelve-hour basis in 1887, trouble ensued. The men refused to sign the annual agreement, and a strike followed December 31, 1887, which continued until May 12, 1888, the plant being entirely shut down except for the mechanical department. When the men finally surrendered and signed the sliding scale inaugurated at that time (by which their pay, in many cases, varies with the selling price of the product) also accepting the 12-hour day, the backbone of Union labor was broken in the Edgar Thomson mills. To C. C. Teeter much of the credit for this first sliding scale must be given.

Captain Jones had often told the officials of his company that if they would only give him the chance he would build them a rail mill that was worthy of the name and would far surpass the old one that they had, and in 1887 he got his chance. In that year the new mill, now known as No. 1, was constructed, with every late improvement of the day installed, and the old mill was slated for the scrap heap.

In the new mill the ordinary three high, positive roll train, run by a single engine, was divided into three trains, the first five passes being made in one three-high 24" train, the second five in a second three-high 24" train, to which the first delivers directly, and the last finishing pass in a two-high train of 24" rolls. Each train is run by its own independent engine, the first and second being 46 x 60", and the third 30 x 48". This mill was nearly automatic, one man handling the levers which lift the tables, move the tumblers, etc. Each roll train had a hydraulic crane for changing rolls. From the bloom furnaces to the hot beds, the roll trains, tables, etc., were in one long, straight building 520 x 60 ft, the hot beds being in a wing at right angles to this. The straightening department was another long building 625 x 47 ft., parallel to the mill. The roll shop was in a wing 60 x 60 ft. on the north side of the roll trains. The steel department got its steam from 70 boilers of various makes. The converters were also changed at this time to 10-ton capacity, to supply the increased demand for steel.

Needless to say, the new mill was fully up to expectations, and in 1889 the annual output of the plant in rails leaped to 277,401 tons.

In that year, the last one of his life, the Captain placed a capstone on a life of charity and benevolence by his humane and vigorous efforts on the occasion of the Johnstown flood. As soon as word was received of this terrible disaster (May 30, 1889) he dispatched a trusted messenger to investigate, and immediately upon receipt of reliable information he systematized the collection of supplies which formed the first relief to come to the stricken people. He shortly assumed command of the Pennsylvania Railroad workmen sent to Johnstown, and did heroic work in alleviation of the suffering of that devastated district.

We come now to the close of this remarkable administration. Jones had taken a new and untried plant, built up an efficient organization, and made a name for the firm all over the commercial world. Just as he had erected the old G. A. R. monument on the hill above Braddock, so did he put Braddock itself on the world's map.

On the night of September 26, 1889, Furnace "C" had been "hanging" for 36 hours, and Captain Jones, Schwab, Gayley, Addenbrook, and others were working around it. A workman was engaged in striking a bar inserted in the tapping hole, to open the furnace up, when Jones, dissatisfied with his efforts, said, "Let me do it," as was his habitual expression. Seizing the sledge he struck the bar, and at the same moment the furnace burst, its contents splashing over his head and shoulders. Springing quickly backward, the Captain struck his head, in falling, upon a modock cinder car. He never regained consciousness, and died in the Pittsburgh Homeopathic Hospital September 28, 1889.

The whole community was appalled and the country shocked by the death of this famous character, and according to one historian a throng larger than the population of the town itself followed the casket to the grave. In this catastrophe more than one man saw the loss of his best friend and counsellor, and, filing past his departed leader cold in death, felt with Marc Antony,

"My heart is in the coffin there with Caesar."

ADMINISTRATION OF CHARLES M. SCHWAB.[1]

OCTOBER 1, 1889-SEPTEMBER 30, 1892.

Under an able master had been trained and developed one of the greatest brains in the American steel industry. Starting in 1880 as stake driver on the engineer corps, (where he worked with a son of Captain Jones) C. M. Schwab's engineering ability and knowledge of men early gained attention, and by the time of Jones' death he had become Chief Engineer of the plant, and assistant to the Captain, having supervision

---

(1) Born in Williamsburg, Pa., 1862.

of the Homestead plant under that official. (The Homestead plant was under the direction of the Edgar Thomson General Superintendent up to October 1, 1892). He was, therefore, an experienced executive when he took charge of the Edgar Thomson establishment on the death of Jones.

The historian is not a little puzzled by the conflicting descriptions that he receives of this man: some say he was a superlatively great engineer, others that he was not; some say he was a great inventor, others that he was not; some say he achieved a high technical development, others that he did not. But a man does not rise from stake driver to General Superintendent in nine years without some very good reason.

The best analysis of his genius is, perhaps, as Mr. Wm. P. Brennan[1] expresses it: He was a great general. He had a true sense of proportion, an appreciation of the relative value of conflicting factors, a mind that could grasp the most complex situation, and last, but not least, he inspired his men with confidence in him and his ability, had perfect knowledge of human nature, and absolute mastery over men. I believe that unskilled in military tactics as he was, Chas. M. Schwab could have assumed command of the Union armies during the Civil War and achieved as great success as Ulysses S. Grant, and incidentally I doubt if he would have wasted 10,000 men in 20 minutes at Cold Harbor. An intuitive grasp of *essentials* and consummate tact made him great.

Schwab was (and is) a thorough going democrat to the very core. To William Powell (clerk to Thomas Addenbrook) he confides: "Do you know, I can hardly realize that here I am General Superintendent of this plant. Why should I be General Superintendent? What do I know so much more than you fellows about this business?"

Of course, to his superior officers he turned quite a different side, and would blandly take credit for anything and everything that came along, but this democracy was real, and not an assumed trait of the man. Gold or titles have never confused or blurred his vision. To him, regardless of wealth or title, every man is still just a human being whom he judges on his own intrinsic value as a man.

He has the sensitive, visionary soul of a great artist, and his consummate tact has arisen from his innate desire to see things "go smoothly.". He always hated "scenes," arguments, or disturbances of any kind. Only a few years ago I heard this lord of millions—yes hundreds of millions—explain and apologize and explain again when he had unwittingly,

---

(1) An old employee; now Accident Clerk at the works.

CHARLES M. SCHWAB.

by the good-natured use of a pet nickname, affronted a choleric old employee of former days. Although, in the eyes of those present, Schwab had not been guilty of the slightest *faux pas*, he seemed exasperated to his very soul by an apparent blunder. For the man has perfect tact; he is an artist, and the instrument on which he plays is *men*.

The band which he organized at the steel works is giving a concert, and standing in the crowd Schwab discovers a lady of mature years. He is distinctly annoyed by the discomfort so elderly a person must be in, and finally going out he invites her in, and gives her a chair.

He is good-natured and big hearted: He and Cosgrove are passing through the mill, when a laboratory employee[1] throws a snowball at one or the other which hits Schwab. Schwab's temper flames up, and the man immediately seeks employment elsewhere. However, the laboratory needs the man, and Cosgrove has the temerity to take the question up with Schwab. "Oh well, take him back, I don't care. But explain to the darn fool that I can't have every Tom, Dick and Harry on the plant firing snowballs at me. Look how many thousand men there are here!" a true and just plea.

The labor world is violently disturbed, and every now and then a committee of men comes up from the mill to demand higher wages. Schwab's first and only thought is to avoid a scene, or any rupture of harmony. He welcomes the men cordially, naturally, gracefully; he gives everyone a chair and passes around a box of fine cigars. There is in his manner no trace of superiority, hostility, or suspicion. He talks with the men about their work, their families, their hobbies, and relates jokes that occur to him. The men are pleased and rather surprised at the pleasantness of their visit. Time passes. The men mention their complaint in a casual way. Schwab listens to them courteously, sympathetically, and frankly explains the situation as man to man, not as employer to inferior. If he can do anything for them he promises to do it; if he can't, he explains just why he can't. He inspires the confidence of the men, and they believe what he tells them. Shortly, taking another cigar, they file out to the accompaniment of cordial "good-byes." Frequently there has been no wage increase, but likewise,—and what is more important to Schwab—no unpleasantness.

C. M. Schwab's operating staff consisted of the following men:— James Gayley, Superintendent Blast Furnaces; M. Killeen, Asst. Supt.

---

(1) Edw. F. Shultz related this incident to me regarding himself the other day.

Furnaces; Thos. Cosgrove, Supt. Transportation; H. W. Benn, Supt. Converting Works; S. A. Ford, Chief Chemist; H. B. A. Keiser, Chief Engineer; Rich. Stevens, Master Mechanic Blast Furnaces; Thos. James, Master Mechanic, Steel Department; Geo. Nimon and A. McWilliams, Foremen Carpenters; Conser McClure, Roll Designer; John Noey, Superintendent Boilers; John Hutzen, T. H. Lapsly and D. L. Miller, Supt. Blooming and Rail Mills; C. C. Teeter, Chief Clerk; Thomas Addenbrook, Foreman Masonry; Roger Bowman, Supt. Finishing Department; Electrician, Wm. Pierce and C. M. Tolman; Secretary, Otto Rhinehart.

In 1890 the old Blooming Mill, with 36″ three-high train (operated by 36 x 72″ engine) was changed to a three-high 40″ mill, C. Mercader being the supervising engineer for that work. The plant at that time consumed about 25,000,000 gallons of water daily, and there were five main pumping stations. The Electric Light Plant[1] contained three Brush 65-light dynamos, running about 175 arc lamps. Power was provided by three 11 x 22″ Buckeye engines. There was a locomotive repair house measuring 54 x 124 feet, and whereas the original plant had had but one broad gauge and one narrow gauge locomotive for yard service, the plant now boasted 12 broad gauge and 14 narrow gauge locomotives.

Meanwhile the development of the Blast Furnaces continued, two more blast furnaces being blown in:

Furnace "H" ....February 27, 1890[2]
Furnace "I" ....August 14, 1890

The whole battery of blast furnaces produced, during Schwab's administration, an average of 54,782 tons of iron monthly.[3]

Only one rail mill was operated during his term of office, the new mill having entirely superseded the old one, which now became known as

---

(1) In January, 1881, Wm. Pierce took charge of the electrical department, and continued until 1892, being superseded by C. M. Tolman, a college man. The electrical equipment in 1880 consisted of one two-light Brush Arc Dynamo installed at the Furnace Machine Shop; it was driven by a line shaft and was the first electrical machine installed at this plant. In 1882 the second lighting plant was installed at the "A" Furnace, consisting of a 45-lamp arc machine, and the third plant was built near the present location of the "B & W." boiler house, consisting of two 65-Lamp Brush arc machines. In 1891 there was installed one 75 K. W. 60 cycle A. C. generator driven by a Porter-Allen engine. During this year the first motor driven soaking pit crane ever built in America was installed at Edgar Thomson, and one of its motors is still in service at the Furnace Department.

(2) Each 22′ diameter of bosh and 90′ high. They had 7 stoves, each 78′ 6″ x 21′. Cast houses were 54 x 180′. Engine house had five E. P. Allis engines, each having a steam cylinder of 40″ diameter, and 60″ stroke. 24 boilers furnished the steam supply, each 28′ long, 54″ diameter, with two 18″ flues. The "F & G" and "H & I" batteries were connected with a steam pipe.

(3) A Gates Mastodon crusher was used for crushing limestone. It had a capacity of 800 tons per day.

"No. 2 Mill." The new mill produced an average of 26,051 tons monthly, as compared with less than 15,000 tons produced by the old mill in its best days.

The plant now employed about 3,500 men, and produced on an average of 1,550 tons of furance iron per day. The record for a single blast furnace was 457 tons for 24 hours, and the best daily rail record 1,417 tons.

Like his predecessor, Schwab was very generous, and gave churches in his town of every denomination many a helping hand. More than one church building, in fact, stands today as a memorial of his generosity and breadth of religious viewpoint.

To the traditions of the office that he held, Schwab added the encouragement of the arts, and at his own expense equipped and organized a fine brass band. Floyd St. Clair, one of his employees, became the leader of this band, and later made a name for himself in the world of music.

After the fatal riots at the Homestead plant in 1892, Schwab, who was well known and liked by the Homestead men from his former work there, was asked to take sole charge of the wrecked organization of that concern. This work he undertook (with the greatest success) October 1, 1892, and James Gayley, Superintendent of the Blast Furnaces, became General Superintendent.

ADMINISTRATION OF JAMES GAYLEY.[1]
(OCTOBER 1, 1892-FEBRUARY 28, 1895.)

James Gayley was probably the greatest technician who ever filled the superintendency. His record at the Crane Iron Works (Catasauqua, Pa.) Missouri Furnace Co., (St. Louis) and E. & G. Brooke Iron Co., (Birdsboro, Pa.) had attracted the notice of Captain Jones, and in 1885 he came to Edgar Thomson as Superintendent of the Blast Furnaces.

In this capacity he made a record as an economist, and reduced the coke consumption to a point that has been little if any excelled since that time. He invented the bronze cooling plate for blast furnace walls, the auxiliary casting stand for Bessemer steel plants, and was the first to use the compound condensing blowing engine with the Blast Furnace. He

---

(1) Born 1855 at Lock Haven, Pa. Graduated as mining engineer from Lafayette College 1876. Subsequently became first vice president of the U. S. Steel Corporation. In 1904 and 1905 was President of the American Institute of Mining Engineers, and from 1905 to 1911 President of the Board of Directors.

JAMES GAYLEY.

also invented the dry-air blast, for which the Franklin Institute awarded him the Elliott Cresson medal.

Under his superintendency the Blast Furnace Department had commanded the notice of the whole metallurgical world, and by his wise selection of stock, and general management, with certain other favoring conditions,[1] his furnaces made record productions. Gayley, in fact, was to the blast furnace what Jones had been to the rail mill.

Brilliant and intellectual as he was, the spirit of education and enlightenment found in him a willing disciple. Not only was he a keenly commercial and technical steel-master, but he was also imbued with the inspiring, uplifting, educational fire that in other days animated such men as Sturmius, Rabelais, Montaigne, Ascham, Mulcaster, Pestalozzi, and Rousseau. Far in advance of his time, he was interested heart and soul in the instruction and education of his men, and under his auspices the finest lectures were delivered, gratis, for them in Braddock Carnegie Free Library. Some of the printed reports of these lectures are still extant, and are the finest brochures obtainable on their respective subjects.[2] Mrs. Gayley, on her part, gave frequent talks on household economy and domestic science.

Never was there a more sincere, earnest, or conscientious man in the superintendent's chair.

The use of molten iron, together with Ferro Manganese, had originated at Edgar Thomson, but under this administration the process was abandoned. (In this connection it should also be noted, in the metallurgical line, that the direct process, i. e., using molten iron direct from the blast furnaces, was first used in America at this plant according to Mr. H. W. Benn, who believes it began in 1881 or '82. He also states that Edgar Thomson was the first plant to cast on cars successfully.)

Mr. Gayley's operating staff consisted of D. G. Kerr, Supt. Furnaces; Rich. Stevens, M. M. Furnaces; Thos. James, M. M. Steel Department; C. M. Tolman, Supt. Electrical Department; John Noey, Supt. Boilers; H. W. Benn, Supt. Converting Works; Geo. Nimon and A. Mc-

---

(1) The Edgar Thomson metallurgist, Mr. J. D. Lewis, states that while the ore in Gayley's time ran sometimes as high as 64 and 65 per cent iron, it now only runs about 50 and 51 per cent. Again, low Silicon iron seems to have been acceptable in those days, and low Silicon permits low coke practice. These conditions, however, in no way detract from Mr. Gayley's accomplishments, for the simple reason that in the day when he won his fame his competitors had, for the most part, the same materials to work with.

(2) The lecture on the geological history of the Pittsburgh district is far better than anything that can now be obtained from the State Geological Department.

THE UNWRITTEN HISTORY OF BRADDOCK'S FIELD. 121

Williams, Foremen Carpenters; Thos. Cosgrove, Supt. Labor and Transportation; Conser McClure, Roll Designer; C. C. Teeter, Chief Clerk; Thos. Addenbrook, Supt. Masonry; D. L. Miller, Supt. Rail Mill; Wm. Connor, Superintendent Foundry; G. E. Harris, Supt. Finishing Department; Chief Draughtsmen and Engineers: H. B. A. Keiser, E. E. Slick, F. DuPeyster Thompson, and Jno. F. Lewis; Secretary, James E. Mitchell.

Gayley had charge of the plant during the panic years that followed Grover Cleveland's election in 1892. Times were very bad, labor was restless, and the Carnegie officials exacting in their demands, and his position was extremely difficult.

Not content with obliterating groves of trees, township roads, and whole rows of dwelling houses, the expanding plant now turned back the very streams from their courses, and in 1893 Turtle Creek's course was moved 1,125 feet east from the old bed back of the Converting Mill to its present location. On May 12, 1891, Carnegie Bros. & Co. had purchased about 7½ acres of land from John Dalzell, chiefly in what is now the Union Railroad Valley yard, and on December 28, 1891, 12 additional acres from Wm. J. McKinney (on the site of the present O. H. plant) and again on July 13, 1892, the Carnegie Steel Company (note the change in name) [1] Limited, secured about 11 acres from Wm. F. Knox in the Union Railroad main track yard and Turtle Creek district.

With this expansion in territory the way was clear for an extension that the plant badly needed, viz: a Foundry Department, and under Mr. Gayley the entire Foundry Department was constructed.

No. 1 Foundry commenced operation July 11, 1893, producing during the remainder of that year 1893 tons. This was probably the first foundry of the kind to make ingot moulds sucessfully with direct molten metal from the furnaces.

No. 2 Foundry commenced operations January 11, 1894, and is used for making general iron castings, and the third and last foundry commenced foundry work March 19, 1894, producing brass and bronze castings. The original Brass Foundry of Mr. Gayley's time was very small, and has since been torn down.

Of this new department, Mr. William Connor, formerly of the Mackintosh & Hemphill Co., became Superintendent.

During Mr. Gayley's administration the abandoned old mill was

---

[1] The Carnegie Steel Company, Limited, was formed July 1, 1892, and was a coalition of Carnegie Brothers & Company, Limited, and Carnegie, Phipps & Company, the capital being $25,000,000.

122   THE UNWRITTEN HISTORY OF BRADDOCK'S FIELD.

again brought into use, producing some 32,000 tons of rails, and entering upon a second lease of life.

Mr. Gayley's exhaustive technical knowledge was desired by the officials in the City Office, and he was accordingly given the post of Ore Agent March 1, 1895, being succeeded at Edgar Thomson by Mr. Thomas Morrison, General Superintendent of the Duquesne Works.

ADMINISTRATION OF THOMAS MORRISON.
FEBRUARY 28, 1895-MAY 31, 1903.

Thomas Morrison was first of all a great mechanician and rail mill man, next a great financier, but withal a hard, practical, common sense man of business, blunt, direct, and outspoken, four square with the world. He had the usual distaste of the man with a mechanical turn of mind for the vagaries of words and phrases and the confusion of official papers. As a rule, he did not dictate his correspondence, being impatient with such affairs, and turning with more cheerfulness to problems of a mechanical or operative nature. He was a strict, fair, and just disciplinarian, and when he left we find his men presenting him with a fine watch and heartily expressing their conviction that he had given everyone a fair deal.

With Mr. Morrison from Duquesne came Mr. G. E. F. Gray[1] as Chief Clerk, who had served in that capacity at Duquesne and Homestead, and was eminently fitted for that position by integrity of character and broad, conservative judgment. This position Mr. Gray has held ever since.

Mr. Morrison's operating staff was as follows:—Assistant Gen'l Sup't, Chas. E. Dinkey; Supt. Blast Furnaces, D. G. Kerr, Geo. Crawford, and H. A. Brassert; Master Mechanic Furnaces, Rich. Stevens, Jno. F. Lewis, A. E. Maccoun; M. M. Steel Department, Thos. James; Chief Electrician, A. E. Maccoun, following C. M. Tolman; Supt. Boilers, John Noey; Supt. Converting Mill, H. W. Benn; Supt. Carpenters, etc., A. Mc-Williams and Reuben Abbiss; Supt. Foundry, Chas. E. Dinkey and Geo. England; Chief Inspector, E. B. White; Chief Engineers, E. E. Slick and Sydney Dillon; Chief Chemists, F. L. Grammar and C. B. Murray; Supt.

---

(1) Passenger service, Pennsylvania Railroad, January 18, 1873, until October, 1879. With Dithridge Chimney Company, 17th Street, South Side, Pittsburgh, from October, 1879, to September, 1881; Inspector and Clerk, Edgar Thomson Works, September 14, 1881, to October, 1886; Chief Clerk, Homestead, October, 1886, until December, 1887; Chief Clerk, Duquesne Works, January 1, 1888, until March 1, 1895; March 1, 1895, Chief Clerk Edgar Thomson Works.

THOMAS MORRISON.

Blooming and Rail Mills, D. L. Miller; Chief Clerk, G. E. F. Gray; Superintendent Finishing Department, Geo. E. Harris; Superintendent Masonry, Thos. Addenbrook; Roll Designer, Conser McClure, L. W. Nageley, F. H. Ghrist; Secretary, James E. Mitchell; Supt. Transportation and Labor, Thos. Cosgrove.

No. 1 Foundry was enlarged early in Morrison's administration (1899) and in 1898, No. 2 Foundry first began the manufacture of iron rolls. The Brass Foundry was torn down in 1902, and the old Power House was converted into the present Brass Foundry, employing about 65 men, and practically bringing the foundry to its present status.

On August 20, 1895, only a few months after Morrison had assumed charge, occurred the distressing explosion at "H" Furnace, wherein six were killed and eight badly burned. If it had been possible, this furnace would have retrieved itself during his term, however, for it completed a nine-years' run on a single lining for over 1,000,000 tons, being the first blast furnace in the world to accomplish such a feat.

During the early part of 1897, the mills' electrical demands had increased to such an extent that a new power house was built on the site of the present plant, the Foundry power house and Mill lighting plant being dismantled. The equipment of the new power house consisted of one 800 K. W. generator, a 400 K. W. generator moved from the Foundry, two 75 K. W. lighting machines and one 150 K. W. lighting machine. The old 250 H. P. generators of the Foundry power house were moved to No. 1 Rail Mill finishing yard, and subsequently scrapped.

A vital improvement effected by Morrison was the double furnace bell, forestalling the escape of gas in charging, which, together with the first automatic skip hoist in America, was put on Furnace "F" in August, 1897. This innovation did away with the necessity of men going on top of the furnace during regular operations.

A great number of electrical installations were put in during this period, perhaps the most noteworthy being the installation on the "B" Furnace, March 9, 1898, of the first *electrically* driven skip hoist in the world. This proved such a success that Morrison subsequently changed the following furnace skips to electric drive:—

Furnace "I", December 4, 1898.
Furnace "A", March 28, 1899.
Furnace "G", September 26, 1899.
Furnace "E", December 5, 1900.
Furnace "D", December 4, 1901.

Furnace "K", December 5, 1902.
Furnace "J", February 16, 1903.

A revolutionary installation was the pig machine, installed at the furnaces 1898. Previous to this the furnace iron had been cooled in chill moulds. The pig machine is an endless moving chain of pig moulds into which the iron is poured from the ladle, passed under water, and cooled.

Again, the blowing engines at the Furnace Department, which formerly had had single cylinders, and were run high pressure, with air tubs equipped with leather valves, were changed at the "A, B and C" in 1896 to independent compound condensing engines, and at the "D and E" to compound condensing steeple engines in 1897. The old type of engine has since been displaced throughout the plant as a result of this campaign.

The greatest plant development in steam economy, however, of this or any other administration was the replacement in 1895 of the old style tubular boilers by the Cahall water tube type. The "A, B and C" boiler house was rebuilt in 1896 and 1897, the "D and E" in 1897 and 1898, the "H and I" in 1902, and the "J and K" in 1902 and 1903. A second great economy effected was the connection of the Mill and Furnace Departments June, 1899, with a 24-inch steam line, thus allowing the removal of most of the coal fired boilers at the mill, and the use of gas fired boilers at the furnaces.

The Union Railroad interlocking plant was thrown into service in Bessemer yard October 26, 1897, and the first train brought in from North Bessemer on that date, which marks an epoch in the transportation system of the plant.

Under Mr. Morrison the first Weiss central condensing plant in this country was established at the Power House 1897. Since that time this type of central counter-current condenser has been installed at all the Blast Furnace steam blowing engine rooms and at all the departments of the mill where steam is used.

In this period of centralization, the Furnace Laboratory and Steel Works Laboratory were combined (1897) and the present laboratory erected, C. B. Murray being appointed chief chemist.

In 1899 the present Converting Mill building, housing four 15-ton converters, was erected for the plant by the Keystone Bridge Company, the building being 165 x 78½ x 31 ft. high, fully equipped with the latest electric and automatic devices throughout. The previous year (1898) the Blooming Mill had been again rebuilt, although still remaining a 40-inch

G. E. F. GRAY.

mill. Furnace "K" was completed and blown in December 5, 1902, and the "J" on February 16, 1903, each being 90' 10" high, the "J" having a 15' hearth while the "K" hearth is 15' 6".

The cry, which had been all for "tonnage" for years past, now began to turn toward "quality." With this in mind, Morrison installed what was known as the "Kennedy-Morrison process" in the rail mill December 5, 1900, which consisted of a cooling bed between the leader pass and the finishing pass, the idea being to put a harder surface upon the rail.

January 8, 1902, an addition was built to the power house, and the second 800 K. W. compound wound D. C. generator, driven by a vertical cross-compound Allis engine was installed. At this time we note that the second lighting line was run to Braddock, (the first line having been run 1894 or thereabouts).

The terrible Furnace "I" accident occurred March 31, 1903, the furnace "slipping" and dust collector blowing out. Nine men were killed in this disaster, and five badly burned.

Late in this administration Mr. W. J. Vance, Chief Shipper, resigned, and Mr. W. L. Miller assumed the duties of that office, which he is still creditably performing.

One of the most important and far reaching innovations of this progressive executive was the weekly meeting of department superintendents for the noon hour meal (generally held on Wednesdays) whereat the difficulties and troubles that beset each department are fully thrashed out for the instruction of all, and thorough harmony and understanding secured throughout the organization. This weekly dinner Mr. Morrison inaugurated October 18, 1899, and it has been most profitably continued ever since. The minutes of these meetings form a most valuable and accurate record for the plant, and it is greatly to be regretted that such a record was not to be obtained for the whole life of the organization.

I regret that lack of space forbids more detail of this vigorous man's term of office. Suffice it to say that under Morrison the plant smashed every record it had ever made, and on reviewing the administration no point appears wherein he did not surpass his predecessors in production. Roughly speaking, the amazing truth is that the plant was speeded up 70 or 80 per cent. While the mills had previously been producing around a quarter of a million tons of rails per annum, under Morrison they put out half a million or so.

Plain spoken and matter of fact as he was, it is the achievements of the man that strike our attention far more forcibly than the reserved

THOMAS JAMES.

D. L. MILLER

THOMAS H. McDONALD.

HARRY W. BENN.

THOMAS COSGROVE.

A. J. BOYLE.

A. J. PREUSSE.

JOHN RINARD.

CHAS. E. DINKEY,
Whose term of service as General Superintendent exceeds all others.

THE UNWRITTEN HISTORY OF BRADDOCK'S FIELD. 129

and unassuming personality which he presented to the world. I have tried to portray, roughly, in a non-technical manner, the results of his regime, and have been most fortunate if I have succeeded in conveying any idea of the cold brilliance of his administration.

ADMINISTRATION OF CHAS. E. DINKEY.
June 1, 1903..

Big executives have a weakness for the man who can get things done, and in June, 1901, Thomas Morrison had brought up the young man who had charge of the Foundry Department and placed him in his own office as Assistant General Superintendent. Two years later, after the formation of the United States Steel Corporation, when Mr. Morrison's extensive personal business demanded all of his time, he recommended his assistant, Chas. E. Dinkey, as his successor.

In the American Manufacturer years before, on October 4, 1889, Jos. D. Weeks had declared that the superintendency of the Edgar Thomson plant demanded greater executive capacity than the presidency of the United States. There now entered that superintendency a man trained under four executives of such caliber, and who, naturally of a reflective turn of mind and keenly observant, brought to that office the noblest qualities of those that had gone before: The force and driving power of Jones, the shrewd tact and generalship of Schwab, the chemistry and detail of Gayley, and the sound common sense and business acumen of Morrison. In him each of these qualities of his predecessors still lived on in one master executive.[1]

For his assistant, Chas. E. Dinkey chose John F. Lewis,[2] who was eminently fitted for such promotion by a rigorous course from early boy-

---

(1) A more complete account of Mr. Dinkey and his methods is given at the conclusion of this chapter.

(2) His service record at Edgar Thomson, as stated by himself, is as follows:—
  1875 Hammer boy, blacksmith shop.
  1876 Clerk in store rooms.
  1877 Machine shop.
  1878 Messenger under Capt. Jones.
  1879 Machine shop.
  1881 Drawing room.
  1883 Machine shop.
  1884 Drawing room.
  1887 Machine shop.
  1892 Drawing room.
  1896 Assistant master mechanic, Furnaces.
  1899 Master Mechanic, Furnaces.
  1903 Assistant General Superintendent.

JOHN F. LEWIS.

THE UNWRITTEN HISTORY OF BRADDOCK'S FIELD. 131

hood in shops and drawing room, and who at the time was Master Mechanic at the Blast Furnace Department. Mr. Lewis is naturally of an inventive turn of mind, and during past years has given to the mill many inventions and improvements, among which may be mentioned the vertical hydraulic ingot stripper (1891) (which alone reduced the force 56 men), steel tie fastening, stock distributing device for blast furnaces, etc., etc. The man lives in a mechanic's world, and thinks machinery as other men think words. His desk is constantly covered with a profusion of the most complicated and unintelligible sketches of gears, drives, trains, etc. of every description. A thorough sportsman, genial, considerate, and wholly democratic, he carries with him an intangible atmosphere of Southern chivalry.

With this period, the historian reaches the most difficult part of his task, for in the administration of Chas. E. Dinkey, up to the present time, not ten, twenty or fifty projects have been undertaken, *but 265 separate and distinct improvements effected of the average caliber of $90,000 or $100,000 each.* It is immediately apparent that in so brief a survey as this history, only the most prominent and interesting features can be touched upon.

His operating staff to date has consisted of the following men:—Assistant General Superintendent, Jno. F. Lewis; Chief Clerk, G. E. F. Gray; Superintendent Blast Furnaces, H. A. Brassert, A. E. Maccoun; Chief Electrician, A. E. Maccoun, E. Friedlaender; Steel Works Master Mechanic, Thos. James, John Richardson; Chief Engineer, Sydney Dillon, L. C. Edgar; Supt. Converting Works, H. W. Benn, L. T. Upton, C. F. McDonald; Supt. Finishing Department, Geo. E. Harris, Jas. V. Stewart; Supt. Blooming and Rail Mills, D. L. Miller; Supt. Masonry, Thos. Addenbrook, P. G. D. Strang; Chief Chemist, C. B. Murray, G. D. Chamberlain, C. E. Nesbit; Superintendent Labor and Transportation, Thos. Cosgrove, Wm. J. Dixon; Chief Roll Designer, F. H. Ghrist, F. F. Slick, I. W. Keener; Asst. Supt. Furnaces, M. Killeen, F. H. N. Gerwig; Foreman Carpenters, Reuben Abbiss; Superintendent Open Hearth, J. W. Kagarise; Special Engineer, Richard Stevens, A. F. T. Wolff; Supt. Foundry, Geo. England, S. B. Cuthbert; Supt. Boilers, John Noey, Geo. S. Kramer; Chief Inspector, E. B. White, J. K. Boyd; Master Mechanic Furnaces, Geo. W. Campbell; Supt. Splice Bar Shop, Edgar S. Wright, Superintendent No. 3 Mill, Frank F. Slick; Secretary, P. A. K. Black.

1903-04. One of the first acts of Mr. Dinkey's term was the changing of the township road from the old location through the mill to the present site, thus giving more yard room and greater area for expansion. The first street car ran over the new tracks July 4, 1903. The foundry was also extended 66 feet during this first year, and at the furnaces a great economy was effected by the installation April 28, 1904, of ten 110,000 gallon settling tanks for treating the acid Monongahela river water with lime and soda ash for boiler feed purposes.[1]

1904-05. The question of roll storage had now become a serious problem, for over 100 different rail sections were rolled at the plant. Accordingly in this year the 24 2-flue boilers at No. 1 Rail Mill were torn out and the Boiler House converted into a roll storage by installing a crane runway and using the old roll shop crane. A new 500-foot wharf and wharf boat were also constructed (besides various other improvements in this year) to take care of the river traffic, at a cost of $97,000.[2]

1905-06. The first gas engine installed at Edgar Thomson was a 21¾" x 30" horizontal tandem Westinghouse of the four cycle constant mixture type. It was started November 13, 1905, and ran until August 7, 1906, when it was returned to the builders for some necessary improvements. It was direct connected to a 250-K.W. generator, and furnished current for operating the Foundry. It was operated on blast furnace gas, and was the first engine of this type to be installed in this country.

The demand for light rails had been exceeding the supply for some years, and accordingly a special light section rail mill, the first electrical mill in this country, was constructed and placed in operation in July, 1905.

For the operation of this mill, Mr. Dinkey had long decided upon Mr. Frank F. Slick,[3] chief roll designer, whose technical education, energy, and versatility appealed to him. The actual appointment of Mr. Slick to this position, however, off-hand and nonchalant as it appeared, and the history of the infancy of that now famous mill,[4] are highly illustrative of both characters:

The mill being practically completed, Mr. Dinkey exclaimed one day

---

(1) Monongahela river water runs as high, at times, as 12 grains acid to the gallon, and about 1,000 pounds lime and 4,000 pounds soda ash are daily required for softening. Each of the ten tanks is emptied and filled an average of three times daily.

(2) The three remaining furnaces were equipped with electrically operated hoists 1904, i. e., Furnaces "C", "F" and "H".

(3) Born 1876, Johnstown, Pa. Was through Johnstown flood. Office boy, clerk, and assistant roller at Cambria Iron Works. Engineering Department, E. T. Works in February 1896; Assistant Engineer, Ordnance Department, Carnegie Steel Co., 1900; In charge of Roll Shop, E. T. Works, 1903. Supt. No. 3 Mill, July, 1905.

(4) An 18-inch mill for re-rolling billets and heavier sections into light rails. Has four roll stands, driven by two 1500 H. P., D. C. Motors. These motors were the first installed in this country for driving main rolls. The main building is 580 ft. x 43 x 26 ft. 8 in. high.

to a group of superintendents: "Well, here's the mill all right, but who the devil will we get to run this condemned sausage factory?"

"Me," said Slick. "I'll run it."

"Take it," said the Boss.

Scarcely, however, had the earnest young superintendent assumed his first charge than the wretched mill groaned feebly and stopped altogether.

Down came Mr. Dinkey. "Well, what's the matter here?"

"We have to make some repairs and get things straightened up, Mr. Dinkey. This mill is in frightful shape," said Slick.

Another day passed, and still no tonnage from No. 3.

Mr. Dinkey then invited Mr. Slick to call. Upon that unhappy man's appearance, he engaged him in some desultory conversation, in the course of which he confided to him that, personally, he greatly admired the picture of still life presented by the brand new mill, with the golden sunlight falling on polished brass and bronze, the silent roll stands fading away in murky perspective, and the stalwart workmen standing about obscured by the shadows of gigantic machines, and that, anyhow, he was the last man to discourage the aesthetic aspirations of his subordinates. He added, however, that in the capacity of superior officer he felt at liberty to make some suggestions in an artistic vein, and took this opportunity to remind Mr. Slick that Corot and many other great painters were wont to introduce a splash of red into the foreground of their masterpieces, which feature, in No. 3, could be best secured by introducing a red hot billet in the first roughing rolls.

The exasperated Mr. Slick heard him through in silence. Then, "Mr. Dinkey, if you'll just give me a chance to get that mill cleaned up right I'll give you the best mill going. I can run it right now if you want a second grade mill, but this isn't going to be that kind of an affair." And he made good his boast, for today No. 3 Mill stands first in the Steel Corporation, and probably ranks first for its kind in the entire United States.

1906-07. On Nov. 16, 1906, upon the resignation of Mr. David F. Melville as Assistant Chief Clerk, Mr. F. A. Power of the Foundry Department was appointed to succeed him, and took office at that time. This lively gentleman has long since justified his appointment by his earnest loyalty and the deeply conscientious discharge of his duty, while his Gargantuan laughter helps remove the dust that is only too prone to settle on the office windows.

Mr. Dinkey's European trip, it should be noted, took place in the summer of 1906.

Two more gas engines were installed in December, 1906, and March, 1907.[1]

Five new ore bridges were installed at the Furnaces in this year of the administration, the bridges in the new yard going into operation Dec. 1, 1906, and in the old yard January 5, 1907. The car dumper was installed in 1907, a giant machine which picks the car up bodily and dumps it, thus saving a vast amount of time and labor. No. 1 Rail Mill was also thoroughly over-hauled and rebuilt for diversified product in 1907.

On March 14, 1907, occurred one of the worst floods of the Monongahela of recent years, the river gauge at the works recording 34 ft. 6 inches. The records show twelve other floods of varying degree in the last ten years.

1907-08. One of the most prominent features of this administration has been the attention given to the safety of the men. An account of the work along this line, alone, would fill a volume, for it is one of Mr. Dinkey's hobbies to make the mill safe. In line with this idea, the Washington Street tunnel was constructed during this year of the administration, affording a safe and convenient passage for the workmen of the Blast Furnace Department.[2]

On January 1, 1908, as though in irony of the attempts to curb him, the Steel demon broke loose in the Converting Department, and an explosion occurred in which three men were killed and eight seriously injured.

1908-09. As a step toward improved quality, the five pass roughing rolls in No. 1 Mill were changed to seven pass, Sept. 5, 1908, with excellent results.[3]

In this year the Cahall boilers at the Mill were moved to the Furnace Department and the extension to the present general office built, ground being broken March 4, 1909, and the office occupied May 8th.[4]

1909-10. Notwithstanding the depression of the panic, improvements at the works kept right on. The 15-ton iron ladles at the Furnaces

---

(1) These engines were horizontal, tandem blowing engines of the four cycle constant mixture type. Cylinders were 38¼" on the gas and air respectively and 54" stroke. A 40 x 54" engine of the same type was installed in the Power Station Nov. 11, 1907, direct connected to a 1500-K. W. D. C. generator.

(2) The famous panic of 1907-08 was on during this year, when improvements and operations were at lowest ebb. In November, 1907 the works started paying in Pittsburgh clearing house scrip, the last of such payments being made Jan. 11, 1908.

(3) That is, the bloom was broken down to about rail size in two more operations than before, and by easier stages.

(4) Furnace "A" was also reconstructed during the early part of 1908, and is now 91 ft. high with a 15 ft. 6 inch hearth and 22 ft. bosh.

had been replaced in 1908 with 35-ton ladles (10 in all) and in this year, 1909, seven electrically operated ladle dumpers were started at the Pig Machine, materially reducing transportation costs and amount of scrap metal produced in handling the furnace iron. The Kennedy-Morrison cooling table, which had been in service for almost a decade, was removed July 24, 1909, and the new direct run operation commenced July 25, 1909.

We are now (1909) entering the period of diversified product from the rail mills, and the Basic Open Hearth plans are approaching completion. For a full understanding of the causes back of these new developments, it is necessary to make a slight discursion at this point:

From the annual report of the American Iron & Steel Institute for 1915, we learn that the domestic consumption of steel rails in the United States, in tons per annum, was as follows for the years 1903-1914, inclusive:

```
1903 .................... 3,057,195
1904 .................... 1,906,237
1905 .................... 3,098,184
1906 .................... 3,654,794
1907 .................... 3,298,500
1908 .................... 1,726,224
1909 .................... 2,725,847
1910 .................... 3,290,712
1911 .................... 2,405,330
1912 .................... 2,885,222
1913 .................... 3,052,635
1914 .................... 1,792,986
```

It will at once be seen that the rail purchases of the country fell off heavily from 1907 on, and as a matter of self preservation the rail mills at Edgar Thomson were compelled to branch off into various products, ordinary billets being rolled in 1907 and '08, tie plates commenced Dec. 31, 1909, and sheet bar Feb. 21, 1910.

When the New York Central sections were introduced, about 1890, owing to the stiffness of those rails they had reduced the Phosphorous to 0.06 and raised the Carbon to an average of 0.55 and even 0.60 in the heavier sections. Other roads followed suit, and claiming that 0.10 Phosphorous rails broke under the severity of northern winters, kept increasing the demand for rails low in Phosphorus content. The Lackawanna Steel Company made a very great amount of these low Phosphorous rails within the next seven or eight years, and the Edgar Thomson Works occasionally rolled some from special ores, but those low Phosphorous ores that were readily available were well nigh exhausted in a short time, and accordingly we find the Lackawanna plant dismantling in 1898 to rebuild at Buffalo, and practically six years elapsed before they were again in full operation. Their former output of rails was distributed among other mills: Carnegie, Cambria, Pennsylvania, Maryland, and Illinois Steel Companies.

The manufacturers declared that the breakages of Bessemer rails were due to the constantly increasing loads and higher speeds imposed upon the rails by the roads, (and incidentally it may be stated that the railroad companies have since virtually admitted this fact). We are not here, however, concerned in the basic metallurgical truths of the matter, but only in the ruling sentiments of the period, and the prevailing fashion in the railroad world. The railroads continued to insist on low Phosphorous rails, and in the year 1907 the situation between manufacturers and roads became so tense that there were many meetings and consultations to determine what could be done to make better rails. The manufacturers said that it was impossible to roll the A. S. C. E. sections with their extreme width and thin bases and put sufficient work upon the head to make them wear well and at the same time have the metal throughout the entire section sufficiently tough.

The Bethlehem Open Hearth plant was in operation in 1907, and the Gary plant for Basic Open Hearth rails was designed. For the 1908 rails many roads specified that the metal in the Bessemer converters should be held $2\frac{1}{2}$ minutes after recarburizing, and also that the number of rails per ingot should not exceed three. The mills could not handle a three-rail ingot at that time, and therefore they rolled the lower two-thirds, only, into rails for such specifications.

The consumers were demanding Basic Open Hearth rails, and for some the Open Hearth steel was made at the Homestead plant and shipped to E. T. Works. This was, of course, an expensive affair for Edgar Thomson, and the Basic Open Hearth plant was shortly designed. The marked reduction in rail orders for 1908 is also accounted for by the panic of 1907-08, and the fact that the western corn crop had been soft, and only suited for feeding purposes, instead of for shipping.

1909-10. Air dump cinder ladles that could be operated from the engine cab replaced the hand dump ladles at the Blast Furnace Department March 10, 1910. The car repair shop was built, and some sixteen other improvements of minor interest effected.

1910-11. The year 1910, among other things, saw the completion of

THE UNWRITTEN HISTORY OF BRADDOCK'S FIELD. 137

the Flue Dust Briquetting Plant[1] and the removal of the Splice Bar shop[2] from Duquesne to Edgar Thomson. To the Edgar Thomson management must be given full credit for the development of the Flue Dust Briquetting process, and the perfection of the high Carbon splice bar, both of which processes have advanced very far beyond what they were on inception at this plant. The Briquette Plant is expected very shortly to have a monthly capacity of 30,000 tons of fine briquettes which will take the place of the best grades of ore used in the Open Hearth or Blast Furnaces.

1911-12. A new Emergency Hospital, for the proper care of the injured employee, was erected during this year, ground being broken Dec. 26, 1911, and the hospital occupied Sept. 16, 1912. The new works club house at Thirteenth Street was commenced in June, 1912, and occupied in November of that year.

On May 28, 1912, came the good news that an appropriation had been granted Edgar Thomson that day for a new Open Hearth Department, an improvement long desired and planned for by Mr. Dinkey, and which had been more or less in contemplation since 1895. Work commenced immediately, ground being broken May 31, 1912.[3] In this year the employment office began operations in the basement of the General Office, June 27, 1912, the present employment office[4] not being occupied until October,

---

[1] The Briquetting plant is situated in Duquesne Borough on the Monongahela Southern branch of Union R. R., and is equipped with machinery for the refining of blast furnace flue-dust, concentrates of which are prepared for Briquette production. There are four furnaces and five presses at the plant, all of which have been remodelled and developed by the works.
The separation of magnetic content is taken care of by six magnetic separators, from which the concentrates are conveyed to mixers and thence to stock bin, where they are ready for feeding to presses. The tailings are disposed of by conveyor belts, and the new Greenawalt sintering plant is now under construction to take care of this material.
Mr. T. J. Davis, who came here from the Northern Iron Co., Philadelphia, has been in charge of the plant since June, 1911.

[2] The Splice Bar shop is 80 x 312 feet, and contains four sets of machines for flanging, shearing, punching, and notching splice bars, either cold or hot working. There are two re-heating furnaces for hot working bars, and oil quenching tank for tempering purposes equipped with steam jet arrangement for snuffing out fire. There are two annealing furnaces. There is a machine shop and various repair tools at the shop. The loading yard has two movable loading conveyors of the chain type which carry bars from one department to another. This plant holds the record for output for any plant of its size in the United States. It is under the supervision of Mr. E. S. Wright.

[3] In this plant, incidentally, was subsequently developed the reverse duplex process (patented) for making low Phosphorous acid Bessemer steel. An order had been received from a foreign customer for steel of 0.06 Phosphorous and under, to be finished by an acid process. To accomplish this the Basic iron was dephosphorized in the stationary Open Hearth furnace, sent to the Bessemer mixers, and high Silicon Bessemer iron mixed with the low Phosphorous Washed Metal, which was then sent to the Converting Works and carried through in the regular manner.

[4] This office has been under the supervision of E. C. Ramage, from the Union R. R. and New Castle Works, and a most efficient system has been introduced.

1913. On June 20, 1912 the old McKinney Club House, that had long served as restaurant and meeting place for the superintendents, was torn down to make room for the new O. H. plant.

1912-13. On Nov. 10, 1912, the present works telephone system and telephone central were installed in the present location in the Club House. In this year of the administration the stocking and shipping yards for Nos. 1 and 2 Mills were constructed, and work commenced on the relocation and improvement of the Blooming Mill while the old No. 2 Rail Mill was also remodeled. During this contruction work, Mr. F. F. Slick was given supervision of the rail mill operations. A fire occurred in this year at the Flue Dust Briquette Plant. In 1913 the Electric Repair Shop, which had been located in the present Power House, was moved to the present location to make room for the installation of additional electrical equipment in the Power House. Electrical ingot strippers were put in operation June 18, 1913.

1913-14. This year saw the completion of the Blooming and old mill improvements, and the completion of the 14-Furnace Basic Open Hearth plant, which is the best Open Hearth plant in the country using coal for fuel, and is conceded by electrical experts to be the best equipped plant, electrically, in the United States. The furnaces are of the stationary type, and the plant includes gas producers, stockyard, calcining plant, and spiegel cupola. Furnaces are rated for 90 to 100 tons per heat. The main building is 150 ft. wide x 1230 ft. long, and is thoroughly guarded with safety appliances throughout. A complete description is given in my article of January 1, 1914, issue of the "Iron Age." Gas was put on the first furnace August 4, 1913, and they started making bottom August 6, 1913. First heat was charged August 15, 1913, and tapped August 16, 1913. The first rail from the new plant, an 85 lb. one for the Norfolk & Western, was rolled August 21, 1913. Owing to the depression in trade, it was not until July 12, 1915, that gas was put on the last furnace.

1914-15. In 1914 the gas cleaning plants at Blast Furnaces were remodelled and their capacities increased to clean the gas for hot blast stoves. (The first plant was installed in November, 1906, and a duplicate plant October, 1907, for gas engine service). A third plant was started Sept. 17, 1914, which gave gas cleaning capacity for all the gas required for hot blast stoves and gas engines. The plants permit the use of much more economical hot blast stoves.

The first part of the mill improvement program was completed this year, and incidentally one of the most revolutionary changes in the rolling department of the works effected with the abandonment of the old Blooming Mill October 10, 1914. The former ingot had been $17\frac{3}{4} \times 19\frac{1}{2}''$, being broken down to a $9\frac{1}{2}''$ bloom in seven passes, while the new 48" bloomer breaks a 23 5-8" square ingot down to about 17" in the first four monkey passes, running at a speed of 4.5 R. P. M. Four ingots were first put through the new monkey rolls August 12, 1914. The 40" bloomer commenced operations August 30, 1914, everything being finally put into operation at this mill October 8th, 1914.

1915-16. The new No. 2 Mill, built for the production of diversified product, was completed this year, starting on regular product January 1, 1916. The new mill is a 32 inch four-stand mill with a motor load of 79 motors driving bloom pushers, charging and drawing machines, bloom cars, table rollers, lifting and tilting tables, hot saw machines, curver, 800-ton billet shear, billet conveyor, delivery tables, etc., and is probably the most modern and thoroughly equipped rail mill in the world.

1916-17. We come now to the close of our review of this able administration of progress and achievement. Among other things, there was started in the summer of 1916, a mammoth 200,000,000-gallon (daily) pumping station near the foot of Thirteenth Street to take care of the work now being done by five smaller pumping stations scattered throughout the plant. This will give the plant a much more economical and efficient water supply system.

1916 marks two improvements that the management had long tried to get: a new general office building and the Pennsylvania subway at Bessemer station. The new office was commenced July 31, 1916, and the Pennsylvania subway thrown open to the public June 12, 1916.[1]

In 1916 the "I" Furnace was rebuilt, with its electric skip hoist and automatic electrically operated bells, and is now the most modern blast furnace in the country. Three more of the same type are under construction. Again, the foundry department has been developed in late years to a point where it has become the best foundry for moulds and stools in the country. Brass and general castings are also a product.

---

(1) In addition to this and countless other innovations for the comfort and convenience of the men, a special safety engineer, John A. Oartel, has been commissioned to look after the safety of the men, under the direct supervision of Mr. Frank F. Slick. The safety department of the works has made a name for itself in the Carnegie Steel Company, and many innovations and suggestions from it have been adopted throughout the Company. The Slick-Bremner safety belt shifter (patented) has been taken up throughout the Corporation. Also, a trained nurse now looks after the health and hygiene of the families of workingmen, and everything imaginable is being done for the moral, physical, and spiritual welfare of the Edgar Thomson workingman.

I believe that the achievements[1] of this administration cannot be more strikingly portrayed (aside from the cursory review I have already given) than by the citation of figures on progress in the electrical department, for as every man knows electricity is the embodiment of speed, economy, and efficiency. These figures from one department alone, speak for themselves, and are a silent and absolute epitome of the progress of the plant under Chas. E. Dinkey.—

	June 1, 1903, beginning of the Dinkey tenure of office.	March, 1917.
Electrical department employees....	50	325
K. W. generator capacity...........	2,400	10,400
Motors installed (number)	140	1,253
Motor horsepower	5,940	56,246
Number of cranes	20	118
K. W. hours generated monthly....	750,000	3,946,700

Needless to say, every record of production that the plant has ever made has been smashed time and again under the Dinkey administration. Sufficient steel rails have been produced to twice encircle the globe and run a half dozen lines from San Francisco to New York, in standard railway sections, or in light weight sections such as produced in No. 3 Mill, to lay a track clear to the moon, if that were possible, while the Blast Furnaces have cast enough iron to reproduce in solid blocks of iron every skyscraper and railroad depot in the city of Pittsburgh, or pave with two-inch iron plates, the Lincoln highway from coast to coast.

---

[1] It should also be noted that the most radical improvement in standard blast furnace lines of the last decade was made under this administration with the blowing in of Furnace "I" May 6, 1907 on her third lining. For that furnace the former 15-foot hearth was widened to 17 feet, and the lower bosh angle widened to over 78 degrees. From a technical standpoint, this was a pronounced departure in furnace construction, and was inaugurated by Mr. Dinkey and Mr. John F. Lewis against the advice of many blast furnace experts.

The new lines immediately proved their worth, however, in increased furnace productive capacity, while they also did away, to a great extent, with the probability of the burden "hanging", the angle for the support of the arch that sustains the "hang" being more nearly straight in the new type furnace. The new design has since proved such a success that it is being rapidly adopted in the steel and iron world.

CHAS. E. DINKEY—THE MAN AND HIS METHODS.

When the caldron of industrial unrest in the Turtle Creek valley boiled over May 1, 1916, and thousands of strikers appealed to the Edgar Thomson men to join them in a sympathetic strike, the employees of that establishment turned a deaf ear to such pleas, and instead of joining the strikers' ranks flew to the defence of the plant, and volunteered by hundreds to serve as guards for the works. For the hate and resentment that had burned in other days was dead, replaced by a loyalty and sincere friendship for the management that would not countenance such a proposal. This is the secret of his success: that through the rank and file of Mr. Dinkey's organization runs a comradeship, a sympathy, and an understanding that lightens the heaviest burdens for every man and signally increases the efficiency of the whole human machine. This accomplishment alone hints at a great executive.

The temper and disposition of the chief executive is transmitted down the line to the lowest paid men in the plant, and I have therefore in this little history gone somewhat into detail regarding the personal characteristics of the men in charge. Aside from this, however, I have wished to portray in this history, a close study of at least one great executive. For the American business executive of the present day, like the intensified products of any other age, the artist of Angelo's time, the poet of the Elizabethan era, the philosopher of old Greece, must some day become a marvel for the world to ponder over.

Most biographers of steel masters call the subject a "genius", throw in a few flowery figures of speech, and let it go at that. And for many characters in the steel business that is a prudent course. But in a book intended for the instruction and inspiration of posterity I intend to follow a different tack, for here, at last, is a character that will bear scrutiny.

For a ready comprehension of his character in general, I would refer you to the mythology of the Greeks. Gifted though their deities were, endowed with superhuman energy and intelligence, they yet retained the vices and the virtues of mankind. On such a broad basis is built the character of Chas. E. Dinkey: though subjected from earliest childhood[1]

---

(1) Born Aug. 4, 1868, on a farm at Bowmanstown, Carbon Co., Pa. His father was Reuben Dinkey, surveyor, farmer, lumberman, and iron mine developer, who was the son of Jacob Dinkey and Susannah Stofflet. Mr. Dinkey's mother was Mary Elizabeth Hontz, nee Hamm. (Vid. "The Dinkey Family,"—S. A. Saeger).

to the gruelling discipline of labor,[1] and filled with an ambition that has driven him to success over every obstacle, by slow successive stages,[2] his thorough human-ness has not been twisted or perverted as is so often the case with men of achievement. He is, in fact, so intensely human that he seems to have condensed in his own individuality the feelings and the energies of twenty men, their varied hopes and fears, joys and sorrows. Whoever knows him well must also understand the psychology of the race.

All these varied and intensified emotions and vital forces he displays with the utter candor and abandon of a child. No suggestion of reserve has ever occurred to him, and with an astounding audacity he will do or say whatever occurs to him at any time or place. In this respect he bears a marked resemblance to his prototype, Captain Jones. While his anger is generally short lived, it is dangerous while it lasts, and those in the hurricane belt travel under close reefed sails.

High strung and acutely sensitive, he is decidedly of the artistic temperament, and for that matter is almost the exact counterpart both in appearance and temperament of a music master I had in childhood. He has a keen sense of the niceties of literature, painting, and dramatic art, although but little inclined to music or poetry. With this temperament, however, he combines the practical, hard common sense of the American man of business.

With the emotions of twenty men, however, he also has the perception, judgment, vision, determination, and optimism of twenty men, and thereby hangs the tale. Backed by a tireless energy, these qualities have made him a great executive.

He always gives you the impression of being larger than the job—that, however complex and dangerous the situation may be, he is still its master.

He has a deep knowledge of human nature, and readily analyzes his man. Bluff and braggadocio are as unavailing as evasion and excuse, and for this reason *nolle contendere* is your best defense under criticism,

---

[1] The family was not rich, and as a boy he undoubtedly did his share on the farm. Reuben Dinkey died while the boy was still a mere child, and he then had to help support a struggling family. In November, 1880, when twelve years old, he was employed by Carnegie Bro. & Company as messenger at the E. T. Furnaces, where he worked until 1883.

[2] 1883 and '84, printing shop assistant and special student of chemistry at Western University of Pittsburgh; 1884 to '87, laboratory assistant; April 1, 1887, to July, 1889, chemist and superintendent steel foundry for Mackintosh Hemphill & Co.; July, 1889, to December, 1889, Ass't Sup't Blooming Mill, Homestead; December, 1889, to Dec. 31, 1893, machinery inspector at Edgar Thomson; Jan. 1, 1894, to Feb. 22, 1899, Assistant Superintendent Foundry; Feb. 23, 1899, to May 31, 1901, Superintendent E. T. Foundry; June 1, 1901, to May 31, 1903, Assistant General Superintendent; June 1, 1903, General Superintendent Edgar Thomson Works.

such being the fairness and generosity of the man, that, like an English judge, if you offer no excuse for your misdeeds, he presently feels impelled to hunt for one himself.

He never asks you to repeat or explain. He listens intently; nothing distracts him from the subject in hand; his thoughts are never scattered, hesitating, or confused: they are centered on the single idea under discussion like the rays from a sun-glass. His mind works at lightning speed; before you have finished the sentence he has anticipated the paragraph, and bored in to the heart of the whole thing with the precision and power of an electric drill.

He has a keen sense of the economy of time, words, and effort. When speaking, he does not drawl, hesitate, or beat about the bush, and when discussing any subject his mind does not stray among words, phrases, or formalities, or, for that matter, dwell upon the reputation or prestige of himself or any other man, but his desire is wholly and simply to get to the heart of the subject as quickly as possible and reach a decision by the shortest route, so that the thing may be laid aside. For he has not now, nor ever did have, any love for work itself; but like U. S. Grant, plunges headfirst and vigorously into every project that it may the quicker be done, for an incomplete affair annoys him.

He does not waste his own or his subordinates' time, generally revolving matters in his mind until he has reached a decision. In this way, despite the countless doubts that must assail him on many projects, he appears always to his officers as the most positive man of decision, so that his men understand what he says to be final, and his orders to be executed with the speed and precision of military commands.

However, if he decides to discuss a subject at all, he encourages his subordinates to speak their minds freely and openly, and although he can hardly use the methods for this end that Tacitus attributes to the old German princes,[1] he attains the same result by always receiving their opinions politely and sympathetically, and not at such times oppressing them with the superiority of his office, or the divergence of his own beliefs.

Furthermore, if he believes a man to excel in anything, whether in a commercial line or in any of the arts, he encourages his development in every way. He nourishes the growth of every man's individuality and

---

[1] "Having feasted, and being thoroughly intoxicated....they frankly disclose their hearts and most secret purposes....On the day following the several sentiments are revised and canvassed...." Tacitus, "Germany," (Of the First Century).

pride, deferring (as Gregory the Great[1] advised) to the personality of each man, handling each according to his character, sometimes even permitting a man to perform things in an awkward manner in order that such a one may learn through his own experience how the task should be done. Nor does he take pleasure in pointing out the mistakes of his inferiors, or impressing them with his own superior knowledge, nor damn with faint praise, but if he approve at all does it whole heartedly and positively. It has been said of him that if there is any good in a man, he can find it and draw it out as the magnet does the steel.

Again, if he notices a man growing expert in any line, he constantly modifies his attitude toward that man, deferring more and more in his opinions to him according to the state of the man's development, presently, perhaps, yielding entirely in specific matters, for he is not afflicted with any short sighted pride regarding his own prestige, but has solely in mind the accomplishment of the thing in itself, and the development of men in his organization who can do that thing well.[2]

Clear and incisive thinker that he is, he bitterly resents the intrusion of the talkative rambler, and likewise is exasperated by verbose or involved writing, sounding words, or cant phrases, especially in business communications. In literature he is more liberal: the prose imagery of De Quincey and the balanced sentences of Gibbon hold an intimate appeal for him, and in lighter moments he will quote a sonorous phrase that has caught his fancy.

He has a broad power of generalship, and a true sense of proportion and perspective, naturally placing events in their proper light, so that he is not troubled by trifles, nor overlooks large and important features of any project.

He has enormously developed his powers of concentration and application. He sticks to one thing until it is done, then turns to the next. Hanging in his office is his motto: "Do it Now."

His physical energy and endurance are prodigious. As a brilliant executive his services are constantly in demand not only for most of the local enterprises that come and go, such for instance as the Braddock Hospital campaign and the Braddock Jubilee celebration, but also for various

---

(1) Gregory I (540-604 A. D.) "The proud and presumptuous are to be admonished in one way, in another the humble and diffident. The presumptuous when too confident despise and revile others—The humble and timid think what they do is very contemptible, and therefore despair....The proud and presumptuous think all their own special thoughts and deeds the best...." *Pastoral Care.*

(2) He has the big executive's knack of effecting an automatic, self-winding organization that can stand on its own legs and run under its own power. This knack, by the way, is one of the dividing lines between the big and the small executive.

THE UNWRITTEN HISTORY OF BRADDOCK'S FIELD. 145

banking and industrial concerns.(1) Notwithstanding these heavy demands on his abilities, he still has energy to spare, and must needs join a dozen or so societies,(2) clubs,(3) and fraternal orders.(4) These not sufficing, he hies himself away every year to the wilds of the Rockies or the Canadian woods, where he sleeps on the ground or the snow, and tramps for miles in strenuous hunts for big game.(5) He has a great reverence for the grandeur of Nature, and in such surroundings he is at last at home.

His mental energy, like his emotions, is 20-man-power. He is an omniverous reader, and remembers what he reads. He knows something about every subject under the sun. He is keenly curious about everything in the universe, and desires to know at once all about anything that may come to his notice. He preserves toward life, in fact, the fresh and unsullied interest of a child that is just learning to read well. With such a spirit, it is impossible to avoid reaching the very highest plane of education.

As a result of this broad development, each man believes that in C. E. Dinkey he has found a brother spirit, and the analyses of his character that I hear generally remind me of the three blind men describing the elephant.(6) The astronomer insists that he is interested in stars, the chemist in chemistry, while the workman is positive that he is interested in steel. None seems to grasp the idea that he might be interested in them all.

---

(1) President, Board of Trustees, Braddock Carnegie Free Library; Director in the following: Braddock National Bank, Bessemer Trust Co., North Penn Coal Co., Western Allegheny Railroad, North Penn Supply Co., Finance Committee, Masonic Hall Association of Braddock. This article was hardly finished before Governor Brumbaugh appointed him to the Welfare Committee of Pennsylvania. At the moment of going to press his successful prosecution of the local Liberty Loan and American Red Cross campaigns furnishes another example.

(2) Alumni Society, University of Pittsburgh; American Institute of Mining Engineers; American Iron & Steel Institute; Major, United Boys Brigade of America; Philadelphia Speedway Association; McKinley Commemorative Association, Hon. Member Major A. M. Harper Post 181, G. A. R.

(3) Americus Republican Club; Pittsburgh Athletic Association; Edgewood Country Club; Duquesne Club (Pittsburgh); Pittsburgh Country Club; German Club (Pittsburgh); Lewis & Clark Club; Braddock Rifle Club.

(4) Braddock's Field Lodge 510, F. & A. M.; B. P. O. Elks 883, Braddock; Shiloh Chapter 257, Royal Arch Masons; Tancred Commandery No. 48, Knights Templar, Pittsburgh; Gourgas Lodge of Perfection, Pittsburgh; Pennsylvania Council Princes of Jerusalem, Pittsburgh; Pittsburgh Chapter of Rose Croix; Pennsylvania Consistory; Ancient Accepted Scottish Rite of Masonry; Syria Temple, Ancient Accepted Order Nobles of the Mystic Shrine, for North America; Arab Patrol, A. A. O. N. M. S.; Royal Order of Scotland.

(5) His home and the steel works club house are filled with moose, bear, deer, elk, and caribou trophies of these hunts.

(6) One blind man felt the elephant's side, and thought he must be like a barn; another found his trunk, and thought he must resemble the snake, while a third was at a leg and thought he must be like a tree........Buddhist Folk Lore.

He is a perpetual optimist, with the occasional fits of depression that are the earmarks of that type. He will entertain a steady hope for the success of some project long after everyone else has given up. The morning after an election, for instance, it is impossible to convince him that his favorites have lost. With this same stubborn, blind hope, and continual trying and experimenting, if it is humanly possible the project actually will finally go through. He is a thorough going pragmatist in the philosophical terminology of that word:[1] if there is no chance he makes one.

Except for this perpetual optimism, his philosophy of life is clearly portrayed in the old Graeco-Roman school of Stoicism. This is the more striking because he seems to have little interest, if any, in the vagaries of metaphysics, and must have concocted his own code. His is no Billiken[2] philosophy of "things as they ought to be," but a stern realization of things as they are and life as it is. He never complains, and the idea of receiving sympathy is highly distasteful to him. Both his sayings, in fact, and the general conduct of his life, recall so vividly the writings of Aurelius[3] that I am incorporating some of the most striking passages here in the text, being so highly apropos and descriptive of my subject:

"Attend immediately to the matter before thee....Have freedom of will and undeviating steadiness of purpose, not to look to anything for a moment but to reason....Not to busy oneself about trifling things.... Unchangeable resolution in the things determined after due consideration....Begin the day by saying to thyself, "I shall meet with the busybody, the ungrateful, the ignorant, the deceitful, the envious, the unsocial. All these qualities they have by reason of their *ignorance*.... Every moment think steadily as a Roman and a man to do what thou hast in hand with perfect and simple dignity and justice....Do every act as though it were thy last....Let nothing be done without a purpose....Whatever happens happens justly, and if thou examine carefully thou wilt find a cause....Do not act as though thou wert going to live 10,000 years....

---

(1) Pragmatism, an anti-intellectualistic philosophy revived by Wiliam James about 1898. The theory may be roughly summarized as one that supports the realization of the idea, and that actualities are in our own hands for shaping; that theories may be made facts, and the world what we think it is and what we choose to make it.

(2) Billiken—A household statuette of an Oriental god much in vogue about 1906 and 1907. The deity was labeled, "The God of Things as They Ought to Be."

(3) Marcus Aurelius Antoninus, noblest of the Roman emperors and chief exponent of the culmination of the Stoic philosophy. His reign was marked by justice and moderation and although he was sole ruler of the civilized and known world, his "Meditations" are remarkable for their modesty, melancholy, and deep sincerity.

Receive honor without arrogance and be ready to let it go....Men exist for the sake of one another. Teach them or bear with them."

He loves life, motion, color, action, and whatever is forceful and dramatic. He takes more than a passing interest in animals, especially of the domestic types.[1] Children always please him, and he is invariably delighted by an invasion from his own family.[2]

Though faithful and unflinching in his resentments as Captain Jones, he is equally resolute in his friendships, and to many a man has been a *fidus Achates*.

He never shows envy for the fortune of any man, and never was there a man with less petty malice in his soul, or less of jealousy. Weak, womanish, cowardly, indecisive characters, charlatans, and quack reformers are his detestation.

His mental life has a basis of facts: he distinguishes clearly between what men say of a thing and that thing in itself: that twenty men calling a house a castle does not make that house a castle. For the most part utterly indifferent to the opinions of men, whether in praise or blame, he realizes entirely that the world cannot honor or humiliate a man, but only the intelligence and virtue of a man can honor him, or his ignorance and crimes disgrace him.

He has highly developed a sense of humor, which at all times lightens the strain of duty. What is more rare, he appreciates the joke just as much if he is at the wrong end of the affair.[3]

Blandly cordial, pleasant, and approachable, he is usually pleased to mask beneath a plausible air of superficiality a nature that is as deep as the proverbial well. He is pre-eminently long-headed, and plans for ten, fifteen, twenty years ahead, so that men often think conditions occur fortunately by mere chance, when he had so designed them to happen long before.

He is eternally willing and eager to learn—any time—any place, and will hear the lowest paid workman on the plant, in hope of getting some new idea.

Trained and disciplined as his mind is, he has always been to his

---

(1) All species appeal to him, especially dogs of the larger, smooth coated breeds.
(2) Married Lelia Ada Boyd, daughter of Robert Boyd of Mt. Lebanon, Pa., June 15, 1899. They have two children, Margaret Elizabeth Eurana and Charles Eugene, Jr.
(3) Hearing that Mr. Dinkey is starting on another hunting trip, S. B. Sheldon, a Duluth steel man, sends him a pop-gun, photograph of a moose, and detailed instructions as to the killing of that brute. This absurd donation has been religiously preserved.

men a developer, and not an exploiter.[1] Surrounded by men most of whom do not approach him in mental brilliance or caliber, his daily life calls for the constant exercise of patience and forbearance, and these qualities are more and more marked as the years roll by. For his own satisfaction, he will occasionally relieve himself by a deep and velvety irony, which often as not passes unnoticed. Gibbon, the "lord of irony," could teach him little of that art.

His ends are attained by various means: sometimes with a Machiavellian subtlety, and again with the blunt directness of a Bonaparte. Lying is the unforgivable sin, and he has the fatally retentive memory of a bull elephant.

Charitable and open handed, his giving is so broad and general that it seems to be assumed as a matter of course. Impelled by his high sense of efficiency, he will sometimes drive his men like a Cossack, but underneath everything lies a kindly and a generous nature. To his young men he is another Jones—versatile, commanding, brilliant, inspiring. Sociable and magnetic, he is at his best in the midst of his fellowmen, although almost equally content with the blessings of solitude. Always considerate of others (sometimes with an exquisite delicacy) the safety of his men at the mill lies nearest his heart, and, as I have mentioned in the description of his administration, he has done everything that the human brain can devise to make the steel mill safe. In safety work, now the cry everywhere, he was a pioneer.

How shall we accurately estimate such a character? I have always thought that the absolute standard was the value of the man to the race, for the individual passes quickly away, like a drop of water through a waterfall, while the race—like the waterfall—remains forever.

When we consider what has most elevated the human race we come down finally to three basic qualities: Reason, which has lifted man above the brute; Hope, which is the basis of courage, ambition and endeavor; and Charity, through which man has become a gregarious animal and learned to give and forbear. Through these three qualities mankind, despite a thousand vices, has eternally progressed. Not that all men have had these qualities, but that somewhere in the race noble souls have always possessed them, and lifted their brothers upward.

These qualities then, are the most precious possessions of the race,

---

[1] Within the last few months I was informed by a big New York executive that the office of Chas. E. Dinkey was one of the very best executive training schools for the young man in the United States.

and whoever has a single one of them should be honored among men. But whoever possesses all of them, and having himself great development of the reasoning faculty has developed and strengthened it in other men—having himself great optimism has encouraged hope, courage and endeavor in those about him, and having charity has borne with the ignorance of his fellow men, taught them, and lifted them up, he has been of the true nobility of our race.

Reason, optimism, charity: these are the cardinal characteristics of Chas. E. Dinkey.

THE MAKING OF THE LOCAL AMERICAN.

BY WM. J. AIKEN, ESQ.

The object of this article is to give briefly a chronological survey of the entry into this neighborhood of the various races that now compose its population, to scan the causes leading to their coming, and to note the processes involved in their Americanization. Like a dramatic performance, into which in regular order are introduced the characters, who remain upon the boards at the close to greet the audience, so by degrees, into the drama of American affairs, as well as upon the stage of local life, each with a part to play, have come the types of all the world; or like a vast choral movement beginning first with a few voices, then, at intervals augmented by others of a different kind, and finally closing with a united chorus, each voice adding something indispensable to the symphonic effect, so, likewise, now join in this vicinity a multitude of tongues telling us the nations of the earth are here assembled.

Mankind, as an animal, is both gregarious and migratory. The history of any race is largely the story of the wanderings of its ancestors, and their final union with each other. Even as a number of modern nations, among which, for example, may be mentioned the English, Spanish, German, and Italian, have resulted from centuries of amalgamation of various peoples, so the same process which produced those nations, but in a far more wonderful way, is now at work upon this soil. The English race of today represents a composite of Angle, Saxon, Dane, Roman, Jute, Celt, Pict, Scot, and Norman, whereas all the races of the world, with their ancestral combinations of blood, are being welded together into a new race in America; and nowhere in our country does the refining crucible burn more brightly or with finer and more marked results than in this immediate district.

The Swedes, Dutch, and English Quakers had the eastern part of Pennsylvania pretty well settled by the time George Washington was born. The settlements were scattered and often consisted of only a few families, but as early as 1740 Philadelphia counted her population by thousands, and we read of the villages of Burleigh, Haddonfield, Chester, Lancaster, Shrewsburg, Squan, Bethlehem, Wyoming, Shamokin, and Wehaloosing. Some of these towns, such as the last one named, contained more Indians than whites, and a number are historic for the terrible massacres of settlers by the Indians.

THE UNWRITTEN HISTORY OF BRADDOCK'S FIELD.   151

The eastern part of the province was thickly enough settled by 1750 to encourage newcomers and the more adventurous settlers to move westward. So it happens that some Scotch and Irish families, having found eastern Pennsylvania well in the hands of others, pushed on over the Alleghanies to the frontier, a pioneer family or two being in this neighborhood when the French arrived to fortify the junction point of the three rivers where, later, was to rise the great city of Pittsburgh. Reliable historical documents inform us that some settlers gave aid to General Braddock's defeated army. After General Forbes captured Fort Duquesne, and the English, having recovered from the defeat inflicted upon Braddock's army, had been successful in their struggle with the French for mastery of the western world, more Scotch, Irish, and English came to settle along the Monongahela near Turtle Creek.

The Indians mingled freely with the white settlers until as late as 1820 gradually, however, dying off or moving further westward. The Penns, by a last treaty with the Indians, had secured from the Six Nations at Fort Stanwix in 1784 quit claims to all lands in Western Pennsylvania not formerly obtained.

The next people to make their appearance in large numbers were the Welsh, who arrived after the opening of the coal mines and the smelting of ore had begun. The numbers of Scotch, Irish, and English increased rapidly, the population of the British Isles, especially Ireland, markedly affecting the immigration. Just before the Civil War a number of German families lived in the district and during the war period hundreds more arrived. Now and then a Dutch family moved over the mountains from central Pennsylvania and a few Hollanders came direct from the Netherlands. It will be noted that the races mentioned so far came from Northern Europe. This was the case until about the year 1870 or a little later. With that year closes the first period or phase of immigration. Beginning with 1870 the additions to our population from alien lands assumes a character differing widely from the earlier period.

A number of reasons may be assigned for the changing appearance of the incoming throng as well as for the added impetus marked in immigration. About the time mentioned above, the great iron industry for which our district is universally famous, began to thrive and a demand arose for labor which the section itself could not supply. Furthermore, the preservation of the Union and the consequent international strengthening of the United States, together with disruptions and dissatisfaction in Europe persuaded many to leave their native land. The overcrowded autocracies and kingdoms of central Europe had nothing to offer even the sturdiest man, physically or mentally, except endless toil for a few cents a day, the scantiest fare, and the harshest burdens of taxation. The great mass of people, weighed down by the sufferings of years, moved under their relentless yoke as if life were a thing unfortunately thrust upon them. In the darkness of their existence glowed a spark of ambition for their children that filled their dreams with brightness. America, land of liberty and opportunity, and all their lives were longing for, beckoned them to come. Great were the resolves of heart. Nobody left his home without a purpose. All came to create a better future for themselves. Wearied with oppression they hailed the lamp of freedom. America's invitation offered the realization promised in their dreaming. By thousands came the home and freedom seekers. An exodus from central, southern and southeastern Europe began such as never before has been witnessed in the chronicles of nations.

Pittsburgh at the beginning of this new phase of immigration was already known as the Smoky City or the Iron City on account of its iron mills, and Braddock contained the largest steel and iron works then in the country. Large numbers of people came to our section. Every day brought some one who had come from a foreign land and spoke a foreign tongue. Sometimes the newcomers arrived by train loads, coming directly from the ship that had borne them across the Atlantic. The numbers from northern Europe and the British Isles continued, but the numbers from southern and central Europe far exceeded the former until the latter made more than seventy-five per cent of all our population gained through immigration.

It is estimated that from 1776 to 1820 the number of arrivals in the United States amounted to two hundred fifty thousand. Of this number fully ninety per cent settled at first in the larger centers of population near the seaboard, and moved westward slowly. In the year 1821 the country received 9127 immigrants, a few hundred of whom came directly to Western Pennsylvania. By the year 1842 the number of arrivals for the year amounted to 104,565, over one third of which number came directly to western towns, Pittsburgh by that time having become a flourishing business city. During the years of the Civil War over 100,000 each year were received and the proportion of westward travelers was large. The numbers continued to increase. There was plenty of room in America, plenty of work was to be had, the greater population made more work for newcomers, and a good report spread over Europe. In 1873 the number of arrivals had increased to 459,803 due to the coming of the central and southern Europeans. During the years 1877 and 1878 the numbers dropped to 141,000 and 138,000 but in 1882 increased to the tremendous number of 788,992. From that time the number never fell below 229,299, which was the number for the year 1898. The million mark was passed in 1905 and the banner year reached in 1907 with 1,285,349. From 1903 they came "a million a year" until 1915, when on account of the great war the number dropped back to 326,700 and for the year ending 1916 the number was 298,826.

Western Pennsylvania originally consisted of the one county, called Cumberland, out of which by Act of 1771 Bedford County was erected, and later by Act of 1773 Westmoreland County. In 1781 Washington County was erected, out of which were carved Fayette and Greene Counties. Allegheny County was erected out of parts of Westmoreland and Washington Counties in 1788, and later, as the population increased, Beaver, Butler, Mercer, Crawford, Erie, Warren, Venango and Armstrong Counties were carved out of the original Allegheny County. This forming of counties gives some little idea of the gradual increase of population and settlement of the territory. People were induced to come westward by public auction of lots held in Philadelphia in 1785, where tracts containing 200 to 350 acres in Western Pennsylvania were sold at prices ranging from three pence to eight shillings an acre and patents were issued to purchasers. Many flourishing cities now stand on ground purchased at these figures. Unsold tracts were gradually disposed of by the Commonwealth on warrants and surveys. Allegheny County was all disposed of by 1813 when an Act was passed to cure any defects that might have existed in these hasty warrant and survey titles. Revolutionary soldiers were encouraged to take up lands by being granted certain 200 to 500 acre tracts free. The Pennsylvania Population Company and the Holland Company took out hundreds of warrants in 1792 and 1793. Examination of the records shows that nearly all these lands were held at that time by Scotch, Irish, or English people, the exception being German or Dutch. Today the records disclose the fact that many of these same lands, for the most part cut up into small pieces or town lots, are held by people who learned to speak English after they arrived in America.

Having outlined the general scope of the populating of our district, it will now be interesting to observe the present composition of the peoples in the three adjoining boroughs, compiled from the census statistics of 1910. Braddock at that time was accredited with 19,837 persons, of whom the native white of native parentage numbered 4,845. There were 6,786 persons made up of those who were of foreign or mixed parentage. The foreign born numbered 7,299, the negroes numbered 421, and the Chinese 6. In North Braddock, out of a population of 11,824, there were 3,811 native white of native parentage, 4,360 native white of foreign or mixed parentage, and 3,365 foreign born, the negroes counting 287 and the Chinese 1. Rankin whose population was 6,042 had 704 native white of native parentage, 1,823 native white of foreign or mixed parentage, 3,072 foreign born white, and 443 negroes. Attention need not be called to the amazing proportion of native white of foreign or mixed parentage and the foreign born to the native white of native parentage. The following statistics for Braddock and North Braddock explain themselves, reliable figures for Rankin not being available: Of the foreign born Braddock had 2,238 from Austria; 12 from Belgium; 45 from Canada; 1 from Denmark; 261 from England; 5 from Finland; 6 from France; 446 from Germany; 21 from Greece; 1529 from Hungary; 481 from Ireland; 445 from Italy; 9 from Roumania; 1225 from Russia; 143 from Scotland; 334 from Sweden; 7 from Switzerland; 70 from Wales; and 21 from various other countries. In North Braddock the countries represented by the foreign born and their numbers were Austria 724; Belgium 4; Canada 19; Denmark 2; England 368; Finland 4; France 40; Germany 579; Greece 9; Hungary 411; Ireland 353; Italy 59; Russia 190; Scotland 250; Sweden 218; Switzerland 45; Wales 55; and other countries 35.

Of the native white both of whose parents were born in foreign lands the numbers follow. For Braddock, both parents born in the countries named, Austria 1049; Canada 15; England 132; France 9; Germany 668; Hungary 1191; Ireland 831; Italy 210; Russia 557; Scotland 106; Sweden 224; Switzerland 1; Wales 79; and all others of mixed foreign parentage 460. For North Braddock, both parents born in the countries named, Austria 646; Canada 7; England 248; France 16; Germany 682; Hungary 208; Ireland 630; Italy 46; Russia 135; Scotland 117; Sweden 237; Switzerland 31; Wales 60; and all others of mixed foreign parentage 315.

From this enumeration it is apparent that the Braddock district is sheltering representatives from nearly all the countries of the globe. Here they dwell together in peace and harmony, gradually being molded and fashioned to conform with the American ideal. Some races take up new customs and follow American principles more readily than others, owing to circumstances, traditions, laws, and racial and family tendencies in the home land. A few have come to exploit the advantages in the United

States, and like the farmer who continually takes a crop from the rich soil but never revives it, so they take all they can get from American life and never return anything. Forgetful of the wrongs they fled in Europe, they aid in nothing in the preservation of human rights in their refuge. Others, selfish, suspicious, and superstitious, hold themselves aloof from the means of progress, and clinging to ancient holidays, former customs, and the very things once odious to them, retard their own development and hinder the advance of the town they dwell in and the nation at large. Again, many are backward and fear to enter into the life of those about them, continuing in their old associations, speaking their mother tongue and making little effort to learn the new language. A large majority, however, especially marked in their children, readily adapt themselves to the conditions found in the new country and are quickly assimilated by the civic public. Much allowance must always be made and judgment never rendered hastily in considering this remarkable union of peoples. It must ever be remembered that they have come from countries differing greatly in customs and laws from the United States and naturally the old ideas are discarded slowly. It is extremely difficult for the average person over thirty years of age to acquire a ready use of a new language and practically impossible for anybody past forty years to learn to speak a new tongue, with any degree of proficiency. Even young people of less than twenty can rarely gain such complete mastery of the new language as not to show their native accent. However, the children of those whose efforts at the American language are slow and broken, show scarcely any accent, and a few years of school, associating with other young Americans, gives them entire use of the language their parents cannot completely master.

The people who have been coming among us represent some of the very best element in Europe. We do not get the maimed, or paupers, or criminals. Our immigration laws are strict and are being made more strict; and are especially aimed at preventing the entry of those who are physically, mentally, or morally unfit to become American citizens or who might become a burden or a nuisance to any community. The underlying question governing admission of persons into this country is the qualification of citizenship. Every alien admitted knows he has passed the first requirements under the law for becoming a citizen. It is his duty, if he intends to make his home in America, to become in due time an American citizen. It is also the duty of American citizens to encourage the alien to become a citizen for it is only by such means that this process of absorption and Americanization can meet with the best results.

Citizenship statistics show that in Braddock for 1910 there were 929 naturalized citizens, 281 declarants or those who have taken out what is commonly called their first papers, 2,781 aliens and 112 unknown. In North Braddock there were 655 naturalized citizens, 215 declarants, 645 aliens, and 107 unknown. In Rankin there were 264 naturalized citizens. These figures show that a great many foreigners remain foreigners. Many instances exist where the parents and one or more children are aliens while other children, having been born here, are citizens. Under most circumstances the aliens have failed to become citizens simply through neglect. Their allegiance is with America, their home and interests are here, they are citizens in all but name and the law. All who find the American principles of government to their liking and appreciate what the stars and stripes stand for should take a further step, and, renouncing forever the ties that bind them to the old world, should take the oath which makes them citizens in the new world.

Of late, influenced by the great war, many who have long been residents here and never were naturalized, have taken out their citizenship papers. The figures in the naturalization office show a diversified array of peoples, as will be seen by the following numbers, taken from a recent report of that office. Out of 205 applicants the number from each country was as follows: Australia 1, France 1, Syria 1, Roumania 2, Norway 1, Turkey 1, Croatia 2, Italy 21, England 7, Denmark 1, Greece 3, Canada 3, Sweden 5, Switzerland 1, Ireland 21, Germany 25, Hungary 37, Russia 21, Scotland 3, Austria 47, Bohemia 1. This proportion of the various races will hold true to about every 200 applicants.

The establishment of evening schools for teaching the language, explaining the naturalization laws, and the requirements, duties, and responsibilities of citizenship has been another influential factor in causing many aliens to become citizens. The Carnegie Free Library of Braddock has supported one of these schools for many years, being one of the first in the United States to offer instruction in citizenship. Various civic bodies and organizations in other cities are now doing such work. The Bureau of Naturalization at Washington, D. C. has outlined a course of study for prospective citizens and is encouraging the public schools throughout the country to furnish evening instruction. The bureau co-operates with the schools by furnishing the list of names of applicants for citizenship in the different districts, and by encouraging the applicants to attend the schools during the period of ninety days which elapses between their petition for second papers and the granting of citizenship. Two years ago the Pittsburgh Public Schools installed an evening school of citizenship and last year Braddock had an evening school for foreigners. North Braddock has had in former years such evening schools and Rankin is planning one the coming year. All of these schools are well attended and much interest is shown by those who come.

The process of Americanization goes on. The races intermingle. The second generation from birth breathes the atmosphere charged with American ideals, principles, laws, customs, language, and liberty. Hyphens disappear. One flag becomes the only flag. Kindly disposed toward their ancestral connections, they hold the land of their birth first in all their thoughts. International brotherhood approaches with the Americanization of the mingled races of the world, making possible the court of nations. The American race representing the unification of the best elements of all peoples is sounding the dominant note in civilization. Peaceable and progressive at home, and respected abroad, the American is known wherever mankind dwells, and such is the race of people we have in Braddock, North Braddock and Rankin.

THE POST OFFICE

BY CHARLES L. CUMMINGS.

No other thing during the past seventy-five years can show the rapid and continuous advancement of the United States Post Office Department. It is told of the visit of General Lafayette to the present site of Braddock in 1825, that he was anxious to dispatch a letter to President John Quincy Adams in Washington. At that time there was no post office between Pittsburgh and Greensburg, and as a consequence it was necessary to send the letter to the former city for mailing. Mails were sent to Washington but once every fortnight, and then by "pony" express. The schedule time for the journey was three days, which was considered very fast. Today a letter mailed in the Braddock post office in the early morning reaches Washington the same afternoon.

It was in the year 1853 that President Franklin Pearce appointed the first Postmaster at "Braddock's Field, Pa." Previous to that date Turtle Creek was the address of mail for the valley, the post office at that point having been established some twelve years before. In 1853 letters were few and far between to the average person, and the Postmaster, while considered a personage of importance by the citizens, required some other means of livelihood in addition to the small amount paid by Uncle Sam for handling the mails. On December 27, 1853, William N. Fleming was appointed as the first Postmaster, and the post office was opened for business on January 18, 1854. Mr. Fleming kept a small store at a point near where the intersection of Tenth street and Braddock avenue now is, and across from the Methodist church. This site was used as a post office until September 1861, when the building was burned, and the then Postmaster Fleming built a structure, part of which is still standing. The latter building is located near the corner of Robinson street and Braddock avenue.

Postmaster Fleming was succeeded by Henry Bailey, whose commission was dated June 21, 1855, and he in turn was succeeded by George M. Young on August 24, 1857. At the opening of the Civil War in 1861 Postmaster Young enlisted for service in the Pennsylvania volunteers, and served until wounded at the second battle of Bull Run. The present historian has been unable to find any further trace of Mr. Young, as to whether he ever returned to Braddock, or whether he died from the effects of his wounds.

Upon the resignation of Mr. Young, President Lincoln named Dr. William J. Lynn, who was commissioned on August 31, 1861. Dr. Lynn it was who moved the post office after the fire mentioned to the building still standing. It is told of the doctor that on some occasions when the mails would arrive he would be out calling on a patient, and patrons of the post office would be forced to await his return. On one occasion, so the story goes, a lady was at a very low point in health, and the mail was not distributed until the following day, the good doctor considering

BRADDOCK POST OFFICE, 1884.

his duty to suffering humanity as far out weighing his duty to the Government. Doctor Lynn served the second longest term of any Postmaster in the history of the local office, his term extending to December 18, 1873, and then it was ended only at his own request, owing to his failing health.

On December 19, 1873 President Grant named as Postmaster William Fritzuis. Mr. Fritzuis was a brother of Mrs. William H. Speer, living at present with her daughter (Mrs. Ellis Y. Hall) at 431 Second street, Braddock. Mr. Fritzuis died the following spring, and he was succeeded as Postmaster by his wife, Mrs. Mary A. Fritzuis, her commission dating from May 4, 1874. Mrs. Fritzuis was the only woman commissioned Postmaster of Braddock, and is now the oldest living one. The lady served until

December 13, 1876, with credit to her sex and to the service. After leaving the service Mrs. Fritzuis married David H. Graham, and now lives at Meamimi, Florida.

On December 14, 1876, James K. Mills, one of the original Mills boys, and whose death occurred a few years since at his home on the corner of Fourth street and Mills avenue, was appointed Postmaster. Mr. Mills moved the Post Office to a site on the corner of Braddock avenue and Ninth Street, during his term. Mr. Mills' service was featured by two or

ORIGINAL LETTER CARRIERS.
Reading from left to right.
ALVA C. NICKEL.   PHILLIP C. RODERUS.   ROBERT PRICE.   HARRY FOGIE.

three very far reaching changes in the post office, the main one being the change of the name of the office to correspond with that of the railroad stations and of the borough itself. On March 7, 1878 the President ordered the name changed from "Braddock's Field," to Braddock, and the post office made the first start toward metropolitan airs by being advanced from the lowest class (the fourth) to that of the third class. Mr. Mills had for his assistant for a time both Wallace K. Benn and William W. McCleary.

Mr. Mills refused to become a candidate for reappointment and on

April 17, 1882, William W. McCleary was named, and the post office moved to a site where the Woolworth five and ten cent store is now located, a building being erected adjoining the old McCleary homestead. During Mr. McCleary's term of office Mr. George A. Todd, now cashier of the Braddock National Bank, served as his assistant.

The years 1882 and 1883 was the time of the depredations of the notorious Gordon gang in and around Braddock. Many business houses were robbed during this period, and the post office was no exception. Mr. McCleary occupied rooms directly back of and above the Post Office. One night he was awakened from his sleep by a noise which he thought was like an explosion in the office below him. Hurrying to a window he found that robbers were in the post office. Picking up the first thing in the room he could lay his hands on, he threw it through the window with the idea of alarming the neighborhood. The noise frightened the robbers and they made their get away, taking with them about $700 in postage stamps and $40 in money. The robbers were later captured, Mr. McCleary helping in the identification, but none of the loot was ever recovered. The Department some time afterwards relieved the Postmaster of the burden of the loss of the stamps, but the money loss was made good by Mr. McCleary.

"Duke," as Mr. McCleary was known, served as Postmaster until April 6, 1886, when the first Democrat was appointed in the person of "Squire" J. M. Hughes. The squire found the duties of the office more exacting than he had either the time or inclination to devote to them, and resigned the first of the following June, and Daniel J. McCarthy, a brother of the present Chief of Police of Braddock, was appointed June 11, 1886, by President Cleveland to fill the unexpired term. "Danny", as Mr. McCarthy was affectionately known by the great majority of the residents of the vicinity at that time, made one of the most popular postmasters in the office's history. At the time of his appointment Mr. McCarthy was conducting a weekly newspaper known as The Tribune, which later he consolidated with the Daily News when he came into possession of the latter paper.

The Republican party coming back into power, there was appointed for the first time on June 10, 1890, a man that nearly every one in Braddock and vicinity associates with the post office, Christian H. Sheets. At the time of the coming of Mr. Sheets as Postmaster the office was still located in the McCleary building, on the site of the Woolworth store, and the total receipts of the office for the year 1890 totaled but $8,654.24. On

January 1, 1892 the office receipts had expanded to over ten thousand dollars, the site of the post office was changed to a location on Library street (or Burton street as then known) and the Department raised the standing of the office from the third to the second class.

On December 1, 1892, the Department authorized the establishment of city delivery in the boroughs of Braddock and North Braddock, and provided for this service the appointment of four carriers. The Postmaster named the following men for the positions: Harry H. Fogie, Alva C. Nickel, Philip Roderus and Walter E. Collins. The first three named are still in the service, carrying mail daily at the local office, having served continuously since first appointed. Mr. Collins was a man well up in years and suffered from the effects of a wound received in the Civil War, and finding the work more arduous than he could stand, resigned some ten days after his appointment, Mr. Robert A. Price being given the vacancy thus caused.

Mr. Sheets served as Postmaster until the thirtieth of July, 1894, when the Democratic party again coming into power, President Cleveland appointed Mr. Moses M. Shaw as Postmaster, only after one of the bitterest contests for a political position in the history of the borough. Among other candidates for the position at that time were ex-postmaster Daniel J. McCarthy, M. M. Kier, and W. A. McDevitt, Henry L. Anderson and William L. Douglass. Mr. Shaw appointed as his assistant Mr. Walter McBeth.

On August 1, 1898, Christian H. Sheets was again appointed Postmaster to succeed Mr. Shaw, a position he held continuously through the line of Republican presidents until February 10, 1915, the longest period ever served by any Postmaster in Allegheny county up to that time.

During Mr. Sheets' service as Postmaster the Post Office was moved from the rooms in the Masonic building to quarters in the Braznell building directly across Library street, remaining there for over eleven years, or until the completion of the Federal Building.

On October 31, 1900, the post office at Rankin Station was discontinued, and free delivery from the Braddock office was installed to serve that borough. Rankin Station had been a post office since August 20, 1886. Mr. Walter S. Colmery was the first postmaster, and was followed in succession by Mr. Owen W. Sheeky, on July 19, 1888, F. G. Bishoff on April 15, 1889, Owen W. Sheeky again on October 17, 1893, and finally by George W. Nash on September 27, 1897.

On December 9, 1907, a bill authorizing the expenditure of $150,-

000 for the construction of a Post Office Building at Braddock, was introduced in the House of Representatives by Hon. John Dalzell, then the representative from this district. This amount was later reduced to $125,000 by the conference committee, and on May 30, 1908, the bill passed Congress. In the fall of that year the Government advertised for sites for the location of the building, and stipulated that sites offered must be approximately 150 feet square, preferably on the corner of two streets, and within eighty rods of the Pennsylvania railroad station. Bids were received for the following sites:

(1) Corner Verona street and Maple way, 120x160 feet, offered by Robert McDonald, for $32,000.
(2) Corner John street and Maple way, 120x160 feet, offered by James A. Russell and Henry S. Leighton, for $34,000.
(3) Corner Sixth street and Maple way, 126x138 feet, offered by Nicholas Glasser, for $40,000.
(4) Corner Halket avenue and Tenth street, 75x185 feet, offered by Mrs. Elizabeth Dowling, for $22,000.
(5) Corner Parker avenue, Moody and Orchard streets, 150x150 feet, offered by Thomas James, for $40,000.

A representative from the Treasury Department visited Braddock, and made an attempt to secure a bid for a site on Braddock avenue, but found the prices prohibitive, $1,100 a foot front being asked for ground at Seventh street and Braddock avenue.

The United States objecting to the amount asked by Mr. James, and having decided that that site best suited the needs of the Department, requested that gentleman to reduce his bid, but met with refusal. The Government then petitioned Court for the appointment of viewers looking to the condemnation of the site, and on August 10, 1910, the viewers allowed Mr. James $37,500.

The bid for the construction of the building complete was given to the Plowman Construction Company, of Philadelphia, Pa., for the sum of $83,293.24. Ground was broken on August 1, 1911, and the building was occupied by the Post Office on June 10, 1913.

On April 1, 1906, the Braddock office was raised to the rank of the first class; on November 4, 1911, it was made a depository for postal savings, and the parcel post was established January 1, 1913.

On February 11, 1915, after an absence of twenty years, Mr. Walter J. McBeth re-entered the postal service, this time as Postmaster, having been commissioned by President Wilson, January 25th. Great changes have been made for the betterment of the postal service during the little over two years of the present postmaster, namely, the establishment of six additional stations for the receipt of mail matter and other services of the postal system; the collection and delivery of mail by automobile, and day and night continuous service at the post office.

On January 18, 1854, when Postmaster William N. Fleming opened the first mail pouch reaching Braddock's Field, one cannot help wondering if he had even a faint dream of the magnitude of the present business. At the Braddock office there are 43 employees, the stamp sales exceed $50,000 annually, nearly a million dollars a year is handled in money orders, besides the thousands of pieces of mail matter handled daily by its employees. No other one item in the history of the local boroughs will better tend to show the magnitude of the growth of Braddock.

THE FEDERAL BUILDING.

BRADDOCK NEWSPAPERS AND THEIR MAKERS.

BY FREDERICK W. OAKLEY.

Newspapers are invariably the pioneers that pave the way in a village or small town, for the more pretentious municipality that usually follows the self-sacrificing efforts of such public-spirited organs, and, if planted in a town already built, aid materially in the way of public morals, as well as in the physical growth of the community, and keep it keyed up to its best possible step on the highway of progress.

"Braddock's Field", at the time of its incorporation, in 1867, was a little different in this respect, from many of its municipal companions in this section of Pennsylvania, and elsewhere, for it had no newspaper to urge the lagging citizen to see that his own welfare and that of his neighbor could be bettered, immediately before or after the incorporation. It was almost a decade after "Braddock's Field" village had been officially incorporated as "Braddock Borough", that the first newspaper had its birth, but practically since that year, the town has been benefitted constantly in every way, by newspapers that have kept the record of almost every year intact, and with but an occasional day's lapse.

It is trite to state that Braddock has had as good newspapers as any other town of its size, but it is nevertheless a fact, because the majority of towns in this or any State, do not meet with the same physical conditions, especially in regard to location, which is a vital factor in the success of a newspaper. Braddock is more peculiarly located, with regard to its newspaper condition, than any other town in a score of states of the Union. In other words, it might be said that a large borough near the confines of a large, first-class city, situated as Braddock and Pittsburgh are, is hard to find, and when found, the municipalities do not each have large, influential and successful newspapers. Those terms apply only to the city, and the large borough is satisfied to have what the adjoining city is pleased to give—which is very little in the way of "home news."

This has never been taken into consideration, as far as Braddock newspapers are concerned by the reading public of the Braddock community, in the opinion of the writer. Braddock, whose corporate limits are not far removed from those of the larger city, has been considered from a newspaper point of view by the city dailies, as an immediate local field in which the latter might work, but without the attention in the news form that the corporate portion of the city always receives.

The people of the Braddock community, ignoring the town's location, and the city newspaper attitude, have subscribed for the city newspapers, then expected the borough or "home paper" not to stick to its local field, which alone it aimed to fill and for which it was founded, but expected it rather to measure up to the stature of a large city daily, covering the world field; which, it might be said here, is never the intent, and is always against the desire of, the smaller country daily or weekly.

A slight digression to illustrate the point. In only three pairs of large cities in the United States, which practically join, do each of those cities maintain large and separate newspapers, with anything like a real circulation, and in each case, none of the papers are as influential in the other city, as they are in the one in which they are published. The "Brooklyn Eagle" is not as widely circulated in New York City, as some of the New York newspapers are in Brooklyn. The St. Paul "Pioneer Press" does not have the circulation in Minneapolis as does the Minneapolis "Tribune" in St. Paul, and likewise, if there is any newspaper of consequence published in Kansas City, Kas., it does not have anything like the circulation in Kansas City, Mo., that the Kansas City "Journal" of the latter city, has in its neighboring city across the river, in Kansas.

And in each of the cases cited, the cities are all large ones, incorporated as such. Where the occasional borough adjoins a large city, the writer has yet to learn of a single other instance in this country, where the small borough has been able to maintain a daily newspaper with only an occasional daily interruption, for 40 years as Braddock has done. As a reminder, it might be said that even old Allegheny City, incorporated as such for quite a century, has never been able to maintain a daily newspaper for a year, the only venture of the kind that can be recalled, being a daily paper that flourished there for ten months, and the editor of that organ spent several months afterwards, doing Braddock newspaper work. Even a weekly newspaper in Allegheny could not live longer than a few months at a time, and there has been none for years in that section of Pittsburgh now known as the "North Side."

All of which indicates that the pioneers of Braddock newspaper work, were worthy successors of those old pioneers, the pathfinders who worked the trackless wilderness of the old days of the frontier period in this country, and who had the American temerity to brave almost inevitable disaster in order to carry out what might seem the practically impossible. And to many fraternal onlookers who saw the game as it was being played in Braddock, it appeared that inevitable business disaster could be the only result from what to them, seemed such a foolhardy risk as the establishment of a daily newspaper in a town situated like no other town of its size in this country. Yet Braddock newspapers have been published from 1876 down to the present, and for more than 30 years a daily paper has been laid at the doorstep of the homes in Braddock almost each day. To the newspaperman of other cities this has been, and is yet, considered a remarkable performance.

The "Centennial Year" saw the first newspaper published in "Braddock's Field" as the borough was still called by the old-time residents. Frederick L. Penney, still living in Somerset county, Pa., and a postmaster at one of the smaller towns near Somerset, was the editor and owner of this organ, which was known as the "Braddock News". It continued from the fall of 1876, until a year later, but Mr. Penney remained in newspaper work in Braddock for two or three years longer. Mr. Penney's "News" had various locations on Braddock avenue, or "Main street" as it was frequently called.

Dr. G. A. Hall, medical practitioner, took up the labors in the "journalistic" field where Fred L. Penney ended his newspaper ownership. Dr. Hall started the Braddock "Sun" in the old Fauset building, at the corner of George street and Braddock avenue, in 1878. Dr. Hall continued to get out a weekly edition of the "Sun" for a year or more, when J. A. Wynne, who married a daughter of Justice of the Peace Thomas J. Louis of John street, took over the "Sun" from Dr. Hall, who had sufficient newspaper experience in Braddock, and operated it from a small frame building on John street near the Pennsylvania Railroad, on property owned by 'Squire Louis, at the rear of the Louis residence, which fronted on George street. Mr. Wynne took charge in the fall of 1879, and was the editor and owner of the "Sun" for about a year, when 'Squire Louis became the owner in the summer of 1880.

The "Sun" continued its home on John street for three or four years, when it was removed to a one-story frame structure on Braddock avenue, on the east side of Eighth street, afterwards the location of Layman's cafe, and later of a furniture store. The structure extended back to Wood alley, the rear being used for the composing and publication rooms, while the front of the building was the office of 'Squire Louis, and also the editorial quarters. The "Sun" was the property of 'Squire Louis until early in 1886, when it was transferred to his eldest son, Frank Ernest Louis, who had previously been associated with his father in the editorial work of the "Sun". After a year spent in the West, F. E. Louis continued the "Sun" at the old location on Braddock avenue, until 1891, when its existence ended.

Col. E. W. Eisenbeis of East Liberty, founded the first daily newspaper in Braddock, in the late summer of 1877. It was the "Braddock Times", and the office was the double story frame building on Braddock avenue, just west of Tenth street. The building is still standing, and for a dozen years after Col. Eisenbeis gave up the publication, the advertising sign of the paper swung to the breeze. The "Times" had an existence of a little less than a year. With Col. Eisenbeis was connected his son, Harry L. Eisenbeis, noted for his stature in those days, for he was some six feet five or six inches tall, and of proportionate girth. The son afterwards for a short time was associated with the late Joseph L. Campbell, Sr., in the publication of the Braddock "Evening Times" on Ninth street.

In late March or early April, 1880, the late Daniel J. McCarthy, a former postmaster of Braddock, and who also served two terms as Democratic jury commissioner in Allegheny county, founded the "Braddock Tribune" a weekly publication, the building in which it was issued being on the south side of Braddock avenue, several doors west of Thirteenth street. Almost across Braddock avenue from the "Tribune" office was the residence of Charles E. Dinkey's mother, the late Mrs. Mary E. Kinsey, in the old Robinson homestead, and her son, Charles E. Dinkey, took it into his head, as many distinguished men before him have done, that he would like to learn the "art preservative of all arts", the printing art. The present general manager of the Edgar Thomson steel plant was connected with the "Tribune" in various capacities for several years, from messenger boy, and "printer's devil" up to acting pressman, until his muse told him that there were likely greater financial returns, and surely more fame or glory, in other fields, than are offered on a weekly newspaper, which in Mr. Dinkey's case has been amply proven true.

Mr. McCarthy continued to publish the "Tribune" in east Braddock avenue, until after his term as postmaster expired, during President Cleveland's first administration, and until it was merged with the Braddock "Daily News", which was established in the summer of 1889, by the late Charles Mills, a son of Isaac Mills, Sr., and grandson of Stephen Mills, Sr., the first settler in 1804, of what is now Braddock, following the actual pioneer, John Frazier, who came to Braddock's Field in 1742, from Bedford county, and became the first white settler west of the Alleghany Mountains.

With Charles Mills in the founding of the "Daily News", was Ells-

ALEXANDER H. SILVEY.   JAMES L. QUINN.   JOSEPH L. CAMPBELL.

JOHN C. LOUGHEAD.   JOEL H. DIETRICH.   FRANK E. LOUIS.

THOMAS LAWRY.   DANIEL JUSTIN McCARTHY.   SAMUEL T. SHAW.

worth Calderwood of Tyrone, Pa., a brother of Mr. Mills' wife. Mr. Calderwood died soon after the "Daily News" was started, and its publication was continued for three years by Mr. Mills, or until his death in 1892. For a year or two the office of the "Daily News" was in the old Wm. C. Schooley Building on the south side of Braddock avenue, between Sixth and Seventh streets, sometimes called the Rauwolf Building, a two-story brick with a double front, afterwards used for hotel purposes. Then the office was removed to the big double-story frame structure erected by Mr. Mills on leased ground, at the corner of Library street, then Burton street, and Maple alley, opposite the Carnegie Free Library, afterwards the site of the First Presbyterian Church.

Mr. Mills died in 1892, and the paper was published by his widow, Mrs. Mary Calderwood Mills, for some months, until near the close of that year, when it was taken over by Daniel J. McCarthy, who removed his "Tribune" publishing quarters from east Braddock avenue to the Odeon Hall Building as the Library street publication building was known. Mr. McCarthy still continued to print the "Tribune'" for a year or so after his removal to Library street, as a weekly edition of the "Daily News", and the "Tribune" went out of existence near the close of 1893.

After the Braddock "Sun" had got a good start, several other newspapers also got into the running, the first of these contemporaries of 'Squire Louis being Alexander H. Silvey, known throughout the western part of the State among his associates as "Sandy" Silvey. Mr. Silvey founded the Braddock "Herald" on June 2nd, 1880, in the frame building which at that time, and for many years thereafter, stood at the southeast corner of Ninth street and Wood alley. The last publication of the "Herald" took place in April, 1888, when Mr. Silvey established the Wilkinsburg weekly "Call" in his home town of Wilkinsburg, and continued the "Call" almost until his death on January 5, 1905, when it was taken up by his son, Thomas Morgan Silvey, who is still the publisher.

With Mr. Silvey was associated for several years on the "Herald", the late Charles Edward Locke, Sr., uncle of the famous Rev. Dr. Charles Edward Locke, of Los Angeles, Cal., a noted divine of the Methodist Episcopal Church. The former Mr. Locke's wife is a sister of Mrs. E. N. Preusse of Holland avenue, Braddock, and of Charles W. Wood, formerly of Port Perry, and of Wm. P. Wood. Mr. Locke was, after his association with Mr. Silvey, city editor and managing editor of the Pittsburgh "Press", and retained those positions for some 18 or 19 years. Mr. Silvey founded the Crawford "Democrat" at Meadville, Pa., and for a time worked on the

Cleveland "Plain Dealer". He was also connected with the Pittsburgh "Christian Advocate and the old "Alleghanian", and later with the "Record" of the East End, Pittsburgh. He was a brilliant member of the old school of newspapers writers.

Following the celebration of Independence Day of 1884, July 5th, to be exact, the "News Net" made its appearance on the streets of Braddock. It was printed as a weekly paper, a five-column folio, by Thomas Lawry, at Robinson street and Bell avenue, North Braddock. Mr. Lawry is now an attorney, and resides in Rankin. For two and a half years the "News Net" gathered every happening of local interest in the upper and lower sections of the town, removing to Franklin street, between Anderson and Robinson streets, the following year.

In January, 1886, Mr. Lawry, who had left a lucrative position at the Edgar Thomson Steel Works converting mills, to try his hand at what the layman calls "journalism", decided to change the name of his youngster while it was yet young, to the "Braddock Journal". As such it grew out of its swaddling clothes until the first of the following year, when the name was again changed to that of the "Braddock Daily Journal." The "Daily Journal" flourished until September, 1887, when Mr. Lawry sold the paper to Harry L. Eisenbeis, a son of Col. Eisenbeis, already referred to as the founder of the Braddock "Times" of 1877, and Joseph L. Campbell, Sr., later justice of the peace in North Braddock for several terms. Mr. Campbell had been for a year or so advertising manager and circulation-maker combined, with the paper on Franklin street.

The "Braddock Journal" again changed its name, in deference to Harry L. Eisenbeis' sentimental tribute to his father, by calling their paper the "Evening Times". The location was changed from Franklin street, North Braddock, to 920 Ninth street, Braddock, the old homestead of Peter Seewald and his family, between the Seewald Building at Ninth street and Braddock avenue, and the later Seewald home at Ninth street and Wood alley, now used as a club-house.

On the second floor of the building occupied by the "Evening Times", in that year, 1887, was published a musical periodical, the "Musical Mirror," by William H. Large, which had moved there about a year before, from Braddock avenue between Tenth and Eleventh streets, after having been established by Mr. Large late in 1885.

The "Evening Times" was published for several months on Ninth street, when its new owners became financially discouraged, and asked the former owner of the "Daily Journal" to take the property off their hands, which condition of relief he extended. After a short period, Mr. Campbell induced William H. Large to try his hand at daily journalism, and the paper moved from its location on Ninth street, to a one-story frame building owned by Justice Louis F. Holtzman, at 960 Braddock avenue, adjoining the old office quarters of Justice Holtzman, and only several yards from the former office of the Braddock "Times" founded in 1877. The "Evening Times" was printed there almost a year, Mr. Large in the meantime having suspended the publication of the "Musical Mirror", and his death brought another change in the ownership of the paper.

For a second time Mr. Lawry was called into executive council, and he took over the plant and again operated it, but retained its name, the "Evening Times". The publishing office was taken from Braddock avenue near Tenth street, to a frame building at 444 Library street, near the Pennsylvania Railroad, owned by the late Edward Lawrence. There it was printed with Mr. Lawry as its owner, for a year or two, the later months of its existence overlapping the first two or three months of the publication of the Braddock "Daily News" by Mr. Mills and Ellsworth Calderwood.

The printing "furniture", type, and presses, of the "Evening Times" were acquired by the "Daily News" in 1889, and the latter newspaper become the only daily newspaper printed in Braddock until January 31, 1893, when the Braddock "Evening Herald" made its appearance. George K. Anderson, a son of a pioneer oil operator of the Franklin and Oil City regions of the early oil days, came from his home in Franklin, Pa., and established the new paper. The writer, who began his printing and newspaper career on Mr. Lawry's "News Net", following its fortunes through the various changes as "Journal", "Daily Journal", "Evening Times" and the "Daily News", gave the name to Mr. Anderson's venture on the storm-tossed sea of Braddock newspaperdom, and became its city editor for the first 16 months of its life, when located in the Stokes Building at 731 Braddock avenue.

There was a change in the ownership of the paper about that time, May, 1894, and while Mr. Anderson remained with the paper for several months as manager, Frank C. Lowing was editor for some 10 months, with C. A. Stokes as president of the publishing firm, which was composed of a number of Braddock business men as stockholders. George W. Penn who came to Braddock from Ohio in 1895, following Mr. Lowing in charge of the news work on the paper, and Elmore E. Greeg, then residing in Braddock, the same year took charge of the "Herald", and remained at the head of affairs until March, 1898, when he severed his connection. C. A. Stokes again took charge of the plant until the spring of 1899, when Arthur F. Emmons became manager for a couple of months, retiring June 24, 1899.

In August of the same year, Joel H. Dietrich, a native of Shenandoah, Pa., and John L. Sechlar, the latter a hotel owner of South Fork, Pa., bought the "Evening Herald" from its firm of business men, and these brought the paper to a high state of efficiency, Mr. Dietrich being a newspaperman of ability and experience, a co-worker in his earlier years with the late Morgan E. Gable, who at the time of his demise last fall, was directing editor of the "Gazette Times", and had been almost from the inception of the old "Pittsburgh Times" owned by the late Christopher L. Magee, its managing editor, and until the merger with the old "Commercial Gazette."

The "Evening Herald", placed on a firm foundation by Messrs. Dietrich & Sechlar, was bought in June, 1903, by Addison L. Petty, now an attorney, residing in Swissvale, and his brother, Joseph Dawson Petty, now of Fishkill, N. Y., connected with New York newspapers, in recent years. The Petty brothers, before embarking in their newspaper canoe in Braddock, had been the owners and editors of the McKeesport "Morning Herald" for a couple of years. In April, 1906, the "Evening Herald", which had changed its location from 731 Braddock avenue when bought by the Petty brothers, to 520 Braddock avenue, opposite the Third ward school building, was merged with the Braddock "Daily News", A. L. Petty leaving for Mexico that year, but retaining his interest, as did his brother, Joseph D., in the "News-Herald" as the merged papers became known. In May, 1907, the firm name became the "News-Herald Publishing Co.", and Melville Clyde Kelly took active charge of the merged papers.

Daniel J. McCarthy, successor to Charles Mills in the ownership of the Braddock "Daily News", left newspaper work for politics in 1896, and the paper became the property of Frank E. Louis, who published it until April 1st, 1899, when Messrs. John C. Loughead and Edward E. Lantz bought the paper from Mr. Louis. Mr. Loughead came to Braddock from Jeannette in the fall of 1893, to assume the foremanship of the composing room of the "Evening Herald", soon after its founding. The autumn of the following year, Mr. Loughead purchased a half interest from Winslow Nicholls in the Eureka Printing Co., a job printing office at 717 Braddock avenue. The following spring, 1895, the publication of a weekly newspaper, the "Weekly Observer", was begun, and the same summer, Mr. Nicholls retired from the business and Mr. Loughead became the sole

THE UNWRITTEN HISTORY OF BRADDOCK'S FIELD. 175

owner of the printing company and the "Observer".

The "Observer" and the "Daily News" became consolidated through the partnership of Mr. Loughead and Mr. Lantz and a few months after acquiring possession of the "Daily News", Mr. Lantz retired from the business, and the publication of the "Observer" was discontinued. On April 1st, 1900, Samuel T. Shaw of Greensburg, a brother-in-law of Mr. Loughead, bought a half interest in the "Daily News", and assumed the position of business manager. Early in 1902, Mr. Shaw sold his interest in the paper to Mr. Loughead.

During the next several years, the "Daily News" forged to the front, and again assumed its place in Braddock newspaperdom, which position it had lost for a time. In January, 1904, one of the latest model linotype, or type-setting machines of the Mergenthaler invention, the first of its kind in the lower Monongahela valley, was installed. The addition of this wonderful machine gave the "Daily News" superior facilities. On May 1st, 1905, Mr. Loughead sold the "Daily News" to L. F. Ross of McKeesport, then connected with the McKeesport "Evening Times", but the following August, Mr. Ross became financially involved to such an extent that Mr. Loughead was compelled to take the plant over again, with a large indebtedness accumulated during Mr. Ross' brief ownership.

A few days later, Mr. Loughead leased the plant of the "Daily News" to the present congressman from the Thirtieth Congressional District, Melville Clyde Kelly, and Winslow Nicholls. May 1st, 1906, Messrs. Kelly and Nicholls bought the "Daily News" plant outright, and Mr. Loughead returned to Jeannette to assume the editorship of the Jeannette weekly "Dispatch", which position he held with a brief interval, until recently, when he became editor of the Greensburg morning "Review".

About the period mentioned, while the "Evening Herald" and the "Daily News" were both flourishing under separate managements, the third daily newspaper made its appearance in Braddock, the only time in Braddock's history that such a condition existed, and the only time that it is likely such a condition were possible in Braddock's newspaper field. The new daily was the Braddock "Evening Journal", established on October 24th, 1905, by James Leland Quinn, in what is now the Leighton Building, at John street and Maple way. With Mr. Quinn was associated his brother-in-law, Charles F. Kramer. The daily "Journal" continued its existence until June, 1908, when the daily was discontinued, and the weekly "Journal" took its place, which is still published by Messrs. Quinn and Kramer, the publication office being on Eighth street, near Talbot avenue.

In December, 1902, the same year that Mr. Loughead acquired full ownership, following the retirement from the paper of Samuel T. Shaw, Melville Clyde Kelly took charge of the news department of the "Daily News". He remained with the paper until the late summer of 1904, and in September of that year established the Braddock "Leader", a weekly paper, with its plant at 444 Library street, the old office of the "Evening Times", published many years before by Thomas Lawry. In September, 1905, Mr. Kelly bought the "Daily News" plant, and merged it with the "Leader", the office being at 317 Seventh street, the former home of the "Daily News".

As already told, the "Evening Herald" then owned by Messrs. Addison, L., and Joseph D. Petty, and the "Daily News", were consolidated in April, 1906, under the firm name of the "Braddock Daily News Publishing Co., Incorporated, as publishers, the plant of the merged papers being at 520 Braddock avenue. Mr. Kelly has been president of the company since the merger in 1906, and has continued also as its editorial manager since that time, even during the period that he served the Tenth Assembly District of Pennsylvania, at Harrisburg, from January 1911, to January, 1913, and also during his first term in Congress as a member from the Thirtieth district, from March, 1913, to March, 1915.

The various weekly and daily newspapers of Braddock, from 1876 down to the present day, have all done a goodly share in the upbuilding of the community, and have given freely, valuable space in their columns, as do practically all newspapers, to further not only the public welfare, but to aid in semi-private enterprises that in a way, may benefit the community, and for which they never get the slightest credit or thanks, and which, invariably, is accepted as the public or private due, something never expected from any other private enterprise or business.

Of course, some of the newspapers have done more than others along the line of local progress, urging in season and out of season, certain public enterprises, and movements that would benefit the whole people, or in some cases, at least most of the community. In this respect might be mentioned all the public improvements that have been made since the Braddock water works plant was built, and incidentally, the splendid manner in which certain Braddock newspapers fought for the people at the time the original street railways were after rights-of-way franchises through the community, the railway companies demanding rights without any benefits or recompense to the public. The financial and alleged graft scandals of those days, were all fought by the newspapers, and the citizens of the present day receive the advantages in decreased taxes.

The present Braddock General Hospital is one result of the activities of the newspapers of Braddock, especially of the old Braddock "Daily News", and in later years of the "Evening Herald", which unselfishly took up the project of the "Daily News", for public weal, for the project originated in the old "Daily News" office during the early years of Mr. McCarthy's ownership, in 1891, to be exact, while the writer was then in charge of the news department of the paper, and a volume in columns of space, was given over a period of some years, to this project, to stir the public mind to the necessity of such an institution, and it might be stated here, with none to question, that in those days the project was bitterly fought, and ridicule from certain quarters was heaped upon the discussions and pleas for a hospital. The writer conducted the propaganda for the project, during the years he was connected with the newspapers of Braddock in an editorial capacity, and knows full well what it meant for the newspapers to take up a project that was unpopular for some years, apart from the support of the noble women who formed the Braddock Hospital Association. It was only in late years, after the way had been hewn out by the old "Daily News" in persistent arguments over years, for a hospital in Braddock, that the hospital idea became a popular one.

The same also was true of the suggestion made by the writer in a series of articles in 1890, written for the "Daily News", while Mrs. Mary Mills was the owner of that paper, that the battlefield on which Gen. Braddock fought, in 1754, be marked by a suitable monument or bronze tablet. In those days there was not the sympathy apparently, between the English-speaking peoples, that there has since developed, especially in recent months, and the suggestion was contemptuously denounced by answering articles in the "Daily News", stating that there was no call for a monument to mark a defeat of a general representing a nation that years afterwards was at war with this country.

The writer of this chapter was threatened with bodily violence in his office many times, by a number of over-enthusiastic, but questionably patriotic citizens, if he did not desist in his propaganda for a monument for the battlefield. The old files of the "Daily News" will show this state of affairs. Still, the world changes, and the acrid sentiments of a generation may be forgotten within that generation, to such an extent that after repeated discussions, in the press, for a monument marking the battlefield of Braddock, of 1754, tablets commemorative of these important events will be unveiled within the coming year.

Braddock newspapers have taken the unpopular side of many movements, because they believed they were right, or for the public welfare, or for the town's good fame, and the true test of a real newspaper is not always following the lead of the people, but leading the people to see the right, or accepting projects and movements for the general public welfare, and moral, social, political and spiritual welfare.

JOHN L. SECHLAR.

A. L. PETTY.

HON. MELVILLE CLYDE KELLY

THOMAS J. LOUIS

JOSEPH DAWSON PETTY.

ELMORE C. GREGG.

GEO. W. PENN.

FRED W. OAKLEY.

SOME OF THE CHURCHES OF BRADDOCK.

1—First M. E. Church.   2—Muhleman Memorial Church, North Braddock.   3—United Brethren Church.
4—Sacred Heart Polish Roman Catholic Church.   5—St. Michael's Greek Catholic Church, Rankin.
6—St. Peter and Paul Greek Catholic Church.   7—St. Joseph's Roman Catholic Church, Braddock.
8—St. Thomas Roman Catholic Church.
9—Congregational Church.   10—Calvary Presbyterian Church.   11—Swedish Lutheran Church.

CHURCHES.

BY REV. JAMES VERNON WRIGHT.(1)

A history of Braddock! And that for fifty years! So many are the influences that go to make up a city; its development, its strength, and its permanency; that care must be taken that all of these be recognized and traced in a survey such as this history claims to make. The Church ministers to the spiritual and moral wellbeing of individuals and communities. The men and women who have made Braddock what it is today—and they are not just a few, who are far-famed, but many humble toilers in mill and shop—were inspired and helped by the sacred ministries of the Church. Our social and industrial development was paralleled by religious fervor and devotion to the ideals of Christianity. The Church has laid deep and broad the foundation of our splendid history. And today our heritage is enriched by the constant appeal of the Churches of this community to the fine things of the spirit.

> What makes a city great and strong?
>   Not architecture's graceful strength,
>   Nor factories' extended length,
> But *men* who see the civic wrong
>   And give their lives to make it right,
>   And turn its darkness into light.
>
> What makes a city full of power?
>   Not wealth's display nor titled fame,
>   Not fashion's loudly-boasted claim,
> But *women*, rich in virtue's dower,
>   Whose homes, tho humble, still are great
>   Because of service to the state.
>
> What makes a city men can love?
>   Not things that charm the outward sense,
>   Nor gross display of opulence,
> But right, that wrong cannot remove,
>   And truth, that faces civic fraud
>   And smites it in the name of God.
>
> This is a city that shall stand,
>   A light upon a nation's hill,
>   A voice that evil can not still,
>   A source of blessing to the land;
>   Its strength not brick, nor stone, nor wood,
>   But justice, love and brotherhood.
>
>   (Author Unknown.)

---

(1) The work of preparing this article was originally assigned to Rev. Percy H. Gordon. Dr. Gordon collected data and had the matter well in hand when, on advice of his physician, he was compelled to relinquish all work and go away for several months for complete rest. Dr. Wright then very kindly took Dr. Gordon's data and prepared the article. (Ed.)

THE UNWRITTEN HISTORY OF BRADDOCK'S FIELD. 181

CHURCHES—BRADDOCK, NORTH BRADDOCK AND RANKIN.

Name.	Location.	Date Organization.	Present Pastor.
First Christian,	Braddock Ave. at Fifth Street	1830	Rev. Henry Mahon.
First United Brethren,	Jones & Hawkins Aves.	1854	Rev. E. B. Learish.
First M. E.,	Library St. & Parker Ave.	1855	Rev. J. Vernon Wright.
First United Presbyterian,	Parker Avenue	1864	Rev. W. H. McPeak.
First Presbyterian,	Library Street	1872	Rev. P. H. Gordon, D. D.
Free Methodist,	Hawkins Avenue	1874	Rev. H. L. Speer.
First Baptist,	Jones Avenue	1881	Rev. Thomas Elliott.
St. Mary's Episcopal,	Lillie Avenue	1881	Rev. F. Welham.
First English Evangelical Lutheran,	Fifth St.	1886	Rev. C. H. Stein.
Emanuel Evangelical Lutheran,	Fifth Street	1886	Rev. F. Englebert.
Swedish Evan. Lutheran Bethel,	Fourth St. & Mills	1887	Rev. Morten Parsons.
Trinity Evan. English Lutheran,	Fourth & Holland	1887	Rev. S. K. Herbster.
First Congregational,	Talbot & Sixth St.	1888	Rev. J. C. Clarke.
Calvary Presbyterian,	Sixth Street	1892	Rev. T. C. Pears, Jr.
Swedish Methodist Episcopal,	Comrie Avenue	1892	Rev. A. P. Lakeberg.
First Methodist Protestant,	Kenmawr Ave., Rankin	1893	Rev. B. K. Bierer.
Fourth Street M. E.,	Fourth Street	1895	Rev. J. J. Buell.
United Evangelical,	Baldridge Ave.	1904	Rev. F. W. Barlett, D. D.
Muhleman Mem. German M. E.,	Grandview Ave.	1914	Rev. D. Worthmann.
St. Luke's Reformed,	Fourth & Camp Ave.		Rev. W. S. Harman.
Brinton Ave. United Presbyterian,	Brinton Ave.		Rev. E. H. Carson.
Corey Ave. A. M. E.,	514 Corey Ave.		Rev. J. L. Jackson.
New Hope Baptist,	Sixth Street		Rev. J. D. Burke.
St. Thomas' Roman Catholic,	Braddock Ave.	1854	Rev. Robert McDonald.
St. Joseph's Roman Catholic,	John Street	1877	Rev. F. J. Eger.
Saint's Peter & Paul Greek Catholic,	John St.	1896	Rev. Stephen Gulovich.
Sacred Heart Polish R. C.,	Talbot & Sixth	1897	Rev. J. A. Rykazewski.
St. Michael's Greek Catholic,	Third St., Rankin	1900	Rev. C. Roskovics.
Russian Orthodox Greek Catholic,	Washington Ave.	1916	Rev. J. K. Antonoff.
St. Brendan's Roman Catholic,	Holland Ave.		Rev. P. Molyneaux.
St. Isadore Greek Catholic,	Talbot & Seventh		Rev. C. Abromaites.
St. Michael's R. C.,	Braddock Ave. & Frazier		Rev. A. Kazinczy.
St. Barnabas' R. C.,	Kenmawr Ave., Rankin		Rev. J. L. Shearinger.
St. Mary of Mt. Carmel,	Margaretta & Sixth		Francisco Beneventano.
Synagogue Agudath Achim,	1023 Talbot Ave.	1894	Rev. J. L. Hillkowitz.
Synagogue Ahavith Acham,	432 Sixth Street		Rev. A. Meyerowitz.
Slovak Congregational Mission Church,	Talbot Ave.	1890	Rev. John Gallo.
St. Paul's Slovak Evan. Luth.,	Halket & 11th	1891	Rev. C. V. Molnar.
Free Gospel Mission Church,	Hawkins Ave.	1902	Rev. F. J. Casley.
Slovak Presbyterian,	Braddock Ave.	1908	Rev. J. V. Kovar.
Mt. Olivet A. Baptist,	Fourth Ave., Rankin		Rev. L. E. Keiser.
Emanuel A. Baptist,	Third Ave., Rankin		Rev. A. D. Brown.
Italian Baptist,	508 Braddock Ave.		Rev. Luke De Amore.
Hungarian Baptist			Rev. Louis Stumpf.

182   THE UNWRITTEN HISTORY OF BRADDOCK'S FIELD.

CHURCHES OF BRADDOCK.

The history of Braddock could not be written without considerable mention of her Churches, whose buildings and equipment are a credit to this thriving industrial center. There are about forty-five Churches and Missions in this community and in their work, they reach most of the nationalities represented in our cosmopolitan population. Long before there was any municipal organization for this community, ministers visited this region and formed the people into Church groups. Sunday Schools were organized, Church buildings were erected, and as the population increased the influence of the Churches became more evident in the upbuilding of the City.

This short chapter has been written from what material has come to the hands of the compiler after most careful and persistent efforts to secure information from each Church in the territory covered by this volume of historic data.

Several congregations trace their history back beyond the year 1850, although the formal organization of the Church may not have taken place until a later date. The First Christian Church is recognized as the oldest Church organization in Braddock. The name of Mills is associated with this Church from the beginning, for it was in the home of Isaac Mills, Sr., where the first preaching was done and the first organization consummated. This was about the year 1830. For eight years these services were held in the Mills home, David Estep, George Forester, James Darsie, and Isaac Erret walking out from Pittsburgh to do the preaching. About 1838 a Church building was erected at Eleventh Street, which after a few years was destroyed by fire. Undaunted by the loss of their building, the congregation decided to build another Church on the same site, which building still stands, occupied now by the Slavonic Catholic Church. After the disposal of this property the present building on Braddock Ave. between Fifth St. and Corey Ave. was erected. This property is valued at $45,000 and is free of debt. In later years the Church started and fostered Churches at Turtle Creek, Wilkinsburg and Homestead. Under its auspices was also organized in 1912 the Italian Christian Church. There are still to be found representatives of the old families in the present organization in such names as Mills, McCune, Shallenberger, and Strathern. The present membership of the Church is 250 and 240 in the Sunday School.

The Braddock Church of the United Brethren in Christ is located at Jones and Hawkins Avenues, North Braddock. This Church was organized in 1854 and now has a property valued at $50,000. The membership of the Church is 438 and there are 552 scholars in the Sunday School.

Five dates stand out in the history of the First Methodist Episcopal Church. They are 1842, when services were held in the old Log-still House on Jones Ave.; 1855, when the Church was organized in the little School House in North Braddock; 1857, when services were held in the First Ward School House, Braddock; 1859, when the first building was erected, Sellers Chapel, on Braddock Ave. at Tenth St.; and 1890, when the present Church building at Library and Parker Avenues was dedicated. "Mother" Barkley, a colored slave, who was brought from Louisville, Ky., by Col. Wallace, was converted and became the first Methodist in Braddock. The first white Methodist convert in Braddock was a Mr. Fink, who was a shoemaker. About 1840 the mother of Mr. J. B. Corey opened up her home in Port Perry and for three years the settlers around Braddock's Field, Brinton, and Turtle Creek and the Methodists from these villages gathered there to hear preaching by the preachers who travelled the circuits. In a little one-story brick school house which would seat about 100 people, Rev. B. F. Sawhill organized the first Methodist Church and Sunday School. The present Church building was erected during the pastorate of Rev. T. N. Boyle and is valued at $55,000, and the Parsonage on Parker Ave. is valued at $8,000. The present membership of the Church is 850 and the Sunday School has an enrollment of 750. The Fourth Street Methodist Episcopal Church was organized and fostered by members and workers from the First Church. This was in the year 1895, when J. W. Miles, D. D., was the Pastor at First Church. This Church has grown to be a flourishing Church of 367 members, with a Sunday School of 384 scholars. The Church has property valued at $6,000.

The First United Presbyterian Church of Braddock was informally organized June 16, 1864, at which time a Commission representing Westmoreland Presbytery received into membership twenty-five persons in the mission. When this was done members were allowed to proceed to complete the organization by the election of elders. The following named persons were elected: Mr. Matthew Henning, Mr. Alexander Claney, Mr. George McCague and Mr. Daniel Cain. These elders were inducted into office July 22, 1864, and the organization was completed. For two years the organization held its Sabbath School and Sabbath services in a two-room school house, on the site now occupied by the First Ward School building on Eleventh Street.

Mr. Matthew Henning donated the congregation a lot on the corner of Eleventh street and the B. & O. Railroad. On this lot the congregation erected a building which is still standing. In August, 1867 the congregation entered its first house of worship in which it worshipped for almost twenty-four years. On April 16, 1893, the congregation dedicated its present church building on Parker Avenue. The congregation has always been self-sustaining, never having received any aid from the boards of the church. The Brinton Avenue Church is a child of this church. The following have been the pastors of this congregation: Rev. Johnathan G. Fulton, stated supply from June 16, 1864 to April 11, 1868. Rev. John S. Easton, D. D., December 21, 1869 to September 5, 1876. Rev. William S. Fulton, December 31, 1877 to October 16, 1898. Rev. George E. Hawes, D. D., December 28, 1898 to October 8, 1911. Rev. Wm. Chas. Wallace, D. D., March 1, 1912 to July 2, 1916. Rev. Wm. H. McPeak, February 2, 1917.

The First Presbyterian Church of Braddock began its career March 8, 1872. In April a petition was presented to Presbytery of Blairsville, asking for the organization of a Presbyterian Church at what was then Braddock's Field. At the home of Mrs. Robinson, September 3, 1872, the organization was effected, with twelve charter members. Services were held for a short time in the school house above the Pennsylvania Railroad, but on March 15, 1873, the congregation began to worship in Seddon's Hall, corner of Main and John Streets. Rev. William F. Kean was the first Pastor of this congregation and served the Church for nine years. During this pastorate ground was purchased and a Church building erected. In the winter of 1892-3 between 40 and 50 persons were dismissed to form what is now the Calvary Presbyterian Church of Braddock. Other ministers who have served this congregation are: Rev. John B. Dickey, 1883-1892; Rev. William G. Reagle, 1893-1906; Rev. L. F. Laverty, 1906-1908; and Rev. Percy H. Gordon, Jan. 12, 1909 until the present time. This Church has grown to a membership of 444 and reports a Sunday School of 307 members, not including Cradle Roll and Home Department.

The Calvary Presbyterian Church, located on Sixth Street, Braddock, was organized October 5, 1892. The first Minister was Rev. O. B. Milligan, D. D. The organization was effected and first services held in Carnegie Hall until the present Church building was erected. There were thirty-three charter members, among them being a number of prominent residents of this community. Other Ministers who have served this Church are Rev. E. M. Bowman, Rev. J. F. Clokey, D. D., Rev. R. P. Lippincott, Rev. F. B. Limerick, and the present Pastor, Rev. T. C. Pears, Jr. The Church now has a membership of 300 and about half that number in the Sunday School.

The First Baptist Church of Braddock was organized June 5, 1881, with 30 members. It was admitted into the Pittsburgh Baptist Association July 29, 1881, at a meeting held in the Christian Church. Rev. A. J. King was the first Pastor, taking up the work in 1882. At once lots were purchased at Talbot Ave. and Seventh St. and plans were drawn for a Church building. A mission Sunday School was formed at Rankin under the direction of Miss Amelia Lee, a Church missionary. This later was organized into a Baptist Church and some of the members of this Church formed the nucleus for the present Swissvale Baptist Church. During the pastorate of Rev. George F. Street, in the fall of 1899, plans were completed for a new Church building, which was dedicated in 1901 and was the home of this congregation until the property was sold, June 15, 1916. Services are now being held in the old United Brethren Church on Jones Ave., North Braddock. The present membership of the Church is 115.

There are several branches of the Lutheran Church in Braddock. The first of these to be organized was the First English Evangelical Lutheran Church. The date of its formal organization was August 15, 1886, when Rev. Luther M. Kuhns was the Pastor. Services were first held in the W. C. T. U. Hall on Braddock Ave., near Tenth St., and later the present Church building on Fifth St., between Holland Ave. and Mill St., was erected. There were 16 charter members. From this small beginning the Church has grown until now the report shows 280 members, with a Sunday School of the same number. The present valuation of the Church property is $10,000. Eight Ministers have served this congregation as Pastors, the present Pastor being Rev. Curvin H. Stein.

The Swedish Evangelical Lutheran Bethel Church was organized March 22, 1877, with 32 charter members. The next year a lot on Sixth Street, near Lillie Ave., was purchased for $1,500, and a frame Church building costing $5,000 was erected. In 1902 the property at Mills Ave. and Fourth St. was bought for $7,800, and three years later, after selling the old Church on Sixth St., work was begun on a new building. Only the basement of the building was completed and the congregation worshiped in this for four years. The main auditorium was finished and the entire Church dedicated May 12, 1912. This beautiful Church is of Gothic architecture and was erected at a cost of $35,000. The property, including the Parsonage, is now valued at $50,000. The Church reports at the beginning of this present year show 400 communicants and 336 children; a total of 736. The Sunday School has 180 scholars with 25 teachers and officers.

The Emanuel Evangelical Lutheran Church of Braddock, Pa., was organized in the month of September, 1886. Prior to that repeated attempts were made to establish a congregation for the German Lutherans at Braddock. The last effort was made by Rev. Schmidt, at that time in charge of a congregation in East Liberty, Pittsburgh, Pa. Services were held on the third floor of the building, still in existence, on the S. E. corner of Talbot Avenue and 9th Street. During September of 1886, Rev. Frederick Brand was called and almost immediately an organization was effected. During the following months of the same year three lots were bought at the corner of 5th Street and Maple Way, and in the beginning of 1887 a frame building was erected. Seven years later, this building proving too small for the growing congregation, a brick building replaced it. This building is still used by the congregation. At that time two additional lots with a house thereon were bought, the house to be used for a parsonage. The original cost was about $20,000, and the present value about $35,000. The present membership of the church is 450 and 125 are enrolled in the Sunday School. There have been three pastors of the congregation as follows: Rev. Frederick Brand, September, 1886-December, 1891; Rev. C. Engelder, December, 1891-September, 1904; Rev. F. Engelbert, October, 1904 to the present time.

The first Episcopal services were held in Braddock in 1881 in a hall on the corner of Ninth St. and Talbot Avenue. These services were held at intervals and were conducted by visiting clergy and occasionally by Cortlandt Whitehead, Bishop of the Diocese of Pittsburgh. In 1890 services were held in a building on the corner of Library Street and Braddock Avenue, now known as the Famous Department Store, but at that time known as the Masonic Building. These services were in charge of Rev. Ingram Irvine.

The first building known as Trinity Church was located on the West side of Sixth Street, opposite Lillie Ave., and was built in 1890 and destroyed by fire in 1891.

A small frame building was then erected on the present site, where the congregation worshipped for the next ten years. In 1901 Mrs. Mary Elizabeth Kinsey, mother of Mrs. Chas. M. Schwab, built and presented to the Diocese the present building on Lillie Avenue, the name of the church being changed to St. Mary's. This building was dedicated June 29,

THE UNWRITTEN HISTORY OF BRADDOCK'S FIELD. 187

1901, and is valued at $30,000. Upon reorganization at this time, the Rev. G. A. Dyess became rector and was followed in order by the Revs. A. C. Stengal, Fred Ingley, A. W. Kierulff, J. C. Fairlie, W. C. Cady and the present rector, the Rev. Frederic Welham.

From the time of its formal organization until 1906 the parish was recognized as a Mission. In June, 1906 the Reverend Fred Ingley became rector, and, under his leadership a vestry was formed and it became an independent Parish.

Like many other Churches, the First Congregational of Braddock had its beginning in the organization of a Sunday School. The meeting was held in the Public School building of the First ward, October 11, 1887. Mr. Thomas Addenbrook was elected Superintendent, which office he filled continuously until 1909. The first session of the Sunday School was held at the home of Mr. Casper Winter on Seventh Street, with 24 present. After this the meetings were held in Sewald's Hall, Ninth St. and Braddock Ave. Here the Church was organized October 18, 1888, there being 29 charter members. The first Pastor in charge was Rev. John H. Young. Previous to 1890 a lot had been bought at the corner of Talbot Ave. and Sixth St. Here a temporary building was erected in ten days by the men and boys of the Church. The Sunday School room of the present Church building was dedicated in November, 1894, and in May, 1902 the auditorium was finished and dedicated. In 1911 the interior of the auditorium was destroyed by fire, but in a few months was restored, a new pipe organ taking the place of the one destroyed. The Church property cost $50,000. The present membership of the Church is 104 and there are 90 members of the Sunday School.

The first meeting held by the Free Methodist Church was on the eve of July 25, 1874, in the public school hall. About $1,000 had been contributed by citizens to build this hall, where public meetings might be held. The hall had not been in use because it was not furnished. These Church people agreed to seat the hall and maintain regular services. The first meeting was conducted by Rev. E. P. Hart, at present a retired Bishop living in California. At that time he was one of the District Elders of the Michigan Conference, coming here through the influence of Mr. J. B. Corey. The first regular Pastor was Rev. A. V. Leonardsen. From the Public School hall the congregation moved to the Corey Chapel, built by Mr. J. B. Corey, and in 1901 found a new location in the present church building on Hawkins Ave. There were 61 charter members and the present membership is 45. The Church property is valued at $6,000.

Rev. W. H. Gladden organized the first Methodist Protestant Church March 10, 1893 in Sewald's Hall. Rev. Leigh Layman was the first Pastor. A lot was purchased at the corner of Sixth St. and Margaretta Ave. and here a building, costing $2,700, was erected and opened June 1, 1896. The building was not completed until 1901. This served as the home of this congregation until the summer of 1904, when the property was sold to St. Mary of Mount Carmel Italian Roman Catholic Church. Services were held for some time in Braznell Hall and Odd Fellows' Hall, and in 1905 the congregation found a new location in Rankin on Braddock Ave., where a new building was erected. This congregation values its property at $14,000 and reports a membership of 170. The Sunday School numbers 125.

The Rev. William Swenson was the first Swedish Minister to visit Braddock. He preached in the First Methodist Episcopal Church in 1892. The next year a Sunday School and Class were organized and Ministers from Pittsburgh and McKeesport looked after the work until Rev. Theodore Peterson was sent here by the late Bishop Walden. Services were held in Stokes Hall, Braddock Ave., and this hall was the home of this congregation until 1912, when the present Church building was procured. This property was purchased from the United Brethren Church for $4,000. The building was recently remodeled at a cost of $2,100. This congregation places the date of its formal organization as January 12, 1897, and reports 13 charter members.

The Muhleman Memorial German Methodist Episcopal Church is located on Grandview Ave., North Braddock. The Church was organized June 15, 1914 with Rev. D. Worthman as Minister. There were 85 charter members and the enrollment of the Sunday School is 130. The first services were held in the Brinton Ave. United Presbyterian Church. A parsonage was built in 1915 and the valuation of the property held by the congregation is $12,000.

The United Evangelical Church was organized in September, 1904 in the building which is still the home of the congregation. There were 14 charter members, and the present Pastor, Rev. F. W. Barlett, D. D., was the first Minister. The Church membership numbers 70 with 175 on the roll of the Sunday School. The property valuation is $9,000.

The present flourishing St. Thomas' Roman Catholic parish is the realization of the plans formulated by the little colony of Catholics who erected their small chapel on Tara Hill on the south side of the Monongahela river in 1854. This mission site was donated by Mr. Thomas J. Kinney, and building material was presented by Mr. West. The steady increase of parishioners augmented the demand for a larger church, on a more convenient site, and resulted in the purchasing of the present church property, by Rev. F. Tracey. In the year 1859 Martin Dowling secured the deed for the land, and April 22, 1860, Father O'Farrell laid the corner stone.

The first Mass was celebrated in the basement of the church, October 14, 1860. Owing to a financial deficit, caused by the War, the parish was threatened with ruin, but was permanently saved by the noble self-sacrifice of Mr. Kinney, who paid the mortgage at the risk of personal bankruptcy. This congregation's pride in their parish was evidenced by an attendance so large that Father Hughes deemed it obligatory to extend the church thirty feet. Expenses were defrayed by the gratuitous services of the coal miners. More prosperous times enabled Father Hickey to formulate plans for a larger church. Foremost among those who were eager to co-operate in the good work, were Mr. and Mrs. Charles Schwab, who generously offered to build the edifice in A. D. 1902. The work was carried on under the admirable direction of Mr. L. F. Holtzman, whose business sagacity secured most satisfactory results to the parish. The structure, Romanesque in architecture, with its exquisite equipments, is a fitting memorial to the munificent donors. The property held by this parish is valued at $200,000. It ministers to 500 families and has 650 in the Sunday School.

The educational advantages afforded by St. Thomas' School have attained their excellence after years of labor. The primitive school under lay supervision was supplanted by the present one during the pastorate of Father Hickey. Rev. Robert McDonald has succeeded in realizing for the parish, not only a thorough grammar grade course, but also a High School, efficiently equipped for a complete scientific and classical course. With true scholarly instincts he has introduced the latest and most complete text-books, free of charge, to the parish children. It is with commendable pride that the people of St. Thomas' parish review the history of their church and school, the present prestige of which they attribute to loyal and earnest co-operation.

Saint Joseph's Catholic Church, Braddock, Pa., was organized September first, 1877, by Rev. Anthony Fischer. The first Mass was held for the newly formed parish of St. Joseph, by the above named Pastor in Sewald's Hall, Cor. Braddock Avenue and Ninth Street, Braddock's Field, as it was then called. The frame church which was in course of construction on George Street, was dedicated by Bishop John Tuigg of Pittsburgh, in August, 1880, and used as a church for thirteen years, and as a school for sixteen more. It was taken down, to make room for the present Parish School, erected in 1909, during the pastorate of Father May.

There were about sixty families at the time of organization and Father Fischer was succeeded by Rev. Jacob M. Wertz on February 3rd, 1888, who, on December 10th of the same year, was followed by Rev. August A. Wertenbach. It was in his pastorate that the congregation purchased the lot adjoining the parish-house on George Street from A. J. Spigelmire, and erected thereon the present permanent Church of brick with stone trimming, covering the whole space, after removing the Spigelmire dwelling across the alley to the lot on Verona Street, where it serves for a convent for the Sisters of Divine Providence who teach the Parish schools.

The Church, which cost about fifty thousand dollars, and took two years to build, was solemnly dedicated on Sunday, December 17th, 1893, by the Right Rev. Richard Phelan, Bishop of Pittsburgh, assisted by eighteen priests: the Rev. P. Kaufmann, C. Coyne, Very Rev. M. Decker, P. Molyneaux, John Faughnan, Geo. Allman, J. Murphy, now Bishop; J. Nolan, Vincent Huber, now Abbot; Father Francis, O. S. B., D. Devlin, R. Wieder, F. J. Eger, S. Schramm, Father Michael, O. S. B., Very Rev. A. A. Lambing, and Very Rev. W. Cunningham, and the Rev. Pastor, Father Wertenbach, to whose untiring energy, the generous co-operation of his faithful people, and the blessing of God through it all, the success of such a great undertaking for such a small congregation, is due. In the winter of 1898-99 Father Wertenbach's health failed, and during his sojourn in the South and Southwest, the parish was attended by the Benedictine Fathers from St. Vincent's and the Capuchines from Pittsburgh. He resigned in April, 1899. Rev. Peter May was appointed Pastor April 8th, 1899. During the pastorate of Father May the congregation kept growing to such an extent that he asked the Bishop for an assistant, and the Rev. William Fromme came in July, 1907. The need of the parish was a school, sufficiently large to accommodate the increasing number of pupils. The present school building, three stories, of brick, commodious, well lighted, heated, ventilated, and fire-proof, containing, besides the school rooms, a large hall, a reading room, a recreation room, a society room, and a gymnasium for the use of the St. Joseph's Young Men's Club, was accordingly erected on the full lot, formerly occupied by the first Church, at a cost of thirty-three thousand dollars.

THE UNWRITTEN HISTORY OF BRADDOCK'S FIELD. 191

After the death of Father May on November 9th, 1911, Rev. F. J. Eger, the present pastor, was appointed on December 21, 1911. The school attendance averages two hundred and eighty pupils, who are in charge of the Sisters of Divine Providence, the Choir of sixteen (male choir) is in charge of Adolph Propheter, Organist. The present Church Committee, elected triennially by the congregation, appointed by the Bishop of the Diocese, consists of the following gentlemen: Lucas J. Walter, Joseph Ketter, Edward Striebich, Philip Escher, Andrew Fischer, Henry Gelm and Henry Wells.

Saint's Peter and Paul Greek Catholic Church was formally organized May 18, 1896. There were seven charter members and Rev. Nicholas Steczovich was the first Pastor. This Church had its beginning when a number of Greek rite Catholic immigrants from Hungary founded the Greek Catholic Union, a Sick and Death Benefit fraternal organization. The property of the old First Presbyterian Church on George Street was purchased for $10,000. The parish has been extended until now a membership of two thousand is reported and three hundred Sunday School Children. The present value of the real estate and buildings is about $100,000.

The Sacred Heart Roman Catholic Polish Church was organized in the month of March, 1897, and was attended by a non-resident pastor from Duquesne, Rev. Anthony Smelsz. The membership grew rapidly and soon lots were purchased at Talbot Avenue and Sixth Street, where the present church was erected, the work of building starting in 1904 and was completed and dedicated with impressive ceremonies the next year. In May, 1906 the present Pastor, J. A. Rykaczewski was appointed to the parish, and under his administration the present school building was erected, where about 450 children in all the eight grades are taught by the Felician Sisters. The rectory on Sixth Street was also built in 1914.

St. Michael's Greek Catholic Church, Third and Mound Streets, Rankin, was organized in 1900, and in 1907, on April 12, all Greek Catholics in Rankin decided to withdraw from the St. Peter and Paul's Church in Braddock, to which they belonged. The basement of the Church was built first, and for about five years the congregation worshipped there. The entire Church was completed in 1911 and the parish home was built in 1915. Rev. John Szabo was the first Pastor and the present Pastor, Rev. Constantine Roskovics, ministers to 130 families, or about 500 souls.

In 1916, April 23, the Russian Orthodox Greek Catholic Church of the Holy Resurrection was organized by Rev. Joseph K. Antonoff. The building was purchased from the Hibernian Society on Washington Avenue, between Eighth and Ninth Streets, and was re-constructed for Church purposes. This building, together with the Pastor's home, is valued at $18,000. A membership of about 1,500 is reported.

There are several Protestant Churches and Missions among the foreign speaking people in this community. Among them is the Bethlehem Slovak Congregational Mission Church. This work was started in July, 1890, by Miss Anna Hodous, a graduate of the Schauffle Missionary Training School for Young Women. Mr. Thomas Addenbrook was untiring in his efforts to effect this organization and has been a constant friend of this work ever since. Twelve members were enrolled at the beginning and now about 35 names are found on the roll. The work started in the home of Mr. John Jelinek, and after meeting in different halls, the present location on Talbot Avenue was secured and a Church erected, which is now valued at $12,000. This mission work inspired other denominations to start similar work; and from this Church members went out and effected the organization of at least five other flourishing Churches in other towns. Rev. Andrew Gavlic, Pastor of the Slovak Congregational Church of Duquesne, is at present looking after the interests of the mission work.

The St. Paul's Slovak Evangelical Lutheran Church was organized in October, 1891, through the special efforts of Mr. Julius Wolf for the Slovaks from Hungary of the Evangelical Lutheran faith. Services were first held in a hall on Washington Avenue and in the Congregational Church on Talbot Avenue at Sixth Street. Very soon this congregation was able to secure the brick church building at Eleventh Street and Halket Avenue, which was originally a school house, but had been purchased by the United Presbyterian Church and changed into a church building. This property cost $8,000 and after repairs and changes were made a pipe organ was received from Mr. Andrew Carnegie, which is valued at $2,000. The present membership numbers over 800 communicants and the property, including Church building, Parsonage and school room, has an estimated value of $35,000. The Sunday School, started only two years ago, numbers 120 children. According to the Church records, during the 26 years of existence, there have been in this Church 2,718 baptisms, 597 marriages, and 679 funerals. Rev. Charles V. Molnar is the present Pastor.

Mission work started among the Presbyterian Slovaks in 1900, services being held in the basement of the First Presbyterian Church. The organization of a Church took place May 15, 1908 with a membership of 62 under the pastorate of Rev. Charles Molnar. A provisional session, composed of members of the First and Calvary Presbyterian Churches assisted in the completion of the organization. A building on Braddock Avenue between 12th and 13th Streets was purchased for $4,500 and was the first home of this mission Church. When in 1910 the Presbyterian Churches of Braddock were transferred from the Blairsville Presbytery to the Presbytery of Pittsburgh, the last named Presbytery erected a brick church building for the use of the congregation and for organized mission work. This Church was dedicated in January, 1913, and has a seating capacity of 250, the basement being used for Sabbath School, industrial work and social meetings. The total value of the Church property is $15,000. Since 1913 Rev. J. V. Kovar has been Pastor of the Church.

The Free Gospel Church on Hawkins Avenue was organized in 1902 by F. J. Casley. There are about 100 in its membership and 48 attend the Sunday School. The valuation of the present Church building is $3,500.

The Synagogue Agudath Achim was organized October 14, 1894. Rev. Jacob M. Bazel was the first minister and served until January, 1917, when the present Rabbi, Rev. J. Leon Hillkowitz took his place. The organization was effected in a room rented for worship purposes at Eleventh Street and Halket Avenue. Later a Synagogue was built on Talbot Avenue, near Eleventh Street, and ground was purchased for a Cemetery at Mucklerat and a Chapel built on this ground. There were 21 charter members and now the report gives 150 members with a Sunday School of 300. The valuation of the Synagogue property is $35,000. At present services are held twice daily in the Synagogue. On Friday evening (Sabbath eve), besides the regular service special children's services are conducted and a sermon is delivered by Rabbi Hillkowitz.

Other Churches whose history is not related in this chapter, are found listed in the complete chronological list on the preceeding pages. Any omissions are due to the failure of Churches or Ministers to furnish the material requested by the writer to make this chapter accurate and complete.

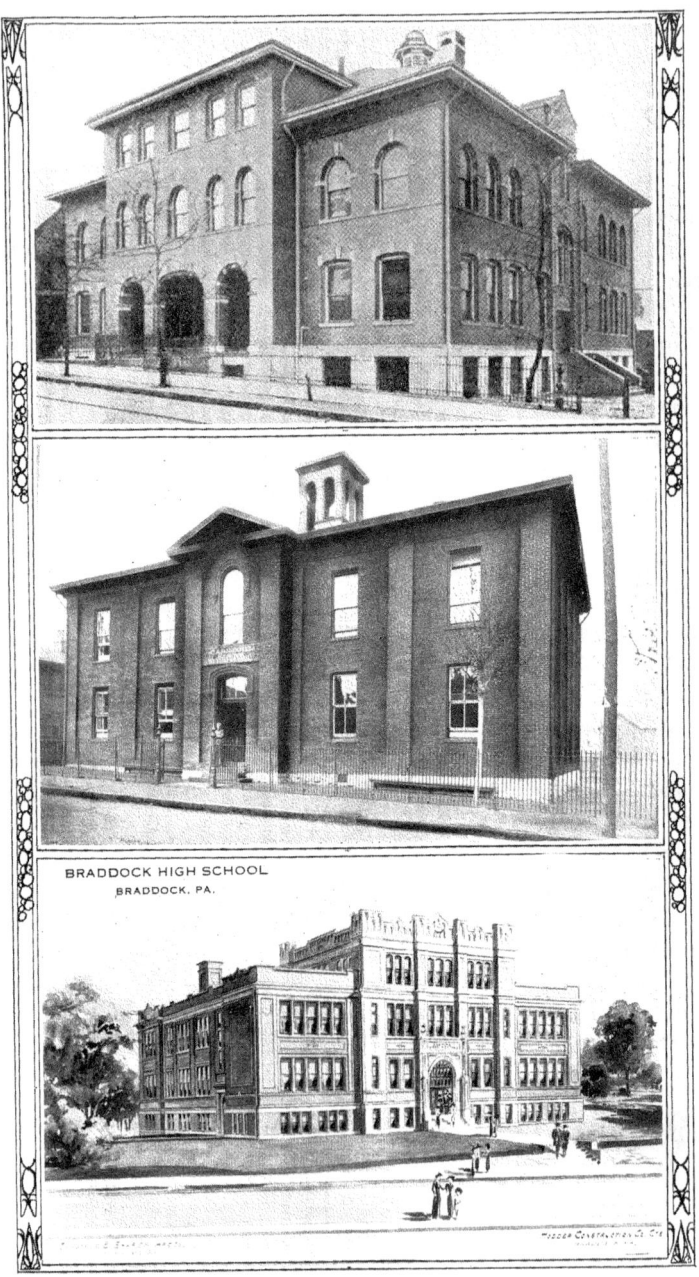

TOP—NORTH BRADDOCK HIGH SCHOOL, BRADDOCK, PA.
MIDDLE—OLD FIRST WARD SCHOOL, BRADDOCK, PA.
BOTTOM—BRADDOCK HIGH SCHOOL, BRADDOCK, PA.

SCHOOLS.

BY GEORGE W. GILMORE.

No better index to the character of a community can be found than what is reflected in the nature and conduct of its educational institutions. Where there is pride in its educational attainments and where these same facilities are stimulated by a healthy desire to grow and become a real factor in civilization backed by a generous tax levy for their maintenance we find a progressive up-to-date community whose citizens are certain to become influential in county, state and nation.

Such a community is Braddock and it is with considerable pride that we point to our institutions of learning both past and present and to the splendid accomplishments they have achieved.

It is true that the maintenance of such a system of schools as this city enjoys is made possible only because the citizens of our city have felt the necessity for culture and refinement and the necessary practical side, made so because of the magnificent industrial growth of the community, and to this end have given liberally of their means for the support of these activities.

Braddock Borough, formerly Braddock's Field, was incorporated in 1867 from Wilkins Township and the only school property falling to the borough in that division was a lot, corner of Eleventh Street and Talbot Avenue, formerly Tonnaleuka and Beaujeu Streets, 138 feet by 275 feet, in the first ward and known as Carnegie sub district, on which was a building 30 by 62 feet. This was the North half of the first building and five years later 1872, an addition to this building was erected at a cost of $4,000. This building was subsequently (in 1903) replaced by the present splendid structure with its equipment for modern school work. In 1881 five lots were purchased on Corey and Braddock Avenues on which was erected in 1883 a ten roomed building, at a cost of $19,500. This was known as the Hamilton building. In 1892 an addition was erected to this building consisting of eight rooms.

In 1893 the Copeland district was annexed to Braddock as the fourth ward, but the schools did not come under the management of the Braddock School district until 1894. This annexation added one building of 8 rooms to the school property.

The records show a continuous healthy growth during the succeeding year so that additional facilities became necessary. The next building was therefore planned on rather a large scale. In 1899 the present splendid property, known as the Henning School was erected. The building and grounds cost approximately $97,400. This building was modern in every detail and contained 14 school rooms, an auditorium and four rooms for high school, together with an office for the Superintendent, a Directors' room and a teachers' parlor.

These four buildings continued to house the growing school population for 14 years until with the added remarkable growth of the high school and the consequent demands made for its broader scope, it was deemed best to remove the high school from the Henning building in order that this building might be given over exclusively to grade school work.

The Board accordingly secured a piece of property fronting on Lillie avenue at a cost of $30,000 on which was erected a modern up-to-date high school building at a cost of about $183,000 making the cost of the present plant together with its furnishings and equipment $213,000. This high school building contains a chapel seating 500, 15 class rooms, 4 splendidly equipped laboratories, two rooms well fitted up as a Commercial department, a library, Superintendent and principals' offices, and Directors' room, together with a completely equipped gymnasium and well organized and furnished domestic science and manual training departments. It was dedicated on May 7, 1915.

It is thus seen that Braddock now has five good school buildings giving accommodation for about 3,000 pupils in 80 school rooms. In all the number of teachers, employed by the district, including special teachers, is 83. Compared with 1867 when we had two school rooms and two teachers it is readily seen what has been our growth.

The first high school in Braddock was opened in 1887 and a three years' course was adopted, which was a normal course. As the number of pupils increased the courses were extended to include a commercial course and a College preparatory course. In 1900 the College preparatory was lengthened to four years so that now the school offers a full College preparatory course of either an academic or scientific trend, a general course and a four year Commercial course. In addition to these three courses, a two year special Commercial course is offered for those who cannot complete the four years' course for want of time. At the time the regular course of the high school was lengthened the grade course was reduced from nine years to eight years. Since the high school was organized it has graduated 370 pupils. The first class to graduate was in 1889 and consisted of eight pupils. At present there are enrolled in the high school 325 pupils with a teaching force of twelve.

Industrial training was introduced in the Braddock Schools in 1901 through the generosity of Thomas Morrison, then Superintendent of the Edgar Thomson Works of the Carnegie Steel Company.

In 1915 the eighth and seventh grades of the district were united in one group and organized into the Junior High School which was housed in the rooms made vacant by the removal of the high school to its present magnificent building. In 1915 a continuation school was organized, which gave instruction for certain definite hours each week to many who were still of school age but were compelled to work part of the time.

In 1916 a school for backward children was organized and has proven of very great help to the less fortunate of our children.

In the Fall of 1916 a school for foreigners was opened in the evenings—the object being the instruction of men and women in the rudiments of English and in the principles of American Citizenship. This school enrolled approximately three hundred.

It is to be noted that a number of men who were, early in life, identified with Braddock schools, later achieved success in other fields of endeavor. Mr. J. S. Johnston went from Braddock schools to the Superintendency of Allegheny county schools. He was succeeded in that office by Dr. Samuel Hamilton, also from Braddock, who has held that position continuously since 1886, more than thirty-one years, and is now the longest in service of any County Superintendent in the United States. He has at the present time, under his direct supervision, more teachers than any other County Superintendent in this country, in spite of the fact that within the territory of the county are two city and nine borough superintendencies. Mr. E. D. Twitmyer went from Braddock to the Portland, Oregon schools, and there has won distinction by his explorations of Mt. Rainier. Mr. E. W. Moore became a successful attorney. Mr. J. W. VandeVenter, who was, incidentally, a singer and choir leader, later gave up teaching for evangelistic work. Mr. G. M. Fowles went into the Methodist ministry and now holds a very important position in connection with the foreign mission work. Mr. F. E. Simcox went into the China mission field, and with his wife, who was his class mate at Grove City college, and their three children, was murdered in the Boxer uprising.

The following have served either as Principal or Superintendent of the Braddock Schools:

PRINCIPALS.

I. N. Cooper 1868-70	J. S. Johnston...........1876-81
A. M. Vantine 1870-71	A. T. Douthitt...........1881-82
S. C. Farrier.............1871-72	Samuel Hamilton 1882-86
J. P. McCord............1872-73	E. B. Twitmyer..........1886-88
L. B. Welsh.............1873-75	A. S. Brubaker..........1888-89
John Bailey 1875-76	J. T. Anderson..........1889-90

E. W. Moore............1890-93

SUPERINTENDENTS.

E. W. Moore......1893-one month	Geo. H. Lamb..........1900-1903
J. S. Keefer(1).........1893-1900	Grant Norris 1903-1912

F. C. Steltz....1912-

The present Faculty of the High School consists of twelve members as follows:

Geo. W. Gilmore, Principal; Myrtle Herbert, German; Margaret Wilson, English; Margaret Cosgrove, Algebra; Mary Brown, English; Harriet Gardner, English; Geo. L. White, Commercial; Emma Pipes, Latin; Olive Taylor, Mathematics; Howard Williams, Science; William Martin, History; Raymond Cox, Civics.

The following persons have been regularly employed as teachers in the Braddock School district:—

Achinson, Jennie; Addenbrook, Louisa; Aiken, W. J.; Allen, Harriet; Bailey, Edna; Bailey, Jennie; Bair, Ethel; Bair, Margaret (Mrs. Eisaman); Baker, Bertha; Barackman, J. B.; Bates, Sadie; Bell, Margaret C.; Bell, Mary I.; Bennett, Jennie (Mrs. Flenniker); Bennett, M. E.; Blattner, Rose; *Bonner, Mary; Bowers, R. E.; Bowler, Rhoda R.; Bowman, Agnes; Brackemeyer, Margaret (Mrs. Geo. Price); Branthoover, Nettie; Bridges, Millie (Mrs. Wm. Hogg); Bridges, Stasia (Mrs. H. F. Fisher); Brisbin, Lillian; Broad, Bessie M.; Brown, Mary; *Brown, Sadie; Bruce, Carolyn; Brubaker, Ella; Brenneman, Emma; Bruxner, Amanda; Bryan, Annie (Mrs. Sherwin); Bryan, Lottie (Mrs. W. G. Purdy); Bryan, Olive (Mrs. Hess); Buzza, Bella M.; Callahan, Elsie (Mrs. J. P. Stephens); Camp, Sallie A.; Campbell, Nannie; Canan, Eva; Carey, John A.; Carmack, Zynett; Carr, Edith C.; Carr, Grace (Mrs. John Killeen); Carrol, Minnie A.; Carruthers, Ruth (married); Carvey, Lillie M. (married); Chester, Edna; Chisholm, Mary; Clancy, Louise; Clarke, Ella; Clark, Ida; Clark, Mame E.;

---

(1) See note at end of this article.

THE UNWRITTEN HISTORY OF BRADDOCK'S FIELD. 199

Clark, Sarah L.; Coble, Mary S.; Cochran, Vista (Mrs. John W. Hanna); Colebank, L; Coleman, Josephine; Conley, Margaret; Cooney, Emma; Cooper, Mrs. M.; Cooper, Wiletto; Corey, Mary E. (married); Cosgrove, Margaret; Coursin, Augusta (Mrs. Wm. Larimer); Covert, Ada; Cox, Raymond A.; Craig, Agnes; Craig, Elizabeth; Craig, Lucy; *Craig, Maude; Cramer, Roxana (Mrs. Bowman); *Cummings, Lizzie; Davies, Ida; Davies, Margaret I.; Davies, Zilla; Davis, Ethel; Day, Evelyn (Mrs. Hoffman); Delo, Margaret; Dieffenbacher, Vallie (Mrs. Wm. Packer); Dillon, Berna (Mrs. Hollis Ardinger); Dixon, Frances L.; Dougherty, Delia (married); Dougherty, Kathryn; Downey, Mary (married); Drewes, Irene W.; Dyess, Nettie; Eagleson, Rebecca; Ellis, Sarah E.; Ellis, Grace; Emeigh, Pearle; Eakin, Milton J.; Fauset, Annie (Mrs. Taylor); Fellabaum, N. Maud (married); Fix, Margaret (Mrs. Ralph Magee); Fixel, G. Wm.; Fornwalt, Mary S.; Foster, Marie (Mrs. Fred Pilgrim); Fowles, M. G.; Frederick, Jessie (Mrs. Miller); *Fritzius, Jennie (Mrs. McGeary); Fuller, Annabel (Mrs. Hendricks); Galbraith, Minnie (Mrs. Heath); Gallager, Gabrielle; Gardner, Emma (Mrs. Reuben Abbiss); Gilfillan, Grace; Gilmore, George W.; Given, Gladys; Glass, Lucy B.; Gorsuch, Nelle F. (Mrs. Roy Musselman); Griffin, Anne M.; Grimm, Della M.; Guss, Anna May; Hall, Clara; Hamilton, Fannie M. (Mrs. T. W. Stephens); Hanna, Nellie (married); Harrop, Hazel P.; *Hart, Clara; Haymaker, Seward; Heath, Helen G.; Henning, Melissa; Henning, C. J.; Herbert Myrtle; Hess, Maude; Hicks, Clara; Higgins, Elizabeth; Hill, Lucy; Hindeger, Annie; Holland, Minnie A. (Mrs. Charles E. Lilley); Holland, Lovina (Mrs. Remington); Holliday, Jane; Horner, Lillie; Hooper, Emma (Mrs. Jas. Brindley); Horrocks, Martha B.; Hough, Mary; House, Marjorie (Mrs. Geo. A. House); Houseman, Ella F.; Huggins, Estella; Hyslop, Anna May (Mrs. Townsend); Irwin, Catherine; Isenberg, Frances G.; Jack, Harriet W.; James, Elizabeth (married); James, Lavina (Mrs. Pollard); Jenkins, M. E.; Jennings, Alice M. (Mrs. Milleken); Jones, Hilda R.; Jones, Julia M.; Jones, Margaret; Kene, Ida M.; Keener, Beckie; Kelly, Elizabeth G.; Kelly, Jessie; Kelly, Louise; Kennedy, Ella F.; Kepler, Mary (Mrs. Parkhurst); Kilcoyne, Annie R.; Kimes, Anna M.; King, Mary E.; Kinter, Edna F. (Mrs. McClelland); Kinter, Ralph F.; Knox, Eileen A.; Koesel, Jeanette; Krise, Daniel H.; Kunes, Anne M.; Lambie, Jeanette; Lamb, Sada M.; Lane, Arvilla A.; Law, Bertha V.; Lea, Anna; Leech, Blanche; Leeger, Marian K.; Leighton, Annie (Mrs. A. M. Stevenson).; *Leighton, Julia; Lenhart, Julia; Liken, Ada; Liston, Julia D.; Little, J. E.; Lloyd, Elizabeth; Long, Stella; Lotsman, Mabel; Lotsman, Zelma; Louis, Blanche (Mrs. McKelvey); Love, Kate M.; Love, Maud;

Lowman, Pearl; Lowry, Georgia; Lytle, Jean M.; Lytle, Kate (Mrs. C. C. Clifford); *Lytle, Sue; Malone, Elizabeth C.; Marks, Stella N.; Marsellan, Perina (Mrs. Bennett); Marshall, Adah L.; Marshall, Mary J.; Martin, Eva; Martin, Wm. J.; *Mathews, Sadie (Mrs. Allewelt); MacCord, Anna; McBride, Bertille J.; McCain, Alice (Mrs. Johnston); McCain, Carrie; McCall, Mary E.; McCarty, Ethel (Mrs. George Dowler); McClain, Margaret (Mrs. William McBride); McCully, Mayme; *McCune, Minnie (Mrs. Samuel Hamilton); McCune, Mrs. Sarah E.; McElhaney, Clare; McElhaney, Helen C.; McIlvoy, Clare; *McKeever, Jennie (Mrs. McKelvey); McKeever, Martha; McKeever, Nannie; McKillop, Elizabeth; McKinley,.Catherine (Mrs. G. E. F. Gray); McKinley, Mary I.; McKnight, Mary R.; McLaughlin, Katherine (Mrs. N. E. Wierbach); McLaughrey, Bessie; McNaugher, W. H.; McWilliams, Maud; *Meacham, Fred A.; Means, Emma B.; Mench, Florence; Meyers, Cora B.; Michener, Kate; Miller, Jessie L.; Miller, Minnie; *Mills, Eliza; Minds, Eliza M.; Mitchell, Carrie; Morgan, Edith F.; Morrison, Ilulia R.; Morton, E. A.; Munson, Emeline (Mrs. Shirey); Murray, Frances; Murtland, Cleo; Musselman, Lois; Neville, Grace; Nevins, Etta L.; Nevins, Lena (Mrs. Alfred Sherwin); Newingham, G. Gertrude; Nimon, Nellie F.; Nolin, Nancy H.; Nugent, Anna (married); O'Neill, Emma N.; Orr, Anna; Osler, Hester; Oster, Ruth; Park, Jennie; Park, Florence; *Patch, Sarah;[1] Patterson, Jennie; Patton, Kathryn (Mrs. Chas. Bair; Pearce, Emma (Mrs. Geo. Jackson); Pennington, Mary; *Petty, Bertha (Mrs. Ray Lynch); Petty, Anna (married); Pflasterer, Annie; Phillips, Alice; Phillips, Mary; Phipps, Mabel E.; Pines, Anna M.; Pinkerton, Floyd V.; Pipes, Emma; Pizor, Lizzie; Pratt, Emma I.; Pyne, Grace; Radcliffe, J. N.; Ralston, Mary; Randolph, Ella (married); Reardon, Mary; Redman, Maggie (Mrs. David Miller); Reed, Edna (married); Reed, Vera N.; Reese, Margaret; Remington, Lois (Mrs. I. W. Keener); Reynolds, Mae; *Rhodes, S. A.; Rich, D. L.; Robinson, Anna May; Rodkey, Florence (Mrs. Ernest Craighead); Roney, Margaret; Rugh, Bessie L.; Schall, M. Agnes; Schoals, Agnes; Scott, Margaret; Shaffer, O. N.; Shallenberger, Laura B.; *Shane, Jennie; Sharp, Genevieve; Sheeran, Elizabeth (married); Shepard, M. A. (Mrs. Reid); Shepard, Elizabeth; Shorts, Clyde P.; Shupe, Abbie; Shultz, Charles; Shryock, Lucy; Sill, Marguerite (Mrs. Limbad); Singer, Mary J.; Simcox, F. L.; Smith, C. L.;*Soles, Ella; Soles, Martha (Mrs. W. S. Blair); Spur, Dillie; Spires, Coral C. (married); St. Clair, Clara (Mrs. W. H. Brown); Stein, Lizzie; Steinmetz, Dillie; Stedeford, Lotta (married); Sterling, Lelah L. (Mrs. Doan); Stevenson, Louella; Stewart, Ina M.; Stewart, Myra I.; Stinner, Mary M.; *Stoody, Louise; Strang,

---

[1] Miss Patch died of pneumonia on Christmas Day, 1916, after twenty years of faithful service as Principal of Copeland Sub-district school.

Mary (Mrs. George Stroup); Strathern, Daisy (Mrs. John Leberman); Stroup, Bessie; Stucki, Anna M. (Mrs. Wm. Husband); Suter, Gertrude (married); Swaney, Catherine (Mrs. Del. King); Swaney, Jessie (Mrs. Thomas); *Sweadner, Eva B.; Sweadner, Mary (Mrs. Ed. Sharah); Taylor, Olive; Taylor, Miss; Teny, Lillie; Thomas, Alice C.; Thomas, Anna B.; Thomas, Martha; Thomson, John; Thompson, Mary H.; Throckmorton, Nanna; Todd, L. L.; Van Deventer, J. W.; Van Kirk, Adeline; Van Voorhis, Viola; Walters, Bertha (Mrs. Hugo); Walton, Sarah; Weaklan, Bertha; Weaver, Lula D. (Mrs. Caldwell); Weil, George; West, Charlotte; Westgate, Helen E. (married); Wheeler, Carrie; White, Dora; White, G. L.; Williams, S. Howard; Wilson, Lizzie; Wilson, Sciota V.; Wilson, Lillian; Wilson, Margaret M.; Winfield, Sadie (married); Wingert, Clara M.; Wood, C. C.; Wood, Thomas; Yarlett, Nannie; Young, Anna.

The present Board of Education of Braddock is: President, Ira. C. Harris, M. D.; Secretary, Samuel D. Hamilton; Treasurer, Harry E. McBride; Vice President, John F. Lowry and William C. Boli, Edward M. Sharrah, and Benjamin H. Jones.

In addition to the present system of schools, Braddock has been fortunate in the possession of several other systems of schools both public and private.

The first educational institution to be established in this community was the Edgeworth Ladies Seminary, the oldest and first boarding school west of the Alleghany Mountains. The school was opened in 1825 at Pittsburgh, by Mrs. Mary Olver, a religious English woman of pronounced educational views. The school remained only a few years in Pittsburgh and was then moved to Braddock's Field and made a boarding school. The tuition was $3.00 per week and it enrolled students from all over Central United States, east of the Mississippi River.

The first catalogue contained the names of many prominent families in Westmoreland, Fayette, Washington, and other counties contiguous to this neighborhood.

The building of the Seminary is still standing on Library Street, and is now the home of Mr. David F. Collingwood. This building is renowned as the house in which the Marquis de Lafayette was entertained while in this community.

In 1836 the school was moved by the founder to Sewickley with the idea that the scope of the school would be thus enlarged.

---

* Deceased.

GREER BUSINESS COLLEGE.

Braddock has only one private school. A private educational institution that can maintain itself for nineteen years in the face of the growth and development of public school facilities must have real merit. When the school was opened it was the general impression that Braddock would not support such a school, because of its close proximity to the city of Pittsburgh, but its successful operation proves that Braddock needed an institution of this character.

There can be no doubt that this school has been serviceable to Braddock and vicinity, as it enables hundreds of young people to give all or part of their time to specific preparation along practical lines. Evidence of this is found in the fact that fully ninety per cent of its 500 graduates are holding desirable positions in this and other communities.

The school was opened October 1898 in a room in the Masonic building, over the First National Bank, now occupied by the Famous department store. Mr. D. Newton Greer, the proprietor, was previously associate proprietor and principal with Mr. M. E. Bennett of the Morrell Institute, Johnstown, Pennsylvania.

In 1900 Mr. Greer had constructed at his own expense an additional story to the building at 837 Braddock Avenue. These quarters becoming too small, in 1908 the third floor of the Russell building, at 836 Braddock Avenue, was leased. These more commodious and pleasant quarters are still the home of the school.

The Greer Business College offers a course of study that is modern in all respects, which is as complete as any school of this character—covering the following courses: Shorthand and Typewriting, Bookkeeping and Office Practice, Business English and Penmanship, Engineering and Mechanical Drawing.

The Annual Commencement Exercises, the first of which were held in the year 1900 (and through the courtesy of the Library are always held in the Carnegie Music Hall,) have become memorable in the Monongahela Valley. They are looked forward to with increasing interest because of their incentive to greater effort and nobler achievement. The Dinkey Gold Medal, the gift of Mr. Charles E. Dinkey, is presented to the graduate who gives the most pleasing performance at these exercises. Men of State and National reputation are engaged to address the graduates.

The graduating class of 1917 numbered 39 students. The Alumni Association was formed in 1915, and its last annual banquet, at Hotel

Schenley, Pittsburgh, June 12, 1916, was a social function of intelligence and refinement.

The social side of the life of the school is not neglected. The A-Gree(r)-a-ble Club which is very active, was formed by members of the school in 1916. To be eligible to membership to this club one must be not only a Greer-a-ble but agreeable as well.

Mr. Greer has become identified with much that pretains to Braddock's welfare, and being active in things outside of the school is enabled to bring an unusual amount of experience into the school. Mr. Reuben D. Abbiss, Graduate of State College, is principal of the Engineering and Mechanical Drawing Department, Miss Mae A. Legal, of the Greer School, secretary of the Alumni Association, is instructor in the stenographic department. Miss Agnes Tallent is an assistant teacher.

The schools of North Braddock borough have been no whit behind the Braddock schools. Indeed, there has always been a healthy rivalry between the schools of the two boroughs. Before North Braddock was organized into a borough, the Bell Avenue school, a large graded school for the township was in operation. Mr. C. B. McCabe held the principalship of this school in the township, and continued to act in that capacity for some years after the borough was organized. In the borough originally was an eight room frame building in the First ward, known as the Brinton Avenue school, and a four room frame in the Third ward, called the Shady Park school. These frame structures have been supplanted with substantial brick buildings which have been enlarged from time to time until each of them now has twenty rooms, and each is further equipped with a large auditorium, which is used as a community center. The borough also has a large commodius High school building, fireproof and thoroughly modern, with gymnasium and auditorium and is now erecting a Junior high school.

Mr. John L. Spitler succeeded Mr. McCabe as Principal of the borough graded schools. On his retirement several years ago, the Board adopted the unique plan of having a separate Principal for each ward, the work being co-ordinated through conferences of the Principals. This method has proven satisfactory under the careful and efficient supervision and co-operation of Miss Isabel White, Principal of First ward school, Miss Elizabeth Wakeham, Principal of Second ward school, and Mrs. Jennie S. Lapsley, Principal of Third ward school.

Under the authority of the school Board, vacation schools are conducted during the forenoons, for six weeks of the summer season, in North Braddock as in Braddock.

North Braddock High school has always been maintained at a high standard. Its management has been and is, kept separate from the grade school supervision. Mr. S. R. McClure was far many years Principal of the High school. He was assisted part of the time by Mr. Jos. F. Mayhugh. Both of these gentlemen are now prominent and successful attorneys, and both are members of the North Braddock school Board, Mr. Mayhugh being President and Mr. McClure Vice President of that body.

Mr. McClure was succeeded as Principal by Prof. E. F. Loucks, and he by Miss Cecil Dean. On the resignation of Miss Dean to accept a position in the Schenley High school, Pittsburgh, Mr. W. E. Albig was engaged as Principal, and is still at the head of this department.

The first class to be graduated from North Braddock High school was in 1894, and had six members. A class has been graduated every year since, save in 1915. At that time a year was added to the curriculum, making it a four-year course. In all, the school now numbers 294 graduates. A very active alumni association is maintained, which encourages the work of the undergraduates by providing valuable prizes. The awarding of these prizes always adds interest to the Commencement program.

The music of the North Braddock schools deserves special mention. Its excellence is in a great measure due to the efficient work of Miss Lillian Frazier, who has had charge of this department for a number of years.

The organization and present teaching force of North Braddock schools are here given:

Directors—J. F. Mayhugh, President; S. R. McClure, Vice President; Dr. J. C. Hartman, John W. Hanna, H. M. Glenn, E. V. White, Jacob C. Coleman, P. A. K. Black, Secretary.

Principals of Grammar Schools—Isabel White, Jennie S. Lapsley, Elizabeth Wakeham.

Principal High School—William Espey Albig.

First Ward, (Brinton)—Isabel White, Principal; Margaret K. Morgan, Mary I. Bell, Julia G. Gallagher, Cora Coulter, Florence E. Saunders, M. Elizabeth Magill, Sara. E. Gordon, Naomi Wilson, Irma J. White, Charlotte Truby, Wilhelmina Falls, Pearl A. Brown, Clade McClary, Belva J. Lanich, Frances Coulter, Bess C. Montgomery, Ina P. Berringer, Marguerite Jameson, Margaret Stephens, Jennie Coe, Lillian M. Donovan.

Second Ward—Elizabeth Wakeham, Principal; Mary L. Campbell, Ray Jenkins, Betha J. Stutzman, Frances Martin, Ethel Christenson, Carolyn Johnston, Ella Mae Rinard, Agnes R. Brandon, Mary E. Bryan, Elsie Alexander, Florence Applegate, S. Eleanor McBride, Lillian Mowry,

Caroline Fellenbaum, Bess B. Cooper, Jennie G. Christy, Madge E. Miller.

Third Ward—Jennie S. Lapsley, Principal; Garnett Anderson, Alma C. Cochran, Ethel Sheplar, Blanche Crozier, Forest Null, Alice E. Johnston, Ocie McCoy, Madge Dean, Jean Dillon, M. Leslie Hutchinson, Margaret McMinn, Myrtle Jones, Rebecca Eagleson, Virginia D. Latta, Lottie E. Atwell, Stella D. McDowell, Lillian L. McCracken, Charlotte Johnston, Mabelle Agnes Means.

High School—W. E. Albig, Principal; J. Foster Gehrett, J. W. Cameron, Lillie Minehart, Etta Reed, Edwin Hurrell, Miss Roberts, O. P. Ballantyne.

Special Teachers—Miss Lillian Frazier, Music; Miss Esther Fromme, Diction and Dramatics; Miss Wertheimer, Physical Instructor.

The growth of the Rankin schools has been no less rapid than that of the other boroughs of the trio. For two years after the borough was organized, the children were sent to the Copeland district, then a township school. In 1894, four rooms were opened in the new Rankin school, with Miss Mary Kennedy as Principal. When Miss Kennedy resigned in 1899 to become the wife of Prof. Samuel Hamilton, then and now the efficient County Superintendent of schools, there were nine teachers. Miss Elizabeth Thompson became Principal in 1899, and continued in that capacity until 1911 when she was succeeded by Prof. R. S. Penfield, who has had supervision from that date to the present. In 1917, the district was withdrawn from County supervision, and a borough Superintendency was created, Mr. Penfield being chosen as the first Superintendent.

In 1900 another large building was erected on the ground beside the original school. A four-room addition was built to this structure in 1913, and in 1915 a large building was constructed on Hawkins Avenue. In addition to a dozen school rooms, offices, and the like, this building has a large auditorium which is the meeting place for all local assemblies.

Rankin, more than any other borough in this section has developed the work of the free kindergarten. This has been rendered necessary by reason of the large percentage of foreign born residents. The teachers find that a year's training in doing things and in learning to comprehend and speak the language, before these children reach school age, is a great help when they come regularly into the school.

Although the borough has not yet provided thoroughly equipped manual training and domestic science departments, instruction is given in sewing and other manual arts. Special attention is given to music, drawing and physical training, under careful supervision.

Rankin has never maintained a High school, but sends pupils above eighth grade to the High schools of the surrounding boroughs, Braddock, North Braddock, and Swissvale.

The organization and teaching force of Rankin schools at the present time is as follows:

Officers of the School Board—E. N. Patterson, President; A. O. Marks, Vice President; H. W. Peters, Secretary; Geo. Watt, Treasurer; R. S. Penfield, Superintendent.

Directors—E. N. Patterson, A. O. Marks, H. W. Peters, H. C. Dixon, M. J. Hughes, Jr., John Henderson, Martin Matelon.

Superintendent, Mr. R. S. Penfield; Assistant Principal, Miss Sarah Palmer; Miss Claire Griffin, Music; Miss Lucetta Arnold, Drawing, 3 days per week; Miss Grace Petty, Sewing, 4 days per week; Miss Mary Shaw, Kindergarten; Miss Stella Duff, Assistant Kindergarten; Miss Agnes Riddle, Miss Marie Escher, Miss Hilda Rodgers, Miss Maude Marks, Miss Ida Williams, Miss Anne Griffin, Miss Mary McLaughlin, Miss Marguerite Todd, Miss Margaret Dieghan, Miss Rose Bonner, Miss Eva Noel, Miss Grace Pruden, Miss Mary Charlton, Miss Josie Brant, Miss Edna Johnson, Miss Mary Gardner, Miss Effie McClune, Miss Laura Heimlich, Miss Margaret McBride, Miss Ellen Anderson, Miss Bertha Stewart, Miss Rhoda Strawbridge, Miss Jane Reno, Miss Adda M. Purdy, Miss Margaret Brown, Miss Helen Brennan, Miss Mae Myers, Miss Leah Greenwood, Miss Mary Hamilton, Miss Carrie Wiley, Miss Margaretta Martin, Miss Rose Roderus.

In addition to the public schools, the Braddock community maintains a number of large parochial schools. Prominent among these is the St. Thomas school which is fully described in connection with the St. Thomas parish in Rev. J. V. Wright's article on the churches. St. Joseph parish also maintains a good school as mentioned in Father Eger's account of the church activities. St. Brendin's parish, under the pastorate of Father Patrick Molyneux also conducts a parish school. All of these schools have buildings separate from the churches.

St. Michael's parochial school was established in 1903, in a separate building, though for six years previous to that time regular instruction was given in the church. The teaching force came from Hungary, Sisters of St. Vincent de Paul society, graduates of Hungarian Normal School. At that time the school had 120 children; there are in 1917, 503. This work among people of this nationality has spread from Braddock to surrounding towns, as Homestead, McKeesport, Mount Pleasant, Donora, and South Side, Pittsburgh. The language used is English with the exception of

Christian doctrine, and the teaching of the children to read and write the language of the country from which their parents came. The school is growing rapidly and will soon require additional buildings. Rev. A. Kazinczy, pastor of the parish, has charge of the school.

Sacred Heart Polish school was established in 1897. The present school building, fireproof, erected at a cost of $45,000.00, was started in 1908. Only one story was built at that time, but it was completed, three stories with nine class rooms, in 1914. The school numbers 450 children, taught by Felician sisters of Detroit. Children are taught through the eight grades, both English and Polish. Rev. J. A. Rykaczewski is the pastor in charge of the parish and the school.

Note on Supt. John S. Keefer—
Prof. John S. Keefer was indentified with Braddock schools for many years, first as teacher in high school, then as Principal of the high school, and later as borough Superintendent. He was cut down in the midst of his usefulness, by typhoid fever. As a slight indication of the esteem, in which he was held a tablet was erected to his memory at the entrance to the Henning building which reads:

JOHN S. KEEFER,
Superintendent............1893-1900
Died April 11th, A. D. 1900.
Erected by Pupils,
Teachers and Principals
of the Braddock Public Schools.

FINANCIAL INSTITUTIONS.
BY E. M. SHARAH.

The financial status of a community is measured by the business done by its banking institutions. Braddock's place in colonial history is well established. Its influence as a manufacturing center, particularly of iron and steel products, is also world wide—many of its steel men, past and present, being known and quoted in Europe almost as familiarly as on the streets at home. In financial circles, too, its banks are recognized as nothing less than phenomenal for a community of its size. Time was when men from foreign countries coming to America and earning money to send back to their families had great difficulty in procuring foreign exchange. Private banks, posing under the sign, "Foreign Exchange Bank," or other equally euphonious and misleading title, handled a large part of this business, and the "breaking" of these banks was a common occurrence. And many a hard working man has paid his money into these wild-cat institutions to bring his family to America only to find after weeks and months of anxious waiting, that his family had never received the money, and that the "Foreign Exchange Bank" had collapsed and the banker was gone. The Braddock National Bank was the first in the country to take up this foreign exchange business systematically, and wrought a complete revolution in the method of handling foreign accounts. The national banks of Braddock, by employing clerks and tellers who can speak to the foreign born men in their own language—whatever part of the world they are from—and by scrupulous care in the handling of these accounts, regardless of the amount of money involved in the transaction, have put all such private banks of this section out of business. In consequence, day laborers, foreign born as well as native, by the thousands, carry a bank account; and they have come to look to their banker as financial adviser just as much as they look to their pastor for spiritual counsel.

The Braddock banks take care of the little people. The man who has but a few dollars to deposit receives the same courteous treatment, the same care, the same sound advice as to investment as does the man with the large account.

The natural result of this sympathy and fair dealing between the banks and their clients has been to create a total deposit in all the financial institutions located here that is, to say the least, unusual. Where else in the world is there a city of forty thousand population that can show a bank deposit of more than twelve million dollars, or more than three hundred dollars for each man, woman and child enumerated?

Even the children are encouraged to start bank accounts, and school deposits and holiday savings club accounts are systematically promoted and fostered. Many banks do not care for the small depositor, for such business is handled by the financial institution many times at an actual loss, but for the fact that larger things develop from these small

JOHN G. KELLY.

GEO. C. WATT.

beginnings; and the Braddock banks have learned from experience, "Once a depositor always a depositor."

Most city banks and many in smaller places close the week's business at noon Saturday. Braddock banks do regular business on Saturday until 4:00 o'clock, then open their doors again at 6:00. Saturday evening at the banks is like a rush at a bargain counter in a department store. It is not unusual to see a line of depositors in front of the receiving teller's window like that at a nickelodeon which has advertised a new Charley Chaplin film. The bank clerks and officers work more hours and more continuously than the men in the industrial plants.

BRADDOCK NATIONAL BANK AND BESSEMER TRUST COMPANY.

Among the conspicuous objects of interest in Braddock is the stately home of the Braddock National Bank, the history of which began in 1873 when Braddock was a village of three hundred inhabitants, and Braddock Avenue was a plank road.

The first banking institution in Braddock was Braddock's Field Trust Company. It was incorporated by a special charter January 1, 1873. Its capital stock was $60,000.00, of which only $50,000.00 was paid in. Its first Directors were, Wilson S. Packer, Robert E. Stewart, Robert P. Duff, John A. Carothers, Henry R. Chalfant, Moses G. Corey, John H. McMasters, J. D. Schooley, M. D., and W. L. Hunter, M. D. Wilson S. Packer was President and John G. Kelly, Cashier. Of these men all are now dead except Mr. Duff and Mr. Kelly.

The Trust Company began business in Seewald's Hotel, the three-story brick building on Braddock Avenue near Ninth Street. It remained in the hotel until 1876, when it was removed to its own building on Braddock Avenue and Tenth Street, a large two-story edifice, now known as Rosenbloom's building.

In 1882 the Trust Company was merged into the Braddock National Bank, which was incorporated on the 28th of November in that year, with a capital of $60,000.00, which in a few months was increased to $100,000.00. The Bank building on Tenth Street was sold, and the Braddock National Bank did business in the Schooley Building until the completion of its new home on the north side of Braddock Avenue near the head of Ninth Street. This building was erected in 1883, and was occupied by the Braddock National Bank for 23 years, until it moved to its present quarters in 1906.

In the year 1909 the Capital was $100,000.00 and the Surplus Fund and Undivided Profits $600,000.00, and at that time a Stock Dividend of 100 per cent was declared by the Directors of the Bank, increasing the capital to $200,000.00, with a Surplus Fund of $500,000.00. At the time of this Stock Dividend the Braddock National Bank stood seventh in the United States on the Roll of Honor of National Banks, as compiled from the figures in the office of the Comptroller of the Currency at Washington, D. C. Since then $100,000.00 more has been added to the Surplus Fund from earnings, making the Surplus Fund at this time $600,000.00.

The Bessemer Trust Company, which is under the same management as the Braddock National Bank, was incorporated November 22, 1905. The Bessemer Trust Company loans money on bonds and mortgages

BRADDOCK NATIONAL BANK.

and acts as executor, administrator, guardian, committee agent, registrar, transfer agent and trustee. It has a cash capital of $125,000.00 and resources approximating $2,000,000.00.

During the early days of banking in this country it was not considered ethical for banks to advertise in any way, but Mr. Kelly, immediately after establishing this bank in Braddock, started a publicity campaign of education, which has been kept up until the present time. The Braddock National Bank was probably the first bank in the country to advertise, by booklets and pamphlets, through personal distribution, the value of thrift among its customers, urging upon them the benefit of industry and economy. The desirability of this kind of educational advertising is now recognized by every banking and financial institution in the country.

What the Braddock National Bank is today is largely due to the aggressive ability of its President, John G. Kelly, who is a financier of accurate judgment, large experience and unquestioned integrity. The Bank today is in the front rank of National Banks. Its cash capital is $200,000.00 and its resources amount to nearly nine million dollars.

(Editor's Note.)—The plain statement of fact contained in this article relative to the Braddock National Bank and the Bessemer Trust Co. was given by Mr. John G. Kelly to Mr. G. W. Penn, who wrote it as it appears. The statement, while scrupulously exact, fails to give sufficient credit to Mr. Kelly, and to Mr. Geo. A. Todd, who have been largely instrumental in building up a financial institution which is recognized throughout the country as one of the best.

Mr. Kelly has been and still is, a man with a vision. Starting in his young manhood as the head of a small financial institution in a small suburban town, he had the daring to dream (the successful man sees visions and dreams dreams) of a great institution in a great industrial center. Strict attention to the work in hand and fair dealing have built up a bank unequalled outside the great cities. When in 1906 the Braddock National Bank moved into its palace at the foot of Library Street—a fireproof, burglar-proof structure, with immense manganese vaults—people called the building "Kelly's Folly". At that time the total deposits of the combined institutions, the Braddock National Bank and the Bessemer Trust Co., were about three million dollars, an amount then considered as enormous. "They" said, "That ends it! You can never get the laboring man and the foreigner to come into a place like this to deposit or to borrow money. He will be frightened away by its very splendor." Again "they" wondered—why build a one-story bank—even if the one story is forty feet to the skylight? Why not use the ground flour for the bank and have four or five stories above to rent either as offices or apartments? The fact that this bank's architecture has been studied and copied widely by banks in other cities, and the further fact that deposits and number of depositors have more than trebled in the last ten years, is the answer to such conundrums.

While in all these and in many other innovations, the directorate of the bank has loyally approved and seconded every advance step, yet the directors themselves are the first to acknowledge and give credit to Mr. Kelly for taking the initiative in every thing that makes for advancement.

Mr. Geo. A. Todd, the cashier of the bank, has been Mr. Kelly's loyal assistant in all matters pertaining to growth and development. Starting as collection clerk in 1887, he has held various positions through promotion,—book-keeper, teller, assistant cashier, cashier,—and is now, though still a young man, regarded as a substantial part of "Kelly's Bank."

The bank building, the erection of which occupied two years, is a magnificent edifice of Grecian architecture, conspicuous among the most handsome bank buildings in the world. It is 60 feet wide and 132 feet deep, with a ceiling 40 feet in height. But no description of it can convey an adequate conception of its beauty and its grandeur. It must be seen to be fully appreciated, and as it is one of the principal objects of interest in Braddock, it is beheld with admiration by thousands of visitors every year.

FIRST NATIONAL BANK, BRADDOCK, PA.

The First National Bank of Braddock, the oldest National bank in the Borough, began business under a charter issued by the United States Government October 4th, 1882; the bank was opened for business on the tenth day of November, 1882, and the personnel of the bank was as follows:

Philander C. Knox, President, Wm. H. Watt, Cashier,
and the following were directors:

Philander C. Knox,	Robert Arthurs,	D. Leet Wilson,
Jessie H. Lippincott,	Ralph Bagaley,	Mort. C. Miller,
	L. Halsey Williams.	

The bank was first located at 906 Braddock Avenue and about six months later moved to the corner of Tenth Street and Braddock Avenue. This building was purchased by the bank, and occupied until April 1st, 1889, when it removed to the Masonic Building, corner Library Street and Braddock Avenue. This building was occupied until 1904, when the present Braznell Building was finished, and the First National Bank of Braddock and the Braddock Trust Company took possession of the room in which the First National Bank is at present located. The capital stock at the beginning was $50,000, which about two years later was increased to $75,000, and still later, to $100,000, the present capitalization. The surplus fund which has accumulated from the earnings, and has been left after the payment of dividends during the entire existence of the bank, amounts to $100,000.00, and the undivided profits to $75,000.00. The deposits since the organization were as follows:

At the end of the first ten years	$205,000.00
At the end of the first twenty years	560,000.00
At the end of the first thirty years	1,235,000.00
At the present time over	2,000,000.00

and the total resources are over two and one-half million dollars.

The Hon. Philander C. Knox, the junior United States Senator from Pennsylvania, and former Secretary of State under President Taft's Administration, was the first President of this bank. The late W. H. Watt, the father of Geo. C. Watt, the present executive officer, was the first cashier, and afterwards became president. Mr. James A. Russell, who is now the chairman of the board, was president from the time of the

HON. P. C. KNOX.

H. C. SHALLENBERGER.

death of Mr. W. H. Watt until the annual meeting in January, 1917, at which time he relinquished the office in favor of Mr. Geo. C. Watt. Mr. Watt has been connected continuously with the bank for the past twenty-seven years.

Mr. F. G. Bishoff, vice president, has been connected with the directorate of the bank for the past twenty years, and Mr. E. C. Striebich, the cashier, has been with the institution for the same length of time. Mr. Striebich started as messenger boy and worked his way up to his present position.

The present board of directors, all local business men of the highest type, and men known for their ability in a business way, are Jas. A. Russell, Geo. C. Watt, F. G. Bishoff, Leo A. Katz and Harry W. Benn.

BRADDOCK TRUST COMPANY, BRADDOCK, PA.

The Braddock Trust Company was organized in January, 1901, and began business the following May. The capital was $125,000.00. It was originally called the Peoples Trust Company, but later changed to the Braddock Trust Company.

Mr. Eli R. Dowler was elected the first president and served until

BRADDOCK TRUST CO.

the time of his death, which occurred while he was on a visit to Florida in February, 1912. Mr. Dowler was one of the best known and most highly respected citizens of Braddock. He was engaged in the lumber business here for many years. Being a keen business man, he was well fitted for the responsible position to which he was elected.

Mr. George C. Watt[1] was elected president to succeed Mr. E. R. Dowler.

Mr. George Nash was elected as vice president and H. M. Scott as secretary and treasurer, and J. M. Clifford, assistant treasurer.

The Trust Company was located in what was formerly the Masonic building at the corner of Braddock Avenue and Library Street, but which is now owned and occupied by the Famous Department Stores. The banking room being small, it became necessary in a short time to look for a larger one, hence they moved to the Braznell building, just across Library Street. They continued in business in that place until May, 1907, when they purchased the Union National Bank and moved to the present location at No. 816 Braddock Avenue, Braddock, Pa.

The Braddock Trust Company took over the Citizens Bank of Braddock in April, 1905.

The deposits on Jan. 1st, 1911 amounted to $720,000.00 and increased to $1,166,000.00 January 1st, 1917. The total resources January 1st, 1917 were $1,400,000.00.

In addition to doing a regular banking business, the Braddock Trust Company has well equipped real estate and trust departments, which are under the management of Mr. W. S. Heath, real estate and trust officer.

This was the first bank in Braddock to take up the trust work, acting as executor, administrator, guardian, trustee, etc., of estates. This did away with the old and unsatisfactory method of having inexperienced persons handling this very important work, thus saving large sums of money which might otherwise have been lost.

The present officers of the Braddock Trust Company are:

President—George C. Watt.

Vice presidents—Harry W. Benn, George Nash and A. J. Spigelmire.

Secretary and treasurer—E. C. Striebich.

Real estate and trust officer—W. S. Heath.

The present directors are: H. W. Benn, F. G. Bishoff, L. A. Katz,

---

[1] Mr. Geo. C. Watt was elected cashier of the First National Bark in 1897, being at that time one of the youngest men in the United States to hold such a position. On the death of his father, Mr. W. H. Watt, in August, 1903, Mr. Geo. C. Watt was made the executive officer of the bank, which position he has held continuously since. The growth of the bank and of the Braddock Trust Co., which is under the same management, during the last fifteen years is the evidence of Mr. Watt's ability as a financier and executive. That Mr. Watt is recognized by the banking fraternity as a man of unusual executive force is shown by the fact that he has been called upon to serve a term as president of Group Eight (Pittsburgh Division) of the American Bankers' Association.—(Ed.)

J. J. Keller, W. A. Kulp, Louis Lorch, Jr., M. J. McBride, Geo. Nash, Jas. A. Russell and A. J. Spigelmire.

STATE BANK OF BRADDOCK, PA.

The State Bank of Braddock, Pa. received its charter July 1st, 1897, and opened for business on July 17th, 1897.

Mr. R. M. Holland was elected the first president and served in that capacity until the time of his death.

Mr. C. A. Stokes, the well known and highly respected real estate and insurance agent of Braddock, was the first vice president, and later was made president at the time of the death of Mr. Holland.

Mr. H. C. Shallenberger, Sr., was elected the first cashier and later succeeded Mr. Stokes as president, in which office he has remained to the present time. Mr. Shallenberger is one of the oldest and best known residents of Braddock. He was always interested in the things that tend to make a better community. He served six years as Burgess.

The bank is located at No. 801 Braddock Avenue. This location was one of the old land marks of Braddock. It was known to many of the older residents as the little Octagon House, and was built by Mr. Parker. Mr. Parker was one of the first settlers of old Braddock's Field.

The bank has a capital of $50,000.00 and a surplus and undivided profits of $30,000.00.

The deposits at the end of the first year amounted to $102,119.67, increased in ten years to $318,550.00 and continued growing until today, when they have a total of $700,000.00.

The present officers are:
President—H. C. Shallenberger, Sr.
Vice president—H. M. Glenn.
Cashier—C. L. Masters.

Directors—P. D. Remington, Geo. L. House, H. M. Glenn, W. R. Magill, Geo. Weil, H. J. Learn and H. C. Shallenberger, Sr.

THE UNION NATIONAL BANK.

The Union National Bank began business June 1st, 1903. The bank was located at No. 737 Braddock Avenue. They continued in business there until their new building at No. 816 Braddock Avenue was completed. Mr. Jas. H. McCrady, president of the McCrady Bros. Co., was elected president, Mr. Chas. Zugsmith, Jr., vice president and Mr. A. A. McKinney, cashier.

They had a paid up capital of $102,500 and increased same to $200,000.

Mr. Geo. Hogg succeeded Mr. Zugsmith as vice president.

Directors: J. H. McCrady, Chas. Zugsmith, Jr., M. J. McBride, A. L. Sailor, W. M. Holmes, Jos. Wolf, John K. Skelley, Geo. Hogg, Emanuel Weiler, J. M. Horner and L. A. Katz.

The bank was taken over by the Braddock Trust Company in 1907.

THE CITIZENS BANK OF BRADDOCK, PA.

The Citizens Bank of Braddock was organized June 5th, 1903, with A. S. Braznell, J. M. Clifford, C. W. Braznell, J. J. Keller and F. S. Bennett constituting the stockholders.

Mr. A. S. Braznell was elected president, Mr. J. M. Clifford, vice president, H. G. Getzel, cashier, and J. M. Clifford, Jr., assistant cashier.

Mr. F. S. Bennett, attorney, was elected as solicitor.

The following directors were elected : A. S. Braznell, J. M. Clifford, J. J. Keller and F. S. Bennett.

The bank was located at No. 721 Braddock Avenue and continued in business there until May, 1904, when they moved to the Masonic building. They stayed there until April, 1905, when the Braddock Trust Co. took over all the assets and assumed all the liabilities of the bank.

A resolution was passed August 1st, 1905, by a unanimous vote of the stockholders, wherein it was decided the institution would go into liquidation.

LIBRARIAN—GEORGE H. LAMB.

THE CARNEGIE FREE LIBRARY, BRADDOCK, PA.

THE OLDEST CARNEGIE LIBRARY IN AMERICA.

THE CARNEGIE FREE LIBRARY.
THE OLDEST CARNEGIE LIBRARY IN AMERICA.
BY GEO. H. LAMB.

In the early eighties, Mr. Andrew Carnegie began his wonderful career of library exploitation by building at Braddock, Pa., the first of the Carnegie libraries in this country. The dominant idea at that time was the equipping of a library for the Carnegie employees and their families; and it was referred to in the newspapers of the period as the Edgar Thomson Works library.

The Braddock library began the circulation of books in March, 1889, with 2,153 volumes on its shelves, and had a circulation during that month of 998. The total circulation for the balance of the year 1889 was 18,738. There were added during that year after the opening, 1,981 volumes, thus starting the year 1890 with 4,134 books.

The library was formally dedicated, and turned over to the community at a public meeting, attended by more than 2,000 people, held in Leighton's rink (the auditorium was not built until 1893) on the evening of Saturday, March 30, 1889.

On that occasion, Mr. Carnegie made an address of considerable length, a few brief quotations from which are here given. The address in full was published in pamphlet form, and is entitled, "An Address given at the Dedication of the Edgar Thomson Works Library." Mr. Carnegie said:—"I hand this library over to you and your successors forever. I have no desire to accumulate more money. We will never be the first to reduce labor. We never have been. The fatal enemy of labor is labor, not capital. I may be ranging the earth, but my heart must ever be directed to the home of my youth, and my thoughts to the prosperity of those industries in which I have not been afraid to invest, and am not now afraid to let my capital remain."

He added further:—"I trust you will not forget the importance of amusements. I hope the room upstairs is to be provided with all the means possible for the playing of a game of billiards and so forth, and for gymnastic exercises. Life must not be taken too seriously. We must have our hours for laughter and frolic. It is a great mistake to think a man who works all the time wins in the race. Have your amusements. Learn to play a good game of whist, a good game of draughts, or a good game of billiards.

"I venture to predict that when generation after generation shall have passed away, this Library will remain and be recognized as a center of light and leading; a never failing spring of all good influences; and perhaps it may serve to remind those generations that are to come, that the duties of capital towards labor, even in this age, are not altogether forgotten.

"Fellow workmen, I now hand over the Library to you and your successors forever."

Mr. Samuel Sweet Green, in his "Public Library Movement", on page 102 says: "In 1881 Mr. Carnegie began his great work of founding and aiding libraries by announcing in the spring of that year his purpose of establishing a free library at Braddock for the benefit of his workmen". Several years were consumed in promoting plans and constructing the building, so that it was not until late in 1888 that everything was ready to be turned over to the management of a Library Board. On December 14, 1888, the Board was organized with the following named gentlemen: Mr. Jas. Gayley, President; Mr. Wm. J. Vance, Vice President; Mr. J. A. Lapsley, Secretary; Mr. W. R. Balsinger, Treasurer; Messrs. Watt Edwards, Wm. A. McDevitt, Thos. McDonald, Wm. M. C. Jones, and Profs. Samuel Hamilton, Edwin Twitmyer, and C. D. Coffey. Prof. E. Twitmyer, on leaving Braddock, was succeeded, July 2, 1889, by Mr. W. E. Morrow. On August 4, 1890, Mr. J. A. Lapsley resigned and Mr. W. L. Lapsley was chosen to fill the vacancy. Mr. B. H. Taylor succeeded Mr. Thos. McDonald, June 3, 1890, and Mr. W. W. McCleery succeeded Mr. W. R. Balsinger, December 9, of the same year. Mr. Wm. M. C. Jones resigned July 7, 1891. His place was left vacant until March 26, 1892, when Mr. Thos. Addenbrook was appointed to fill the vacancy. Mr. Addenbrook is still on the Board, after a period of continuous service of more than twenty-five years, a longer term than that of any other member up to the present time.

March 31, 1894, Mr. W. S. Brown and Mr. D. F. Collingwood were appointed to places left vacant by the resignations of Mr. McDevitt and Prof. Coffey, and A. B. Stevenson, Esq., succeeded Mr. Watt Edwards, March 5, 1895. On April 2, 1895, Mr. E. H. Anderson, the retiring librarian, accepted a position on the Board of Trustees. On December 15, 1897, W. S. Dalzell, Esq., was chosen to fill the vacancy that had existed since the resignation of Mr. W. L. Lapsley, July 12, of that year.

On May 19, 1899, the Board of Trustees was reorganized with the following members: Mr. Thos. Addenbrook, Mr. Chas. A. Anderson, Mr.

W. S. Brown, Col. Thos. Cosgrove, W. S. Dalzell, Esq., Mr. Fred W. Edwards, Mr. Jas. Gayley, L. F. Holtzman, Esq., Mr. D. G. Kerr, Mr. Jas. H. McCrady, Mr. Thos. Morrison, Mr. W. E. Morrow, Dr. A. W. Schooley, Mr. C. M. Schwab, Edward J. Smail, Esq., A. B. Stevenson, Esq., Maj. R. E. Stewart, Mr. Wm. J. Vance.

Mr. Jas. Gayley, who served the Board of Trustees as its president from its organization in 1888, having moved away from Braddock, resigned the presidency and membership on the Board, January 14, 1902. Mr. Thos. Morrison was elected president and Mr. Jas. E. Mitchell was chosen to membership on the Board. A little later the resignations of Mr. Schwab and Mr. Morrow were accepted and Mr. Chas. E. Dinkey and Mr. G. E. F. Gray were appointed to the vacancies. In 1906, Mr. John F. Lewis became a Trustee in the place of Mr. Kerr, resigned. Mr. Morrison retired from the presidency of the Board in April, 1907, but continued as one of its members. At the same time Messrs. Mitchell, Anderson and Dalzell resigned, and Messrs. P. A. K. Black, F. F. Slick, and A. E. Maccoun were elected in their respective places. Mr. Chas. E. Dinkey was then chosen as president of the Board, which position he has held continuously since.

The year 1910-1911 witnessed three changes in the personnel of the Board. Maj. R. E. Stewart, who had been a member of the Board since 1899, died March 30, 1910. Mr. W. J. Vance, who had served on the Board from its inception in 1888, a continuous term of twenty-two years, moved to Missouri, and A. B. Stevenson, Esq. also left Braddock, resigning after a continuous service of twelve years. Messrs. Reuben Abbiss, H. W. Benn, and Leo A. Katz were appointed to the vacancies thus created. In 1912, on April 30, occurred the death of Mr. Fred. W. Edwards, after thirteen years of service as Trustee. Mr. C. A. Stokes took his place on the Board. March 2, 1913, death claimed Col. Cosgrove, a member of the Board since 1899. Mr. F. A. Power succeeded him.

In the twenty-eight years of active library work there have been six librarians, and the work has twice been directed for short periods by the first assistant librarian. The first librarian was Miss Rose Phillips. She was succeeded in July, 1890 by Mrs. Anna M. Hay, who continued in charge until November, 1891. The work of the library was then directed by Miss A. W. Hezlep, assistant librarian, until May, 1892, when Mr. Edwin H. Anderson took up the work and continued it until he was called to organize the Pittsburgh library in 1895. Mr. Anderson was succeeded by Miss Helen Sperry, who resigned to organize the Homestead library in

1898. The Carnegie Club was first opened in 1893, and while occupying a part of the library building, and under the same Board of Trustees, it had a separate management, and was a distinct institution. On January 1, 1898, the duties of Chief Librarian and Superintendent of Club were merged into one office, and the late Mr. Walter Crane was appointed as head of the combined institution. Mr. Crane continued in this position until his death, which occurred suddenly October 19, 1902. The work was then continued under the direction of assistant librarian, Mr. Chas. L. Cummings, until March 1, 1903, when Mr. Geo. H. Lamb assumed the duties of Librarian and Superintendent of the Carnegie Club, which position he has held continuously since.

The Braddock library has three distinct branches in as many surrounding towns, Wilkinsburg, Turtle Creek, and Monongahela, and a station at Elizabeth, Pa. These several municipalities provide rooms for the branches and pay the salaries of the local librarians, the main library supplying the books and doing the work of cataloging. The Wilkinsburg branch was opened September 10, 1899; Turtle Creek branch, April 16, 1900; and Monongahela branch, May 7, 1902.

The Braddock library was one of the earliest to come into active co-operation with the schools, and for years has done and is still doing a vast amount of such work. The work of this library in this field has been somewhat different from that of most libraries, in that it began by placing the most elemenatry reading books obtainable in the hands of the youngest classes that could use them, whereas most libraries introduce the work first into the upper grades, reaching the little people after some years of the advanced work, if at all. This library pursues this school work along three distinct lines. First, the library supplies supplementary reading matter in sets of thirty copies of a classic, for class use. In later years the library has encouraged the schools to provide many such readers for themselves, thus relieving the library of a part of this expense. Second, it provides books in cases, well adapted to the various grades, 45 books to the case. These are placed in the school room at the beginning of the school year, the teacher acting as assistant librarian, are given out to the children weekly to be taken home, read, and returned to the school. The books remain in the school as long as desired, or until the close of the term. Third, the library has for some years given systematic class instruction to the High school pupils in the content and use of the library. This instruction comprises a series of eight or ten lessons, outlined by the library and printed in pamphlet form. The class comes to the library for this instruction, doing regularly assigned laboratory work in research, and receiving credit for the same as part of the regular course in English.

The period of time covered by the Braddock library has witnessed nearly all there is of Public Library history. The first tax-supported free public library was founded in the town of Peterboro, Mass., in 1833, followed thirteen years later by the town of Orange, Mass., and four years after that by the town of Wayland. The purpose and aim of all of these was distinctly didactic. The members and patrons were to be instructed in useful knowledge, and those in charge of the libraries were to select the books with that end in view. The effect of this method was to limit the use of the library to persons of studious habits, or to those who had some definite purpose to serve. A library that should provide amusement and recreation for its patrons as well as instruction was not conceived until a later date, was first propounded in Boston in 1851, and was not put to the practical test until some years later. This is the type of the free public library as it is known to-day.

When the foundations of the Braddock library were laid in 1887, there were only 2,981 libraries in this country, and of these only 649 were free and tax-supported. Of the whole number 440 had between 5,000 and 10,000 volumes each; 353 had from 10,000 to 50,000, while only 47 liraries in the entire country had more than 50,000 volumes. Braddock library now has nearly 70,000 volumes, being larger now than any library in the entire United States was when it was organized, with the exception of less than a score.

Another matter that seems strange to people of to-day is that not only were there no free libraries in Pennsylvania when Braddock library was built, but there was no statute law even permitting a free library to be supported by taxation. The first enactment legalizing such a tax levy was passed in 1887, and applied only to cities. The levy then was permissible only for maintenance of an existing library, but not for erecting a library building. It was not until 1895, six years after the Braddock library began circulating books, that the universal library law was enacted making it legal for a borough or school district to build, equip, and maintain a free public library at the expense of the tax payers. At that, Pennsylvania was not far behind most other states, for in 1887 it was one of twenty that had library laws of any kind; and its law of 1895 was the most liberal and the most far-reaching of any that had been enacted in any state up to that time.

THE UNWRITTEN HISTORY OF BRADDOCK'S FIELD. 225

The period covered by this library's history has witnessed many other changes that have been revolutionary in this field. The library school, the trained librarian, uniform systems of classification and record keeping, library indexing, open shelves, children's libraries and children's librarians, State free library commissions, State Library Associations, all these have had their origin and development within this less than a third of a century. While the American Library Association, the one force that has been the most potent instrument of all for the development and unification of library work had its origin as late as 1876, and has done all of its important work within the time limit named. It is thus seen that the Braddock library has been a participant in nearly all of library history in this country, and has been a pioneer blazing the way, and going forward without chart or compass in many of its activities.

It has often been remarked that the tendency of library reading is to lead the patron to a better and better grade of literature. Not all of fiction is trifling, and not all of classed literature is heavy or really worth while. But the dividing line is usually made between fiction and nonfiction. By this record, this library has repeated the history of others, in that the percentage of fiction has gradually been reduced from more than 80 to less than 50.

On April 29, 1914, the library held its silver jubilee celebration in honor of its twenty-fifth year of active work, and, as this is the "Oldest Carnegie Library in America", the twenty-fifth anniversary of the Carnegie Library Movement.

Braddock has been the scene of many important gatherings and startling and stirring events, from the day of its christening in a baptism of fire on that weltering July 9, 1755, down through the gathering at the time of the Whiskey Insurrection, past the recruiting of troops at Camp Copeland in civil war times, and civic and industrial gatherings of later days, but Braddock as a community never entered more heartily or with greater unanimity into any single undertaking than in this twenty-fifth anniversary of the founding of the library.

Previous to the day of the celebration, three triumphal arches had been erected, one at the foot of Library Street, and two on Braddock Avenue. These were beautifully decorated and illuminated. Every business house in the town was profusely decked with flags and bunting, while enlarged lithographs of Mr. Carnegie were to be seen everywhere. Private residences, especially those along the line of march of the parade, were also dressed in holiday attire. All business houses in Braddock and all the schools were closed during the afternoon, the town making of it a holiday.

The celebration had three distinct features; first, the parade, second, the meeting in the auditorium, third, the banquet.

A reviewing stand was erected in front of the library on which were seated Mr. Carnegie, the library Trustees and invited guests. Past this stand marched the immense parade consisting of the police and fire departments of the three boroughs, a bagpipe band, clans and orders, the officials of the three boroughs and the G. A. R. men in carriages, Sons of Veterans and Boys' Brigades, thousands of mill workers, and several thousand children from the public and parochial schools, with many bands and drum corps interspersed, all succeeded by a long line of beautifully decorated automobiles.

Each of the school children carried a flag, a pennant, or a banner having a large lithograph of Mr. Carnegie as its dominating feature. As the schools passed the reviewing stand they were massed there and under the direction of Mr. Geo. S. Speidel, sang "America" and "Auld Lang Syne." The automobiles left the line of march after passing the reviewing stand and took a longer route than the marchers, rejoining them at the lower end of Braddock Avenue. After the parade was over all the bands, more than a hundred pieces, were massed and gave an open air concert for the thousands of people who were unable to gain admittance to the auditorium.

While the audience was being seated in the Hall, Mr. Carnegie took his place on the platform where he met many of his friends of former years, the old time employes of the Edgar Thomson Steel Works. For it is to be remembered that not only was Braddock the recipient of the first Carnegie library in America, but the steel mills of Braddock were the first to bring fame and fortune to the great iron master and his co-partners.

At this meeting, Mr. Chas. E. Dinkey, President of the Board of Trustees, presided. Prof. W. L. Mayer rendered musical numbers on the great organ. Addresses were made by Col. H. P. Bope, vice president of the Carnegie Steel Co., by Dr. John A. Brashear, the great scientist of Pittsburgh, and a life-long friend of Mr. Carnegie, by Mr. C. M. Schwab, the first President of the United States Steel Corporation, a former Braddock man, and at one time a member of the Board of Trustees of the library, by Dr. Samuel Hamilton, Superintendent of the Allegheny County Schools, and by Mr. Carnegie.

Mr. Carnegie's address was full of tenderness and breathed of his love for the scenes of his early successes and for the friends who were with him at that time. Much of his address contained reminiscences of his early friend, the late Capt. William R. Jones. He could not have touched on a theme that would please a Braddock audience more than by referring to the great Captain. Although Captain Jones has been dead for more than a quarter of a century, to this day, a public speaker in Braddock is sure of at least one round of applause if he can under any pretext bring the Captain's name into his address. For Mr. Carnegie to relate anecdote and incident in the Captain's life was to carry his audience right with him back to that early day.

"I don't know how every one thinks about the way I spend my money", continued Mr. Carnegie, "But I'm willing to put this library and similar institutions against any other form of benevolence. It's the best kind of philanthropy I can think of, and I'm willing to stand on that record.

"This is a grand old world and it's always growing better, and all's well since it is growing better. And when I go for a trial for the things I've done on earth, I think I'll get a verdict of 'Not guilty', through my efforts to make earth a little better than I found it".

On the reviewing stand, in response to a short address of welcome to the distinguished guest, made by Dr. F. K. Whitfield, burgess of Braddock, Mr. Carnegie said, "I want to say that being a citizen of Braddock is no mean asset. I am proud to be a man of Braddock, and in my travels through Europe and every other continent, Braddock has been my cry.

"I am very sorry Mrs. Carnegie is not here to see this grand celebration. You know, like all other women, Mrs. Carnegie is awfully wise; and when I tell her of this honor she will say, 'Go on, now, Andy, you were excited and imagined these things.' But imagination can't describe this occasion, and I am glad to be among my fellow employees once again."

The closing event of the Jubilee day was a banquet, held in the gymnasium, under the auspices of the Braddock Merchants' Association, working in conjunction with the library Board of Trustees. Two hundred and fifty guests were entertained at this banquet. Addresses were made by State Superintendent of Schools, N. C. Schaeffer, Col, H. P. Bope, Mr. C. M. Schwab, for Governor John K. Tener, Rev. Charles Wallace, Mr. Alvah C. Dinkey, President Carnegie Steel Company, Hon. Thos. L. Montgomery, State Librarian, and others, Mr. Geo. C. Watt acting as toastmaster.

Bulletin 25, 1915 (whole number 652) of the Bureau of Education, Washington, D. C., is devoted to a study of public, society and school libraries. The figures used are for the year 1913. From this bulletin it is learned that there are in the United States more than 18,000 such libraries, as compared with less than 3,000 in 1887, only 25 per cent of which were at that time "Free". Of these 18,000, 111 Public, 80 Society, and 90 School libraries have more than 50,000 volumes each. Braddock is 1 one of the 111 Public libraries thus designated.

Of this list of 111 large libraries, Braddock library stands:—
Sixty-fourth in number of volumes.
Thirty-seventh in circulation.
Seventeenth in juvenile circulation.
Forty-second in percentage of population enrolled as borrowers.
Sixty-ninth in cost of maintenance.
Eighty-second in number of employees doing the work.

The Carnegie Club is under the same management as the library and occupies a part of the building, but is a distinct institution. The Club represents one of the earliest efforts of a great industrial plant to provide healthful and sane amusement and recreation for its employees. It was first conceived as a co-operative organization for the procuring of household supplies. The mercantile feature was soon abandoned and the Club became a place for social recreation and physical development exclusively. The library is entirely free to any one wishing to avail himself of its privileges. The Club is for its members only, and from these a membership fee is exacted, the charge being insufficient, however, to meet expenses were it not for outside help.

The Carnegie Club is conducted somewhat on the plan of a Y. M. C. A., with a difference. It does no distinctly religious work. It admits ladies to membership, they being limited, however, to swimming pool and gymnasium privileges, and for fixed periods. At another point the Club differs radically from a Y. M. C. A., in that it demands no certificate of character or other recommendation as a prerequisite to membership, the management holding to the view that the fact of application for membership is the evidence of the individual's need of the Club's help. In this way a class of men is reached who would be scared away from an institution where more rigid requirements are exacted. As a result the morale of the membership may be and doubtless is, somewhat lowered, but the assistance is rendered where the want is greatest.

The Club maintains all the best means and equipment for indoor

THE UNWRITTEN HISTORY OF BRADDOCK'S FIELD.   229

sports and games; such as gymnasium, bowling alleys, billiards, game rooms, swimming pool and baths, all of which are free to members, except that a small fee is charged for the use of the bowling alleys and billiard tables.

First started as a Club for Carnegie employees exclusively, all restrictions have long since been removed, and any one wishing may now acquire membership regardless of residence or occupation.

The librarian has, since 1898, been also Superintendent of the Club. He is aided by a Club Manager who devotes his entire time and energy to the Club, and by a Physical Director who gives his efforts to work in the gymnasium and swimming pool. The Manager has an assistant, and there is a lady director for the ladies' classes in the gymnasium and a lady attendant for the women and girls in the pool. As evidence of the stability and permanence of the work it may be stated that the present Club Manager, Mr. David Shelby, has been connected with the Club for ten years, Mr. F. J. Cartwright was Physical Director for sixteen years, succeeded four years ago by Mr. L. B. Cundiff, who is still in the work, while Mrs. Barbara Mosellin has been lady attendant in the swimming pool since it was first opened in 1893.

The Library and Club have come to mean more than what these terms generally imply, and this institution is a real community center. The Braddock Merchants' Association with a salaried Secretary and Clerk, has headquarters, furnished free, in a room of the building. All kinds of assemblies and committees, such as the Braddock Medical Society, the Braddock Druggists' Association, the Jewelers' organization, the Aquatic Club, the Women's Club, and many other business and professional combinations hold regular or periodical sessions in some of the committee rooms; while the large auditorium is the community meeting place for all general assemblies. The hall is used, too, for amateur theatricals, lectures and concerts, whether for school, church, lodge, or other society.

The Carnegie Round Table, an association of business and professional men, has for fourteen years held monthly meetings in the gymnasium, from October to March, gathering for a 6:00 o'clock dinner followed by addresses, papers, and discussions on important topics of the day.

The Matinee Bowlers, made up of business and professional men, meet on the Club Alleys every working day between 12:00 and 2:00. They have scarcely missed a day, except when the alleys were undergoing repair, for thirteen years.

THE BRADDOCK GENERAL HOSPITAL.

BY W. T. MORGAN, M. D.

The first public suggestion for a hospital for Braddock was from the pen of a young newspaperman, Fred W. Oakley, then engaged in that capacity by the Braddock Daily News, of which the late Daniel J. McCarthy was editor and publisher. That was about the year 1890. Later, to be exact, August 3rd, 1893, there appeared another article by the same writer anent the same subject. Still later, on December 11th of the same year, Mr. Oakley, in a column article made a special plea in behalf of a hospital for Braddock, following up the subject the next day in another article of equal length, suggesting that a hospital be built in the coming year, and that in view of Mr. Carnegie's liberality toward Churches, an appeal to him in behalf of a hospital might result in generous financial help.

That there were no immediate results was not surprising, for, at that time, as at a later date, there were not a few who were disposed to look upon such a possibility as rather of the nature of a fanciful dream, and I know, from personal knowledge, that even Editor McCarthy was far from enthusiastic on the subject.

Whether it was a coincidence, or a sequence to the original suggestion, is a matter of small moment, but the fact remains that the hospital movement had its inception on Saturday, October 6th, 1894, when according to the Braddock Daily News, a gentleman, described as "a Hebrew merchant of Braddock" expressed himself to a representative of that paper, as being so much in favor of a hospital for Braddock, that he tendered a subscription of $200 for the cause, and promised an additional twenty-five dollars annually for maintenance purposes, the announcement being made in the Daily News of October 8th, 1894.

Subject to the wishes of the gentleman, his name was withheld, and the subscription credited as "anonymous". In time, of course, the owner of this particular "Anonymous" name leaked out, and the original subscriber to the hospital fund proved to be Mr. Jacob Katz the tailor. The gentleman died in Philadelphia several years later.

Following the lead of his Hebrew brother, Mr. Louis Amshall immediately came forward with a subscription of like amount.

The next day, the day after, and, in fact, almost daily until October 16th, 1894, when the ladies of the town took hold, new names were added to the list of original subscribers to the hospital fund until the following names were to be found on the honor roll:

Jacob Katz $200.00, Louis Amshall $200.00, S. T. Fiero $5.00, J. K. Fisher $50.00, H. B. Goldberg $100.00, Louis Schmidt $25.00, P. J. Hafner $25.00, David Goldrath $25.00, Employees of Jacob Katz $25.00, J. B. Corey $100.00, Jacob Friedman $25.00, S. Maltinsky $25.00, Jacob Litvitz $25.00.

The spantaneous generosity of our Hebrew citizens towards the hospital project is strikingly illustrated by a glance at the foregoing list of familiar names, and it is pleasing to record that our friends of that nationality have never ceased their interest or liberal financial assistance to the institution.

On October 16, 1894, we read in the Braddock Daily News that "The good women of Braddock have come to regard the movement to build a hospital for Braddock as one well worthy of their attention and support, and a meeting was held last evening at the home of Mrs. Thomas James, of Parker Avenue, for the purpose of furthering the object, at which the following ladies were present:—

Mrs. Thomas James, Mrs. N. H. Treese, Mrs. H. Scritchfield, Mrs. Jacob Katz, Mrs. David Goldrath, Mrs. Thomas Cosgrove, Mrs. A. H. White, Mrs. Richard Stevens, Mrs. W. E. Morrow, Mrs. Emma Zimmerman, Mrs. R. A. Clay, Mrs. D. F. Collingwood, Mrs. Amos Laughner, Mrs. A. S. Braznell, Mrs. M. E. Kinsey, Mrs. P. S. Todd, Mrs. W. R. Edwards, Mrs. A. P. Maginni, Mrs. John Laux and Mrs. A. W. Schooley.

At this meeting an organization was perfected and the following officers elected:

President, Mrs. Thomas James; Vice President, Mrs. H. Scritchfield; Secretary, Mrs. R. A. Clay; Treasurer, Mrs. A. P. Maginni.

At about this time the Homestead News, commenting editorially upon the movement had this to say:

"Our neighboring town Braddock is going ahead in a vigorous manner with its hospital enterprise. Through the influence of the Braddock Daily News one thousand dollars have already been subscribed and now the ladies of the town are taking hold."

A second meeting of the ladies was called at the home of Mrs. Thomas James for October 22nd, 1894.

In order to enlist the interest of as many as possible, wide publicity of the meeting was made, and on Sunday, the day preceding the meeting, announcement of the same was made in every church, with the result that

BRADDOCK'S FIRST HOSPITAL.

about forty were present at the meeting, representing, practically, every religious body of Braddock.

Mrs. James, who was the previously elected president, realizing, as she stated that to carry on the work successfully would require more time than she had at her command, resigned from that office, and Mrs. W. L. Lapsley was elected to fill the vacancy.

Ways and means for raising money were thoroughly discussed, resulting in a decision to hold a week of fair and bazaar, designating a particular night for each denomination, except in the case of the smaller churches, in which instance two or more would combine for a particular night, and the following ladies were appointed a general soliciting committee to secure contributions suitable for the occasion and the cause.

Mesdames: Allen Kirkpatrick, James Gayley, C. W. Woods, C. M. Schwab, J. B. Corey, J. N. Shallenberger, J. M. McCrady, S. D. Hamilton, C. A. Stokes, George Larimer, W. J. McBeth, Andrew Kramer, A. J. Spigelmire, D. F. Melville, Ed. B. White, A. S. Brubaker, A. J. Boyle, P. S. Todd, J. L. Campbell, W. S. Brown, W. H. Speer, Josiah Crosby, A. S. Braznell, Daniel Oskin, Tilgman Kulp, Ada Lucas, C. C. Fawcett, W. S. Stewart, G. E. Bair, Chris Hager, C. H. Clifford, B. F. Price, W. T. Morgan, S. J. Shaw, Eli Boyd, W.S. Packer, Sr., J. R. King, J. H. Rankin, J. W. Miles, O. B. Milligan, O. H. Phillips, W. G. Reagle, H. M. Bowden.

Merchants and others, both in and outside of Braddock, were most generous in their contributions either in money or supplies for the bazaar and fair, each appearing to vie with another in trying to see which could help the most.

The Turner hall was secured for the occasion and, on Tuesday, November 20th, 1894 the bazaar and fair, in charge of over one hundred of Braddock's fairest daughters, opened in a blaze of glory, amid a small army of most enthusiastic women, and closed on the Saturday night following, in a shower of gold upon a tired but very grateful body of workers.

The militant and determined spirit of the ladies in charge was emphatically illustrated by a little experience they had on Monday, the day preceding the opening of the bazaar. Notwithstanding a contract had been signed, sealed and delivered, giving the ladies the right of possesion of the hall from Monday morning until twelve o'clock on the following Saturday night, a mixup had occurred by the letting of the same for Monday night to some Society for the purpose of a dance, and when the committee of ladies in charge of setting up booths, tables, etc., arrived at 6:30 o'clock Monday morning prepared to perform their part of the

BRADDOCK GENERAL HOSPITAL—WEST WING.

work, they were confronted with the surprising information that the hall had been rented to other parties for that particular day and night, and that they would not be allowed to enter and take possession at that time. The fact that they did enter and take possession, and that the bazaar and fair opened on schedule time, is only one more illustration of the truth of that old adage that "When a woman wills, she will, you can depend on it".

After deducting a little matter of $123.64 for expenses, thirty-four hundred and nine dollars and seventy-four cents ($3,409.74) was the net total of receipts for the week's work.

This amount, together with $240.00 collected by the late A. B. Stevenson, Esq., a donation of $100.00 from the Second Avenue Traction Company, and the $1,000.00 previously subscribed, gave the prospects for a hospital a very promising outlook.

Interest in the hospital project still continued at high tide for some time. The proceeds from lectures, concerts and theatrical performances were freely donated, and several merchants contributed a portion of the profit from sales made on one or more particular days. Many of those ladies, however, who rode upon the highest crest of the first wave of hospital enthusiasm were, apparently, well satisfied to relegate all further active interest in the project to others, and as time passed on, fewer and fewer were found to take that active interest in the affair so necessary to its fulfillment, so that, at the end of a few years, but a small company of faithful ones remained active of that galaxy of workers which started out so valiantly to give to the physical sufferers of Braddock and vicinity the haven of refuge it was sincerely felt they so much needed.

In the meantime something over six thousand dollars had been garnered for the cause which, through the courtesy of friends of the project was placed in the care of the Carnegie Steel Company where, at a good rate of interest, it continued to grow in amount until April 4th, 1905, when the auspicious time had arrived that it could be put into active use for the purpose for which it was solicited.

Diminished in numbers but undaunted in spirit the remaining handful of faithful women, through one source or another, gathered into their treasury a good many extra dollars, some of which was used in the year 1897 for the very laudable purpose of paying for the services of three professional nurses who, at the instance of the Braddock Relief Association were engaged to care for a number of sick of the town.

While thoroughly appreciative of the fact that the few thousand dollars already in hand were but a drop in the bucket, as it were, of the

BRADDOCK GENERAL HOSPITAL—EAST WING.

amount necessary to accomplish the purpose for which they set out, optimism with a big "O" was the keynote of the few remaining workers and, as an evidence of their implicit confidence in the final success of their efforts, application for a charter for the organization was made and, through the efforts and courtesy of the late R. E. Stewart, Esq., who, always generously donated his professional services in all business connected with the hospital project, one was granted bearing the date of December 21st, 1898, having attached thereto the following named ladies as applicants:

Florence M. Bell, Gertrude R. Corothers, Mary K. Collingwood, Elmira Scritchfield, Elizabeth James, Mary M. Schooley, Virginia Riston, Jennie Scott Lapsley, Kate M. Treese, Mary J. Holtzman, Margaret Cramer, Susan C. Kulp, Margaret M. Scott, Caroline M. Stewart, Kate McIlfred.

Notwithstanding that the charter plainly stated that "Any person willing to assist in the work of the association, and contributing such sums as fixed by the by-laws, may become members of the association", a popular but erroneous impression prevailed that, inasmuch as application for the charter was made exclusively by women, only those of the gentler sex were entitled to membership in that body, with the result that women alone continued to make up the membership of the association.

In January 1899 the first election held under the new charter resulted in the selection of the following officers: President, Mrs. Corothers; First Vice President, Mrs. Scritchfield; Second Vice President, Mrs. Riston; Recording Secretary, Mrs. Kulp; Financial Secretary, Mrs. Schooley; Corresponding Secretary, Mrs. Bell; Treasurer, Mrs. James.

Interest in the hospital, of course, continued but without any pyrotechnical display and the quiet effectual efforts of that small body of faithful women was fittingly recognized when in the year 1903 the Braddock Board of Commerce elected to take a hand in the movement. In the fall of that year a street fair and carnival was held under its auspices for the benefit of the hospital fund, which netted in the neighborhood of $1,500, the amount being held in the treasury of the Board of Commerce, it being the intention of the board to increase that amount before placing it in the hospital fund.

Just at this time, a new element was injected into the enterprise. The physicians of Braddock realizing, perhaps, more than any others, the crying need for a haven of refuge for the sick and wounded of this community, decided to appeal through their Medical Society to both the Braddock Hospital Association and the Board of Commerce and, if possible, induce both bodies to unite their forces at once, and their funds, for the benefit of the cause and, in this way accentuate the ultimate object of both parties, and a committee of the following members of the Medical Society, Drs. H. F. Fisher, L. G. Rubenstein and W. T. Morgan, was appointed by the President, Dr. A. W. Schooley, for that purpose.

No difficulty was experienced in bringing both bodies to a mutual agreement. The ladies who, financially, had the upper hand, were perfectly willing to throw their lot and interest into the common fund on condition that the Board of Commerce raise an amount equal to that in the hands of the Hospital Association which, at that time was something over $11,000. The Board of Commerce, recognizing the justness of the proposition, immediately set about to fulfill their part of the agreement, and a committee of that body, by a solicitation among the business and professional men throughout the district, was soon able to report their readiness and ability to perform their part of the proposition, the committee of the Board having in hands an amount, not only equal to that possessed by the ladies, but an additional $10,000 which had been contributed to the cause by W. E. Corey, the president of the United States Steel Corporation.

A hospital for Braddock was now assured. A committee representing the Board of Commerce, the Braddock Hospital Association and the Braddock Medical Society was elected to select a site. A number of locations were considered and inspected. After a careful survey of each, the Mills homestead was decided upon as the most suitable.

The Mills homestead was one of the substantial landmarks of this region, beautifully situated on the top of an eminence at the corner of Fifth Street and Holland Avenue, in the centre of a plot of ground about 250 feet square and was easily accessible to all parts of the three boroughs.

The purchase price of $30,000 being acceptable, this committee consisting of Mrs. Mary M. Schooley, representing the Hospital Association; Mr. Leo. A. Katz, the Board of Commerce, and Dr. W. T. Morgan, the Medical Society, together with the owners, Mr. & Mrs. Louis Drexler, on November 23rd, 1904, signed articles of agreement to purchase the same at the price asked, a stipulation in the agreement being that in consideration of a donation of $2,500, by the owners, the same to be deducted from the purchase price, the hospital was to furnish and maintain a ward in the hospital as a memorial to Mrs. Rachel A. Clay, the mother of Mrs. Louis Drexler, and the first secretary of the original Braddock Hospital Association.

Purchase of the property being agreed upon, on February 6th, 1905 a petition for a charter for the Braddock General Hospital—the title for the new organization—was made upon the application of the following who constituted the first Board of Managers of the Hospital: Geo. Hogg, Mary M. Schooley, Leo. A. Katz, Elizabeth James, W. T. Morgan, M. D., David F. Collingwood, Fogel G. Bishoff, Louisa E. Kelly Donovan, Fannie Newman, Elmira Scritchfield, Louis G. Rubenstein, M. D., Alfred W. Schooley, M. D., George Moore, J. A. Miller, M. D., and Harry F. Fisher, M. D., and a charter was granted March 11th, 1905 by President Judge of Common Pleas Court No. 2 Robert S. Frazier.

A deed bearing date of April 14th, 1905, conveying the property to the Braddock General Hospital completed the transaction of the change of ownership and, at a cost of, approximately $7,000 the building was remodeled to meet its new requirements.

It was, indeed, a gala day for Braddock when on June 27th, 1906, the Braddock General Hospital was opened for inspection and for business.

It soon became apparent that in a very short time the little hospital of, practically, 30 beds, would be wholly inadequate to supply the demand upon it. This condition of affairs created an embarassing position for the Board of Managers, for with a purchase money Mortgage of $17,500 still on hand, and no visible means in sight to liquidate it, to say nothing of finding extra funds for new building purposes, the prospects for increasing the facilities of the hospital were not very encouraging. Gradually beds for the sick and injured were at a premium. Every bed in the hospital was occupied, and cots were provided in every conceivable corner to accommodate those who insisted upon getting in, and many were being daily turned away.

Succumbing, at last, to the clamorings of a suffering public, the Board of Managers of the hospital decided to endeavor to meet the demands upon the institution, trusting that Providence, in the garb of one or more good Samaritans would volunteer to lift the added burden it would incur.

Plans for a new building were prepared and, at a cost of $40,000, a new wing was added to the hospital, affording accommodation for about 70 beds, or more than double the capacity of the original hospital, besides furnishing more commodious quarters for administrative and other purposes.

With these, apparently ample accommodations, it was deemed unnecessary to continue the original hospital as such, and it was, and still is, utilized for dormitory purposes for student Nurses who, up until this time, were housed in rented quarters near the hospital.

A few years later, the Board of Managers of the hospital were again confronted with the same old problem of supply and demand. Overcrowding was again becoming the rule rather than the exception, so much so that, at times, notwithstanding every private room was occupied and every bed in the wards was filled, beds and cots were placed in the sun parlors, corridors and alcoves and, on not a few occasions, the office of the directress of nurses, the doctors' Library and the Board room were pressed into service for those who, literally, demanded admission, and there was still a waiting list of those who laid claim to "the next bed". While the normal capacity of the hospital was 70 beds, as many as 90 patients at one time were housed under its roof.

The proposition to conduct a week of so called "Whirlwind Campaign," for the purpose of raising the necessary funds to add an additional wing to the hospital was duly considered and accepted, and one was staged for a week in October, 1913. A small army of workers under the efficient leadership of C. E. Dinkey, Superintendent of the Edgar Thomson Works of the United States Steel Corporation labored most valiantly, and secured cash and pledges to the amount of $68,000. Of this amount $63,000 has actually been collected.

Realizing that this amount would be totally inadequate even to build the contemplated addition, to say nothing of its equipment for service, and having also in mind the already existing debt of $29,333 charged against the hospital, the Board was very reluctant to place another burden on the institution which, eventually, must be borne by the public at large. But because of the continued crowding of the hospital and the increasing demands for more and more accommodations, coupled with the fact the Board realized its obligation to the contributors to the Campaign fund to utilize the money collected for no other purpose than that for which it was solicited, the Board unanimously concluded to carry through the work of adding another wing, with the result that on April 19th, 1917, in the presence of several hundred friends the second wing, at a cost of nearly $90,000, was dedicated to the services of suffering humanity, thus adding 60 more beds to its capacity.

No pains were spared to make this new wing a model in every respect. From the first floor which contains the main and diet kitchens, together with the dining rooms, to the top floor of the building on which are to be found the operating rooms and pathological laboratories, everything is as modern and up-to-date as it is possible to be made, even to the lighting signal system for the use of patients, in place of the antiquated electric call bell. In fact every part of the equipment is of the latest and best.

The following are some of the institution's benevolent friends who maintain either a ward, a room, a bed or a cot in the hospital as a memorial to some loved one, or for some equally noble reason.

Mr. and Mrs. Louis Drexler for Rachel A. Clay, Jewish Ladies Auxiliary I. O. O. B., Mr., and Mrs. Ferd Newman, Woman's Club of Braddock, Braddock Ministerial Association, Mrs. Henry Brown, Mrs. Fannie Handel, Valetta Commandery K. of M. No. 129, Ladies' Auxiliary of the Braddock General Hospital, Mr. F. G. Bishoff, Mr. J. Windt, Mr. Steinmetz and family, Dr. H. W. Morrow, Womens Christian Temperance Union, Bernath Weiss.

The staff and officers of the hospital are as follows:—
Surgery—A. W. Schooley, M. D., H. E. Dean, M. D., J. B. Smith, M. D., T. H. Snowwhite, M. D.
Medicine—L. G. Rubenstein, M. D., J. C. Nicholls, M. D.
Gynecology—W. T. Morgan, M. D., H. F. Fisher, M. D.
Eye, Ear, Nose and Throat—D. A. Metzgar, M. D.
Pediatrics—W. T. Pyle, M. D.
Pathology—S. R. Mills, M. D.
Radiography—F. K. Whitfield, M. D., B. M. Bartilson, M. D.
Laboratory Technician—Miss Anna May Young.
Superintendent of Hospital—Miss Margaret W. Woodside.
Assistant Superintendent—Miss Sophie E. Ripper.
Directress of Nurses—Miss Emma E. Church.
Assistant Directress of Nurses—Miss Amy Linsenmeyer.
Dietitian—Miss Martha L. Morgan.
Operating Room Nurse—Miss Lina G. Enders.
Night Superintendent—Miss Irene Kierman.
Clerk—Miss Dorothy Newman.

The hospital training school for Nurses, like the hospital, has received the official endorsement of the State, and has graduated, thus far, fifty-eight nurses. The first class received their diplomas in April, 1910 and a class has been graduated annually since that year.

The Board of Managers of the hospital consists of fifteen members, comprising an equal representation of the Contributors at large, the Medical Society and the Ladies Auxiliary—this latter a working body of women supplanting the original Hospital Association. The names and officers of the present Board are as follows:

F. G. Bishoff, Mrs. Elizabeth James, D. A. Metzgar, M. D., W. T. Morgan, M. D., George H. Lamb, E. J. Striebich, C. B. Guttridge, F. K. Whitfield, M. D., H. E. Dean, M. D., Mrs. Elmira Scritchfield, Mrs. Louise Bachman, Wm. Conner, Miss Florence E. Mench, J. C. Nicholls, M. D. President W. T. Morgan, M. D., Vice President George H. Lamb, Treasurer Fogel G. Bishoff, Secretary Miss Florence E. Mench.

The first Superintendent of the hospital was Miss Mary J. Weir, serving in that capacity from the opening of the institution until July 1910, and it was due not a little to her executive ability that the hospital was early placed upon a good working basis. Miss Wier resigned to become the bride of Dr. Clinton S. Kerr, of Emlenton, Pa., and Miss Ellen Hunt was elected as her successor. Miss Hunt was a lady of exceptional qualities. Her kindly disposition and gentle manner during the three years of her official connection with the hospital had endeared her to all those with whom she came in contact. Miss Hunt died suddenly in July, 1913, while on a visit to friends during her vacation. By her death the hospital sustained a loss that was sincerely and greatly felt by all connected with it.

Miss Margaret W. Woodside, the present Superintendent assumed the duties of the office in December, 1913, and has demonstrated her ability to grasp and control the requirements of the rapidly growing demands of the institution.

GEO. HOGG.

Mr. George Hogg was the first President of the Board of Managers and during the time he served in that capacity there was no detail in the installation of the hospital and its subsequent management requiring his consideration that he did not give his personal attention. He easily demonstrated himself to be the right man, in the right place and at the right time. After serving as president for about a year Mr. Hogg, on account of the pressure of his personal business, resigned from that office and Mr. George Moore was de-

---

(Editor's Note.)—To one man more than any other—Dr. Wm. T. Morgan, the present president of the Braddock General Hospital and author of this chapter—is due the consummation of the Braddock hospital idea. Dr. Morgan has given credit to others, deservedly so, but with his commendable and natural modesty, he has entirely eliminated himself from the chapter as a leading factor in the ultimate completion and success of the hospital. Dr. Morgan took up the project when it was in abeyance, revived it through various mediums, and kept the movement going with such impetus that it came to full realization. No better tribute for Dr. Morgan's untiring, unselfish zeal for the hospital can be given than the hospital, completed and serving humanity, which will always be a lasting testimony to his purely altruistic labors.

servedly elected in his stead. Early interested in the hospital project Mr. Moore not only labored unremittingly to bring the enterprise to a successful conclusion, giving liberally of his time and his money to the work, but continued that same interest with unabated zeal to the end of his life. Even during the last few months of his life, when he was, physically, unable to give his personal attention to the affairs of the institution as became the office of president, he was as solicitous of the welfare of the hospital as though it were his own personal affair.

GEO. MOORE.

Mr. Moore died January 25th, 1914, and by his death the hospital lost one of its real friends, and the legacy he helped make possible for the physical unfortunates of Braddock and vicinity will ever remain a monument to his unselfish interest in the cause of suffering humanity.

DR. W. T. MORGAN.

Since the death of Mr. Moore, the writer[1] has worn the mantle of the Presidency with as much grace as is possible for him to do, and, fully appreciating the responsibilities attached thereto, has endeavored, at all times, to perform his duty as he sees it.

While the three organizations mentioned were the leading influences in promoting the original hospital, there are a host of others who deserve great credit for their heroic efforts to make the present institution a reality.

The merchants and citizens of Greater Braddock should not be neglected in the list of those who so nobly planned and worked that Braddock might be possessed of such an institution.

The newspapers, also, lent valuable assistance and the publicity given every step aided greatly in keeping the hospital idea ever before the people. When the subject is entirely summed up it will be clearly seen that the Braddock General Hospital is the result of the united efforts of all, and there is scarcely a man, woman, or child in the entire district who has not, in some way, made possible the glorious monument on the hill, and it is pleasing to record that the Braddock General Hospital is open to the afflicted of all classes and conditions, regardless of creed, nationality, color or financial standing, each and every one receiving the kindness

---

(1) See Editor's Note on opposite page.

and consideration that his or her case demands and from the day the first patient was admitted on June 28th, 1906, until the present time when nearly 12,000 have received medical and surgical care under its roof and 500 have first seen the light of day within its walls, the hospital has proved itself to be what its friends have always claimed for it, a much needed institution.

MEDICAL HISTORY OF BRADDOCK.

BY S. ROY MILLS, M. D.

The Physician, like the "Proverbial Poor", we have always with us, for go where you will, there within call will be found one who bears the burden of our infirmities, both physical and mental.

In the not very distant past this individual was considered one of the Honored Members of the community and as such, was accordingly respected and looked up to. He was a welcome visitor at all times, either professionally or otherwise. Very often he was held before the children as an example for good, and in some cases used as a whip to lead erring youngsters in the right paths, but always was the surname Doctor applied with a sense of honor, amounting almost to reverence. To-day the term is used indiscriminately to designate numerous classes of callings and occupations, regardless of the educational requirements, be it a simple three months or prolonged over a course of seven years.

Think what you will of the Physician, let the Cynic say that his "Mistakes are all buried", and we emphatically deny this, (they live on forever as Living Mill-stones)—yet are you bound to admit that he is the first to be called and the first to respond in the time of need but always the last to be thought of, if at all, when accounts are to be settled. In this connection I was very much amused at the account given mè by one of our most successful and best known Practitioners, in relation to his first year of practice which he spent in a nearby city. It seems that in this year he worked as hard and saw as many patients as he has ever seen since in a like time and received for this the magnificent sum of $235.00, which you can easily see did not even pay for the upkeep of his horse. Time certainly has made no material change in this respect.

In going back over the Medical History of this vicinity I find the earliest mentioned Physicians are Drs. Murray, Rush Marchand and William Penny. Of these, nothing can be found except that Dr. Marchand was spoken of as being especially proficient in the treatment of dog-bite (From an account of J. B. Corey) and that his colleague Dr. Penny was something of a Lay Preacher as well, and was frequently to be found in the pulpits of the various churches when their Pastors were indisposed.

Next on the scene comes William Gore, who at this time, (slightly before 1860) was located at what is now Monroetown, and who later removed to Turtle Creek and then to Braddock. He is remembered by the residentors as the Chesterfield of the profession, as he was always attired in the most correct dress and at all times was the Perfect Gallant. Death called him after but a few years of practice in this vicinity.

THE OLDEST LIVING PHYSICIANS OF BRADDOCK.
IN REGARD TO TIME OF SERVICE.

A. W. SCHOOLEY.
1871.

E. W. DEAN.
1876.

About this time, we find that another Physician has made his appearance and is located in Port Perry, in the person of J. C. F. Maggini. Dr. Maggini was graduated from the Ohio Medical School in 1841 and established himself in Cincinnati for about a year, when he removed to Fayetteville in the same State. Here he remained until about 1859, when he brought his family to Port Perry and here practised until his removal to Braddock in 1875. All of his family were well known here, especially B. A. Maggini, who is at present one of our prominent and successful hardware dealers. Doctor Maggini died in 1877.

From this time on Braddock seems to have had an especial call for Physicians. Dr. J. D. Schooley, the father of the present well known

THE UNWRITTEN HISTORY OF BRADDOCK'S FIELD. 247

Practitioner, A. W. Schooley, located here in 1861. He graduated from Starling Medical School and practised in Cadiz, Ohio for about six years before coming here. His first office was in the McCune House on Jones Avenue, but after a year here, he removed to his own property on Braddock Avenue, and later added to his practice the management of a drug store, located at the same site. The Grim Reaper relieved him of his arduous duties in 1880.

At about the same time that we find Dr. Schooley, Doctor J. W. Linn put in his appearance, located a little farther along Braddock Avenue, and like him also maintained a drug store along with his office.

James Matlack opened an office in the Old Robinson House in 1868 and remained here for several years when he removed to Turtle Creek and continued to practise until his death in 1877.

Next comes W. A. Sandles, who had an office at the head of Ninth Street, and later on Verona Street. One of the "Old School", Dr. Sandles has left behind a most enviable reputation. He is spoken of as one of the most likeable as well as successful men of his time. His death surely caused a distinct loss to this community.

Doctor Kimmel located here in 1868, but remained only until 1871, when he removed to the West.

A. W. Schooley, the Oldest Living Practitioner of this district and the first example of a son following his father in the practice of medicine in Braddock, graduated from Jefferson Medical School in 1871 and came to Braddock in the same year, going in with his father on Braddock Avenue. He was born at Everett, Penna., coming to Braddock in 1861, and has lived here ever since, with the exception of the last few years, when he removed his residence to East Liberty, though he still maintains his office here. Few indeed are the children or the younger grown-ups of this vicinity who are not friends of this Grand Old Member of our Profession. Shall any of us forget that familiar snow-white beard or that ever present friendliness, which are so characteristic of our esteemed colleague? As he is to-day, so do I remember him from my youth and must say that Time has certainly not made any very appreciable change in him, not even in appearance.

The year 1876 finds E. W. Dean located on Library Street in the building just next to what is now Strights Pharmacy, but in about a year he removed to what is now the Stewart building at the head of Eighth Street. A short time later, he was installed in his own property on Library Street, where he still maintains his office, although it has been somewhat changed about because the building has been but lately remodeled into the Masonic Temple. Doctor Dean, next to Dr. Schooley, is the Oldest Living Physician of Braddock in regard to time of service. He is the father of Dr. H. E. Dean, one of the most successful of the "Younger Physicians"—the second example of father and son practising medicine in this vicinity.[1] Dr. E. W. Dean took a special course in Eye, Ear, Nose and Throat at the New York Polyclinic from 1887-90 and returned to Braddock to specialize in this branch of medicine and surgery.

We find among the local physicians quite a few who are distinctly Local Products, as it were, i. e., born here and educated in this district. These are H. E. Dean, C. C. Gardner, Ira Harris, F. K. Whitfield, John Zeok and myself.

Again, there are physicians in other localities, who were raised and educated in this community. Among such are Drs. Griffith, Frank Mervis and Frank Patterson. Also, Dr. Jacob Rosenbloom has achieved distinction in Biological chemistry and toxicology, while Dr. Grover C. Weil is a prominent and successful surgeon. Both of these are at present located in Pittsburgh. The writer's brother, Dr. W. W. Mills, is located in Duquesne.

To keep an accurate record of the physicians who have come and gone is almost an impossibility, as there were many whose sojourn here lasted less than a year, and many who remained only a few months in all. Dr. F. S. Rossiter, who had an office in the McDonald building during 1909-11 and then went to Swissvale, has reopened an office at the site recently vacated by Dr. A. E. Bulger, who has joined the army.

It would seem on the surface that Braddock had more than its share of physicians, but on closer view we find that the pro-rata number of people per doctor is well above the general average for the same in this part of our country.

Following is the list in brief:

---

(1) The life history of Braddock doctors presents other interesting family connections which should be known, though Dr. Mills' modesty prevents his referring to them. In the Mills family are two doctors, brothers, Dr. S. Roy, and Dr. Wm. W., both raised in Braddock, graduates of Braddock High School, and of the University of Pittsburgh. The Doctors Bair, both practicing in Braddock, are also brothers. In this case there is a whole family of doctors, as two other brothers are engaged in the profession, while a sister is the wife of Dr. Jas. N. Stanton of Pittsburgh, and another sister is the wife of Dr. I. M. Eisaman, a Braddock dentist. Dr. A. W. Hinman, who has been practicing veterinary surgery in Braddock for twenty-three years, has four brothers who are doctors of medicine. Dr. Harold H. Lamb can claim a long line of close relationship among the profession, two uncles, three great uncles, and nine cousins.—(Ed.)

THE UNWRITTEN HISTORY OF BRADDOCK'S FIELD.

Name	University	(1) R (2) H	Year Located Here	Practice	Death or Removal
J. C. F. Maggini	Ohio Medical	R	1859	General	Died 1877
J. D. Schooley	Starling	R	1861	General	Died 1880
J. W. Linn	Jefferson	R	1861	General	Died 1880
Jas Matlack	Jefferson	R	1868	General	Died 1877
W. A. Sandles	Jefferson	R	1869	General	Died 1891
Dr. Kimmel		R	1869	General	Moved West, 1871
A. W. Schooley	Jefferson	R	1871	General	
E. W. Dean	Hahnnemann	H	1876	Eye, Ear, Nose, Throat	
J. W. Weddel		R	1876	General	Deceased
W. M. Corothers	Jefferson	R	1877	General	Died 1902
E. O. Anderson	Hahnemann	H	1877	General	Died 1897
J. H. McLaughlin	Cincinnati	R	1877	General	Died 1913
B. F. Price	Cincinnati	R	1882	General	Died 1909
Christian Hagar	Dublin	R	1885	General	
Chas. H. Clifford	Jefferson	R	1888	General	
W. S. Stewart	Medico-Chi	R	1888	General	Moved West, 1910
C. B. Weida	Jefferson	R	1889	General	Died 1905
W. T. Morgan	Maryland	R	1889	General and Gynaecology	
G. E. Bair	Jefferson	R	1890	General	
P. C. Cope	Pittsburgh	R	1890	General	
J. A. Miller	Pittsburgh	R	1891	General	Died 1917
Geo. Tell		R	1891	General	Died 1907
Anna Watts	Hahnemann	H	1892	General	
B. M. Bartilson	Jefferson	R	1893	Medicine and Surgery	
G. H. McGeary	Hahnemann	H	1893	Gen'l ..Wilkinsburg, 1917	
D. A. Molyneaux	Dublin U.	R	1894	General	Died 1913
J. Behane	Dublin U.	R	1894	General	Died 1906
W. A. Clementson	Jefferson	R	1895	Genito-urinary, Died 1912	
H. F. Fisher	Pittsburgh	R	1895	Gynaecology	
C. A. Meals	Jefferson	R	1896	General and Surgery	
A. J. Korhnak	Jefferson	R	1898	General	
J. C. Hartman	Pittsburgh	R	1899	General	
J. C. Nichols	Pittsburgh	R	1899	General	
D. A. Metzgar	Pittsburgh	R	1899	Eye, ear, nose & throat	
Max Horowitz	Bellevue	R	1900	General	Removed 1903
L. G. Rubenstein	Pittsburgh	R	1901	General	
Samuel Howard	Shaw	R	1902	General	
E. W. Ellis	Pittsburgh	R	1902	General	Removed 1904
T. S. Hicks[3]	N. Y. Homeo.	R	1903	General	
H. H. Turner	Jefferson	R	1904	Eye only	
W. M. Proctor	Hahnemann	H	1905	General	Died 1911
F. K. Whitfield	Louisville	R	1905	General and X-Ray	
Ira Harris	Louisville	R	1905	General	
C. E. Bair	Jefferson	R	1906	General	
H. E. Dean	Pennsylvania	R	1906	General and Surgery	
H. S. Isaacs	Pittsburgh	R	1906	Gen., Killed in Accident 1912	
J. B. Smith	Pittsburgh	R	1908	General and Surgery	
C. C. Gardner[4]	Pittsburgh	R	1910	Genito-urinary	
A. E. Bulger	Pittsburgh	R	1910	General	Army 1917
A. A. Wall	Shaw	R	1910	General	
W. J. Lowrie	Medico-Chi	R	1911	General	
S. R. Mills[5]	Pittsburgh	R	1911	General and Pathology	
O. I. Polk	Pittsburgh	R	1912	General	
R. N. Lowrie	Medico-Chi	R	1912	General	
J. P. Egan	Medico-Chi	R	1913	General	
F. L. Morrow	Pittsburgh	R	1914	General	
T. H. Snowwhite[6]	Pittsburgh	R	1914	General	
John Zeok	Louisville	R	1914	General	
S. A. Godlewski	Valparaiso, Ind.	R	1915	General	
M. S. Bowers[6]	Pittsburgh	R	1917	General	
H. H. Lamb	Pittsburgh	R	1917	General and Pathology	

(1) R—Regular.
(2) H—Homeopath.
(3) Enlisted in Cavalry.
(4) Enlisted in Naval Reserves.
(5) Enlisted in Navy.
(6) Enlisted in Army.

FRATERNAL SOCIETIES.

BY REUBEN D. ABBISS, JR.

I. O. O. F., Braddock's Field Lodge No. 529, Inst. Nov. 17, 1856.

F. & A. M., Braddock's Field Lodge No. 510, warranted June 5, 1872.

I. O. O. F., McMaster's Encampment No. 239, instituted April 23, 1873.

O. of I. A. Monongahela Council No. 122, instituted June 21, 1879.

G. A. R., Major A. M. Harper Post No. 181, instituted July 31, 1880.

R. A., Edgar Thomson Council No. 512, instituted August 10, 1880.

Ladies of G. A. R., instituted September 1, 1883.

N. S. S. of U. S. A., Slavian Assembly No. 21, founded Jan. 20, 1889.

The Maccabees, Bessemer Tent No. 92, organized Feb. 16, 1889.

C. M. B. A., Branch No. 65, instituted July 8, 1889.

S. M. A. S. S., Branch No. 35, organized Feb. 9, 1890.

K. of P., Husband Lodge No. 386, instituted Feb. 13, 1892.

S. E. U., St. Paul's Branch No. 4, organized Oct. 30, 1892.

A. & I. O. K. of M. Valetta Commandery No. 129, instituted Feb. 23, 1893.

St. J. R. C. U. of A. Branch No. 6, organized March 14, 1895.

I. K. S. J. Cisle 197, organized Aug. 3, 1895.

A. & I. O. K. of M., Melrose Commandery No. 179, instituted Nov. 27, 1895.

G. U. O. O. F. Triumphant Lodge No. 3954, instituted Jan. 26, 1896.

T. B. H. Arrius Court, No. 4, organized Feb. 4, 1896.

Z. B. S. S. Branch No. 34, organized May 17, 1896.

G. C. U., St. Ann's Society No. 108, organized December 20, 1896.

S. E. U., Branch No. 47, organized Feb. 1898.

F. W. C. of C., No. 163, organized Mar. 22, 1898.

L. V. H. H. R., No. 1334, instituted April 11, 1898.

I. O. of G. T. North Star Lodge No. 2, instituted June 24, 1900.

I. O. B. B., Braddock Lodge No. 516, instituted Sept. 8, 1901.

S. E. U., John the Baptist Branch No. 92, organized June 5, 1902.

S. & D. of L., instituted June 27, 1902.

I. O. B. B. Ladies Auxiliary, instituted Jan. 15, 1903.

B. P. O. E., Braddock Lodge No. 833, instituted Nov. 19, 1903.

S. of V., Capt. W. R. Jones Camp No. 218, instituted Mar. 19, 1904.

K. of C. Braddock Council No. 711, organized Nov. 27, 1904.

THE UNWRITTEN HISTORY OF BRADDOCK'S FIELD. 251

F. O. E., Braddock Aerie, instituted June 23, 1905.
G. of St. A. Branch No. 821, organized Sept. 10, 1905.
E. S. L. U., "Bethesda" Branch No. 6, organized Jan. 21, 1906.
I. O. S. D., Mon City Lodge No. 3, organized June 11, 1907.
L. O. O. M., Braddock Lodge No. 57, instituted October 7, 1908.
M. W. of A., Camp No. 13413, instituted Nov. 6, 1908.
P. R. C. U., St. Joseph Society No. 449, instituted 1908.
I. O. St. L. Barton Union Council No. 694, organized 1908.

MALTA TEMPLE

R. & G. C. S. B. of Western Pa., organized April 18, 1909.
R. & G. C. S. B. St. John's Society, organized May 1909.
P. A. C. C., instituted Sept. 30, 1910.
A. O. H., Ladies Auxiliary, instituted May 16, 1912.
E. S. U., Branch No. 73, organized May 19, 1912.
K. of St. J., St. Mary's of Mount Carmel Commandery, No. 199, instituted July 7, 1912.
D. of I., Braddock Court No. 244, instituted July 19, 1914.

I. O. M. B. Lodge of Braddock, re-organized Feb. 24, 1917.

There are in America more secret societies and a larger aggregate membership than in all other civilized countries of the World.

Our land of liberty and democracy afforded a most congenial, receptive and unrestricted field for the active development of a prevailing anti-ism and for the popular formation of societies of the fraternal order. The great majority were founded, operated and have existed on the honest principle of fraternal love and association. These have, therefore, very naturally contributed materially in the consolidation, agreeable association and the general betterment of such a cosmopolitan and conglomerate crowd as that which, augmented from time to time by immigration, to-day forms the population of some hundred millions of Americans.

Some time since it was reported that there were 650 well known, regularly formed and generally recognized fraternal orders in the United States, with an aggregate membership of 8,000,000. There were in existence at that time, additional smaller orders with an enrollment of about 3,000,000 members making a grand total of 11,000,000 American citizens, or about one tenth of the entire population of the United States. The estimated amount of insurance is stated to be about $7,000,000,000.

More than 30,000 members are annually added to the rolls of the Masonic Fraternity alone, and quite as many join the Odd Fellow Societies. About one-half as many add to the annual membership of the Knights of Pythias. The smaller societies secure an increase of recruits every year in almost the same proportion.

Although the American Fraternities have the same basis and fundamental principles common to the Friendly Societies of England and Scotland, and are in fact the outgrowth of British secret and non-secret friendly societies; yet they possess features which are purely and distinctly American.

As in Great Britain, the American Societies are organized on the Lodge System with grips, passwords, and rituals. The foundation and existence of these societies is a contract to pay by means of assessments a stipulated amount of insurance to the beneficiaries of the deceased members, and in some instances sick, disability and funeral benefits.

The general aim of these societies is to cultivate the spirit of fraternity; by encouraging the social, the intellectual, the esthetic, they increase the popularity of their respective organizations.

The Masons, Odd Fellows, Elks and Maltas, of Braddock, all own their homes of which they are justly very proud. Most of the other Orders are very strong financially and some of them contemplate the erection of a home in the near future.

Independent Order of Odd Fellows, Braddock's Field Lodge No. 529, was instituted Nov. 17, 1856. The Charter Members were: John W. House, Daniel Kuhns, Morris Brannon, John C. Campbell, Miles Fawcett, William Sarver, James Carson, Lloyd Jamison, Samuel Baden, James Petty, Samuel Watts, Daniel Mansfield, H. Bailey, Jacob Linheart, James McCleary, Samuel Kuhns.

ELK'S CLUB.

The following officers were elected: John W. House, Noble Grand; Daniel Kuhns, Vice Grand; Morris Brannon, Secretary; John C. Campbell, Financial Secretary; and Miles Fawcett, Treasurer.

The officers at present are: Thomas N. Strathern, Noble Grand; Edward M. Graffis, Vice Grand; W. S. Lowman, Rec. Secretary; Reuben Abbiss, Financial Secretary; and Philip D. Heyne, Treasurer.

Braddock's Field Lodge No. 510, Free and Accepted Masons, was warranted on June 5, 1872, with the following charter members: Esli P. Black, William F. Lang, John H. Cooper, Thomas J. Dowler, Henry M. Lytle, William B. Lucus, Christopher C. Fawcett, Sharply M. Packer, Newton I. Roberts, Edward J. Allen, John Bladridge, Jr., Thomas K. McVay, Thomas J. Lewis, William F. Hope, Samuel W. Elliot.

The first officers were: William F. Lang, Worshipful Master; John H. Cooper, Senior Warden; Thomas J. Dowler, Junior Warden; Christopher C. Fawcett, Treasurer; William F. Hope, Secretary.

The present officers are: David Dudgeon, Worshipful Master; James H. Rose, Senior Warden; Clarence F. Bernatz, Junior Warden; Henry C. Shallenberger, Treasurer; [1]Thomas J. Dowler, Secretary.

McMaster's Encampment No. 239, I. O. O. F. was instituted at Turtle Creek, April 23, 1873. The first meeting of this organization in Braddock was held Mar. 21, 1885.

CHRISTOPHER C. FAWCETT.(2)

The first officers and charter members were: David Mackey, C. P.; James S. McCauley, Sr. W.; S. H. McCabe, H. P.; David Allen, Jr. W.; John Gibb, Scribe; George W. Ament, Treasurer; John Glunt, Alexander Cunningham, W. A. Crusan, N. G. Harrison, David McMunn, Taylor McIntosh, George Crake, H. Maxwell, R. N. Lewis, and Henry Lane.

The present officers are: George K. Butler, C. P.; Edward M. Graffls, H. P.; Clarence N. Sickler, Sr. W.; Warren D. Kellar, Jr. W.; Reuben Abbiss, Scribe; and R. Olin Glenn, Treasurer.

---

(1) Thos. J. Dowler died March 28, 1917, having served the lodge as secretary continuously for forty-five years.
(2) Only living charter member of Braddock's Field Lodge No. 570, F. & A. M.

THE UNWRITTEN HISTORY OF BRADDOCK'S FIELD.   255

Order of Independent Americans, Monongahela Council No. 122, was instituted in Seewald's Hall June 21, 1879, by Daniel G. Evans, State Councilor, of the Junior O. U. A. M. assisted by Smoky City Council No. 119. In June 1904 the Council affiliated with the majority of Councils in Pennsylvania by forming the O. of I. A., in order that the real objects and purposes of the parent organization could be carried out in a successful manner.

The present officers are C. W. Cochran, Con.; G. H. Gardner, V. C.; O. K. Hyland, Recording Secretary; Roy M. Lowers, Secretary; L. M. Potter, Financial Secretary; Adam Mehlman, Treasurer; Clyde House, Cond.; R. L. Witters, Warden; L. E. Reeves, I. S.; J. M. O'Donovan, O. S.; H. J. Frye, Chaplain; J. G. Kerr, J. I. Nulls, Harold Greig, Trustees; J. F. Lowers, Rep. S. C.; L. M. Potter, Alt.

Major A. M. Harper Post No. 181, Department Pennsylvania G. A. R.

In pursuance of Special Order No. 58, Headquarters Department of Pennsylvania, Grand Army of the Republic, issued to Thos. J. Gist of Post 59, of McKeesport, Pa., a provisional Post was instituted July 31, 1880 for the purpose of mustering into the G. A. R. Order, Post 181 of Braddock, Pa.

The Comrades of the detail were from the Posts of Pittsburgh, East Liberty, McKeesport and were as follows: Thos. J. Gist Post 59, Commander; W. W. McClellan, Post 3, Sr. Vice Commander; G. S. Gallupe, Post 88, Jr. Vice Commander; S. A. Wills, Post 3, Adjutant; W. L. Hurd, Post 59, Quartermaster; L. D. Radinsky, Post 59, Surgeon; Q. Lutz, Post 117, Chaplain; W. W. Tyson, Post 88, Officer of the Day; A. C. Monland, Post 151, Officer of the Guard; T. Eastwood, Post 59, Sergeant Major.

The following were then mustered into the G. A. R. as Post 181, of Braddock, and were duly instructed in their duties as comrades of the Order of the G. A. R., by the above details of comrades: C. Bennett, J. C. Bash, August Brocksmith, Robert Bates, T. C. Clark, J. M. Clark, G. A. Douglass, G. S. Fritzius, Wm. Ford, Wm. Flanigan, T. W. Graham, J. W. Hawthorne, G. F. House, C. F. Hugo, Wm. Holmes, G. W. Johnson, J. S. Jones, H. T. Kulp, V. C. Knorr, C. C. Lobinger, J. L. McFeeters, W. L. Murdough, J. F. McGuire, Consor McClure, W. T. Meradith, J. J. Mills, J. W. Mathews, David Nichols, R. H. Owens, John Powell, J. H. Rankin, Christian Raichle, W. H. Speer, W. A. Sandles, Henry Slater, H. C. Teeter and Casper Winters.

The first officers of the Post were as follows: David Nichols, Past Commander; Wm. Holmes, Sr. Vice Commander; H. C. Teeters, Jr. Vice

JAS. A. RUSSEL.*

P. G. SYLVIS.*

THOS. J. DOWLER.

ROBT. J. KINTER.

WM. COLBERT.*

JAS. W. FAWCETT.*

*Oldest living members Braddock's Field Lodge, I. O. O. F., No. 529.

THE UNWRITTEN HISTORY OF BRADDOCK'S FIELD.   257

Commander; G. S. Fritzius, Adjutant; J. J. Mills, Quartermaster; Dr. W. A. Sandles, Surgeon; W. H. Speer, Chaplain; J. W. Hawthorne, Officer of the Day; R. H. Owens, Officer of the Guard; C. F. Hugo, Sergeant Major; J. L. Jones, Quartermaster Sergeant.

At the second regular meeting of the new Post a Committee consisting of Jones, Teeter, Murdough was appointed to select the name of some deceased comrade for whom to name the Post. This Committee submitted the names of A. M. Harper and O. Noyse, the latter being withdrawn, that of A. M. Harper was adopted unanimously.

The following comrades were prominent in business and industrial affairs of Braddock: Capt. W. R. Jones, Capt. T. H. Lapsley, Capt. J. L. McFeeters, Isaac Mills, Jr., John Little, John Rinard, Rev. S. P. Slade, Rev. J. L. Long, Rev. J. L. Miller, Dr. W. A. Sandles, Dr. W. L. Hunter, Dr. W. W. Meyers, Dr. B. F. Price, V. C. Knorr, David Nichols, T. W. Graham, J. N. Griffith and H. T. Kulp.

Following are the names of the Comrades who have filled the office of Commander from date of muster until the present time: David Nichols (1880, 6 months, deceased); Harry C. Teeter (1881-82, 2 years deceased); T. H. Lapsley (1883-84, 2 years, deceased); W. H. Speer (1885, 1 year, deceased); G. F. House (1886, 1 year); J. L. Jones (1887-88-89, 3 years, deceased); W. L. Murdough (1890, 1 year); R. W. Jones (1891, 1 year, deceased); W. J. Redman (1892, 1 year, deceased); R. C. Jackson (1893, 1 year, deceased); J. M. Clark (1894, 1 year, deceased); A. M. Bryan (1895, 1 year, deceased); J. W. Mathews (1896, 1 year, deceased); A. H. White (1897, 1 year, not a member); V. C. Knorr (1898, 1 year); A. M. Carline (1899, 1 year, not a member); Isaac Kramer (1900, 1 year, deceased); G. B. Hargett (1901, 1 year); S. T. Hart (1902, 1 year); H. J. Sharah (1903, 1 year); William Bennett (1904, 1 year, deceased); W. R. Collins (1905, 1 year); W. L. Murdough (1906-07, 2 years); D. L. Provance (1908, 1 year); W. L. Murdough (1909, 1 year); John Rinard (1910, 1 year, deceased); Jacob Hentz (1911, 1 year); B. A. Jobe (1912, 1 year); Joel Cruckshank (1913, 1 year); J. N. Griffith (1914, 1 year); P. W. Pike (1915, 7 months, deceased); J. N. Griffith (1915, 5 months); W. L. Murdough (1916, 1 year).

The present officers are: W. L. Murdough, Commander; Hamilton Mutterfield, Sr. Vice Commander; W. R. Collins, Jr. Vice Commander; B. A. Jobe, Adjutant; V. C. Knorr, Quartermaster; J. H. Rankin, Surgeon; D. L. Provance, Chaplain; B. F. Spangler, Officer of the Day; J. N. Griffith, Patriotic Instructor; J. J. Soles, Officer of the Guard; J. N. Griffith,

B. F. Spangler, W. R. Collins, Post Trustees; J. H. Rankin, W. R. Collins and Jacob Hintz, Cemetery Trustees.

From the date of muster up to the present time there were 286 comrades enrolled, but only forty-three (43) are still living, namely Jackson Allshouse, Jackson Anderson, Wm. Benson, Hamilton Butterfield, W. R. Collins, Joel Cruckshank, Patrick Conley, C. C. Fawcett, Henry Frank, J. N. Griffith, T. M. George, Ezekiel Gray, G. F House, J. H. Hoes, S. T. Harte, Wm. Huey, Jacob Heinz, James Hurley, B. A. Jobe, V. C. Knorr, H. T. Kulp, John Kountz, W. L. Murdough,[1] Wm. Mayer, John Mensdorf, Wm. McCauley, John McCaplin, Thos. McClelland, George Petty, D. L. Provance, Wm. Phillips, J. H. Rankin, Christian Raichle, H. P. Rigby, Hezekiah Scritchfield, B. F. Spangler, J. J. Soles, Wm Soles, Phillip Sadler, W. H. Thompson, C. T. Taylor, C. J. Williams and John Watkins.

The Honorary Members are Chas. E. Dinkey, L. F. Holtzman, W. H. Sharah, Frances Bebbett, George English, and Miss Tillie Harrison. The latter was taken in when a very small girl and was called the daughter of the Post.

Royal Arcanium, Edgar Thomson Council No. 512, was instituted Aug. 16, 1880, by Deputy Grand Regent, Owen Handcock of Pittsburgh, the charter members being: E. W. Eisenbeis, George A. Lewis, George W. Bond, John Dodds, Daniel Berthhold, Matthew I. Davis, Courtlandt F. Lukens, Stewart D. St. Clair, Matthias Bankert, J. D. Riley, Victor C. Knorr, Dr. George Gladden, Frank Wandrocke, Samuel Bowers, Robert A. Hart, Frank Keyser.

The Officers elected were: Regent, E. W. Eisenbeis; Vice Regent, Matthew I. Davis; Orator, Dr. George Gladden; Past Regent, Courtlandt F. Lukens, Secretary, George A. Lewis; Treasurer, Victor C. Knorr; Collector, J. D. Riley.

The living Past Regents of the Council in order of seniority are; J. F. Roberts, F. F. Sneathen, W. Leslie Miller, Edgar S. Wright, J. R. Emmert, Thomas J. Wood, Harry V. Barr, George S. Speidel, John T. C. Bowman, Erastus F. Loucks, M. Clyde Kelly, Harry E. Gwynne, Robert Bennet, David Creelman.

The present officers are: Lewis P. Fisher, Regent; Wm. J. B. Macauley, Vice Regent; Sherman T. Stroup, Orator; David Creelman, Collector; E. M. Sharah, Treasurer; J. C. McCormick, Jr., Secretary; C. A. Duffy, Chaplain.

---

(1) Mr. Murdough, who furnished this account of the Post, died June 8, 1917, in consequence of overexertion in the celebration of last Memorial day.

THE UNWRITTEN HISTORY OF BRADDOCK'S FIELD.

The Ladies of the G. A. R. were organized and instituted as the Loyal Ladies League, September 1, 1883, by the State of New Jersey as an aid to the Grand Army of the Republic.

The Charter Members were: Mrs. Emma Douglass, Mrs. Esther Murdough, Mrs. E. H. Ling, Mrs. Helena Lobingier, Mrs. T. Graham, Mrs. Ellen B. Soles, Mrs. Sue C. Kulp, Mrs. J. W. Meredith, Mrs. Jennie Slater, Mrs. Mary Nichols, Mrs. Margaret House and Mrs. Christiana Bryan.

At the Convention held in Altoona, Pennsylvania in 1886, a Department of Pennsylvania, Ladies of the G. A. R., Circle No. 4, was instituted, the fourth circle in Pennsylvania and the first in Western Pennsylvania. It was termed the "Mother Circle" and instituted many of the Circles of Western Pennsylvania. Circle N. 4 was allied to Post No. 181 of Braddock and shared all the work pertaining to Grand Army.

There were forty-two (42) Charter Members but the passing years have reduced our number to twenty-six (26), but the work for which we were banded together, The Post, The Widows and Orphans of Old Soldiers, is enduring. The Home at Hawkins stands as a monument to the Ladies G. A. R.

The first officers were: Mrs. Emma Douglas, President; Mrs. Helena Lobingier, First Vice President; Mrs. Annie Jones, Second Vice President; Mrs. Ellen B. Soles, Chaplain; Mrs. Sue C. Kulp, Secretary; Mrs. Christiana Bryan, Treasurer and Mrs. Anna Rankin, Conductress.

The present officers are: Mrs. Sarah Campbell, President; Mrs. Leona Hugo, Sr. Vice President; Mrs. Nellie Thomas, Jr. Vice President; Mrs. Jennie Graham, Chaplain; Mrs. Melisia Provance, Secretary; Mrs. Sue C. Kulp, Treasurer; Mrs. Maud Thomas, Patriotic Instructress; Mrs. Sarah Hoffman, Conductress; Mrs. Laura Leffler, Asst. Cond.; and Isabel Humbert, Guard.

Slavian Assembly No. 21 of the National Slovak Society of the United States of America is the oldest Slovak beneficial society in Western Pennsylvania. It was founded January 20, 1889, through the efforts of Messrs. Joseph Wolff, John F. Rybar and John Valecek, with thirty-five (35) charter members. It was founded as a sick benefit organization but on October 1, 1890, soon after the organization of the National Slovak Society, it affiliated with that body and became Slavian Assembly No. 21 of that body. Affiliated with the Slavian is a childrens' society called the Young Folks Circle.

The officers are John Kulamer, President; John Cupak, Vice President; Michael Borsuk, Recording Secretary; Michael Stecz, Financial Secretary; John A. Gimesky, Treasurer; Peter Dzmura, John Korman, Blasius Britanik, Auditors; and Paul Balint, Elder of the Young Folks Circle.

The Maccabees, Bessemer Tent No. 92, was organized February 26, 1889, with twenty-one (21) charter members and the following officers: John L. Jones, Sir Knight Commander; J. K. Fisher, Sir Knight Past Commander; John Hilgenberg, Sir Knight St. Commander; E. S. Bracken, Sir Knight Record Keeper; E. M. Brackemeyer, Sir Knight Finance Keeper; Dr. J. W. Weddle, Sir Knight Chaplain; Dr. J. W. Weddle, Sir Knight Physician; W. R. Edwards, Sir Knight Sargent; T. Kulp, Sir Knight Master at Arms; J. W. Mathews, Sir Knight First Master of Guards; Chas. Davis, Sir Knight Second Master of Guards; G. F. Larimer, Sir Knight Sentinel; David Creelman, Sir Knight Picket.

The present officers are: John Moenick, Sir Knight Past Commander; Albert J. Bachofer, Sir Knight Commander; Thos McCafferey, Sir Knight St. Commander; Wm. L. Callahan, Sir Knight Record Keeper; Frank A. Reilly, Sir Knight Chaplain; Homer Carpenter, Sir Knight Sargent; Dr. J. A. Miller, Sir Knight Physician; George Frye, Sir Knight Master at Arms; Joseph Seamon, Sir Knight First Master of Guards; Joseph Fisher, Sir Knight Second Master of Guards; John Langley, Sir Knight Sentinel; Nickolas Bongartz, Sir Knight Picket; Samuel Benson, Homer Carpenter, and A. F. Bachofer, Trustees.

Catholic Mutual Benefit Association, Branch No. 65 was instituted July 8, 1889, with the following charter members: John A. Carr, Edw. D. Nugent, Wm. J. Wall, Rodger Daugherty, John Fullard, Owen Larkin, Jos. Syden, James Nugent, Chas. W. McGarvey, John C. Logan, Jas. Kinney, Jas. Gorman, John Griffin, Sr., Patrick Martin, Patrick O'Shea, M. J. Daugherty, Peter Hammill, Wm. McMullen, M. J. Munhall, Wm. Dunn.

The first officers were: John A. Carr, President; Wm. J. Wall, Recording Secretary, Edw. D. Nugent, Financial Secretary; Jas. Kenney, Treasurer.

The present officers are: M. J. Simon, President; John Mullin, First Vice President; John Carr, Second Vice President; Vern Ridge, Recording Secretary; P. J. O'Connell, Financial Secretary; Richard J. Butler, Treasurer and W. F. Clark, Chancellor.

Saint Michael Archangel Slovak Society Branch No. 35, which is the largest branch of the Catholic Slovak Union, was organized February 9, 1890 with sixty (60) members. The fifst President was John Barlok; Stephen Vanyo, Financial Secretary; Frank Shikula, Recording Secretary; John Pilas, Treasurer.

THE UNWRITTEN HISTORY OF BRADDOCK'S FIELD.   261

The present officers are John Lukac, President; Paul Hatala, Vice President; Joseph J. Semes, Recording Secretary; Andrew S. Hajdu, Financial Secretary; Imrich Mamrak, Association Secretary; Andrew Puhalla, Treasurer; John Kovaly, First Trustee; Ludwik Martinko, Second Trustee.

Knights of Pythias, Husband Lodge No. 386, was instituted February 13, 1892.

The Charter Members were Albert Queery, George Earl, Joe Evens, John Maxwell, John M. Reed, Jacob R. Smitley, Ebenezer Wilson, Wm. T. Morgan, Elmer Metz, H. T. Barnhart, Charles L. Shoop, Christ Forney and J. G. Wallace.

The officers were: George Earl, C. C.; John M. Reed, V. C.; John Maxwell, Prelate; J. R. Smitley, K. R. S.; E. L. Wilson, M. F.; W. T. Morgan, M. E.; I. Reed, M. A.; H. T. Barnhart, I. G.; Elmer Metz, O. G.

The officers at present are: David George, C. C.; Edward Payne, V. C.; Chas. Lewis, Prelate; H. H. Fogie, K. R. S.; W. J. Lewis, M. F.; Samuel Barlow, M. E.; Samuel Branthoover, M. A.; Arthur Fram, I. G.; C. F. Smith, O. G.; Simon Stump, Chas. Lewis, and Wm. Husband are Trustees.

St. Paul's Branch No. 4 of the Slovak Evangelical Union was organized October 30, 1892, with the following charter members: Andrew Sedlak, Andrew Varga, John Mizoff, George Sec, John Goga Smith, John Marcin, Sr., Stephan Cop, John Marton, Michael Sedory, John Sedory, Michael Kachman, George Goga, John Smetana, Stephen Gall, George Varga, John Sedlak-Onderuf, Joseph Demcak, George Maco.

The first officers were: Rev. L. Novomeskey, President; Stephen Cop, Vice President; George Vargo, Secretary; John Marton, Treasurer; Andrew Damankos, Financial Secretary.

The present officers are: Stephen Kusnier, President; John Stark, Secretary, Andrew Duraj, Jr., Financial Secretary; John Tompos, Treasurer.

Valetta Commandery, No. 129, Ancient & Illustrious Order Knights of Malta, was instituted February 23, 1893, with 59 charter members, ten of whom are still living. The officers were: Sir J. N. Griffith, Past Commander; Sir M. F. Michael, Sir Knight Commander; Sir Jacob Shipman, Generalissimo; Sir Henry Miller, Captain General; Sir Wm. Porter, Prelate; Sir D. F. Melville, Recorder; Sir A. H. Parker, Treasurer.

The present officers are: Sir E. B. Calihan, S. K. C.; Sir John Somerville, Generalissimo; Sir Chas. Stewart Jr., Captain General; Sir F. A.

Meacham, Prelate; Sir Albert Liston, Treasurer and Sir E. T. Engelhart, Recorder. Valetta Commandery has been especially honored by the election of the following to the Supreme and Grand offices of the Order.

Sir David F. Melville, Grand Commander Pennsylvania 1899. Supreme Commander, Continent of America 1903.

Sir B. M. Bartilson, M. D., Grand Commander Pennsylvania 1904, Supreme Commander, Continent of America 1908.

Sir H. F. Fisher, M. D., Grand Commander Pennsylvania 1914.

St. Albert's Roman Catholic Benevolent Society, Branch No. 6 of St. Joseph's Roman Catholic Union of America, was organized March 14, 1895, and was the first Polish Society in Braddock. The first officers were: Frank Sumeracki, President; Anthony Pater, Vice President; Thomas Polanski, Secretary; Ludwick Wlazlinski, Treasurer; Anthony Krzyzosiak, and Philip Kanarkowski, Trustees.

The Society was chartered by the Common Pleas Court of Allegheny County, Mar. 13, 1897. The charter members were Anthony Pater, Ludwick Wlazlinski, Peter Dudek, Anthony Krzyzosiak and John Drozen.

The present officers are: Anthony Krzyzosiak, President; Felix Josienski, Vice President; Joseph Balawajder, Secretary; Michael Peli, Financial Secretary; Frank Czapliwski, Treasurer; Philip Kanarkowski and Frank Wisniewski, Trustees; Joseph Rosin and Frank Kultis, Directors of Sick.

Spolok Sv. Rodiny Jezis, Maria a Jozef Cislo, 197 I. K. S. J., was organized in St. Michael's Parish, August 3, 1895 with 33 charter members and the following officers: John Pipko, President; Andrew Zajac, Secretary; George Opet, Financial Secretary; Jozef Popovich, Treasurer.

The present officers are: John T. Oranez, President; John Kizasoniak, Secretary; George M. Kallock, Financial Secretary; Jozel Manik, Treasurer.

Melrose Commandery, No. 179, Ancient & Illustrious Order Knights of Malta, was organized by Alexander McPhee, November 27, 1895, with sixty-five (65) charter members, eighteen (18) of whom are still active in the affairs of the Commandery. The following were the first officers: George Nash, Sir Knight Commander; G. W. Brown, Generalissimo; August Mann, Captain General; R. P. Everett, Prelate; Frank Boardman, Recorder; Chas. B. Guttridge, Asst. Recorder; Giddeon H. Jaquay, Treasurer; A. Allison, Sr. Warden; Thos. Watkins, Jr. Warden; F. E. Wollerton, Standard Bearer; John Peterson, Sword Bearer; Fred Miller, Warder; R. Miller, Sentinel; Ruben Guttridge, First Guard; E. S. Metz, Second Guard.

THE UNWRITTEN HISTORY OF BRADDOCK'S FIELD. 263

The present officers are: Martin J. Fisher, S. K. C.; James Baxter, Generalissimo; Edgar Reed, Captain General; Arthur Fram, Prelate; David H. Drylie, Recorder; John Neckeraeur, Asst. Rec.; Harry C. Dixon, Treasurer; Fred M. Lucas, Sr. Warden; William Crawford, Jr. Warden.

Grand United Order of Odd Fellows, Triumphant Lodge No. 3954, was instituted Jan. 26, 1896, with the following charter members: H. J. Rector, Jessie Roy, James L. Roy, P. H. Homes, W. W. Jackson, Thomas Humes, J. H. Brown, R. H. Greer, James Florence, Sandy Jones.

The present officers are: William McWright, N. G.; James H. Hairston, V. G.; R. G. Puryear, Chaplain; John J. Willis, N. F.; Samuel Moore, P. N. F.; Kaleb Booker, W.; Alexander Weathers, Advo.; J. E. Sackwell, Treasurer; William Stanton, E. S.; William H. Barton, P. Secy.

Arrius Court No. 4, Tribe of Ben Hur was organized Feb. 4, 1896 in Carline's Hall, Ninth and Washington Streets with sixty (60) charter members. The first officers were: Chief, Louis Sulzbacher; Judge, Robert J. Kinter; Teacher, Walter J. McBeth; Scribe, David F. Melville; Keeper of Tribute, Joseph M. Hollander; Captain, Henry H. Meyers; Guide, George M. Nimon; Physician, Dr. B. M. Bartilson.

The present officers are: Chief, Robert J. Kinter; Judge, Samuel R. Raer; Teacher, William E. Phillips; Scribe, T. H. Whittaker; Keeper of Tribute, George W. Kutscher; Captain, Edward F. Mickey; Guide, Daniel Harris; Physicians, Dr. B. M. Bartilson, and S. R. Mills.

Zivena Beneficial Slovak Society Branch No. 34 was organized May 17, 1896, with the following members: Helen Dzmura, Julia Gimesky, Mary Lesso, Mary Sedlak, Mary Novak, Carrie Pustinger, Mary Malby, Mary Sinetana, Elizabeth Varga, Anna Spirko, Anna Matias, Mary Galla and Anna Gajdos.

The first officers were Helen Dzmura, President; Mary Lesso, Secretary; Julia Gimesky, Treasurer; Mary Sedlak, Financial Secretary.

The present officers are: Mrs. Mary Parlak, President; Mrs. Elizabeth Cibula, Vice President; Mrs. Ludmila Rehak, Secretary; Mrs. Susie Sklenar, Financial Secretary; and Mrs. Mary Havir, Treasurer.

Greek Catholic Union, St. Ann's Society No. 108, was organized December 20, 1896, with 51 charter members and the following officers: Helen Dzmura, President; Anna Hrenyo, Financial Secretary; and Anna Gynrik, Treasurer.

The present officers are: Mary Leyko, President; Mary Sokol, Recording Secretary; Agnes Verosky, Financial Secretary and Anna Dzmura, Treasurer.

Branch No. 47 of the Slovak Evangelical Union was organized February 30, 1898 by the following: Stephan Cop, George Vargo, Michael Novotny, Andrew Damankos, Michael Damankos and Michael Sedori.

The first officers were: Stephan Cop, President; Michael Damankos, Secretary; Andrew Damankos, Financial Secretary; George Varga, Treasurer.

The present officers are: George Marton, President; Alois Cibula, Secretary; Matej Hadbavny, Financial Secretary; George Galla, Treasurer.

Finest of Wheat Court of Calanthea, No. 163, was organized March 22, 1898, with the following members: Mr. C. O. Hawkins, Mrs. Mary Tombs, Mary Scott, Joseph Scott, Sadie Jackson, Katie Boone, Thena Yates, Thos. Yates, Lourenia Hawkins, John Tombs, Alvenra Roy, Pattie Kizer.

The present officers are: Mrs. Fannie L. Nevels, W. I.; Mrs. Lillie Gipson, W. In.; Mrs. Bettie Richerson, W. O.; Mrs. Janie Ashly, R. of D.; Mrs. Clara Hanston, R. of A.; Mrs. Havenia Norris, R. of D.; Mrs. Fannie Maloy, S. D.; Mrs. Pollie Seimes, J. D.; Mrs. Louise Gaehright, W. E.; Mrs. Mary Hariston, W. C.; Mrs. Jackson Blackburn, J. D.; Mrs. W. H. Norris, W. H. & P.; Mrs. Mary Jones, W. Trustee.

Lillie of the Valley, H. H. of Ruth No. 1334, was instituted April 11, 1898, with the following members: Annie Christian, Mollie Wayne, Nellie Williams, Barbara Anderson, Patrick Holmes, Fannie Fletcher, Alvenya Roy, Janie Roy, Moses King, James Florence, Jackson Crawford, Mary Jones, Alice Reed.

The following are the present officers: Ada Dear, M. N. G.; Clara Pyrear, P. M. N. G.; Elizabeth Pyrear, W. N. G.; M. L. C. Norris, N. G.; Sadie Jackson, W. K.; Nellie Williams, W. Treasurer; Mamie Brown, W. P.; Mamie Washington, W. N.; Mary Meright, R. S.; May Wilson, L. S.; Mollie Barton, R. S. L.; Annie Christian, L. S. S.

North Star Lodge No. 2, of the International Order of Good Templars, was instituted and given the number 107 under the jurisdiction of Pennsylvania and Delaware and District Lodge Number 3, on the 24th day of June 1900, by the District Chief Templar, Carl Thebon.

Upon petition from the Swedish-speaking lodges in District No. 3, permission was given to form a Swedish district lodge. The Swedish District Lodge No. 3, Jr., was instituted November 30, 1901. In September 1912, upon petition from the Swedish speaking lodges under the jurisdiction of the Grand Lodge of Pennsylvania and Delaware, permission was given to form a separate Swedish Grand Lodge. The new Grand Lodge

THE UNWRITTEN HISTORY OF BRADDOCK'S FIELD.   265

was chartered and named, 'The Pennsylvania Scandanavian Grand Lodge', having Pennsylvania and Delaware under its jurisdiction. New charters being issued, the North Star Lodge became number 2 and the District Lodge No. 3 Jr., became District Lodge No. 1.

The first officers were: Gust Gronland, Chief Templar; John R. Nelson, Vice Templar; Jenny Gronland, Supt. of Juvenile Work; Otto Sthal, Chaplain; Conrad Hultgreen, Secretary; Axel Broman, Assistant Secretary; Fritz Wahlgren, Financial Secretary; Hanna Westlund, Treasurer; Lina Wahlgrun, Marshal; Chas. Hultgreen, Deputy Marshal; Algot Johnson, Guard; Sigfrid Hamilton, Sentinel; Oscar Edstrom, Past Chief Templar; and Oscar Westlund, Deputy G. C. T.

At present the officers are: George Johnson, Chief Templar; Julia Axelson, Vice Templar; Maria Wallin, Supt. of Juvenile Work; Oscar Edstrom, Chaplain; Fabian Axelson, Secretary; J. V. Bjorling, Asst. Secretary; Andrew Wilson, Financial Secretary; Olaf Lindberg, Treasurer; Hulda Peterson, Marshal; Edvin Johnson, Deputy Marshal; Conrad Hultgren, Guard; Robt. G. Karlsson, Sentinel; Gust. Hammarstrom, Past Chief Templar; John R. Nelson, Dep. G. T. C.

Platform of the International Order of Good Templars.

1. Total abstinence from all intoxicating liquors as a beverage.

2. No license in any form under any circumstances, for the sale of liquors to be used as a beverage.

3. The absolute prohibition of the manufacture, importation and sale of intoxicating liquors for such purposes; prohibition by the will of the people expressed in due form of law with the penalties deserved for a crime of such enormity.

4. The creation of a healthy public opinion upon the subject by the active dissemination of the truth in all the modes known to enlightened philanthropy.

5. The election of good honest men to make and administer the laws.

6. Persistence in efforts to save individuals and communities from so dreadful a scourge, against all forms of opposition and difficulties until our success is complete and universal.

Braddock Lodge No. 516, Independent Order B'nai B'rith, was instituted on September 8, 1901, with the following Charter Members: Leopold Newman, Herman Hochstetter, Morris Rosenbloom, Leo A. Katz, L. J. Goldsmith, H. H. Meyers, Herman Koenig, Louis Schmidt, Dr. L. G. Rubenstein, Simon Spatz, S. Schoemann, S. Meyers, Julius Hoechstetter,

Louis Bachman, Herman Arnowitz, Ferd Newman, Samuel Levi, Joseph M. Steinetz, I. W. Simons.

The following were elected to office on date of Institution: President, Leopold Newman; Vice President, Dr. L. G. Rubenstein; Monitor, Louis Schmidt; Secretary, I. W. Simons; Treasurer, Leo A. Katz.

The present officers are as follows: President, Morris Adler; Vice President, Bennett Zeff; Monitor, J. M. Steinetz; Recording Secretary, Henry S. Sulzbacher; Financial Secretary, Sigmund Schoemann; Treasurer, Charles Klein; Assistant Monitor, Morriss Weiss; Warden, Herman Berliner; Guardian, Julius Schmidt; Trustees, Simon Spatz, Sigmund Schoemann, Hermann Arnowitz.

Braddock Lodge is part of District Number Three, which comprises the States of Pennsylvania, West Virginia, New Jersey, and Delaware; it maintains an Orphanage and Home for Friendless Children, located near Erie, Pennsylvania, on Ninety-five (95) acres of land; the buildings being on the Cottage system.

John the Baptist Branch No. 92 of the Slovak Evangelical Union was organized June 5, 1902 with the following officers and members: Mathew Bednar, President; George Suran, Vice President; John Durisek, Secretary; Martin Holly, Financial Secretary; Stephan Klimek, Treasurer; Paul Babek, John Klimek, John Hnupa, George Babek, Thomas Foltin, Samuel Brusko, John Vicik, John Kuric, Paul Pavelka, Paul Gabriel, John Bednar, John Ilencik, Stephan Kravarik, Adam Mahalik, Paul Turan, Stephan Duga, John Galla, John Gajdos.

The present officers are: Paul Shnatka, President; Michael Piecky, Vice President; John Tomka, Financial Secretary; Stephan Duris-Findak, Treasurer.

Sons and Daughters of Liberty was instituted June 27, 1902, with the following charter members: A. H. List, Q. A. Griffith, Mamie A. Benson, Anna Matchet.

The first officers were: John W. Johnson, Councilor; Minnie Berthold, Secretary; I. E. Griffith, Financial Secretary; G. C. Taylor, Treasurer.

The present officers are: Alice E. Welshouse, Councilor; Daisy E. Barnhart, Secretary; J. D. Malady, Financial Secretary; Mamie A. Benson, Treasurer; Hannah Simpson, Asso. C.; Amanda Frye, Guide; Mary Muir, O. Guard; Phoebe Bathorst, Inner Guard; Mae Moneres, Vice C. and Elizabeth Kirkpatrick, A. V. C.

Ladies Auxiliary of Independent Order of B'nai B'rith was instituted on January 15, 1903, with the following members: Mrs. Max Altman, Mrs. Herman Amshel, Mrs. Louis Schmidt, Mrs. H. H. Meyers, Mrs. Louis Goldsmith, Mrs. Leo Katz, Mrs. Louis Sulzbacher, Mrs. Mat Levy, Miss Carris Goldsmith, Mrs. Lee Newman, Miss Daisy Rosenbloom, Mrs. Jacob Blattner, Mrs. Louis Bachman, Miss Pauline Blum, Julia Brown, Mrs. J. K. Fisher, Mrs. H. Friedberg.

The first officers were: President, Mrs. Lee Newman; Vice President, Mrs. Harry Friedberg; Treasurer, Mrs. Joe Lubic; Secretary, Mrs. Daisy Rosenbloom.

The present officers are: President, Mrs. Hattie Meyers; Vice President, Mrs. Wm. Gershuny; Secretary, Mrs. Samuel J. Beedeman; Treasurer, Mrs. Mat Levy; Chairman of Relief, Mrs. Lena Hechtman and Chairman of Membership, Mrs. Mildred Fisher.

Braddock Lodge No. 833, Benevolent & Protective Order of Elks, was instituted in Turner Hall, November 19, 1903, with a membership of eighty-one (81).

The instituting officers were: D. D. G. Exalted Ruler F. T. McAllister, assisted by P. D. D. G. E. R. Chas. W. Ashley (deceased) of Homestead Lodge, and Elks of prominence from all the lodges of Western Pennsylvania.

The first regular meeting was held in Braznell Hall, November 27, 1903 with Exalted Ruler T. G. Aten, presiding, assisted by the following corps of officers: W. B. Connelly, Esteemed Leading Knight; E. D. Nugent, Esteemed Loyal Knight; L. L. Todd, Esteemed Lecturing Knight; C. H. Sheets, Tiler; R. S. Maggini, Esquire; John L. Colmery, Inner Guard; Thos. L. Larimer, Outer Guard; Rev. J. A. Burgoon, Chaplain; J. L. Daugherty, Organist.

The present officers are: H. H. Keller, Exalted Ruler; Jas. L. Quinn, Esteemed Leading Knight; Joseph A. Bumbera, Esteemed Loyal Knight; E. J. Spigelmire, Esteemed Lecturing Knight; Frank McCallen, Secretary; Will Sullivan, Treasurer; Philip Roderus, Tyler; Peter G. Canfield, Esquire; Thos. J. McCarthy, Inner Guard; John A. Lancaster, Chaplain; L. F. Holtzman, Fred C. Lou, Thos. E. O'Conner, M. J. Nugent, Samuel Markle and John J. Keller, Trusteees.

Capt. W. R. Jones Camp, No. 218, Penna. Division, Sons of Veterans, U. S. A.

This camp was mustered in March 19, 1904, by Past Commander W. R. Wilhide of Camp No. 162, assisted by the officers of Camp No. 33 of Allegheny.

Among those present were the following members of Major A. M. Harper Post 181, Grand Army of the Republic of Braddock, Pennsylvania: William Bennet, A. L. Corovance, W. A. Thompson, H. B. Rigby, Joseph Steele, G. E. Dean, John Oskin, Sr., H. J. Shamlee, Jac. Hanns, Robert H. Holmes, Joseph Cruikshank, Charles Hugo, Sr., Henry Frank, W. J. Redman.

The charter members of this Camp were:

M. F. Oates, O. P. Benson, J. T. Hillman, G. Redman, J. H. Sherman, C. McCauley, F. D. Eifley, J. L. Alexander, G. Shearer, W. L. Burress, J. C. Hugo, I. J. Parsons, J. W. Milliken, C. Oates, A. H. Cargo, A. J. Fisher, I. D. Berlin, J. Oskin, Jr., W. F. Woomer, G. A. Thompson, W. Griffith, P. J. Qualey, S. Q. Berlin, W. Shea, J. Q. Davis, R. C. Warner, H. G. Hart, G. S. Jones, C. S. Burres, A. W. Eifey, E. J. Griffith, John Spangler.

From whom the following officers were chosen: Commander, I. J. Parson; Senior Vice Commander, Michael Oates; Junior Vice Commander, W. E. Griffith; Camp Council, J. W. Milliken, John Q. Davis, A. J. Fisher; First Sergeant, A. H. Cargo; Quarter Master Sergeant, O. P. Benson; Chaplain, Arthur J. Fisher; Sergeant of Guard, J. Q. Davis; Corporal of Guard, S. Q. Berlin; Color Sergeant, P. J. Qualey; Camp Guard, Charles Jackson; Picket Guard, G. W. Thompson; Principal Musician, Charles Burriss.

The present officers are: Commander, Lee H. Gibson; Senior Vice Commander, John T. Bennett, Sr.; Junior Vice Commander, John T. Bennett, Jr.; Patriotic Instructor, Thos H. Snowwhite; Secretary, J. Raymond Hunter; Treasurer, Ira T. Berlin; Chaplain, George H. Gardner; Color Bearer, H. L. Wagner, Sr.; Guide, Harry Jones; Inside Guard, Paul Jones; Outside Guard, Walton Parks; Principal Musician, Robert Bennett; Camp Council, George H. Gardner, T. H. Snowwhite, Paul Jones.

Knights of Columbus, Braddock Council No. 911, was organized November 27, 1904, with forty-seven (47) Charter Members. The following men occupied the offices when the Council was instituted: John A. Loew, Grand Knight; Edward C. Finnin, Deputy Grand Knight; Thomas J. Tierney, Chancellor; John T. Finnin, Financial Secretary; Joseph Tronsberg, Jr., Recorder; M. J. McBride, Treasurer; Chas. C. Miller, Lecturer; Frank A. Riley, Advocate; William Kennan, Warden; John S. Sheekey, Inside Guard; Philip J. Sweeney, Outside Guard; Peter Fey, Frank X. Spitzer and Geo. V. Milligan, Trustees.

The present officers are: Eugene J. Munhall, Grand Knight; William J. Gilmartin, Deputy Grand Knight; John R. McMullen, Chancellor; John W. Ryan, Financial Secretary; Victor G. Wise, Recorder; Frank J. Shuster,

Warden; John T. Finnin, Treasurer; Patrick J. O'Connell, Lecturer; Thomas F. Dougherty, Advocate; James J. Donovan, Inside Guard; James Leech, Outside Guard; Jacob A. Mohr, George Huber and Charles P. Parrish, Trustees.

Braddock Aerie, Fraternal Order of Eagles, was instituted June 23, 1905, with fifty (50) Charter Members. P. A. Killeen was the first Worthy President, P. K. Flannery, Past Worthy President; B. K. Barkman, Secretary and John F. Nugent, Treasurer.

The present officers are: Thos. A. McDonough, Worthy President; John W. Kilburn, Worthy Secretary; J. J. McCarth, Treasurer and Dr. F. K. Whitfield, Physician.

Guards of St. Anthony, Branch No. 821, Polish Na'tl. All., was organized on September 10, 1905, through the efforts of Alex Walewski, Walter Malczewski, and Toney Pater. The Charter was signed by the following: Alex Walewski, Walter Malczewski, Toney Pater, John Kosakouski, Frank Russczyk, Joseph Stick, Frank Lemanski, Boleslaw Ksiezopolski, Leon Podowski, Karl Skarlinski, Leopold Roman, Jan Lucilowski, Tony Pokrzywnicki, Boleslaw Kocmirowski.

The first officers were: Alex Malewski, President; Walter Malozewski, Financial Secretary; Walter Pater, Treasurer; Military Officers, Tony Pater, Major; Alex Malewski, Captain.

The officers at present are: Leon Padowski, President; Walter Malczewski, Financial Secretary; Stanislaw Kolski, Treasurer. Military Officer, Boleslaw Drzewinski, Captain.

"Bethesda" Branch No. 6 of the Evangelical Slovak Ladies Union was organized January 21, 1906 with the following charter members: Elizabeth Valiska, Louisa Balent, Mary Gajdos, Elizabeth Demcak, Mary Cop, Sr., Susie Koren, Sr., Mary Mally, Anna Daniel, Barbara Paukuch, Anna Vagasky, Anna Balent, Susie Havian, Susie Portik, Mary Bobak, Bessie Boor, Anna Galla, Kattie Vdoviak, Mary Liska.

The first officers were: Bessie Boor, President; Mary Gajdos, Secretary; Louisa Balent, Financial Secretary; Anna Daniel, Treasurer.

At present the officers are: Mrs. Mary Sedlak, President; Miss Anna Gajdos, Secretary; Mrs. Louisa Balent, Financial Secretary; Mrs. Bessie Molnar, Treasurer.

Iron City Lodge No. 3 of Independent Order of Sons of David was organized June 11, 1907, with the following Charter Members: Eleck Steiner, Isadore Stanlight, Henry Shermer, F. H. Swartz, Charles Kohot, J. M. Steinetz, Ralph Swartz, Julius L. Zelmonovitz, Adolph Kline,

Lowis A. Lebowitz, Joseph Shaffel, Lowis Schafer, Armole Steinetz, Morris Lefkowitz, Mossen Yossen, Moses Feldman, Lowiz Kline, Meyer Kline, Jacob Swartz, Samuel Markle, William Katz, Bernard Rosenberg and Philip Young. From whom the following were elected: J. M. Steinetz, Ex-President; Henry Shermer, President; Eleck Stanlight, Vice President; F. H. Swartz, Secretary; and William Katz, Treasurer.

The officers at present are: Isadore Ecker, President; Martin Silber, Vice President; J. M. Steinetz, Recording Secretary; Julius L. Zelmanovitz, Financial Secretary, and Max Lazear, Treasurer.

Loyal Order of Moose, Braddock Lodge No. 57, was instituted Oct. 7, 1908, with the following officers: John S. Nichols, Past Worthy Dictator; J. Edgar Little, Worthy Dictator; Horace G. Read, Vice Worthy Dictator; R. G. Ranwolf, Prelate; A. L. Erwin, Sgt. at Arms; H. W. Peters, Inner Guard; Bernard Altman, Outer Guard; James L. Sheekey, George H. House, Samuel Pringle, Trustees; Charles J. Carr, Secretary; George D. Stroup, Treasurer.

The present officers are: Wm. E. Miller, P. W. D.; Frand Woolford, W. D.; Louis F. Shearer, Vice D.; Wm. Allbeck, Prelate; Andrew Kress, Outside Guard; John J. Lawler, Inside Guard; John P. Ruhley, Alvin Flick and F. H. Johnson, Trustees; Thos. Chambers, Treasurer; Charles J. Carr, Secretary.

Modern Woodmen of American, Camp No. 13413, was instituted Nov. 6, 1908, with the following officers: G. S. Jones, Consul; A. A. Schilling, Adviser; A. McCabe, Banker; R. C. Jones, Clerk. The present officers are: L. L. Jones, Consul; C. W. Reader, Past Consul; J. W. Boehm, Adviser; H. A. Burkhart, Banker; O. R. Wilson, Clerk.

St. Joseph's Society No. 449, Polish Roman Catholic Union, was instituted in 1908, with the following officers: Blasius Rodak, Francis Zygrnunt, John Dziadosz, Karl Vcoski, Jacob Pytka.

The present officers are: Ladislav Panek, President; Stanley Glod, Vice President; Stanley Lesniak, Secretary; and Karl Vcoski, Treasurer.

Independent Order St. Luke, Barton Union Council No. 694, was organized in 1908, with fifty-six (56) charter members.

The first officers were: Bertha Howard, W. Chief; Naomi Fleeks, V. Chief; Isaac S. Medlig, W. R. Secretary; Agnes Morris, Financial Secretary; Sadie White, W. Treasurer; Cora Bilhipo, Sr. Cond.; Kitty Jordan, Jun Cond.; John Carter, W. Advocate; Lucy Turner, Inside Sentinel; Mary Taylor, Outside Sentinel; Polly Sims, Keeper Wardrobe; George King, W. Chaplain; Alice Banks, W. Mother.

THE UNWRITTEN HISTORY OF BRADDOCK'S FIELD. 271

The present officers are: Bertha Howard, Degree Chief; Martha Murphy, W. Chief; Anna Brown, V. Chief; Naomi Brown, R. S. and Fin. Secretary; James Kidd, W. Treasurer; Namomi Washington, W. Chaplain; Sarah Holmes, Sr. Conductor; Sarah Christian, Jr. Conductor; Cora Bilhipo, Inside Sentinel; Annie Lewis, Outside Sentinel; Mary Lee, Keeper Wardrobe; Adaline Brown, W. Mother.

Roman and Greek Catholic Slovak Brotherhood of Western Pennsylvania, under the patronage of Saint George, was organized April 18, 1909.

The following Committee was appointed to have the organization incorporated, Stephan Miklusko, John Tomas, Stephan Leskovsky, Joseph Bodnar, Paul J. Jablowsky, Joseph Palchak, M. G. Pivovarnik, M. S. Ondrej, L. J. Kraly, George Kovalyik, John Lukac, Andy Palencar, Steve Ondrej, Andrew Basala, John Kovaly, George Palfy.

The first Supreme Officers were: Joseph Palchak, President; George M. Kalock, Vice President; M. G. Pivovarnik, Secretary; Ladislaus J. Kraly, Financial Secretary; Michael S. Ondrej, Treasurer; Joseph Bodnar, Stephan Miklusko, John Tomas, Stephan Ondrej and Andrew Palencar, Trustees.

The present Supreme Officers are: Rev. George D. Barlock, Chaplain, Ellsworth, Pa.; John Tompos, President, Braddock, Pa.; Andrew Minarcak, Vice President, Duquesne, Pa.; Anna Soboslay, Vice President, Duquesne, Pa.; Andrew S. Hayden, Rec. Secy., Braddock, Pa.; Ladislaus J. Kraly, Financial Secretary, Braddock, Pa.; Joseph J. Semes, Treasurer, Braddock, Pa. The Trustees are: Michael Bendik, Chairman of Auditors, Duquesne, Pa.; Adam Vleek, Donora, Pa.; Anna Straka, Braddock, Pa.; Zuzanna Lukac, Duquesne, Pa.; Andrew Mikalik, Woodlawn, Pa.; Rev. A. Kazincy is President and Emery Mamrak, Secretary of the Literary Committee.

The members of the Supreme Court are: George Eidely, President, Donora; Ella L. Broszo, Braddock; Mary Popovic, Donora; George Fedor, Trafford; Michael Pocatko, Rankin; John Kozusko, Unity Station; Katy Macko, Rankin.

The Roman and Greek Catholic Slovak Brotherhood consists of thirty-eight (38) Branches, twenty-seven (27) of which are in Allegheny County, four (4) in Westmoreland County, four (4) in Washington County, one (1) in Beaver County, one (1) in Mercer County and one (1) in Cambria County.

St. John Society, Branch No. 1, Roman and Greek Catholic Slovak Brotherhood, was organized May 1909, with the following officers: Stephan N. Pollak, President; Stephan Leskoosky, Vice President; John Kovaly, Secretary; John Lukac, Financial Secretary; Joseph Bodnar, Treasurer; John Tomas, Andrew Basala, Trustees; Stephan Hornak, Flag Bearer; Mike Papay, Guard.

The present officers are: Ladislaus J. Kraly, President; John Tomas, Vice President; John Kovaly, Secretary; George Jurko, Financial Secretary; Andrew Basala, Treasurer; Joseph Barbus, George Kraly, Trustees; Joseph Qhelka, Collector of Dues; Mike Papay, George Simchak, Committee of Sick; John Zajac, Captain.

The Polish American Citizen Club, was chartered September 30, 1910. The object of this organization is to teach the Poles how to become American Citizens.

The Organizers were: P. Dudek, A. Krzyzosak, P. Kanarkowski, W. Ulanowicz, J. Stick, St. Ulanowicz, F. Zygmunt, J. Bosinski, M. Jozwiak.

The first officers were: P. Dudek, President; K. Szczesmy, Secretary; P. Kanorkowski, Treasurer.

The present officers are: Koz. Stankiewicz, President; St. Mandela, Vice President; S. A. Kolski, Secretary; P. Kanarkowski, Treasurer; John Polanski and F. Szulc, Directors.

Ladies Auxiliary A. O. H., was instituted May 16, 1912, by Mrs. Louisa Donovan.

The first officers were: Mrs. Louisa Donovan, President; Mrs. Anna Conohan, Recording Secretary; Miss Rose McNeil, Financial Secretary; Miss Louis Kelly, Treasurer.

The present officers are: Mrs. Margaret M. Keefe, President; Mrs. Mary Kennedy, Vice President; Mrs. Clara Niles, Recording Secretary; Mrs. Anna G. Durgan, Financial Secretary; Mrs. Mary Miller, Treasurer.

The Sending of the Holy Ghost, Branch No. 73, of the Evangelical Slovak Union was organized May 19, 1912, with the assistance of Michael Hudak and Martin D. Findak. Following are the officers and charter members: Anna Hudak, President; Sophie Mako, Financial Secretary; Anna Vydareny, Secretary; Susie Sako, Treasurer; Anna Kostelny, Anna Rubansky, Anna Bicijan, Anna Matusik, Susie Ochodnicky, Anna Remias, Elizabeth Balya, Katie Klimek, Susie Kovar, Susie Hamara.

The present officers are: Mrs. Anna Hudak, President; Mrs. Anna Tomka, Secretary; Mrs. Eva Duris-Findak, Financial Secretary; Mrs. Anna Strnatka, Treasurer.

THE UNWRITTEN HISTORY OF BRADDOCK'S FIELD. 273

Knights of St. John, Saint Marys of Mount Carmel Commandery No. 199, was instituted July 7, 1912, with 56 members. The following officers were then elected: John P. Dougherty, President; John J. Hughes, First Vice President; Peter McKeown, Second Vice President; Henry P. Glenn, Recording Secretary; Thomas F. Dougherty, Financial Secretary; George C. Bachhofer, Treasurer; James J. Dunn, John B. De Nardo, Patrick Cody, Daniel G. Eshman, and Michael Torch, Trustees; Michael Torch, Captain; Bartholomew F. Harrigan, First Lieut; Jerry Marcellus, Second Lieut.; Patrick Cody, First Seargent and Frank X. O'Shea, Second Seargent.

The present officers are: George C. Bachhofer, President; Thomas P. Brannigan, First Vice President; Chas. V. Weakland, Second Vice President; Leo. P. Hughes, Recording Secretary; John J. Gollogly, Financial Secretary; John P. Dougherty, Treasurer.

Daughters of Isabella, Braddock Court No. 244, was instituted July 19, 1914, with forty-seven (47) Charter Members from whom the following officers were elected: Mary Holtzman, Grand Regent; Mary O'Connell, Vice Regent; Mary Stinner, Prophetess; Clara Spitzer, Historian; Margaret McBride, Financial Secretary; Mary Wagner, Treasurer; Mary Morgan, Monitor; Rev. Robt. McDonald, Chaplain.

The present officers are: Mary O'Connell, Grand Regent; Helen Brennan, Vice Regent; Marie Escher, Prophetess; Helen Glynn, Historian; Gertrude Duffy, Financial Secretary; Clara Spitzer, Treasurer; Mary Wagner, Monitor; Mary Rutter, Sentinel; Jennie Ryan, Margaret Zorn, Ella Lally, Julia Gordon, Mary Larkin and Lela Ackley, Trustees; Mae Kramer, Organist; Rev. Robert McDonald, Chaplain.

Independent Order Moses Ben Amron Lodge of Braddock.

This order was affiliated with the Independent Order of Free Sons of Juda of New York City until Feb. 4, 1917, when it was re-organized with 426 Charter Members. The officers are: Bernard Swartz, President; Bennie Zeff, Vice President; Julius Zelmanovitz, Recording Secretary; J. M. Steinetz, Financial Secretary; Andrew Shermer, Treasurer.

The "Daughters of the American Revolution" the largest and most influential patriotic society of the world, will in the near future be represented in Braddock by a chapter to be known as the "Tonnaleuka" Chapter of D. A. R. The work of organizing is under the direction of Miss Florence E. Mench, "Chapter Regent." A charter membership of twenty-five is assured.

FIRES AND FIRE-FIGHTERS.

BY HARRY H. KELLY.

The fast-swinging fire bell in the schoolhouse tower clangs brazenly, and sleepy Main Street wakes to life.

Out from the little frame shops and offices hurry shirt-sleeved men carrying buckets. Up the street they run, a curious crowd tailing out behind, boys shouting and dogs barking. Past an orchard stretching away up the slope from the street the bucket-brigade speeds and draws up panting before a frame cottage, the roof smoking and little tongues of flame licking over the shingles. From out the babble of shouts a strong man's voice rises:

"Get in line, men. Clear the way, there".

The shirt-sleeved men form a long line, one end at a well back of the house, the other at a ladder on which perches the tall figure of the man who directs them. The chain of buckets moves swiftly from hand to hand and up to the man on the ladder, who with rhythmic movement slashes the water on the burning shingles and throws the empty bucket over his shoulder, to be caught below as it falls. Five minutes and the fire is out, the wet roof still smoking. The line breaks up into little groups which move slowly back down the shady street towards the single string of stores and offices in the business section. Here and there they linger in amicable gossip while the owner of the house views the damaged roof.

Once again Main street settles down to its interrupted afternoon nap.

The year is 1880. The shirt-sleeved men are bucket-brigaders, the first fire-fighting organization in Braddock.

The brigaders never really organized themselves into an official body, but judged by the standards of the time, their work was efficient. Once, during the fire which swept the planing mill of H. B. Grannis in Penn street, they saved from destruction a tiny frame house standing in an alley 18 feet from the blazing mill, by keeping its roof deluged with water from their buckets. That was the night of September 22, 1880, when the efforts of the brigaders reached their climax. They had fought many fires, most of them small ones, but a few of which caused heavy damage. In their early history, in 1874, they had fought the flames in the planing mill of Joseph B. McCune, but failed to save it. In those days, if the fire secured much headway, nothing could stop its progress until it

THE UNWRITTEN HISTORY OF BRADDOCK'S FIELD.   275

burnt itself out. But this fact never prevented the brigaders from working for hours, carrying buckets of water and dashing them in the face of the flames.

The bucket brigade could not last. With the growth of industry and business following the opening of the Edgar Thomson Steel Works and other mills, the way was paved for a more efficient and powerful organization. The burning of the block between John and Library streets on Braddock avenue in 1884 brought the need of an organized fire department forcibly to the attention of borough citizens. The successful completion of the water works was also a contributing factor in the forming of an organized band for fighting fires.

Thus was the Braddock Volunteer Fire Department organized. It was at the instigation of Isaac Mills, burgess of Braddock, that a public meeting was called on July 1, 1885, for the purpose of forming a volunteer fire department. The preliminary plans were gone into at this meeting, but it was not until July 10, when 40 men met in the borough council chambers, in a two-story brick structure at 728 Braddock avenue, across the street from the present municipal building, that definite action was taken. Seventy-nine members were enrolled, and the following officers were elected: President, Thomas J. Dowler; Vice President, Peter Seewald; Secretary, Daniel J. McCarthy; Treasurer, L. F. Holtzman; Trustees, George L. House, Frank L. Bridges and S. D. Hamilton. At a third meeting, held July 22, James Morrow was unanimously elected the first chief of the department, with A. H. White and Charles Upton as assistants, Zack Oskin, foreman of Hose Company No. 1, Thomas Britt, foreman of Hose Company No. 2, and Henry Fix, foreman of the hook and ladder truck company. The original members of the department were as follows: Zack Oskin, John Lawlor, Charles Arensberg, Frank Wentzel, Patrick Norton, James Black, John M. McKelvey, John Yinger, Patrick Farrell, Patrick Collins, Robert Morrow, Charles Yinger, Daniel McCarthy, Henry Miller, Harry Lewis, John Quinn, Elmer Leech, Al James, James Gorham, John Kinney, William Young, J. C. Riston, T. J. Dowler, T. W. Sharp, Charles Upton, J. K. Fisher, Henry Fix, Samuel Frederick, W. A. McDevitt, James Morrow, H. T. Bruggeman, C. H. Sheets, George L. House, Peter Seewald, L. F. Holtzman, M. J. Dowling, Thomas Britt, L. C. Fritzius, Frank Lewis, W. H. Sharah, Frank L. Bridges, James Collins, Al H. White, C. C. Fawcett, Jacob Katz, James Martin, George R. Fauset, Oscar Dart, George F. House, Washington Lewis, H. C. Teeter, V. C. Knorr, James McCarthy, Mart Flannigan, George Oskin, Jr., Walter

Brown, William Monroe, S. D. Hamilton, Frank Shilling, Fred Opperman, John Mangion, P. McCaulley, James H. Bennett, J. G. Seibert, John Donovan, Patrick Hughes, William H. Miller, Conrad Schilling, George Hoffman, James Dowling, Alfred Carr, J. M. Yarlett, Edward Oskin, Jr., R. E. Spear, A. Dorritz, Samuel Shearer, D. G. Fisher, H. H. Bair and James Phillips. In addition to these, sixty-seven others, whose names are as follows, were added to fill vacancies and to increase the department membership: William Yarlett, David Masters, D. Z. Musselman, William Lapsley, Charles Gourley, W. T. Oskin, Frank Harrop, W. L. Sechler, Albert Oskin, Robert Redman, Frank Redman, Mark L. Kulp, Albert Speidel, Joshua McCune, W. A. McCune, Denny Dowling, Mell F. Riley, George N. Riley, H. C. Teeter, George Dowler, John Little, Dr. E. O. Anderson, C.

BRADDOCK FIRE DEPARTMENT AND MUNICIPAL BUILDING, 1914.
Left to Right—John W. Morris, Chas. D. Barthold, Geo. C. Spangler, and Chief T. K. Martin.

H. Clifford, George W. Day, Dr. E. W. Dean, William Howat, Sr., H. C. Shallenberger, D. L. Miller, A. P. Maggini, A. M. Carlins, John Dinges, E. J. Smail, J. M. Hurley, Adam Appel, George B. Gibson, Fritz Tegethoff, Neal McGinley, John Griffin, Christ Thier, James Purcell, Harry Farr, John Sechler, William Connors, Joseph Riston, William Wymard, Philip Roderus, Jacob Walters, Harry Fleck, Thomas G. Aten, Samuel G. Owens, William C. McAdams, Wilson Packer, E. M. Brackemeyer, Andrew Mercer, George W. Kutscher, D. M. Kier, Thomas Ward, W. W. McCleary, William Lang, Wash Wentzel, A. B. Price, E. J. Hamm, E. S. Bracken, John Dick, Rob A. Hart, John Howard and P. A. Gillen.

A chemical tank, which in action proved something of a failure, was the first piece of equipment to take the place of the buckets of the early fire-fighters. One of the first acts of the new volunteer department was to purchase a two-wheeled hose reel, a four-wheeled hose reel and a four-wheeled hook-and-ladder wagon. This apparatus, all drawn by hand, was housed in a frame addition to the old municipal building. The removal of the department in 1892 to a frame building across the street, situated on property purchased by the borough shortly before and which is now the site of the present municipal building, marked the summit of achievement for the volunteer firemen, but it was also the beginning of the end for them.

The department had now been organized seven years, and had reached a high level of efficiency. The whistle on the water-works at the river bank called out a force of trained fire-fighters whose flying feet carried them in record time to the scene of fire. The department had become one of the centers of the town's activities. An annual ball in winter and a picnic at Kenney's grove in the summer attracted more than local attention. The department numbered many of the most prominent business and professional men. It was the hey-day of the volunteer force.

There are no fires now like the old ones, the surviving members of the Braddock volunteers lament. They tell of the Joseph Wolf fire on July 31, 1890, which started at Twelfth street and Washington avenue and destroyed forty houses, entailing a loss estimated in those days of low values at $75,000. On January 8 of the same year the Grannis planning mill had again been swept by fire, with $15,000 damage. Old members tell of their return one rainy evening from a picnic at Idlewild in Westmoreland county, to be met by the sound of the fire whistle and to turn in and work all night in efforts to save the Protestant Episcopal church in Sixth street and neighboring buildings. Disastrous fires at the Eli Dowler planing mill and the Dawes Manufacturing Company's plant, and scores of smaller blazes, were fought during the ten years of the company's existence.

But the period of popularity and power was fleeting. Soon after the removal of the firemen's headquarters across Braddock avenue, two horses were purchased—innocent cause of the ultimate dismemberment of the company. A four-wheeled hose-reel, the pride of the department, was donated by H. C. Frick of Pittsburgh, prominent steel and iron manufacturer. This necessitated a driver and caretaker who would spend all his time in the service of the department. Upon his selection the firemen divided. There were too many candidates for the job, and with the election of Oliver McMichaels as the first paid driver, the dissension among the members grew to alarming proportions. After that, it was only a matter of time until the department would be made a part of the borough government, with paid employes.

This was the action taken by the Braddock borough council on June 3, 1895, when the first paid fire department in Braddock was created with a membership of six. The department now employs twelve men. Its equipment now consists of two motor-trucks, which supplanted the last horse-drawn apparatus, the hose-reel donated by H. C. Frick and an aerial-ladder truck. The volunteer department's activities automatically ceased with the formation of the paid department. It was never officially disbanded, and remains in existence as an organization today, although the members have not met for more than a score of years.

Almost simultaneously with the termination of the Braddock volunteer department, an organization modelled along the same lines was formed in Rankin. One hundred and fifty borough citizens met in the schoolhouse September 26, 1895, and organized the Rankin Volunteer Fire Department, which is still active and which remains the only fire-fighting force in the borough. The names of 100 men presented for membership were accepted; most of these have continued in the organization ever since, and the total membership at present is 90. The first officers were Jess Illingsworth, President; E. F. McBride, first vice president; Axel Allison, second vice president; C. B. Guttridge, secretary; Thomas Watkins, treasurer; William Sullivan, chief; A. M. Parker, foreman hose cart No. 1, and James Nash, foreman hose cart No. 2. The department owns an auto truck, two fire horses having been sold in 1916, and employs a paid driver.

RANKIN VOLUNTEER FIRE DEPARTMENT.
Left to Right—Lewis Alshouse, assistant chief; David Frederick, driver; Jas. Hughes, Elmer Walters, R. S. Guttridge, Theodore Tierney, Daniel Eshman, Benjamin Remlinger, and Thomas Ludwig.

NORTH BRADDOCK FIREMEN'S CHAMPION RACING TEAM.
Left to Right, Bottom Row—Abel, Christy, Stewart, Sanders, Carrier.
Middle Row—Evertts, Graham.
Top Row—Jones, McKinney, B. Kurt, L. Kurt, Kramer, H. Kurtz, Dorin, Smith, Lungen, Boon, Haffey, McDonald.

The North Braddock Volunteer Fire Department was formed in 1899 by the following men, who acted as the first officers: President, W. J. Vance; vice president, W. R. W. Steiner; secretary, John F.

THE UNWRITTEN HISTORY OF BRADDOCK'S FIELD. 279

Lowers; treasurer, Joseph L. Campbell, Sr.; chief, Clement S. Newton; member of by-law committee, J. O. Jones. The other members of the department at that time were Lee L. Hayden and James Maxwell. Following the division of the borough into three wards, the department was separated into three companies, each housed in its own building. The one auto truck owned by the department, stationed in the central station in the municipal building, Second ward, answers all calls in the borough and covers a district almost as large as any other three boroughs combined in Western Pennsylvania. As in Rankin, the truckdrivers are the only paid members of the department. North Braddock firemen have won numerous trophies and championship cups with racing teams and other crack organizations at the annual firemen's conventions.

One of the first men to take an interest in the Braddock Volunteer Fire Department was William H. Sharah, who was one of the original members. He was the first president of the Western Pennsylvania Fireman's Association, organized in 1894, and has been its secretary for 21 years. He was president of the State Firemen's Association in 1894, and is a member of the International Association of Fire Chiefs. He was born in Port Perry March 24, 1863, and resides at present at 218 Sixth street, Braddock.

None of the local fire departments have ever lost a man while fighting fires.

The fire departments in the boroughs have grown far beyond their original limits. Braddock avenue is no longer a dirt road, covered thick in summer with slack brought from the coal mines back in the hills. The firemen have lost in a large measure their social and political power. Only memories remain of the picnics and balls, the merry-makers ferrying across the Monongahela river or making impressive entries on horseback and in buggies into town on cold winter nights. In Braddock at least, the romance has gone forever from the stern business of fighting fires.

1913—PUNXSUTAWNEY CONVENTION.

Left to Right—Frank Graham, Joe Litzki, Louis Kurtz, John Gindas, John Burke, P. J. O'Connell, J. J. McDonough, J. C. Jones, and Daniel J. McCue.

WOMAN'S ACHIEVEMENTS.
BY MRS. SAMUEL HAMILTON.

"Everything in the world depends on woman."
"The history of woman is the history of the world."

All over the world a change is taking place in the social position of woman. It is not merely the question of political standing—which like prohibition is almost decided—for every sensible person today in our country is quite willing to grant that woman is certainly entitled to vote; but it is rather as an essential agency in all social and civic betterment that this change is most noticeable. Woman's vote is here in a score of states and coming tomorrow in all the rest. Woman has ever been a subject of great and absorbing interest—a problem, a mystery—to man. She has been a great factor in events of the past both good and bad, great and small; and she will be a greater factor in the future. She has been discussed more than any other subject in the world.

How then would it be possible to give a complete history of Braddock for the past one hundred seventy-five years without a chapter devoted to the influence and work of woman! She certainly was man's helpmate in the beginning for that first settler, John Frazier, would never have remained on his tract of land at the mouth of Turtle Creek in 1742 had it not been for Nelly, his bright and happy wife. It was she who encouraged him to remain among the red people instead of returning to Lehigh Valley whence he came. It was she who shared his toil and helped to make the wilderness blossom like the rose.

After his cabin was built, her task was to keep the hearth-fire bright, the home comfortable and to encourage John when his body was tired and his spirits low with the hard toil of the day. Her task was to mould the hearts and lives and shape the character of her little children. Such a task you will agree is the greatest task in the world on account of its far-reaching importance. Transcendently it is above everything in the universe.

Since our topic is woman, we will speak only of the daughters of this pioneer family. Nancy and Marie under the guidance of such a worthy mother were instructed in the arts of sewing, spinning, knitting, dairy-matters and kitchen concerns. Each was possessed of much personal beauty and both were singularly intellectual for those times, having been taught by the wise and learned Tonnaleuka.

So beautiful and attractive was Marie that Dame Rumor says that Washington, stopping to rest at the Frazier cottage on his way to Fort Le Bouf, became so enamored of the fair maiden, that some months later he returned, capitulated, and laid his—heart at her feet. Talk about achievements! was there ever a greater than this?

HOME.

After six decades the Frazier family has disappeared. In 1804 Isaac Mills with his family settled in this region, soon followed by others. In 1852-54 the settlement had more rapid growth and for years woman's influence was felt chiefly in the home. Emerson says, "Men are what their mothers make them", and the mothers of these older inhabitants were anxious, earnest, hard-working, self-sacrificing women who were desirous of having their children succeed in life. Wait until we reach the eternal mountains then read the mothers' names in God's hall of fame and see how many have come from the old town of Braddock.

"The bravest battle that ever was fought,
  Shall I tell you where and when?
On the maps of the world you'll find it not
  'Twas fought by the mothers of men.

Nay not with cannon or battle shot,
  With sword or noble pen,
Nay not with eloquent word or thought
  From mouths of wonderful men.

But deep in a walled up woman's heart
  Of woman that would not yield.
But bravely, silently bore her part—
  Lo, there is the battle field.

No marshalling troops, no bivouac song,
  No banner to gleam and wave;
But oh! these battles, they last so long,
  From babyhood to the grave."

CHURCH.

In 1857 the churches began to rise slowly, very slowly, one after another, until today Braddock is known as the "City of Churches," having no less than forty-four. These church edifices, built mostly of brick and stone with heavenward-pointing spires are monuments, silent yet eloquent monuments, to the perseverance and energy of the earnest women workers of the congregations.

Each brick and stone and spire, had it a tongue, would cry out in trumpet-like tones and triumphantly testify to the desperation, and perspiration with which that anxious, zealous, and over-worked body of women known in church circles as "The Ladies' Aid" had toiled in their behalf. Oh! companions in industry. Think of the sewings, quiltings, concerts, oratorios, musicals, bazaars, suppers, dinners, festivals, lawn-fetes, rummage sales, etc., etc.! Think of the ducks and geese plucked, the turkeys and chickens beheaded. Think of the bread, pies, cakes, puddings, waffles, cranberries, slaw, fried oysters and what not consumed!

Has the Medical Association ever awakened to the *real* cause of Braddock's need for a hospital? Oh, "Ladies' Aid"! A paragraph or a page would never do justice to your long and zealous labors. It would take the pen of an Elliot or a DeStael and a volume the size of a Webster's Unabridged Dictionary to hold a dissertation sufficiently long to extol in proper manner your works.

"We've put a grand addition on the good old church at home,
It's just the latest kilter, with a gallery and dome,
It seats a thousand people, the finest in all the town.
And when 'twas dedicated, why we planked ten thousand down;
That is, *we* paid five thousand, every deacon did his best,
And the Ladies' Aid Society, it promised all the rest.

They'll give a hundred sociables, cantatas, too, and teas,
They'll bake a thousand angel cakes and tons of cream they'll freeze;
They'll beg and scrape and toil and sweat, for seven years or more,
And they'll start all over again for a carpet on the floor.
No it isn't just like digging out the money from your vest,
When the Ladies' Aid gets busy and says, 'We'll pay the rest.'

Of course we're proud of our big church from pulpit up to spire,
It is the darling of our eyes, the crown of our desire;
But when I see the sisters work to raise the cash that lacks,
I somehow feel that the church is built on women's tired backs,
And sometimes I can't help thinking, when we reach the region blest,
That men will get the toil and sweat and the Ladies' Aid the rest."

Aside from helping to erect churches and keep them in repair, the women of Braddock have always been interested in other lines of Christian work, as both the Home and Foreign Missionary Societies will testify. Neither time nor space permits of a description of the work done by these societies.

It is sufficient to say that the work in Braddock is far-reaching and varied. Christ said, "Go ye into all the world and preach the Gospel", and the women of Braddock churches are endeavoring through these organizations to do their part in spreading the Gospel of Christ.

There can be no greater achievement on earth than to do the will of the blessed Master and surely the members of these organizations will hear the words "Well done" for their glad and faithful services in His vineyard.

SCHOOLS.

In 1867 the first school building was located in what is now the First Ward, Braddock, and since that time women have been employed chiefly as teachers. Starting with a faculty of but two teachers—Miss Margaret B. Bell and Miss Eliza J. Mills—Braddock, North Braddock and Rankin have at the present time a corps of one hundred and ninety-three teachers, all but thirteen of whom are women.

It is only about one hundred years since the girls in Massachusetts were sitting on the school house steps listening to their more favored brothers drone their lessons. Later they were allowed to take the boys' places in the school while the latter were needed in gathering in the harvest. But what a marvelous change has taken place in the education of woman in that time!

Who now sneers at the intellect of woman? Who laughs at a blue stocking? Who denies the insight, the superior tact, the genius of woman? What schools are better kept than those taught by woman? Today as a teacher she holds the very first place in all the agencies that make for the betterment of Braddock.

"It is her duty to impart useful knowledge, to train mind and soul and body, to impart pure ideas and high ideals of manhood and womanhood, to transform a mass of untrained children, many of whom are the offspring of a long line of untrained parents, into a nation of men and women able physically, mentally and morally, not only to recognize the deep responsibility of citizenship, but also to contribute their share toward furthering the development of home, of country, and of civilization."

That the teachers of Braddock and North Braddock are performing this work nobly and successfully in the midst of such a heterogeneous people is an assured fact. Their task is a hard one, but they receive the gratitude of a grateful people. Their reward is mainly in a full realization of a great work well done. To be the superintendent of a great industry, or the president of a large bank or corporation is a great achievement, but to be a live, capable teacher is to be a real benefactor of mankind!

W. C. T. U.

To walk the streets of Braddock and count the saloons and wholesale liquor houses at the present day one would not think that this fair city until 1878 had been free from the influence of liquor.

When the great steel mill was planted at the head of Thirteenth

Street, Braddock, it brought with its prosperity man's curse, woman's enemy and the children's educator in vice and crime—the saloon.

The plea of the saloon is well stated in the following stanza:

> "Wanted, some bright boys, full of cheer,
> To stand at my counter as drinkers of beer,
> To fill up the ranks without further delay
> Of the army of drunkards passing away.
> A hundred thousand a year will just supply
> The loss to our trade from the drunkards who die."

A noted evangelist has said, "The saloon is the sum of all villianies. It is worse than war or pestilence. It is the crime of crimes. It is the parent of crimes and the mother of sins. It is the appalling source of misery and crime in the land and the principal cause of its crime. It is the source of three-fourths of its crime and of course it is the source of three-fourths of the taxes to support that crime."

The mission of the saloon is to fill the jails, penitentiaries, insane asylums and other charitable institutions with human derelicts.

Who has to pay the bills? The landlord who does not get the rent because the money goes for whiskey; the butcher, the baker, the grocer, and the charitable persons who take pity on the children of drunkards and the tax-payer who supports the insane asylums and the poor-houses, that the whiskey business keeps full of human wrecks.

In these days when the question of saloon or no saloon is at the fore in almost every community the mind returns to a nation-wide organization known as the W. C. T. U., which had its origin in the great temperance crusade in 1874, and had, yes, still has a very earnest band of workers in Braddock.

There are a few of us who can remember the time when the patient, long-suffering wives and mothers of the drunkards of this country assisted by their sympathizing, but more fortunate sisters, marched in solemn conclave, two by two, into the saloons and offered prayers to God for help in stopping the liquor traffic. The spirits of these brave women were never dampened by the water, beer and whiskey thrown upon them, but often, very often, by the sneers and jeers of friends (?) in the family and church.

Our dear Francis Williard, who was national president of this wonderful body of women from 1879 until her death in 1898 was at the time of the crusade a teacher in the Methodist Female College in Pittsburgh, and was first initiated into the temperance work in a crusade on Weiss's saloon on Market Street, Pittsburgh.

The W. C. T. U. is today the largest society of women in the world managed and controlled by them and having in the United States alone in 1916 a paying membership of 445,000.

The badge of the society is a bow of white ribbon—the motto is, "For God and Home and Native Land". The trysting hour is at noon when white-ribboners all over the world lift their hearts in prayer that God will bless the temperance cause. Today a glance at "the wet and the dry" map of the United States shows that an all-wise God hears that prayer and is answering it. A wonderful illustration of prayer answered!

In 1874 the task seemed so large, so dark, so hopeless, so improbable. Today almost———accomplished.

Braddock's branch of the W. C. T. U. was organized in the Methodist Episcopal Church December 6, 1881, and was composed of the following women:

Mrs. Arvilla Harrop	Mrs. Keziah Boli
Mrs. Sarah Bowman	Mrs. Helen Soles
Mrs. Elmira Scritchfield	Mrs. J. T. Riley
Mrs. Virginia Riston	Mrs. E. Robinson
Mrs. Sue G. Kulp	Mrs. Ellen Jones
Mrs. Mark Bennett	Mrs. S. Reynolds
Mrs. Flora Lewis	Mrs. Joseph McCune
Mrs. Rachel Clay	Miss Eliza Mills
Mrs. Kate Treese	Miss S. Parker
Miss Eliza Henning	Miss R. Stephens
Miss B. Sharp	Miss A. Seddon
Miss O. Bryan	Mrs. W. Murdough
Mrs. G. Sherwin	Miss Sue Lytle

Meetings were held in Braddock's first bank building at the head of Tenth Street and Braddock Avenue.

Mrs. J. F. Riley, Mrs. E. Robinson, Mrs. Joseph McCune were the first three presidents in order named. Mrs. S. Bowman and Mrs. Rachel Clay were secretaries. Mrs. Arvilla Harrop was the treasurer. The first state convention was held in Pittsburgh December 15, 1881.

This body of women working under great, very great difficulties, received very little recognition from the Braddock people. At that time the cause for which they were working seemed a losing one. Being in sore straits for funds, a committee composed of Mrs. Harrop, Mrs. Clay and Mrs. Bowman called upon Mr. Thomas Carnegie to ask his assistance.

"A friend in need is a friend indeed." He proved this friend by giving them $300 at this time. Later he sent them $200, telling them to call upon him whenever they were in need. This they did many times over, and in his death they lost a very loyal friend.

What can be said of the work of these women? "By their works, ye shall know them." In the pursuance of the "Do Everything" policy, these women sewed for, and clothed the poor, made naked by King Alcohol; fed the hungry, made so by the same cause; nursed the sick and housed the homeless. They carried petitions year after year, against licensing liquor houses. Oh, the need of woman suffrage! In 1889, thinking to get the people awakened to the importance of temperance, they brought Francis Murphy to the town for a six weeks' campaign, and at its close The Blue Ribbon Society had control of the temperance work in the town.

In 1909 the W. C. T. U. comes again to the front in the temperance work. Re-organized through the efforts of Mrs. Bowersox and Rev. Quick, it now has a membership of sixty women from all the church denominations.

President—Mrs. Donaldson
Secretary—Mrs. Zuerner
Corresponding Secretary—Mrs. Speer
Treasurer—Mrs. Holden

These women visit the sick and crippled throughout the town and hold religious services on Saturday afternoon in the Braddock Hospital. They assist in the maintenance of the "Providence Rescue Home" on Mount Washington—a very worthy institution. Temperance literature to the amount of 3,000 pages a month has been circulated by them and they have just furnished a room in the new hospital at a cost of $100. These worthy women are constantly doing deeds of kindness and acts of mercy too numerous to mention, proving themselves worthy active members of the great W. C. T. U.

Have the women working in the cause of temperance throughout the nation achieved anything worth while? One glance at the map on the following page answers the question.

Remember "In union, there is strength". This valiant band of organized women press zealously forward. Each branch, supplying its quota of good work for the temperance cause: knowing that "Love beareth

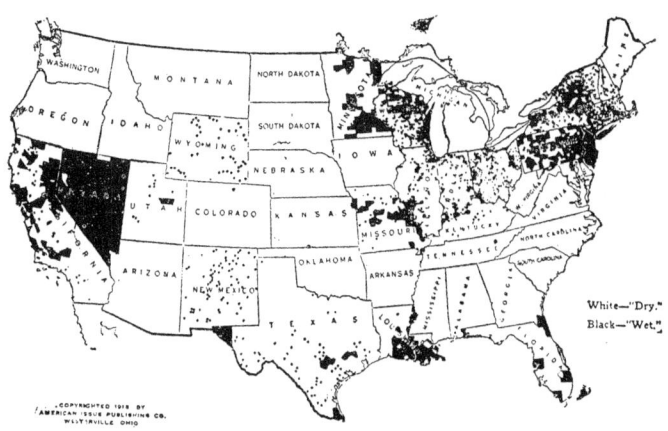

all things; believeth all things; hopeth all things; endureth all things;" and that if they continue in their good works, the great annalist of the future dipping her pen in the sunlight of humanity and love shall write in the clear blue side-by-side with the name of this great and glorious nation one word—SALOONLESS.

A SALOONLESS NATION, IN 1920.

'Twas an inspiration of divine creation,
  When the Christian throng decreed,
That this boon of heaven, unto mortals given,
  Be from liquor's bondage freed,
That this land of plenty be in nine-teen-twenty,
  In the name of Christ our King,
A saloonless nation, it's a proclamation,
  Hear the joyful millions sing.

G. A. R. HOME.

On the north side of the Pennsylvania Railroad at Hawkins Station stands a large commodious building known as the G. A. R. Home. This Home was erected and dedicated to the indigent mothers, wives, sisters and daughters of the honorably dismissed soldiers of the Grand Army of the Republic by the women of the G. A. R.

This valuable property has from its erection been a quiet and inviting refuge for the helpless, bereft, or decrepit women whose claim for admission has been the relationship held to a veteran of the Civil War. The Home was founded with the express desire to prevent the descendent of a soldier's family from ever crossing the threshold of an almshouse in this nation which was ransomed by their blood.

In 1890 the Stahl Homestead at Hawkins was purchased for the nominal sum of $9,500. It was furnished and equipped, and on June 28, 1890 was dedicated with imposing ceremonies. Immediately it was used for the purpose intended—a haven of rest. On Thanksgiving Day, November 28, 1890 five soldiers' widows and one soldier's mother (four of whom were from the Allegheny County Poor House) ate their Thanksgiving dinner in this Home as guests of the women of the G. A. R. With growing demands the institution has been enlarged and improved until now it houses one hundred ten inmates and is valued at $75,000.

To the women of the G. A. R., and particularly to those of Major A. M. Harper Circle No. 4 of Braddock, and to Mrs. Elmira Scritchfield, Mrs. Sue Kulp, and Mrs. Ella Soles may be ascribed the credit of seeing this laudable movement launched and carried to its consummation. The work of the Braddock Circle is strenuous and is ever on the increase, since only a small membership remains from the long list of early years. The needs of the Home are a life work for this small band of earnest workers.

Annually these women have conducted a supper on the lawn of the Home at which from 500 to 600 people are fed on provisions donated from Braddock homes entirely. The solicitation of this food and the giving of the dinner demand not only energy but forethought and executive ability on the part of the members of this Circle. Through their efforts a donation of food is received each year from Braddock, North Braddock and Rankin schools. All goes for the maintenance of the Home and is a wonderful help.

The foregoing does not show the limitation of work done by the Circle. This band of women knows no limitation in its line of service. A cry for help is never unheeded; whether it be for a basket of groceries, or days and nights of strenuous activity in dire disaster or smaller aids in kindness and sympathy.

Achievements! This home stands an eloquent monument to the enterprise as well as womanly patriotism of this band of willing workers who conceived the idea and carried out its consummation. To the women of the G. A. R. and to the Braddock women in particular we pay grateful tribute for upholding the honor of this patriotic order and perpetuating its memory in such an institution.

WOMAN'S CLUB.

In 1894, a few years after the Carnegie Library had been built, two townswomen, Mrs. A. B. Stevenson and Mrs. A. W. Schooley, in conversation as to the benefit of the library to the community bethought themselves that a woman's club in connection with the same might prove not only a benefit to women, but indirectly one to the town.

At their suggestion, Mrs. Edwin Anderson, wife of the librarian, called a meeting at her home on North Avenue for the purpose of organizing a literary club for the women of Braddock.

On February 12, 1894, the following women met in the parlors of Mrs. Anderson's home and organized a club which after twenty-three years still lives and is known as the Woman's Club of Braddock.

Charter Members:

Mrs. Edwin Anderson
Mrs. A. B. Stevenson
Mrs. A. W. Schooley
Mrs. Adah Preusse
Mrs. Richard Stevens
Miss Louisa Addenbrook
Miss Minnie Dinkey

Mrs. James Gayley
Mrs W. Morrow
Mrs. W. Lapsley
Mrs. A. M. Scott
Mrs. R. M. Holland
Miss Maggie Lukens
Miss Elizabeth Corey

Mrs. A. J. Spigelmire

At a second meeting held in the home of Mrs. Adah Preusse on Holland Avenue a constitution and by-laws were adopted, a program for study selected and the following officers elected:

President, Mrs. Edwin Anderson
Vice President, Mrs. James Gayley
Secretary, Miss Louisa Addenbrook
Treasurer, Mrs. A. J. Spigelmire

This club, being the only literary club in the Monongahela Valley for several years, grew in size, admitting members from Turtle Creek, Edgewood, and Wilkinsburg, and the interest aroused in the study of good literature cannot be over-estimated. "Give a person this taste and the means of gratifying it, and you can hardly fail of making him a happy person. You place him in contact with the best society in every period of history, with the wisest, the wittiest, the tenderest, the bravest and the purest characters which have adorned humanity."

One day during each club year was known as "Visitors' Day". Each member was permitted one guest and a varied and delightful program was rendered followed by a social hour. As other clubs began to organize in the neighboring towns, the officers of these clubs were also invited and thus the meeting grew in size and importance.

The Club joined the State Federation in 1899 and the National Body in 1900. Delegates to these conventions always returned with enthusiastic reports of civic work which was being accomplished in various parts of the state and this aroused the members of the Woman's Club to the fact that a purely literary club is more or less a selfish one benefitting the members and their friends only, and that a true civic spirit inculcated into the same would make it of greater benefit to the community.

On one memorable "Visitors' Day" the entire membership of the neighboring clubs was entertained in Carnegie Library and from this meeting arose an organization known as "The Federated Clubs of the Monongahela Valley". (1900) This Federation was entertained by one of the sister clubs each year; a general program was presented and civic affairs were freely planned and discussed. This organization grew in size and importance, and, when "The Congress of Clubs of Western Pennsylvania" was formed in Pittsburgh, "The Federated Clubs of the Monongahela Valley" disbanded in its favor, but the civic spirit it had fostered grew, and what is more conducive to good in a community than a true civic spirit?

No adequate idea can be given of the work that is being done by clubs, and societies of women—scholarships established, hospital beds endowed, traveling libraries started, sewing and cooking schools maintained, day-nurseries supported, schoolrooms decorated, nurses supplied to the poor, playgrounds established, clean-up days organized, birds cared for, yard improvement encouraged, all, all for the betterment of the community; for intellectual and moral growth—*not one for graft.*

When Braddock was laid out (if it ever was, one thinks from the look of it that it just "growed") no thought was ever given to parks or breathing spots for the poor of the congested districts. The yards are small where there are yards and we are sorry to say there are sections where there are no yards. Playgrounds, therefore, are very necessary in a city like Braddock. His Satanic Majesty is just as busy today as ever in finding mischief for idle hands to do. Play is a safe guard against crime; therefore the children should be given places in which to romp and play.

GIVE THEM A PLACE TO PLAY!

"Plenty of room for dives and dens (glitter and glare and sin!),
Plenty of room for prison pens (gather the criminals in!),
Plenty of room for jails and courts (willing enough to pay!)
But never a place for the lads to race; no, never a place to play.

Plenty of room for shops and stores (Mammon must have the best!),
Plenty of room for the running sores that rot in the city's breast!
Plenty of room for the lures that lead the hearts of our youth astray,
But never a cent on a playground spent; no, never a place to play!

Plenty of room for schools and halls, plenty of room for art;
Plenty of room for teas and balls, platform, stage, and mart.
Proud is the city—she finds a place for many a fad today,
But she's more than blind if she fails to find a place for the boys to play!

Give them a chance for innocent sport, give them a chance for fun—
Better a playground plot than a court and a jail when the harm is done!
Give them a chance—if you stint them now, tomorrow you'll have to pay
A larger bill for a darker ill, so give them a place to play!"

In 1909 the Woman's Club decided that the children of the town should have a public playground. The public was aroused to the need through the press, but playgrounds cost money; and alas! no open-hearted, open-handed philanthropist appeared. The women cast about them, but there was neither a Hetty Green nor a Mrs. Russell Sage in their midst. Recalling that Goethe says "Energy will do anything that can be done in the world", they girded their loins and started forth to secure the playgrounds.

A little button bearing the sweet face of an unkempt child and the words, "Wanted—a playground" was the scheme adopted. 'Twas only a button—a little button! But it was truly wonderful the way in which that sweet face crept into the hearts of the people and the way in which the buttons appeared upon their coats signifying their sympathy with the movement. Under the guidance of the teachers, thousands of these buttons disappeared in the hands of the school children. The playground idea appealed to them. Where is the child who does not love to play?

At the close of the button campaign, the shekels were counted. Lo! there were five hundred and thirty-five dollars—almost enough to equip and run a playground for the summer. An entertainment given by Mr. and Mrs. Cartwright in Carnegie Hall netted $100. Each member of the Woman's Club subscribed five dollars and the following donations were solicited:

Sand	Carnegie Steel Co.
Sand Boxes	Braddock Lumber Co.
	McBride Lumber Co.
Swings	Mrs. Allen Kirkpatrick
Balls	Roderus and Klaban
Baskets	Katz and Goldsmith

Thus fortified the women hired a superintendent and two assistant teachers and for six weeks six hundred children played to their hearts' content under the supervision of these trained teachers and the club women, upon the grounds of the First Ward School in Braddock. That was real labor for the club women, but they closed with the determination to have two playgrounds the following summer. Playgrounds had come to stay.

> "Still humanity grows dearer
> Being learned the more."

The next summer (1910) the Club took care of two playgrounds—one in North Braddock and one in Braddock; in 1911, two in North Braddock and two in Braddock; in 1912, two in North Braddock and two in Braddock; in 1913, three in North Braddock and two in Braddock. Please take notice that the movement, like Topsy, just naturally "growed".

Now there are two important questions:—How much did the playgrounds cost? Where did the Club get the money? The cost in money was $2,391.47. The cost in physical strength, in mental labor and in time cannot be estimated. The members of the Club gave freely of all. The civic committee, which was composed of Mrs. Vankirk, Mrs. Ida Morgan, Mrs. A. M. Scott deserves great praise for its earnest and exhaustive labors.

Where did the money come from? Buttons, entertainments and personal contributions were the sources of wealth. The School Boards worked side-by-side with the women and rendered splendid financial assistance.

At the close of 1913, the Club felt that the work of development was finished, that they had succeeded in awakening the people and the Boards of Education in both boroughs to the importance and necessity of the playground activities and that the time was now ripe to hand it over to the School Boards, where the whole movement properly belonged. The Boards accepted the trust and have taken excellent care of the movement. The Club, however, shall always be proud of its child and wish it long life and prosperity.

"Clean-Up Day" was the next thing attempted by the women. "Free Ride to the Dump" drew the usual crowd. The way those Braddock alleys and cellars belched forth their germ-laden contents was truly appalling. The City Fathers had consented to haul the rubbish free of charge and it took weeks and weeks to do it. Cost? The cost of playgrounds is but a trifle in comparison.

The Woman's Club has ever been mindful of the hospital and its needs. For years it had donated $10 for Christmas decorations and has helped with decorative work. In 1917 they donated $367 to furnish the maternity ward and expect in the future to undertake the up-keep of the same. These things have been done and many others planned for Braddock's welfare by this band of optimistic workers. Blessed optimism! that amid all the short-comings of human nature sees the best, lifts souls upward and helps to make the world sunny by its singing:

> "When a bit of sunshine hits ye,
>   Glancing sidewise from a cloud;
> When a bit of laughter gits ye,
>   And your spine is feelin' proud,
> Don't forget to up and fling it
>   At a soul that's feelin' blue
> For the minute that you sling it,
>   It's a boomerang to you".

Captain Jack Crawford's conclusion is correct. The optimism that cheers others onward and upward is always a boomerang of blessing and helpfulness to the individual who embodies it.

This is an age of clubs—clubs for the rich; clubs for the poor; clubs for pleasure; clubs for profit. Some clubs are a blessing to a community; others are a curse. Some are are a hindrance; some are a help. For the Woman's Club of Braddock, there is but praise. Its doctrine is to help, not to hurt humanity. It's not a printed, but a living gospel—the art of right living. Can there be greater achievement than this?

> "They talk about a woman's sphere as though it had a limit
>   There's not a place in earth or heaven
>   There's not a task to mankind given,
> There's not a blessing or a woe,
> There's not a whisper yes or no,
>   There's not a life or birth,
>   That has a feather's weight of worth,
> Without a woman in it".

"Sow good services; sweet remembrances will grow from them."
—Madam DeStael.

BRADDOCK HOSPITAL.

While we will concede to man the credit of first suggesting a hospital in Braddock, we will have to maintain that without the enterprise, courage, indomitable will, and persistent energy of the Braddock women, it would now be a thing unknown.

Mrs. Thomas James, Mrs. Scritchfield and Mrs. Treese were the trio of our town's women to whom credit must be given for taking the preliminary steps in organizing the work for the Braddock Hospital.

From the pulpits of the various Braddock churches went forth a call that all women interested in a hospital movement should meet at the home of Mrs. Thomas James, Parker Avenue, October 15, 1894.

At this meeting the enterprise was fully discussed and it was decided to have a hospital. A second meeting was called at the home of Mrs. James October 21, 1894. At this meeting a society known as the

Braddock Hospital Association was formed, and the following officers were elected:

President, Mrs. Jennie Lapsley,
Secretary, Mrs. Rachel Clay,
Treasurer, Mrs. Al Maggenni,
Financial Secretary, Mrs. A. W. Schooley.

A charter was applied for and received through the kindness of the late Major R. E. Stewart. This charter reposes today in the new safe in the Braddock General Hospital and bears the following names in mute testimony of their good works:

Florence Murto Bell	Jennie Scott Lapsley
Gertrude Roberts Carothers	Kate W. Treese
Mary K. Collingwood	Mary J. Holtzman
Elmira Scritchfield	Margaret Kramer
Elizabeth James	Susan C. Kulp
Mary M. Schooley	Margaret Bell Scott
Virginia Riston	Kate McIllfried

Caroline Markle Stewart

"So shines a good deed in a naughty world".

After the organization, there came the struggle for existence. The women discussed ways and means whereby they could earn enough money to build and equip a hospital where the men injured in the mills could be properly and quickly cared for.

"When pain and anguish rive the brow,
A ministering angel thou——".

Hundreds of Braddock women were interested and for a time all went well. Everyone was anxious and willing to work. The first effort—a bazaar in Turner's Hall—netted the sum of $4,500. Entertainments of various kinds—concerts, waffle-suppers, lectures, lawn-fetes—followed each other in rapid succession until the ladies had in hand the sum of $10,000, no mean sum, but only a drop in the bucket to buy a building and equip it as an up-to-date hospital. Interest in the scheme began to wane. One by one the enthusiasts dropped off until a faithful nine remained—Mesdames Schooley, Scritchfield, Kulp, James, Newman, Kelley, King, Steinmetz and Treese.

Rumors were abroad that the undertaking was too gigantic, that the town would never be able to care for it and that the money on hand had better be used for another purpose, but these faithful few said, "No! we will keep the money for the purpose intended".

They selected the following officers:
President, Mrs. Schooley,
Vice President, Mrs. Scritchfield,
Secretary, Mrs. Kulp,
Treasurer, Mrs. James.

For nine years this little Gideon band met regularly once a month in the parlors of Mrs. Schooley, transacted what little business there was, kept the money well invested and so managed to keep the little spark of love for maimed and unfortunate humanity still burning.

"Persistency! thy name is woman."

About 1903 the Braddock Medical Association awoke to the fact that Braddock was sorely in need of a hospital and while they had been dreaming, their sisters were clad in armor and forth to the fight had gone. Realizing as never before that a place in the ranks awaited them, and in fact awaited every man in Braddock, if the desired object was to be obtained, they succeeded in getting the Board of Commerce to throw off its lethargy and together they started in pursuit of their more progressive sisters and by forced marches were able to overtake them.

A committee called upon the women to see what agreement could be made and learned that the women would very gladly co-operate, providing the men would donate an equal sum of money to the cause and give the women representation on the Board of Managers of the hospital.

Three committees were appointed for the purpose of adjusting matters:

Braddock Hospital Association—Mesdames James, Schooley, Scritchfield, Newman and Kelley.

Braddock Medical Association—Doctors Morgan, Nicholls, Miller, Rubenstein and Fisher.

Board of Commerce—Messrs. George Hogg, George Moore, D. F. Collingwood, L. A. Katz and H. J. Learn.

As a result of the meeting of these committees the Braddock Hospital Association disappeared and the Braddock General Hospital Association was born with a Board of Managers consisting of fifteen people, five of whom were women.

When the Braddock Hospital Association was disbanded, the members organized into an Auxilliary to the board of managers of Braddock General Hospital in order to continue their work and to place their five members each year as co-workers on the board of managers.

At the time the building was equipped, the members of this Auxiliary worked two or three days each week under the direction of Miss Weir, Superintendent of the Hospital, sewing bed-fittings, muslins, gowns, table linen, etc. The material had been purchased from the merchants of the town at cost thereby saving many dollars; it was paid for with money from the treasury of the Auxiliary. Aside from the work they did, the women of the Auxiliary have made cash donations amounting to $2,698.59.

The women of Braddock have given to the hospital up to date the following sums:

    $11,500.00 earned by women.
    2,500.00 donated by Rachel Clay.
    2,698.59 earned by Auxiliary.

$16,698.59

This money so zealously kept was after many years used for the purpose for which it was earned—a building in which suffering humanity could be nursed. That building, erected on Holland Avenue, devoted to the care and healing of the sick, stands a monument to these few, brave, persistent women who "hewed to the line no matter where the chips fell" and remained true to their convictions—that Braddock did need and must have a hospital. They wish no blare of trumpets for their humane acts. Their work is sufficient praise.

The entrance of woman into public life has taken place within the last thirty years and is gaining a momentum whose ultimate force cannot be prophesied.

That she is a human being, as well as a woman, and must have duties as such toward human beings outside of her own home circle, and toward her town and community, has proved a blessing to the world, and has been the cause of great social reforms.

    Who first started prison reform? Elizabeth Fry.
    Who aroused the world against slavery? Harriet Beecher Stowe.
    Who led the temperance reform? Frances Williard.
    Who organized the first Women's College? Mary Lyons.
    Who was "The Angel of Crimea"? Florence Nightingale.
    Who organized the Red Cross Society? Clara Barton, etc. etc. etc.

That she has intellectual ability as well as duties to humanity and that she ranks high in many of the pursuits of life are self-evident. One of the greatest writers in political economy since Adam Smith was a woman. The greatest novelist in England, since Thaceray, was a woman. One of the greatest writers in astronomical science was a woman. In art she ranks second to none, as the names of Rosa Bonheur and Harriet Hosmer testify. One of the greatest financiers of the twentieth century was a woman. Some of the ablest rulers of the world have been women, as the names of Elizabeth, Catharine II, and Victoria recall.

President of this country? Why not? If for any reason at some future time the country finds any one woman particularly fitted to be President, there is no reason why she should not rule as queens have ruled.

The wife of William Penn assumed the management of colonial affairs after his death, executed the task with tact and business capacity. Watson says, "She became in fact our governor, ruling us by her deputies or lieutenant governors during all the term of her children's minority."

If women were to govern the world's affairs in place of men, it would without doubt in most cases be done well.

This is an age of woman. There have been and still are great changes to be made in the status of woman, as this great war is going to show. There are great advantages to come from woman having power and voice in the affairs of the world.

What other women have done Braddock women can do! There is not a better class of women in the world—noble, intelligent, conscientious, self-sacrificing, willing women, alert to the needs of the day! That woman has borne an equal share of the burden of Braddock's development none can deny; that she leads in the progress that ennobles the life of the borough all must admit; that her great interest in her home and its youth and the moral welfare of her city will produce giant strides in social uplift in the future, we prophesy. In a word woman is Braddock's best gift— "man's joy and pride in prosperity; man's support and comfort in affliction".

THE EVOLUTION OF LOCAL BUSINESS.

BY CHARLES ROSE.(1)

At the very beginning of this article, we wish to state clearly that its purpose is purely historical, and consequently has absolutely no advertising object connected with it. Since the history of any community's commercial development is largely the story of the various business enterprises of its residents, many names of individuals and firms, must necessarily be mentioned. Quite likely many names that ought to be here are omitted because of lack of space, as well as lack of definite data concerning them. Furthermore, the stores spoken of are not discussed because they are or were certain stores, but because their appearance in or disappearance from the district indicates to a degree the evolving necessities and changed or changing demands and requirements of the trading public, much as a barometer evidences the varying conditions of the atmosphere.

To find the beginning of business in this district, we must go back to the middle of the eighteenth century, when some adventurous traders made their way over dangerous trails from Philadelphia to the westward of the Alleghanies, to trade with the Indians. As the red men, becoming dependent upon civilization, grew accustomed to certain articles furnished by the itinerant merchants and as more settlers moved into the district, it became apparent to the astute traders that a permanent trading post might be profitably established. The French had early chosen the junction point of the Monongahela, Allegheny, and Ohio rivers as an advantageous business as well as military position. After the French and English territorial disputes had been settled, more of these posts were placed at what were regarded as likely places. Most of these frontier stores were fairly well fortified in case some undesirable customers on the war path appeared, their frescoed countenances fairly equaling the most striking facial effects accomplished by our modern devotees of the paint pot, and making their presence known by a noise somewhat resembling the circus calliope. These undignified and unprofitable interviews with the redskins occurred about as frequently in the early days as automobile bandit hold-ups occur now, but the gradual increase in population made them, after a while, a matter of history.

---

(1) Mr. Rose, the longest time merchant now doing business in Braddock, furnished much of the material for this chapter from early reminiscences. The story was written by Wm. J. Aiken, Esq., and Mr. Geo. H. Lamb.

Besides the early trading post at Pittsburgh, another was located at the mouth of Turtle Creek on the Monongahela River, near old Port Perry, the exact point being now covered by railroad yards incident to the Edgar Thomson Steel Works. Another held forth further up the river near where Brownsville is today. The post at Port Perry and the post at Pittsburgh were the centers of trade for this immediate valley. For many years the town of Port Perry, on account of the commercial impetus given it by this early trading post, as well as on account of its superior location to the neighboring villages, kept most of the business. As late as 1820, people for many miles around went either to Pittsburgh or to Port Perry to do their marketing. The settlers in Braddock's Field, the settlers across the river and from all directions, bought their salt, sugar, tea, coffee, gun-powder, tobacco, and nails at Port Perry.

Twenty-five years before the Civil War, Braddock's Field was a country village straggling along the township road parallel with the river. The houses of the village, for the most part, were located near the road. The land between the road and the river was mostly swampy, but when drained, made good farm soil. It was fertile, furnished good pasturage for cattle, and made several orchards famous for their excellent fruit. North of the road, the land sloped upward to the large farms that spread over the hills. By 1845, these farms were noticeably smaller in area and houses were more numerous. The hillsides soon became dotted with dwellings and the dusty township road, forming the main street in the village below, now and then took on an active business air. As the village grew, more highways were necessary to accomodate the growing population and those who could make their living in town built their houses in more or less regular order upon certain fairly well defined streets, and the one time farmers began to lay out plans of lots. By the time recruiting began for the Rebellion, Braddock had acquired the appearance of a prospering town and contained enough people to support a diversified class of stores. The township road then and long afterwards called Main Street, now known as Braddock Avenue, has remained the principal business thoroughfare. Most of the stores were located between what are now Ninth and Eighth Streets. Very few were successful above Ninth and any located much below Eighth were regarded as too far out of town. No stores had appeared amongst the scattered dwellings on the hills, and Copeland was still in the country.

Like all country towns, Braddock's first store was of that general type where the farmer lad could bring a few dozen of eggs, some butter, a load of potatoes, or some corn, and either receive cash in exchange or trade for anything from a pocket knife, a whetstone, or a pound of sugar, to a suit of clothes. While the salesman, who was also proprietor, as well as political prophet of the community, was weighing out the sugar, his customer might slip into the back room where the heavy scales and numerous barrels were kept, and there try on a pair of jeans. The village belle, whose tastes in fashion could not be satisfied with the conservative calicoes, ginghams, and roomy shoes handled in town, had to go to Pittsburgh, traveling by stage-coach or by river packet, unless the family possessed their own conveyance.

The blacksmith shop in combination with a wagonmaking business was always busy, but never rushing. The ringing anvil and the flying sparks fascinated many a boy whose swelling ambition filled his dreams at night with vision of himself as a brawny bare-armed man, applying a hot shoe and sniffing smoke from the singeing hoof. There was no hurry around the shop. The farmer who had taken a load of grain to the packet for shipment to Pittsburgh, left his team to be shod. No hurry to get back to the farm. Besides, acquaintanceship must not suffer just because he did not live in the crowded town. His favorite store usually chosen for the reason that the members of his particular political party gathered there, had to be visited, or perhaps he called at the harness maker's shop to dicker on a set of new harness, or possibly the tavern attracted him. He often visited the livery stable, scenting prospects of disposing of a doubtful horse at a good profit. The tavern and livery stable were frequently combined under the same enterprising management, and sometimes the undertaking business was included with the livery.

The barber led perhaps the easiest life in town. Those were the halcyon days of the grandfathers, when a grandfather was not a real grandfather without a flowing beard, when the young man proudly cultivated the hair on his face, and when mothers used the shears and mush bowl regularly every two months, except in the wintertime, upon the tops of their sturdy sons. Joke-picture artists in the Sunday supplements had not yet set the style for cutting children's hair. A barber who could not play a quadrille or a Virginia reel and call the figures was of little use to the rising village.

It was a common sight in old Braddock to see a herd of cattle, a hundred head or more being driven along the road. There was a slaughterhouse near the river and in these times before the packing house was de-

THE UNWRITTEN HISTORY OF BRADDOCK'S FIELD. 301

veloped every butcher dressed the meat he sold. The meat shop storage room was filled with ice cut from the river in winter. It was the only business house that had much need of ice, but there were a number of private icehouses, all filled in the winter time with ice-blocks cut from the frozen stream. The meat supply was kept alive and killed as the demand arose so that very little of it was stored. Ice was needed only for preserving meat soon to be sold, and the supplies of salt meat did not need ice. Large quantities of salt pork cured in the old fashioned way were brought in by the farmers, and the butchers themselves were always in the market for hogs, sheep, calves, and cattle.

As the town thrived and the opening of the coal mines increased commercial demands, it was apparent that the onetime village was becoming firmly established as a business center. The general stores in the old style gradually ceased to do business and the merchants entered into various separate lines of trade. The following stages always mark commercial progress: first, the general store; second, the diversified stores; third, as the town becomes large and thriving, the last stage is marked by the introduction of the same idea as the general store, but called the department store.

About the year 1869, Braddock was well entered upon its second stage of business development. One evidence of this advance is the fact that William Rose in that year established a shoe business at the corner of Main and Allequippa Streets, now known as Ninth Street. He died in 1877 and the store was run for four years by William Millick, Trustee for the estate of William Rose. In 1881 the present proprietor, Charles Rose, took charge of the business. The following prices of shoes were taken from an advertisement in 1887 of Charles Rose's shoe store: Babies' shoes, 50c; Boys' and Girls' shoes, 75c to $1.50; Men's calfskin boots, $2.50; Men's fine dress shoes, $2.00 to $2.50; Men's working shoes, $1.50 to $2.00; Women's fine shoes, $2.25. It is needless to remark here in this year 1917 that the same goods sell at anywhere from three to five times the mentioned figures.

In the month of February, 1881, Franklin Wentzel began business at the head of Ninth Street on Main Street and moved into his present location in 1887. His catering, confectionery and baking business thrived, showing that the demands of the population had outgrown the meager home necessities of the old town. A. S. Goehring was established in the eighties in the ice-cream business between Tenth and Eleventh Streets on Main Street.

The gustatory requirements of the community are now further cared for by Nill's bakery, an institution of long standing, and by Ellenberger's bakery, a more recent establishment.

In passing, it is necessary to mention Ward's Cafe. This famous restaurant started many years ago in a place so small that it was dubbed the "Hole in the wall". Its present standing reminds one of Mark Twain's etymology of the word restaurant; taurus, a bull, and res, a thing; hence a bully thing. Ward's is known far and wide as the best eating place at moderate prices to be found anywhere—and traveling men always try to "make" Braddock at noon, so as to lunch here. Never closed, the rush between midnight and 2:00 A. M. and again at breakfast is as great as at the noon hour or the evening meal. Mr. Thomas Ward, the popular caterer who established the place and built up the trade, sold out a few years ago and went to California; but his successors, Messrs. John Gaffney and Clark Harding, have kept the place up to the standard adopted in the beginning, and Ward's cafe is still the popular eating place, and is abundant proof that money can be made by serving meals without any bar or other side issues. Other restaurants are the Corey Avenue restaurant, and the Olympia, one of a chain. Some of the hotels also cater especially to the noon day lunch for business men. Among such are the Ebner, Butler, and Opperman hotels.

THE FAMOUS.

THE UNWRITTEN HISTORY OF BRADDOCK'S FIELD. 303

The firm of Katz & Goldsmith,—composed of Leo A. Katz, born in Pittsburgh, Pa., 1857, and Louis J. Goldsmith, born in New York City, 1852,—under the trade name of "The Famous", opened in Braddock at 872 Braddock Avenue, October 12, 1881, in a store twenty by sixty feet, with clothing and men's furnishings. At that time Braddock had no lighting system or water works. The illumination was by lamp light only. The store was lighted by tin pipes suspended from the ceiling filled with kerosene, to which wick burners with lamp chimneys were attached. It was considered the best lighted store in Braddock. Brackets holding lamps illuminated the windows. The store prospered from the start. It was in the early days of the Edgar Thomson Works, with monthly pay days. In a few years they outgrew their quarters and occupied the double store of the Baldridge Building at 871-873 Braddock Avenue, opposite Ninth Street. It was then the largest store in Braddock, with the distinction of having the largest plate glass windows. The business continued to prosper and larger quarters were again needed and an addition was added to the rear. Illuminating gas had been introduced into Braddock and the town felt metropolitan. In a short time larger quarters were again necessary and the Kerr Arcade Building at 807-809 Braddock Avenue was secured in 1893, the year of the panic. New lines were added and the building was altered to meet the ever increasing trade. In 1896-1897 new stories were added and it blossomed out as a Department Store. In rapid succession the Routh property on the west and the Masonic Hall Association Building on the east were acquired and transformed to meet the requirements of a modern department store. In 1914 Josiah L. Goldsmith was admitted to the firm and the firm is thus constituted today. The store's area (when the contemplated changes are carried out) will be one hundred sixty by one hundred twenty feet, three and four stories high with basement, all used for selling, with modern lighting and heating system and a warehouse on Talbot Avenue and Pine Way. The growth of the store typifies the growth of the town probably better than anything else, in the period from kerosene oil to illuminating gas and from the latter to the electric lighting. Lanterns carried by pedestrians was the only lighting in 1881 and when the stores turned out the lights the town was dark indeed.

A good illustration of the old adage "Tall oaks from little acorns grow" is afforded by the Department store of Thos. W. Nugent & Co., familiarly known as "Nugent's, Braddock's Best Store."

Conceived in a small and unpretentious way, in a small store with

NUGENT'S DEPARTMENT STORE.

only a few lines, the business has steadily grown year by year until today, when it stands forth in this community as a fine example of a Modern Department Store.

The business was founded in 1894 by Mrs. Mary Nugent, and has been conducted ever since that time by her and her sons and daughters.

The place in which the business had its beginning was a small store at 823 Braddock Avenue, in the site now occupied by the First National Bank. The lines carried at that time were Millinery and a few lines of Ladies' Wear.

In a few years the business had grown so that larger quarters became necessary, and a more spacious store was found at 851 Braddock Avenue, where the firm moved in 1898. New departments were now added, principally Dry Goods and Men's Furnishings.

From that time the store has had a continuous growth, new departments and additional space being added every year. The Lytle Opera House, which included the second floor of the store at 851 Braddock Avenue, and also of the adjoining store, was added, making the largest store-room in Braddock.

In the year 1906, the pioneer furniture store of Masters & Lewis, which occupied the next room at 853 Braddock Avenue, was purchased by Nugent's, and thus additional space was gained, and also more lines were added to the many carried.

The two storerooms on George Street were soon found necessary, and by this time the store occupied almost the entire block.

However, the store still continued too small for the ever-increasing business, so it necessarily followed that plans were made in 1915 for the erection of a modern three-story Department Store. A site was chosen at the corner of Braddock Avenue and John Street, in the next block from the old building.

The new structure was completed in September, 1915, and was built of white enamel brick, with large show-windows forming an Arcade front. The store has modern fixtures throughout its three floors finished in mahogany.

The successful growth of The Famous and Nugent's into thoroughly modern department stores marks the entry of Braddock into the class of large commercial centers.

Harry J. Learn, a well-known resident of the town, for many years has conducted a dry goods business that began successfully and has had a steady and flourishing growth.

A. J. Spigelmire, who began business in the eighties, has conducted a growing business ever since, having a general store and handling dry goods and carpets.

Of the old stores that are now out of business, familiar to the earlier residents, may be mentioned the clothing store of Katz & Wormser, the dry goods and millinery store of Thomas Wagner, the general dry goods store of Spitzer & Speidel, the dry goods store of J. W. McCune, the Kerr Arcade, a dry goods store occupying a part of the present site of The Famous, and Blattners Department Store, a member of which firm now conducts a men's furnishing store.

Among the clothing and men's furnishing stores of long and successful standing in the town may be mentioned Bachman's, Sullivan, Jones & Ryan, C. V. Weakland & Co., Fromme's, and Fromme & Newman's, all located on Braddock Avenue.

The first furniture store in Braddock was that of James A. Russell, which he opened in connection with his undertaking establishment as was quite the custom in the '60's and '70's. There are now several exclusive furniture stores in the town, among which may be mentioned,

Noland Furniture Co., Stephens Furniture Co., Braddock Furniture Co., Globe Furniture Co., and R. E. Thompson.

 H. M. Glenn and Braddock Paint & Glass Co. specialize on house decorations. Roderus & Klaban of Braddock, and C. B. Guttridge of Rankin, have flourishing trade in periodicals, stationery, blank books, and office equipment. John M. Balsamo, starting with a small tobacco store, has built up in connection with it a good trade in papers and periodicals. A. B. Crow has for many years conducted a harness making plant and store.

 Jas. A. Russell was succeeded in the undertaking business by his son, Robert M. Russell; and he a few years ago, sold out to W. L. Dowler, who is now widely known as a funeral director. Others in the same line are Marshall Brothers, A. P. Pustinger, Stephen Vanyo, and Zorn & Glasser.

 Another line of trade requiring the business sense of the specialist is jewelry. This department of commerce is carefully looked after by Fritz Liljedahl, Kopsofsky's, D. H. DeNardo Co., Karl Hess, A. Goldstein, A. Schmidt, and his brother, in a separate store, L. Schmidt.

 A line of commercial work that has had much to do with the growth of the community, as it does in all sections, is the real estate developments. The man who lays out vacant property into lots and induces people to build homes, even with little capital, paying for them by monthly installments, is a community builder, and his work is abiding. If the man who makes two blades of grass grow where only one grew before is a philanthropist, what shall we say of him who makes hundreds of homes grow where none were before? Some of Braddock's most successful men have acquired competence by handling property for others, and incidentally have been potent factors in the town's development. Nearly all renting and exchanging of property is done through these brokers. The only thing these men have to complain of now is that there are not enough houses for rent to go round, and there are not any more large undeveloped tracts where lots, convenient and desirable can be had at moderate prices. Among the men who have succeeded as realty brokers may be mentioned L. F. Holtzman, Esq., C. A. Stokes, R. M. McNulty, J. M. Clifford, J. N. Griffith, S. E. Stewart, Jones & Davis, C. R. Baldridge, John T. Unangst, John J. Walker, Ebdy & Ketter, P. D. Remington, Geo. B. Whitfield, Jr., W. S. Heath, manager of the Real Estate Department of the Braddock Trust Co., and John B. McMillan and M. B. Groat who succeeded E. A. Stroud & Co. Many of these men write insurance in connection with their realty work. Mr. E. D. Nugent specializes in insurance, as does Mr. Jos. Wagner.

The large amount of real estate and financial deals put through naturally requires the services of many attorneys at law. Of these, Braddock has a goodly number, some of them men of prominence at the bar, others young practitioners with brilliant futures ahead. Among the lawyers may be mentioned Francis Bennett, E. J. Smail, S. R. McClure, Jos. F. Mayhugh, E. J. Stebick, George Weil, P. D. Remington, J. E. Little, Thos. Lawry, Jas. A. Nugent, Ralph J. Brown, John K. Benn, Jas. J. Cosgrove, W. J. Aiken, Thomas Daugherty, Viers Edwards, W. Lloyd Miller, Roland A. McCrady, Bernard McKenna, A. H. Rosenberg, Julius Spatz, Henry Gelm, H. A. Dean.

As this chapter is intended to cover the points not touched upon by the writers of other special themes, it seems proper here to include a list of Braddock Dentists. That is one profession that is not now, nor likely soon to be overcrowded. In this profession, prevention is better than cure; and it is still a long way to go, before the mass of people will learn that regular visits to a careful, conscientious dentist are far better and cheaper than waiting until it is too late. A number of men formerly engaged in the practice of dentistry in Braddock have gone elsewhere. Among such are, Dr. J. R. King, and Dr. A. H. Speer, now located in California; Dr. H. H. Sargent and Dr. E. G. Masters, now in Pittsburgh, and Dr. Geo. A. Sloan, who is engaged in other lines of work. Present day dentists include the following:—Dr. R. J. King, Drs. Coulson and Fonda, Dr. Chas. E. Rose, Dr. I. M. Eisman, Dr. S. W. Frank, Dr. H. S. Kopsofsky, Dr. H. T. McCune, Dr. M. H. Robin, Dr. R. M. Urmson, Dr. Len Calihan, Dr. Leo Shonefeldt, Dr. L. S. Flower.

For many years Charles Haas, still a resident of the town, conducted a successful shoe business, being succeeded by the Hillsman Shoe Store. The Borland Walk Over Shoe Store, owned and conducted by Joseph H. Borland, is another shoe business that by its development marks the growth of Braddock. The Star Shoe Corner, the Book Shoe Store and Carlson's are all thriving Braddock Avenue shoe stores, showing that Braddock people insist upon being well shod.

In the hardware line Frank Shilling for many years ran a store near Ninth Street. Fulton Brothers conducted a successful hardware business for many years, forming later the firm of Fulton & Maginni, now Maginni's Hardware Store. The firm of Edmunds & Williams, a store of long standing, was succeeded by Richard Edmunds, who has successfully continued the business. William Strathern has had a flourishing store for many years and the store of J. A. Loew, now J. A. Loew's Sons, is another modern hardware business. The firms of Wills & Shelby, Kost & Costello, and Dudgeon Brothers, and G. Roy Walker are successful in the general plumbing business.

The development of the automobile has given rise to a new industry during the last decade, and garages, auto supply stores and repair shops have sprung up everywhere. One of the first firms to embark in this line in Braddock was H. S. Leighton & Company. Handling a complete line of Overland cars and supplies and operating a repair shop, their plant is one of the busy places. Wm. J. Tracey & Company, with the Ford, the Chalmers, and the Dodge cars, are also doing a big business, while the Buick interests are looked after by the Seewald Motor Company. Speicher & Daniels, young men of ability and energy, have recently opened an establishment devoted exclusively to the repairing of automobiles.

The town has progressed along all lines of trade, no line exhibiting this fact any more than the thriving condition of its many drug stores. Among those of long standing are the stores of George W. Kutscher, W. A. Kulp, George Klein, John Weyels, Charles Weyels, E. A. Hering, Hollander Drug Company, Cyrus Edmunds, James Sheekey, S. A. Stright, and Matthew Cassidy. Of the old time stores may be recalled Maginni's Drug Store, and the store of V. C. Knorr. David Musselman is an old time drug store proprietor and the name of J. D. Simon will be remembered by many. John Walker, at present in the real estate business, sold his store to Harry Poorman, who conducts the business now, and W. A. Kulp has recently sold one of his stores, it now being known as the Miller Drug Store.

The Carnegie Cooperative Store, located where Woolworth's Five & Ten Cent Store is now, flourished a number of years, but finally closed and settled up with the stock-holders. It made money in its day but went out of style. Daniel Oskin conducted a grocery store near Ninth Street thirty years ago. Of the older general stores, may be mentioned the old stock company store of Smith and Worthington, and the store of W. A. McDevitt & Co. The grocery store of John Brennan above Eleventh Street was long a familiar sight.

Stores were slow to make their appearance in North Braddock and then only grocery stores or drug stores did much good, but in the eighties P. Walters Grand Double Stores did a good business on Rebecca Street, the following price list being taken from an advertisement of that store in

THE UNWRITTEN HISTORY OF BRADDOCK'S FIELD. 309

1887: 17 lbs. granulated sugar, $1.00; 11 cans tomatoes, $1.00; 16 lbs. prunes, $1.00; best sugar cured hams 11½c per lb.; bacon 11c per lb.; rye flour, per sack, 65c. However, in those days wages were about one-half what they are now. Furthermore, those were the days of the market basket and the telephone was a rarity. The delivery wagon or auto quick delivery was not considered essential to the success of the grocery business. People did their buying then over the counter and not over the telephone.

The development of the grocery business has paralleled the industrial and civic growth. The community now supports two large wholesale grocery companies, L. H. Bishoff & Company, and The W. E. Osborne Company. The most extensive retail grocery business is doubtless that of F. G. Bishoff & Company. Mr. Bishoff started this work in 1886. At first, he was buyer, salesman, and a man of all work, the amount of trade not justifying the employment of even a boy. The delivery clerk had not yet been invented. He and his wagon came later. To-day, this store carries a pay-roll of thirty-five to forty, and employs eighteen automobiles, including solicitors' run-abouts, delivery cars, and heavy auto trucks for bringing in the supplies. The store occupies the entire ground floor of the large Bishoff Block.

Jones Brothers of North Braddock, have also built up a big trade from small beginnings in the same way. They, too, have erected a large block, using what they need for their store and letting out other parts of the building for dwelling apartments. A. J. McQuiggan has a flourishing trade, specializing in poultry. Other successful grocers include Liston Brothers, Geo. P. Roby. H. Campbell, F. S. Colmery, Max Miller, Morris Adler, besides a great many that cater especially to trade in distinctly local sections or among the families of European nationalities.

Calahan's arcade is a busy place which includes a butter store, a meat market, a delicatessan department, and other distinct lines.

Green goods and fruits are handled by specialists, chiefly Italians and Greeks. A. Andolina is a wholesaler in this line. Nucci & Ferrera have a large retail trade. Both of these firms have been in business in Braddock for many years, starting in a small way in a new field and in a strange land, and are now recognized as substantial American business men. Their families have grown up around them, their children have gone through the schools and the high schools, and the families are thoroughly American.

The Diamond Ice Company, operated by H. J. Wagner, does an extensive business. In the hot days the ice man is as welcome as is the doctor in time of sickness.

The welfare of animals is not neglected, and anything needed for them can be had from the Braddock Feed & Supply House, C. M. Marriott & Sons, or J. C. Muir.

Recently the chain stores have appeared, such as Woolworth's five and ten, Butler's grocery and the A. & P. They locate either in the residence or business districts. The residence streets in Braddock that have not one or more grocery stores are few.

The Braddock Laundry, under the management of Mr. J. R. Robinson, is one of the thriving industries of the community. It employs sixty people, uses auto-trucks for gathering and delivering goods, and is fully equipped with modern machinery and appliances.

The interests of the merchants are promoted by the Braddock Merchants' Association, a live-wire organization. W. H. Sullivan is President and J. E. McDonald the salaried Secretary, who devotes all his time to promoting mercantile interests. The Association has taken over most of the functions of the Board of Commerce, though the latter body, now quiescent, has accomplished much in the past and may be still relied on in an emergency.

Thus has Braddock and the community grown from a mere rural village with dusty roads and kerosene lamps, into a modern commercial center teeming with business on its crowded streets, and at night lighted up with up-to-date electric systems. The old time general country store has given place to the metropolitan department store. The stores in special lines of business are flourishing and increasing in number. The real estate offices are busy, the barber shop gives tickets for your turn, the garage has grown up beside the blacksmith shop, the drug stores sell anything in the medicinal line that may lie in the gamut from soap and sundaes to kodaks and automobile horns, the telephone bells are never silent, the song of the phonograph is in the air, the ice-man visits daily, the moving picture shows are beyond the most fanciful dreams of the early resident, the ten cent stores are thronged, and the department stores meet all the requirements of the most exacting customer. Buy in Braddock is a good slogan. It means continued growth.

CONCLUSION.

BY GEO. H. LAMB.

Having passed in review all the papers submitted in this modest attempt to preserve the important features of the local history of the last half century, it seems proper that the editor should add a few words, not by way of apology for what has been written, nor for what has been left unsaid, but explanatory of the labor performed and the results accomplished.

When it was determined early in 1917 to hold a semi-centennial celebration of the incorporation of Braddock, and later a quarter-centennial of the organization of Rankin borough, and incidentally the one-hundred-seventy-fifth anniversary of the building of Frazier's cabin, the present editor was appointed chairman of the history committee for that celebration, with power to select his assistants. With much care, the staff of editors whose names head the various chapters was chosen, and this book is proof of the wisdom of the selections made.

When the history committee got together they planned two distinct lines of action; first, to write the heretofore untold story of the later development of this region; and, second, to erect suitable tablets for the marking of certain historic spots, hitherto neglected. To each member of the committee was assigned the specific task of writing one chapter. The committee began its work enthusiastically, each planning to have his story completed early in April, that the book might appear on the stands in time for the celebration in June. When war was declared with Germany, and the executive committee of the Jubilee decided to postpone the event for a year, the work of this committee was so well advanced that it seemed wise to go forward with its every detail, but the stress was somewhat relaxed and time for the completion of the work was extended. Accordingly, this history appears, and the historic tablets are erected in 1917 as originally planned.

The members of the committee had a wide margin to work on, being restrained only by two rules which were to be rigidly adhered to. First, no one was to permit a statement to appear which was not fully verified, so that it could be strictly relied on. Members of the committee were reminded of Mark Twain's dictum, that the trouble with reminiscences is not that people know too much, but that they know so many things that aren't so. The second rule was, nothing shall appear in the volume that can, in any way, be construed as an advertisement. Names were to be used freely, and personal reminiscences and individual touches to be given ad libitum, but these were to be matters of historic importance, and not incidents inserted because of friendship or favoritism.

In so far as the editor is able to observe, these rules have been carefully followed; and while the names of hundreds of present and former citizens appear, not one is printed "by request", and no individual or firm is written up because of "influence". The response of the old residents and of business men to the interviews, the interrogatories, and the questionaires of the different members of the committee, has been hearty and encouraging. The historians have spent days in running down obscure and half-forgotten facts. A few of the articles might have been a little fuller if every one appealed to had supplied the desired information as requested. Doubtless many things have been left unsaid which, told, would have added to the history's value. But the character of the members of the committee is such as to win the confidence of the community, and they have been untiring in their efforts to get the facts.

As was foreseen, the labors of different writers frequently overlap; and there is more repetition than would have been the case in the event of the writing of the whole book by one person. This is not wholly a detriment, but emphasizes the wide-spread influence that emanates from an individual or from any important event, and, by showing how one deed or incident reacts on another, furnishes cumulative evidence of the wide-reaching force of the community.

For record, it is important here to note the second part of the committee's work, the placing of the historic tablets. Four bronze tablets are now cast, which are to mark as many important events. The first of these commemorates the building of Frazier's cabin, and incidentally points out the place where Braddock's army crossed the river. The exact spot where the cabin stood is on the banks of the river, within the grounds of the Edgar Thomson Steel Works. As the location is inaccessible, the tablet is erected along Braddock Avenue, on the concrete wall surrounding the works, and reads:—

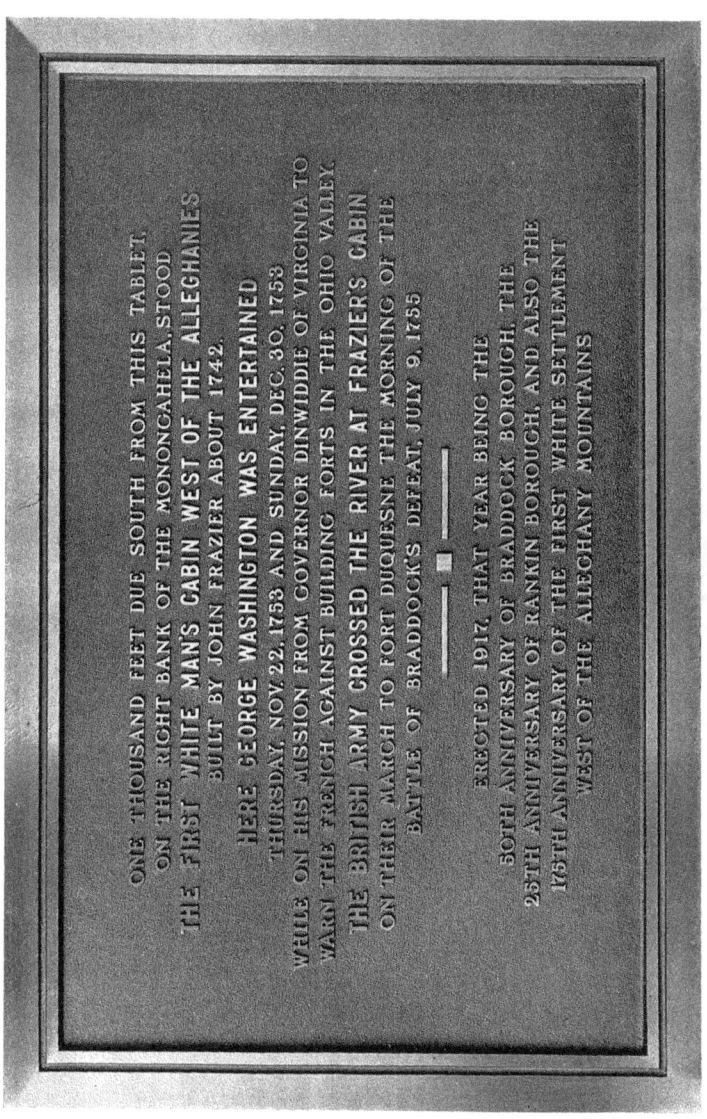

ONE THOUSAND FEET DUE SOUTH FROM THIS TABLET,
ON THE RIGHT BANK OF THE MONONGAHELA, STOOD
THE FIRST WHITE MAN'S CABIN WEST OF THE ALLEGHANIES
BUILT BY JOHN FRAZIER ABOUT 1742.

HERE GEORGE WASHINGTON WAS ENTERTAINED
THURSDAY, NOV. 22, 1753 AND SUNDAY, DEC. 30, 1753
WHILE ON HIS MISSION FROM GOVERNOR DINWIDDIE OF VIRGINIA TO
WARN THE FRENCH AGAINST BUILDING FORTS IN THE OHIO VALLEY.

THE BRITISH ARMY CROSSED THE RIVER AT FRAZIER'S CABIN
ON THEIR MARCH TO FORT DUQUESNE THE MORNING OF THE
BATTLE OF BRADDOCK'S DEFEAT, JULY 9, 1755

ERECTED 1917, THAT YEAR BEING THE
50TH ANNIVERSARY OF BRADDOCK BOROUGH, THE
25TH ANNIVERSARY OF RANKIN BOROUGH, AND ALSO THE
175TH ANNIVERSARY OF THE FIRST WHITE SETTLEMENT
WEST OF THE ALLEGHANY MOUNTAINS

The location of the second tablet is on Sixth Street, North Braddock, just above the Pennsylvania Railroad. The wording of this tablet is:—

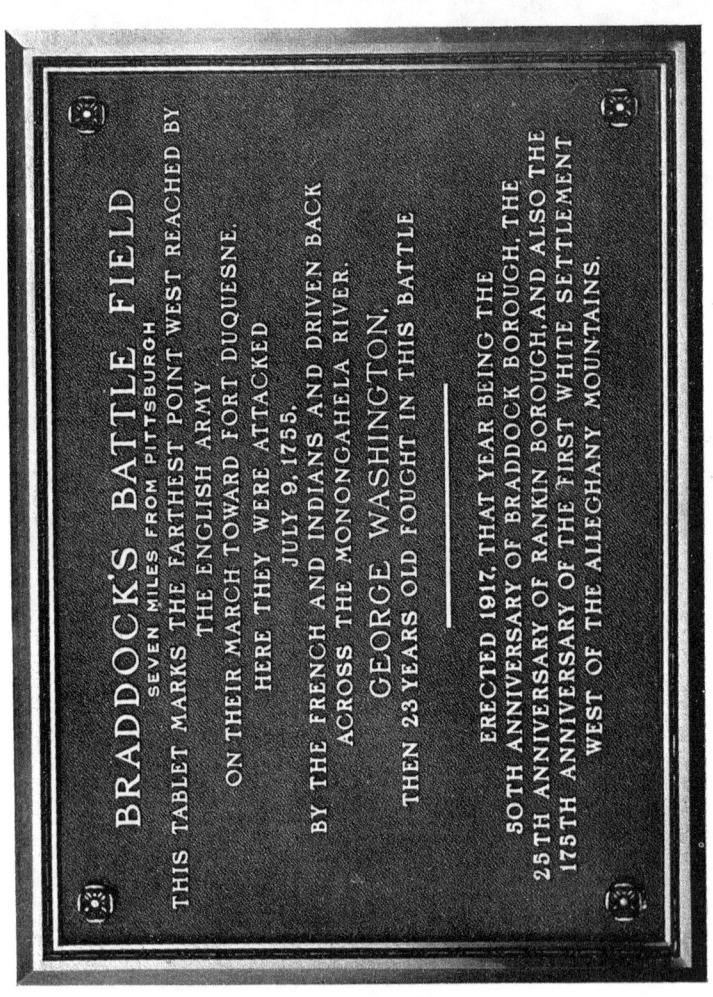

BRADDOCK'S BATTLE FIELD
SEVEN MILES FROM PITTSBURGH
THIS TABLET MARKS THE FARTHEST POINT WEST REACHED BY
THE ENGLISH ARMY
ON THEIR MARCH TOWARD FORT DUQUESNE.
HERE THEY WERE ATTACKED
JULY 9, 1755,
BY THE FRENCH AND INDIANS AND DRIVEN BACK
ACROSS THE MONONGAHELA RIVER.
GEORGE WASHINGTON,
THEN 23 YEARS OLD FOUGHT IN THIS BATTLE

ERECTED 1917, THAT YEAR BEING THE
50TH ANNIVERSARY OF BRADDOCK BOROUGH, THE
25TH ANNIVERSARY OF RANKIN BOROUGH, AND ALSO THE
175TH ANNIVERSARY OF THE FIRST WHITE SETTLEMENT
WEST OF THE ALLEGHANY MOUNTAINS.

The third tablet, marking the location of Braddock's spring (which is now sewered away and gives no surface indication) is placed on the concrete foundation of the new Edgar Thomson Steel Works office building, where Braddock Avenue crosses Thirteenth Street, and reads:—

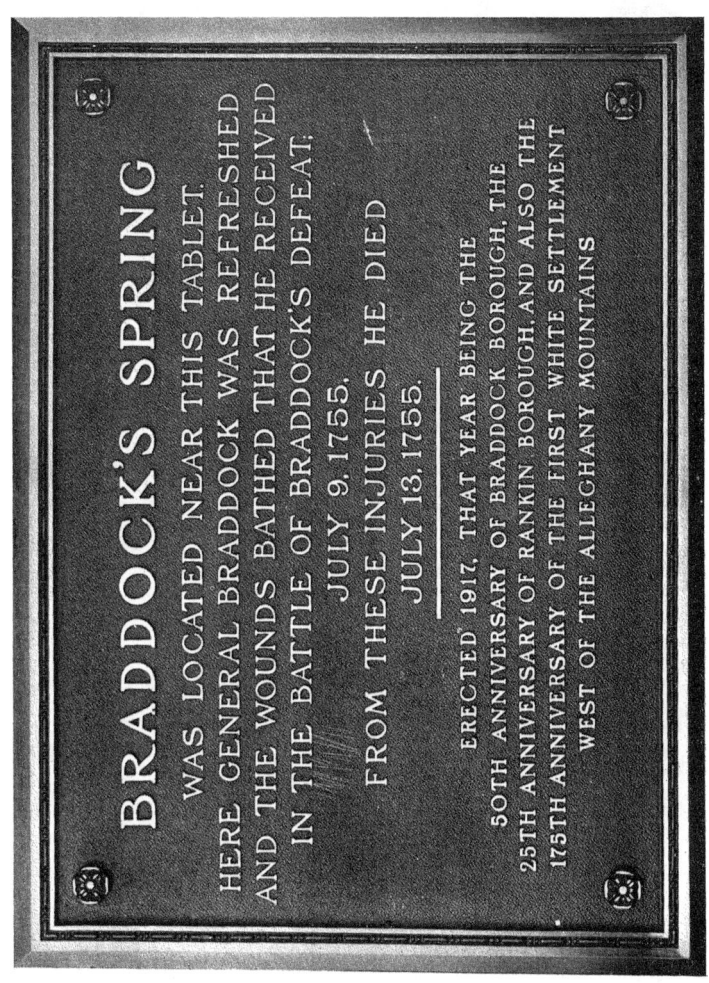

BRADDOCK'S SPRING
WAS LOCATED NEAR THIS TABLET.
HERE GENERAL BRADDOCK WAS REFRESHED
AND THE WOUNDS BATHED THAT HE RECEIVED
IN THE BATTLE OF BRADDOCK'S DEFEAT.
JULY 9, 1755.
FROM THESE INJURIES HE DIED
JULY 13, 1755.

ERECTED 1917, THAT YEAR BEING THE
50TH ANNIVERSARY OF BRADDOCK BOROUGH, THE
25TH ANNIVERSARY OF RANKIN BOROUGH, AND ALSO THE
175TH ANNIVERSARY OF THE FIRST WHITE SETTLEMENT
WEST OF THE ALLEGHANY MOUNTAINS

The fourth tablet marks events of a later date. It is placed on the wall of the Wallace mansion, several times referred to in this work, and reads:—

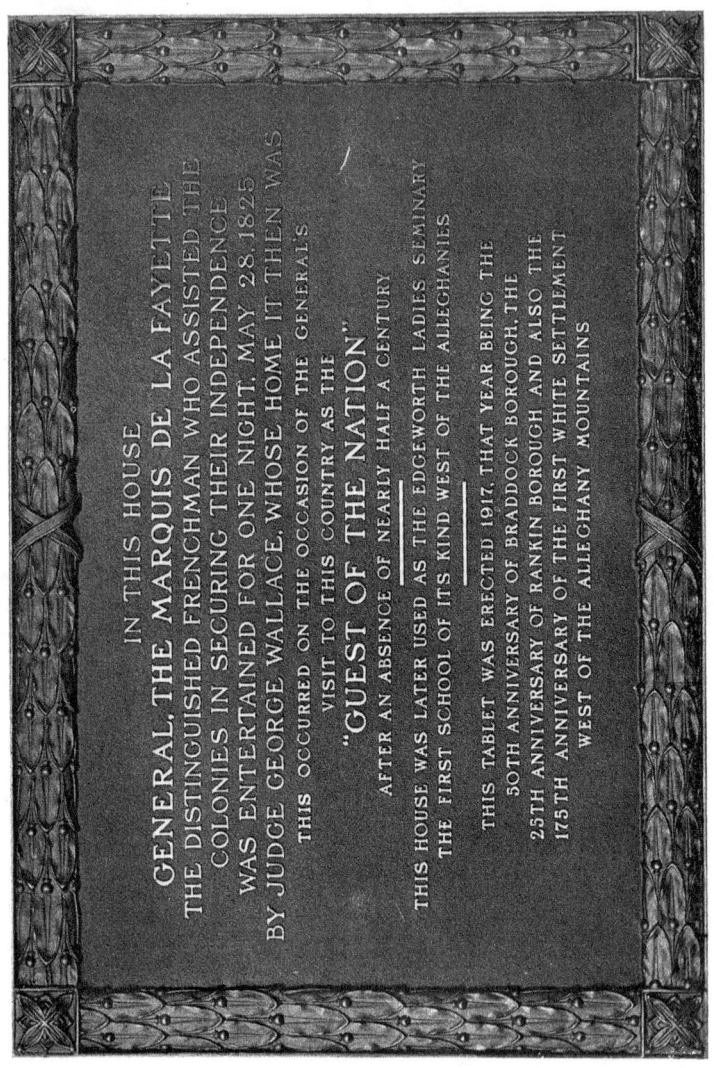

IN THIS HOUSE
GENERAL, THE MARQUIS DE LA FAYETTE
THE DISTINGUISHED FRENCHMAN WHO ASSISTED THE
COLONIES IN SECURING THEIR INDEPENDENCE
WAS ENTERTAINED FOR ONE NIGHT, MAY 28, 1825
BY JUDGE GEORGE WALLACE, WHOSE HOME IT THEN WAS
THIS OCCURRED ON THE OCCASION OF THE GENERAL'S
VISIT TO THIS COUNTRY AS THE
"GUEST OF THE NATION"
AFTER AN ABSENCE OF NEARLY HALF A CENTURY
THIS HOUSE WAS LATER USED AS THE EDGEWORTH LADIES SEMINARY
THE FIRST SCHOOL OF ITS KIND WEST OF THE ALLEGHANIES
THIS TABLET WAS ERECTED 1917, THAT YEAR BEING THE
50TH ANNIVERSARY OF BRADDOCK BOROUGH, THE
25TH ANNIVERSARY OF RANKIN BOROUGH AND ALSO THE
175TH ANNIVERSARY OF THE FIRST WHITE SETTLEMENT
WEST OF THE ALLEGHANY MOUNTAINS

INDEX.

A.

Abbiss, Reuben 122, 131, 222
Abbiss, Reuben D. 203, 250
Abromaites, Rev. C. 181
Adams, A. R. 78
Adams, Chas. 78
Adams, John 24
Adams, John W. 78, 86
Adams, President John Quincy 158
Addenbrook, Louisa 289
Addenbrook, Thos. 23, 100,
and note 101, 108, 109, 113, 114, 117,
121, 124, 131, 187, 221.
Adler, Morris 309
A-Gree(r)able Club, ...203
Aiken, A. P., ...53, 56
Aiken, Wm. J. 4, 150, 298, 307
Aites, Wm. R. 43
Albig, W. Espey 3, 31, 204
Alexander, James 57
Alexander, J. L. 41
Alleghanies 3, 11, 13,
32, 151, 169, 201, 298, 313, 314, 315, 316
Allegheny Chronicle 102
Allegheny City 167
Allegheny County 153
Allegheny River 298
Allegheny River Railroad 59
Alliquippa, Queen 11, 25
Allison, Axel 278
Alman, Rev. Geo. 190
Alman, Sam. R. 90
Allshouse, Lewis 278
Alters, Mrs. Harry 62
Alumni Association 202, 203
Amalgamated Association 110, 112
American Chain Co., Inc. 92
American Library Association 225
American Steel & Wire 88
Amshall, Lewis 230, 231
Anderson, C. A. 221, 222
Anderson, E. H. 221, 222
Anderson, Mrs. E. H. 289
Anderson, Dr. E. O. 249, 276
Anderson, Geo. K. 173
Anderson, H. L. 42, 162
Anderson, Joseph 23
Anderson, Leonora M 42
Andolina, A. 309

Antis, David 19
Antonoff, Rev. J. K. 181
Appel, Adam 276
Arensberg, Chas. 275
Argall, A. J. 42
Armstrong Company 153
Arthurs, Robert 213
Aten, Thos. G. 40, 276
Atlantic & Pacific 310

B.

Bachman, Mrs. Louise 242
Bachman's 305
Bagaley, Ralph 213
Bailey, Henley 158
Bailey, John 198
Bair, Dr. C. E. 248, 249
Bair, Dr. G. E. 91, 248, 249
Bair, Mrs. G. E. 233
Bair, H. H. 276
Baker Chain Wagon Mfg. Co. 92
Baldridge Building 303
Baldridge, C. R. 43, 306
Baldridge, John 24, 30
Balsamo, John M. 306
Balsinger, W. R. 221
Baltimore & Ohio R. R. 66, 67, 69
Bank of Pittsburgh 13, 21
Barkley, "Mother" 183
Barlett, Rev. F. W. 181
Barnes, Phineas 98, 107
Bartilson, Dr. B. M. 43, 241, 249, 261
Baughman, Elizabeth 20, 21
Baughman, Hiram 78
Baughman, Peter 20, 21
Bayard, George 23
Bayard, Stephen 32
Beattie, Robert 58
Behane, Dr. J. 249
Bell Ave. School 203
Bell, Florence 237, 294
Bell, George H. 8, 13, 14, 23, 24, 27, 30
Bell, Mrs. Geo. H. 24
Bell, Margaret 14, 22, 283
Bennevantano, Rev. Francisco 181
Benn, H. W. ....
108, 117, 120, 122, 127a, 131, 214, 216, 222
Benn, John 22

Benn, John K.	307
Benn, Wallace B.	160
Bennett, F. S.	218, 307
Bennett, James H.	276
Bennett, Mrs. Mark	285
Bennett, M. E.	202
Berg, H. A.	86
Berg, P. T.	108
Berkey, James	19
Berthold, Chas. D.	276
B. & L. E. Railroad	70
Bessemer Process	96
Bessemer, Sir Henry	96
Bessemer Trust Co.	210, 212
Best, A. L.	24, 42
Bierer, Rev. B. K.	181
"Billy Smith" Cottage,	18
Bishoff, F. G.	3, 42, 57, 162, 214, 216, 239, 241, 242, 309
Bishoff, L. H.	42, 57, 309
Bishoff, Wm. H.	57
Black, John	62
"Black Bab"	23
Black, James	275
Black, P. A. K.	131, 204, 222
Black, S. J.	60
Blattner's Department Store	305
Blue Line Street Railway	76
Board of Managers, Hospital	239, 240, 241, 242
Boat Yard	84
Boli, B. W.	60
Boli, Mrs.	23, 285
Boli, Wm. C.	201
Book Shoe Store	307
Bope, Col. H. P.	226, 227
Borland Shoe Store	307
Bouquet, Colonel	31
Bowden, Mrs. H. M.	233
Bowers, Dr. M. S.	249
Bowman, Rev. E. M.	184
Bowman, John T. C.	60
Bowman, Roger	117
Bowman, Mrs. Sarah	285
Boxer Uprising	197
Boyd, Mrs. Eli	233
Boyd, Jame K.	131
Boyd, Jane	14
Boyd, Mary	14
Boyle, A. J.	127a
Boyle, Rev. T. N.	183
Brackemeyer, E. M.	276
Bracken, E. S.	276
Braddock & Turtle Creek Railway	73
Braddock Board of Commerce,	237, 238, 310
Braddock Borough	40
Braddock Burgesses	40
Braddock Daily News	21, 230, 231
Braddock Electric Railway	75
Braddock Feed & Supply House	309
Braddock Furniture Co.	306
Braddock, General Edward	9, 11, 12, 13, 31, 151, 177, 315
Braddock General Hospital	21, 177, 230, 232, 234, 236, 237, 238, 239, 242, 243, 293.
Braddock Glass Co.	87
Braddock Hospital Association	177
Braddock Lumber Company	74, 89, 291
Braddock Machine & Mfg. Co.	90
Braddock Manufacturing Co.,	90
Braddock Merchants' Assn.	227, 229, 310
Braddock Ministerial Association	241
Braddock National Bank	161, 208, 210, 211, 212
Braddock Paid Fire Department	278
Braddock Paint & Glass Co.	306
Braddock Planing Mill Co.	89
Braddock Post Office	159, 163
Braddock Relief Association	235
Braddock Trail	66
Braddock Trust Co.,	213, 215, 216, 218
Braddock Volunteer Fire Department	275, 278
Braddock Wire Co.	87
Braddock Wire Plant	89
Braddock's Defeat	12, 313, 315
Braddock's Field	7, 8, 11, 13, 14, 18, 20, 22, 23, 24, 25, 158, 160, 164, 166, 169,195, 201.
Braddock's Field Trust Company	210
Braddock's Spring	315
Bradford, David	14, 74
Brand, Rev. Frederick	186
Brashear, John A.	226
Brassert, H. A.	122, 131
Braznell, A. S.	218
Braznell, Mrs. A. S.	231, 233
Braznell, Benj.	24, 25, 91
Braznell Building	213, 216
Braznell, C. W.	218
Braznell, Hall	188
Brennan, John	40, 308
Brennan, William P.	114 and note
Brenneman, George	56
Bridges, Frank L.	275
Brinton Ave. School	203
Britt, Thos.	275
Broden, E. H.	3, 88, 89
Brooklyn Eagle	167

THE UNWRITTEN HISTORY OF BRADDOCK'S FIELD. 319

Brown, Allan ...17
Brown, Rev. A. D. ...181
Brown, Harry ...56
Brown, Mrs. Henry ...241
Brown, Rev. Joseph ...61
Brown, Thos. B. ...42
Brown, Ralph J. ...307
Brown, W. H. & Sons ...55
Brown, W. S. ...221, 222
Brown, Mrs. W. S. ...233
Brown, Walter ...276
Brown, Zachariah ...17
Brubaker, A. S. ...198
Bruggeman, H. T. ...275
Bryan, Miss O. ...285
Bryans, Wm. A. ...62
Buchanan, Jas. W. ...13, 23, 27
Bucket Brigade ...274
Buell, Rev. J. J. ...181
Bulger, Dr. A. E. ...248, 249
Bull Run ...158
Burke, Rev. J. D. ...181
Burke, John ...279
Burleigh ...150
Butler, General B. F. ...27
Butler's ...302, 310

C.

Cady, Rev. W. C. ...187
Cain, Daniel ...183
Cain, Patrick ...56
Cain, Thos. M. ...42
Callahan's Arcade ...309
Callahan, Dr. Leonard ...307
Callery, James ...86
Camp Copeland ...8, 78
Campbell, Geo. W. ...131
Campbell, H. ...309
Campbell, Jos. L., Sr. ...
...169, 170, 172, 173, 279
Campbell, Mrs. Jos. L. ...233
Carlins, A. M. ...276
Carlins Shoe Store ...307
Carnegie, Andrew ...
  10, 25, 69, 96, 98, 104, 110, 220, 221,
  225, 226, 227, 230.
Carnegie, Mrs. Andrew ...227
Carnegie Bros. & Company ...110
Carnegie Club ...10, 223, 228, 229
Carnegie Co-operative Store ...308
Carnegie Free Library ...
  ...10, 156, 171, 219, 220, 223, 225, 227
Carnegie McCandless & Co. ...9, 98
Carnegie Round Table ...229

Carnegie School ...22, 195
Cariegie Steel Co. ...
...9, 38, 86, 121, 197, 235, 291
Carnegie, Thos. ...96, 98, 104, 110, 285
Carothers, John A. ...210
Carothers, Gertrude R. ...294
Carr, Alfred ...276
Carr, Chas. J. ...3, 46
Carrie Furnaces ...21, 86
Carson, Rev. E. H. ...181
Cartwright, F. J. ...229, 291
Cartwright, Mrs. F. J. ...291
Casley, Rev. F. J. ...181
Cassidy, Matthew ...308
Caulfield, J. P. ...88
Chalfant, Henry R. ...210
Chamberlain, G. D. ...131
Chambers, Thos. ...88
Chandler, G. J. ...93
Charles H. B. ...93
Cheney & Baldwin ...29
Chess, H. B. ...90
Chess, N. P., Jr. ...89
Chess, P. F. ...89
Chess, Walter ...90
Chieftain Packet ...51
Churches ...179 to 193 inclusive
  List of ...181
  Also ...52-61, 281
Church, Chas. R. ...60
Church, Emma E. ...241
Church, Harry ...60
Citizens Bank ...216, 218
Civil War ...14, 28, 29, 151, 152, 299
Claney, Alexander ...183
Clarke, Wm. Sons & Co. ...86
Clarke, Rev. J. C. ...181
Clay, Mrs. Rachel ...
...231, 238, 241, 285, 294, 296
Clementson, Dr. W. A. ...249
Clemson, D. M. ...91
Cleveland Gas Coal Co. ...30
Cleveland, Pres. Grover ...51, 162, 169
Cleveland Plain Dealer ...172
Clifford, Dr. Chas. H. ...249, 276
Clifford, Mrs. C. H. ...233
Clifford, J. M. ...216, 218, 306
Clokey, Rev. J. S. ...184
Clugston, John A. ...59
Clugston, Robt. ...58
Clugston, Sarah C. ...58
Clugston, William ...58
Coal Mining ...51
Cochran, Chas. & Co. ...109

Cole, Thos. 60
Coleman Hailman & Co. 102
Coleman, Jacob C. 204
Coleman, William 96, 98
Coleman, W. H. 47
Collin, Simon C. 108
Collingwood, D. F. 14, 201, 221, 239
Collingwood, Mary K., (Mrs. D. F.)....
....231, 237
Collins, Mr. 98
Collins, James 275
Collins, Patrick 275
Collins, Walter 22, 53, 79, 162
Colmery, F. S. 309
Colmery, W. S. 162
Colored Republican Club 46
Colonel Baird 51
Conner, William 242, 276
Connor, William 121
Consolidated Expanded Metal Co. 89
Conway, Wm. P. 41
Cook, Colonel Edward 32
Cook, Thos. 14
Cooper, D. F. 56
Cooper, I. N. 198
Cooper, Gen. Joseph T. 79
Cope, Dr. P. C. 249
Copeland School 195
Corey, A. A. 30
Corey, A. A., Jr. 86
Corey, A. A. & Company 25, 30
Corey & Adams 37
Corey, Adaline 56
Corey Avenue Restaurant 302
Corey Chapel 87
Corey, Elizabeth 289
Corey, J. B. ....
  23, 26, 27, 30, 49, 50, 69, 183, 187, 231, 245
Corey, Mrs. J. B. 233
Corey, J. B. & Co. 28
Corey, M. G. 40, 210
Corey, W. E. 56, 59, 238
Corey, Mrs. 52
Corrothers, Gertrude R. 237
Corrothers, Dr. M. W. 249
Cosgrove, James J. 307
Cosgrove, Thomas ....
  22, 98, 108, 111, 116, 117, 121, 124,
  127a, 131, 222.
Cosgrove, Mrs. Thomas 231
Coulson, Dr. 307
Coultersville 50
Councils (borough) 40, 42
Coyne, Rev. C. 190

Craig, John 51
Cramer, Margaret 237
Crane, P. 88
Crane, Walter 223
Crawford Democrat 171
Crawford, Geo. 122
Cremer, J. 108
Crosby, Mrs. J. 233
Crow, A. B. 306
Crown Wall Plaster Co. 90
Crum, John 14
Cummings, Chas. L. 158, 223
Cundiff, L. B. 229
Cunningham, H. M. 60
Cunningham, Rev. W. A. 61, 190
Cunningham, S. M. 60
Curtis, F. J. 93
Cuthbert, S. B. 131

D.

Dalzell, John 47, 121
Dalzell, W. S. 221, 222
Darcy, James 182
Dart, Oscar 275
Davidson, Samuel 51
Davis, Chas. L. 87
Davis, Ezra 56
Davis, T. J. ....(note) 137
Davis, W. A. 88
Dawes Mfg. Co., ...94, 277
Day, A. J. 88
Day, Geo. W. C. 276
DeAmore, Rev. Luke 181
Dean, Cecil 204
Dean, E. W., Doctor.....................................
  ....246, 247, 248, 249, 276
Dean, H. A. 307
Dean, Dr. H. E. 241, 242, 248, 249
Decker, Rev. M. 190
DeDeken, Albert 108
Delafield, Herbert 74, 75
Dempster, Alexander 22, 25, 28
Dempster, Samuel 93
DeNardo, D. H. 306
Derrickson, John 52
Devlin, Rev. D. 190
Diamond Ice Co. 310
Dias, E. A. 60
Dick, John 276
Dickey, Rev. John B. 184
Dickson, Jas. B. 56
Dickson, Stewart & Co. 30, 61
Dickson, Wm. 56
Diethrich, Albert 65

Dietrich, Jos. H. 170, 174
Dillon, Sydney 9, 122, 131
Dinges, John 276
Dinkey, A. C. 95, 227
Dinkey, Chas. E. ....
..............3, 91, 95, 122, 202, 222, 226, 240
   Administration 129
   Character and Methods.....................141
   Affiliations 145
Dinkey, Mrs. Chas. E...............(note) 147
Dinkey, Minnie 289
Dinwiddie, Governor....................8, 11, 313
Dixon, H. C..206
Dixon, William J..................3, 41, 56, 131
Donnellan, Jno. S..........................42, 46
Donovan, John 276
Donovan, Louise 239
Doritz, A. 276
Double, Peter 60
Douglass, William L. 162
Douthitt, A. T. 198
Dowler, E. R....................22, 78, 91, 215
Dowler, George 276
Dowler, J. G. 22, 40
Dowler Lumber Co................................85
Dowler Planing Mill Fire.....................277
Dowler, Thos. J..................22, 40, 85, 275
Dowler, W. L. 306
Dowling, Denny 276
Dowling, Elizabeth 163
Dowling, James 276
Dowling, Martin 17, 189
Dowling, M. J...................................... 275
Drexler, Mr. and Mrs. L...............238, 241
Dudgeon Bros. 308
Duff, Robert P. 210
Dunbar, Frank 78
Dunn, James and Patrick....................102
Duquesne Forge 85, 87
Duvall, U. G. 42
Dyess, Rev. G. A...................................187

E.

Easton, Rev. J. S..................................184
Eaton, Katherine 17, 18, 22
Ebdy & Ketter 306
Ebner Hotel 302
Ebner, John 20
Eddstrom, Chas. 88
Edenborn, William 87
Edgar, L. C. 131
Edgar Thomson, J. 98, 99

Edgar Thomson Steel Works...................
..............................9, 11, 19, 38, 43
   Article, 96, 169, 172, 197, 240, 299, 312, 315.
Edgar Thomson Steel Works, Ltd........104

EDGAR THOMSON WORKS TECHNICAL INDEX.

For additional personal names—see General Index.

Accidents............................114, 124, 127, 134
Bloom Mill.............102, 117, 125, 138, 139
Blowing Engines 118, 125
Boilers...102, 125, 134
Briquette ....(note) 137
Car dumper 134
Club House 137, 138
Converting works 100, 118, 125
Dinkey, C. E.:
   Administration 129
   Man and Methods............................. 141
Direct Metal 120
Diversified Product 135
Electrical........117, 124, 125, 127, 138, 140
Floods 134
Furnace (Blast) Improvements ....
....118, 120, 124, 140
"A" 109, 124
"B" 109, 110
"C" 109, 110, 113, 132
"D" 111, 124
"E" 111, 124
"F" 111, 132
"G" 111, 124
"H" 117, 132
"I" 117, 124, 127, 139, 140
"J" 125, 127
"K" 125, 127
Foundries 121, 124
Gas Cleaning 138
Gas engines 132, 134
Gayley, James, Administration..............118
General Office 110, 134, 139
Hospital 137
Jones, W. R., Administration...............107
Kennedy-Morrison Process 127, 135
Labor (1876) 110
Laboratory 125
Ladles 135, 136
Locomotives 117
Masonry 98

322 THE UNWRITTEN HISTORY OF BRADDOCK'S FIELD.

McKinney Club House 138
Mill No. 1 ....112, 118, 134, 138
Mill No. 2, ...139
Mill No. 3 132
Mill No. 4 ....102, 117, 118
Mixer (Jones) 111
Morrison, Thos., Administration............122
Open Hearth Plant........................137, 138
Ore, Changing Character of, (note 1)..120
Ore Bridges 134
Original Plant 102
Production ....
    Jones 108
    Schwab 118
    Gayley 120
    Morrison 127
    Dinkey 140
Panics, 1873 100
    1907 ....(note) 134
Pig Machine 125
P. R. R. Subway..139
Reverse Duplex Process........................137
Road (Old) Changed..............................131
Roll storage 132
Safety department ....(note) 139
Schwab, C. M., Administration..............113
Settling Tanks 132
Sliding Scale 112
Splice Bar Shop, ...(note) 137
Steel, Pittsburgh District, History of
  (early) Superintendents, Department,
    Jones 108
    Schwab 116
    Gayley 120
    Morrison 122
    Dinkey 131
Telephone System 138
Turtle Creek Moved 121
Union Railroad Connections..................125
Water Supply 117, 139
Washington Street Tunnel 134
Wharf 96, 98, 132

Edgeworth Ladies Seminary..........201, 316
Edmundstone, Capt. 13
Edmunds & Williams..............................307
Edmunds, Cyrus 308
Edmunds, Richard 307
Edwards, Fred W. 46, 74, 222
Edwards, Watt, ...221
Edwards, Mrs. W. R..............................231
Egan, Dr. J. P...249
Eger, Rev. F. J.................181, 190, 191, 206
Eisaman, Dr. I. M.........................248, 307

Eisenbeis, Col. E. W........................169, 172
Eisenbeis, Harry L.........................169, 172
Elector Packet 51
Elizabeth Packet 51
Ellenberger's Bakery..............................302
Elliott, Rev. Thomas 181
Ellis, Charles 75
Ellis, Dr. E. W...249
Elrod, J. N...56
Emmert, P. F. 40
Emmens, A. F. 174
Enders, Lina G..241
Engelder, Rev. C....................................186
England, Geo. C............................122, 131
Engelbert, Rev. 181, 186
Episcopal Church Fire..........................277
Erret, Isaac 182
Escher, Philip 191
Eschman, Daniel 278
Estep, David 182
Eureka Printing Co................................174

F.

Fairlie, Rev. J. C....................................187
Falcona, A. 88
Famous, The 216, 303, 305
Farr, Harry 276
Farragut, Commodore 27
Farrell, J. A...88a
Farrell, Patrick 275
Farrell, William 89
Farrier, S. C...198
Faughman, Rev. Jno. 190
Fauset, Geo. R..275
Fawcett, Ann..16
Fawcett, C. C...................................22, 275
Fawcett, Mrs. C. C.................................233
Fawcett (or Fausett) Thos.............18, 28
Federal Building 165
Felician Sisters 191
Fiero, S. T. 231
Fighting (Street) 45
Fink, Mr. 183
Finley, Rev. Frank G..............................51
Finnin, Edward 53
Finnin, John T...53
Finnin, Wm. 56
Fireman Picnic and Ball......................277
First National Bank..............202, 213, 304
First Presbyterian Church 171
First Ward School, N. B......................203
First White Settlement.................314, 315
Fischer, Andrew 191

Fischer, Rev. Anthony 189, 190
Fisher, D. G. 276
Fisher, Rev. Grant E................................61
Fisher, Dr. H. F.....238, 239, 241, 249, 295
Fisher, J. K..231, 275
Fitch, Col. Thos. 87, 88, 89
Fitch, Henry 275
Flannigan, Mart 275
Fleck, Harry 276
Fleming, W. M. 158, 164
Floods (Monongahela) 134
Fogey, Harry 160, 162
Fonda, Dr. 307
Forbes, General 13, 151
Ford, S. A., ...108, 117
Ford, Wm. 78
Forester, Geo. 182
Forney, Christ 74
Forsyth, Robt. 79
Fort Duquesne 9, 11, 12, 25, 31, 151, 314
Fort Le Boeuf 11
Fort Necessity 31
Fort Pitt 13, 31
Foundry (Edgar Thomson) 121
Fowles, G. M. 197
Foye, Henry 72, 74, 75
Francis, Father 190
Franey, Wm. 57
Frank, Dr. S. W...307
Fraternal Societies—All such societies are named chronologically as constituted, at beginning of article on page 250. Names of officers and members not indexed.
Frazier, John (and Family).......................
............8, 11, 25, 169, 280, 311, 312, 313
Frazier, Lillian 204
Frazier, Judge Robt. S.........................239
Frederick, David 278
Frederick, John 100, 108
Frederick, John M..................................40
Frederick, Samuel 275
Frick, H. C. 95, 96, 277, 278
Friedlaender, Eugene 131
Friedman, Jacob 231
Fritchman Farm 50
Fritz, Geo. 40
Fritzius, Geo. 40, 56
Fritzius, Jordan 21, 56
Fritzius, L. C. 275
Fritzius, O. B. 56
Fritzius, William 22, 56, 159
Fritzius, Mary A. (Mrs. Wm.)......159, 160
Fromme, Rev. Wm. 190

Fromme & Newman 305
Fromme's 305
Fulton & Maggini 307
Fulton Bros 307
Fulton, Reverend J. G.............................184
Fulton, Rev. Wm. S...................................184
Furlong, Major 14

G.

Gable, M. E. 174
Gaffney, John 302
Gallagher, Mary 56
Gallagher, Timothy 56
Gallo, Rev. John 181
Gardner, Dr. C. C. 248, 249
Gates, John W. 88
Gauermann, Henry 91
Gayley, James ....
........95, 108, 113, 116, 118, 129, 221, 222
Gayley, Mrs. James...............120, 233, 289
Gazette-Times (Pittsburgh) 174
Gelm, Henry 191
George, John 56
George, King of England.........................13
George, Miles 56
George, Thomas 53, 56
Gerwig, F. H. N...131
Getty, J. P. 78
Gettys, W. E...108
Gettysburg 7
Getzel, H. G. 218
Ghrist, F. H. 124, 131
Gibbs, E. A. 93
Gibson, George 79, 276
Gibson, J. 40
Gibson, Lester 79
Giles, John 19, 29
Gillen, P. A. 276
Gillespie, T. A...93
Gilmore, G. W. 195
Gilmore, James, Sr.....................................62
Gilmore, James, Jr. 62
Gindas, John 279
Gist, Christopher 11, 31
Gladden, Rev. W. 188
Glasser, Nicholas 163
Glenn, H. M. 204, 217, 306
Globe Furniture Co. 306
Godlewski, Dr. S. A.................................249
Goehring, A. S. 301
Goldberg, H. B. 231
Goldrath, David 231
Goldrath, Mrs. David 231

324   THE UNWRITTEN HISTORY OF BRADDOCK'S FIELD.

Goldsmith, Lewis, J. 303
Goldsmith, Josiah L. 303
Goldstein, A. 306
Goodwin, H. W. 60
Gordon, Rev. P. H. 180, 181, 184
Gore, Dr. Wm. 245
Gorham, David H. 160
Gorham, James 275
Gourley, Chas. 276
Govier, J. W. 88
Graham, David H. 160
Graham, Frank 279
Grammar, F. L. 122
G. A. R. Home 287
Grannis, Bros. 85, 274, 277
Grant, President U. S. 159
Gray, G. E. F.
    ....122 and note, 124, 126, 131, 222
Gregg, E. E. 173, 178
Greek Catholic Union 191
Greensburg Turnpike 59, 62
Greer Business College 202
Greer, D. Newton 73, 202
Griffin, J. E. 74, 276
Griffith, Dr. 248
Griffith, J. N. 306
Groghan, Geo. 31
Grove City College 197
Guest of the Nation 8, 316
Gulovich, Rev. Stephen 181
Guthrie, John P. 78
Guthrie, R. S. 278
Guthrie, Sam T. 78
Guttridge, C. B. 3, 42, 46, 242, 278, 306
Guttridge, R. S. 278

H.

Haas, Chas. 307
Haddon, Thos. 78
Haddonfield, ... 150
Hafner, P. J. 231
Hager, Dr. C. 249
Hager, Mrs. C. 233
Hall, Mrs. Ellis Y. 159
Hall, Dr. G. A. 168
Hamburg 53
Hamfeldt, George 86
Hamilton, S. D. 62, 91, 201, 275
Hamilton, Mrs. S. D. 233
Hamilton, Samuel....197, 198, 205, 221, 226
Hamilton, Mrs. Samuel...................205, 280
Hamilton School 195
Hamm, E. J. 276

Hand, Hope 19
Handel, Mrs. Fannie 241
Hanlon, James 19
Hanna, John W. 204
Hanna, Mrs. John W. 3
Hannatown 30
Hardin, Col. M. D. 79, 81
Harding, Clark 302
Harman, Rev. W. S. 181
Harris, Geo. E. 121, 124, 131
Harris, Dr. Ira 201, 248, 249
Harris, Morgan 111
Harrison, Chas 78
Harrison, John 23, 40
Harrison, Squire Richard 53
Harrison, President Benjamin 51
Harrison, President Wm. Henry 37
Harrity, Morgan 43
Harrop, Mrs. Arville 285
Harrop, Frank 276
Hart, Rev. E. P. 187
Hart, Michael 38
Hart, Robert A. 276
Hart, Samuel 17, 56, 79
Hartman, Dr. J. C. 204
Harvard University 9
Hawes, Rev. G. E. 184
Hawkins, Col. G. W. 24, 58
Hay, Anna M. 222
Hayes, A. 90
Haymaker, Hon. J. C. 61, 62
Haynes, F. B. 88
Heath, Robt. 49
Heath, Capt. Samuel 49
Heath, Sam. J. 49
Heath, Sam. L. 54
Heath, W. S. 49, 216, 306
Heigh, Jos. 85
Henderson, J. D. 60, 206
Henning, Eliza 285
Henning, Matthew 16, 17, 23, 183
Henning, Mrs. M. 17
Henning School 196
Herbster, Rev. S. K. 181
Hering, E. A. 308
Hess, Karl 306
Heverly, A. 43
Hezlep, Miss A. W. 222
Hezlepp, Joseph 62
Hickey, Father 189
Hicks, Dr. T. S. 249
Hill, F. B. 89
Hillkowitz, Rev. J. L. 181
Hillsman Shoe Store 307

Hinman, Dr. A. W. 248
Hodder Construction Co. 93
Hoffman, Geo. 276
Hogg, Geo...................93, 217, 218, 239, 242
Hogg, Mrs. Geo. 295
Holland Company 153
Holland, R. M. 22, 217
Holland, Mrs. R. M..................................289
Holland, Wm. A. 22, 40
Holland, Wm. G. 22
Hollander Drug Co. 308
Holleran, Eliza 17
Holley, A. L. 96, 98, 102
Holmes, W. B. 90
Holmes, W. M. 90, 218
Holtzman family 14
Holtzman, L. F., Esq..................................
........3, 14, 41, 46, 173, 189, 222, 275, 306
Holtzman, Mary J. (Mrs. L. F.)..237, 294
Horner, J. M. 218
Horowitz, Dr. Max 249
Horr, Ignatz 46
Horton, James 20
Horse Racing 107
House, Geo. F. 78, 275
House, Geo. L. 217, 275
House, John 19
Howard, John 276
Howard, Dr. Samuel 249
Howard, T. L. 41
Howatt, Wm. 91, 276
Huber, Rev. Vincent 190
Hughes (contractor) 98
Hughes, Father 189
Hughes, James 278
Hughes, John 18
Hughes, Squire J. M.................................161
Hughes, M. J., Jr.......................................206
Hughes, Patrick 276
Hultgren, C. 88
Hultgren, Fred 88
Hungarian Normal School 206
Hunnell, I. N. 43
Hunt, Miss Ellen 242
Hunter, Geo. 14
Hunter, H. R. 3, 43
Hunter, J. C. 60
Hunter, Dr. W. L. 60, 63, 210
Hunting, ...62
Hurley, J. M. 276
Hurell, R. E. 88
Husband, W. S. 93
Hutzen, Hiram 100
Hutzen, John 91

Hutzen, Noah 100
Hyland, W. V..42

I.

Illingsworth, Jess 278
Independence Hall 7
Indians 150
Ingley, Rev. Fred 187
Iron City 152
Irvine, Rev. Ingram 186
Isaacs, Dr. H. S..249
Italian McKinley Club.............................46

J.

Jackson, Rev. J. L....................................181
Jackson, Wm. 86
James, Al 275
James, Elizabeth (Mrs. Thos.)...............
..........................231, 237, 239, 242, 293, 294
James, Jack 79
James, Thomas..
    100, 108, 111, 117, 120, 122, 127a, 131, 163.
Jamestown 7
Jaquay, Gideon H. 46
Jefferson Guards 54
Jefferson House 57
Jefferson, G. W. 88
Jewish Ladies I. O. O. B......................241
Jobe, Captain 62
Johns, Reynold 42
Johns, Samuel 42
Johns, W. H. 42
Johnson, Chas. 74
Johnson, James 79
Johnson, Robert 58
Johnson, William 58
Johnston, J. S. 197, 198
Jones, Benjamin H..................................201
Jones Brothers 309
Jones, Cora ....(note) 109
Jones, Daniel N. 100
Jones, Mrs. Ellen 285
Jones, J. C. 279
Jones, J. C. F. & Sons..............................308
Jones, John O. 42, 279
Jones, Philip 60
Jones, William M. C.................................60
Jones, Capt William R..............................
    45, 95, 100, 107, 113, 118, 120, 129, 142, 227.
Jones & Quigg 102
Jumonville 31

K.

Kagarise, J. W. 131
Kane, Thos. 42, 79
Kansas City Journal 167
Katz & Goldsmith 291, 303
Katz, Jacob 230, 231, 275
Katz, Mrs. Jacob 231
Katz, Leo. A..
........3, 214, 216, 218, 222, 238, 239, 303
Katz, Mrs. 295
Kauffman, Rev. P..................................190
Kazinczy, Rev. A. 181, 207
Kean, Rev. Wm. F..................................184
Keefer, J. S. 198, 207
Keener, Isaac W....................................131
Keiser, H. B. A...............................117, 121
Keiser, Rev. L. E....................................181
Keller & Milliken 28, 90
Keller, John J........................3, 90, 216, 218
Kelly, Chas. 19
Kelly, Harry H. 274
Kelly, John G...3, 96, (note), 209, 210, 212
Kelly, M. Clyde.......3, 47, 174, 175, 176, 178
Kelly, William ....(note) 96
Kennedy, Julian.........95, 106, 108, 109, 111
Kennedy, Mary (See Mrs. Sam'l Hamilton).
Kennedy-Morrison Process 127
Kenney, T. E...86
Kenney, Mrs. T. E...................................52
Kenney, Thos. J......................................24
Kentucky Boat 32, 33
Kenyon, W. H. 60
Kerr Arcade 303, 305
Kerr, Dr. Clinton S................................242
Kerr, D. G................89a, 95, 120, 122, 222
Ketter, Joseph 191
Kidd, Peter 57
Kier, D. M. 41, 276
Kier, M. M. 162
Kierman, Miss Irene 241
Kierulff, Rev. A. W. 187
Kilburn, J. W. 88
Killeen, M. 111, 116, 131
Kimmel, Dr. 247, 249
King, Rev. A. J......................................185
King, J. R. 307
King, Mrs. J. R...............................233, 294
King, John 53
King, Dr. R. J..307
King, Wm. M..56
Kinney, John 275
Kinney, Thos. 78, 188, 189
Kinsey, Mrs. Mary E.............169, 186, 231

Kirkpatrick, Allen 23
Kirkpatrick, Mrs. Allen 8, 14, 233, 291
Kirkpatrick Mansion 54
Klein, George 308
Kloman, Andrew 98, 104, 109
Knights of Labor 112
Knorr, V. C. 275, 308
Knox, Philander C. 95, 213, 214
Knox, Wm. F...121
Kohrnak, Dr. A. J..................................249
Kolb, Ellsworth 24
Kolb, Emory 23
Kolb, John 23, 79
Kopsofsky, Dr. H. S...............................307
Kost & Costello 308
Kovar, Rev. J. V....................................181
Kramer, Chas. F....................................175
Kramer, Geo. S. 131
Kramer, Margaret 294
Krohe, John 43
Kuhns, Rev. L. M..................................185
Kulp, Mark L...276
Kulp, Susan (Mrs. Tilgman).....................
......................................233, 237, 285, 288, 294
Kulp, W. A. 3, 91, 216, 308
Kurtz, Louis 279
Kutscher, Geo. W. 3, 276, 308

L.

Lacock, Prof. John K..................................9
Ladies Auxiliary, B. G. H......................241
LaFayette, General.........8, 14, 54, 158, 316
Lakeberg, Rev. A. P..............................181
Lamb, George H.......................................
....3, 7, 49, 50, 198, 220, 223, 242, 298, 311
Lamb, Dr. Harold H......................248, 249
Lambing, Rev. A. A...............................190
Lang & Miller...20
Lang, Wm. 276
Lantz, E. E....................................174, 175
Lapsley, J. A...221
Lapsley, Jennie S. (Mrs. W. L.)..............
..................78, 203, 233, 237, 289, 294, 295
Lapsley, Captain Thos............................
..............................21, 100, 104, 108, 117
Lapsley, William..............100, 221, 276
Large, W. H..................................172, 173
Larimer, Mrs. George............................233
Larimer, John 59, 62
Lauck, Reverend 24
Laughner, Mrs. Amos 231
Laux, Mrs. John 231
Laverty, Rev. L. F.................................184
Law, Alexander 78

THE UNWRITTEN HISTORY OF BRADDOCK'S FIELD.

Lawler, Matthew ...14
Lawlor, John ...275
Lawrence, Edward ...173
Lawry, Thos. ...170, 172, 173, 176
Layman's Cafe ...168
Layman, Rev. Leigh ...188
Lazear, Sollinger & Patton ...84
Learish, Rev. E. B. ...181
Learn, H. J. ...3, 217, 305
Learn, Mrs. ...295
Lee, Amelia ...185
Leech, Elmer ...275
Legal, Mae A. ...203
Leighton, F. K. ...42
Leighton, H. S. ...163, 308
Leighton's Rink ...220
Leonardson, Rev. A. V. ...187
Lewis, Anthony ...62
Lewis, Mrs. Flora ...285
Lewis, Harry ...275
Lewis, John F. ...
...3, 121, 122, 129, 130, 131, 140, 222
Lewis, Jonathan D. ...(note) 120
Lewis, Washington ...275
Lexington ...7
Library, Braddock (See Library, Carnegie Free).
Library, Carnegie Free ...
...10, 156, 171, 219, 220, 223
Twenty-Fifth Anniversary ...225, 227
Library, E. T. Works ...220
Limerick, Rev. F. B. ...185
Lincoln, President A. ...51, 57, 159
Linn, Dr. J. W. ...19, 159, 247, 249
Linsemyer, Amy ...241
Lippincott, Jessie H. ...213
Lippincott, Rev. R. P. ...184
Liston Bros. ...309
Little, John ...100, 276
Little, J. E. ...40, 307
Litzki, Joe ...279
Litvitz, Jacob ...231
Lobingier, C. C. ...78
Lock No. 2 ...54
Locke, C. E. ...171
Lock, C. E., Sr. ...171
Loew, John ...57
Loew, John A.'s Sons ...307
Loughrey, Chas. ...56
Lorch, Louis, Jr. ...216
Lothrop, Sylvanus ...38
Loucks, E. F. ...204
Loughead, John C. ...170, 174, 175, 176
Louis, F. E. ...168, 170, 174, 275

Louis, Thos. J. ...53, 168, 171, 178
Lowers, John F. ...279
Lowing, Frank C. ...173
Lowman, W. S. ...41
Lowrie, Dr. R. N. ...249
Lowrie, Dr. W. J. ...249
Lowry, John S. ...78, 201
Lowry, Nathaniel ...78
Lowry, Mrs. Nathaniel ...78, 81
Lucas, Mrs. Ada ...233
Lucy Furnaces ...109
Ludwig, Thos ...278
Lukens, Maggie ...289
Lutz, Chas. W. ...88
Lutz, Jerry ...46
Luzerne Packet ...51
Lytle Opera House ...304
Lytle, Sue ...285

Mc

McAdams, William ...20, 40, 276
McAfee, John ...88
McArthur, Noah L. ...92
McBeth, W. J. ...3, 162, 163, 233
McBride Bros. ...90
McBride, E. F. ...278
McBride, Harry E. ...201
McBride Lumber Co. ...291
McBride, M. J. ...216, 218
McCabe, C. B. ...203
McCague, George ...183
McCain, Daniel ...22
McCandless, David ...98, 110
McCandless, Gardiner ...110
McCarthy, Daniel J. ...
161, 162, 169, 170, 171, 174, 177, 230, 275
McCarthy, J. J. ...41, 161, 275
McCauley, Alexander ...23, 78
McCauley, James ...78
McCauley, P. ...276
McCleery, James ...18, 20, 40
McCleery, Mrs. James ...18
McCleery, W. W. ...20, 160, 161, 221, 276
McClintic-Marshall ...10, 92
McClintick, Chas. ...63
McClintick, Flora ...63
McClintick, Garfield ...63
McClintick, Joseph ...58
McClintick, Sadie P. ...63
McClintick, Squire J. C. ...62, 63
McCloskey Coal Works ...52, 57
McCloskey, John ...51, 52, 57
McCloskey, Squire Joseph ...57

McCloy, W. R., Glass Works..............87
McClure, Conser 117, 121, 124
McClure, S. R., Esq.,..........25, 204, 307
McClure, Washington 22, 40
McCollum, Lillian 89
McCollum, Mark 89
McCollum, William 89
McCombs, Wm. 78
McConnell, F. B...............91
McCord, J. P. 198
Maccoun, A. E.............111, 122, 131, 222
McCoy, Frank 76, 77
McCracken, John 79
McCrady Bros. 14, 85
McCrady, Edward 14
McCrady, James H.........85, 217, 218, 222
McCrady, Mrs. J. M...............233
McCrady, "Mother" 14
McCrady, R. A. 307
McCue, Mrs. C. 51
McCue, Daniel, Jr...............279
McCune, Davis 78
McCune, H. T. 307
McCune, Jesse 40
McCune, John F. 42
McCune, Joseph 40, 274
McCune, Mrs. Joseph 283
McCune, Joshua 276
McCune, J. W. 305
McCune, Mrs. Sarah H..............22
McCune, W. A. 276
McCutcheon, Samuel 14
McDevitt, W. A. 162, 221, 275, 308
McDonald, C. F. 131
McDonald, Jas. E...............310
McDonald, Rev. Robert.........163, 181, 189
McDonald, Thos. 127a, 221
McDonough, J. J...............279
McDonough, P. 88
McDowell, Eliza 16
McDowell, Mary 16
McDowell, W. W...............16
McElroy, Wm. 58, 62
McFadden, Thos. 36
McFeetters, Captain J. L...............79
McGeary, Dr. G. H...............249
McGinley, Neal 276
McGowan, R. E. 58
McGreevy, Pat 56, 79
McGreevy, Robert 53
McHose, K. M...............93
McIlfred, Kate 237, 294
McIlvrie, Peter...............88
McIntyre, Neil 14

McKeesport Morning Herald..............174
MacKellar, Patrick 89
McKelvey, John M...............275
McKim, Alexander 85
McKinley, President Wm. 51
McKinney, A. A...............217
McKinney, John...............98, 111
McKinney, Robert...............98
McKinney, Wm. J...............121
McKinneys' 24, 28
McLaughlin, Dr. J. H...............249
McLaughlin, Patrick 56
McMasters, John H...............210
McMasters, Thomas 62
McMichaels, Oliver 277
McMichaels, Sledge 56
McMullen, A. P...............60
McNany, Henry 72, 74
McNulty, R. M...............306
McPeak, Rev. W. H...............181, 184
McQuiggan, A. J...............308
McVay-Walker Foundry..............20, 85
McWilliams, A. 117, 121, 122
McWilliams, James A...............42

M.

Magee, C. L...............174
Magill, W. R...............217
Maggini, Mrs. A...............231, 294
Maggini, A. P...............276
Maggini, B. A...............56, 246
Maggini, Dr. J. C. F...........19, 56, 246, 249
Maggini Hardware Store, ...307
Maggini, Robert...............56
Mahon, Rev. Henry...............181
Mangion, John 276
Mangus, Jacob 56
Mann, August 88, 89
Mann, Wm. I...............108
Marchand, Dr. Rush...............245
Mark Twain 302, 311
Marks, A. O...............206
Marks, Philip 24, 53
Marks, Wilson 53
Marriott, C. M. & Sons...............309
Marshall Brothers 306
Martin, James 275
Martin, Thomas K...............41, 276
Martin, William 100
Masonic Building.........213, 216, 218, 303
Masters, C. L...............217
Masters, David 276
Masters, E. C...............307
Masters & Lewis...............305

Matelon, Martin ...206
Mates, J. C. ...60
Matinee Bowling Club ...229
Matlack, Dr. James ...247, 249
Maxwell, Jane ...279
May, Captain John ...32
May, Rev. Peter ...190, 191
Mayer, Mrs. Joseph L. ...57
Mayer, W. L. ...226
Mayerowitz, Rev. A. ...181
Mayhugh, Jos. F. ...42, 43, 57, 91, 204, 307
Mayhugh, William ...57
Maxwell, Hugh ...62
Meals, Dr. C. A. ...91, 249
Meese, H. P. ...4, 82
Melcher Bros. ...93
Mellon, Judge Thos. ...27, 29
Melville, D. F. ...133, 261
Melvin, Matthew ...56
Melvin, Sarah ...56
Mench, Florence ...242, 273
Mercader, C. ...117
Mercer, Andrew ...276
Mervis, Dr. Frank ...248
M. E. Church, Port Perry ...52
Metzgar, Dr. D. A. ...241, 242, 249
Michael, Father ...190
Michilimackinac ...8
Mifflin, Governor ...13
Miles, Rev. J. W. ...183
Miles, Mrs. J. W. ...232
Miller, Mr. ...54, 100
Miller, C. O. ...93
Miller, D. L.
...100, 117, 121, 124, 127a, 131, 276
Miller Drug Store ...308
Miller, George ...42, 51, 52
Miller, Henry ...88, 275,
Miller, H. B. ...3, 42
Miller, Dr. J. A. ...239, 249, 295
Miller, J. C. ...60
Miller, John B. ...91
Miller, Max ...309
Miller Mort C. ...213
Miller, R. V. ...91
Miller, William ...85
Miller, W. L. ...24, 26
Miller, W. Leslie ...127
Miller, W. Lloyd ...307
Millick, William ...301
Milligan, J. Knox ...3, 42, 46
Milligan, J. W. ...41
Milligan, Rev. O. B. ...184
Milligan, Mrs. O. B. ...233

Milligan, Robert ...24
Milliken, Homer A. ...90
Mills, Charles ...21, 169, 171, 173, 174
Mills, Eliza ...21, 283, 285
Mills, Elizabeth ...18, 21
Mills, Isaac, Jr. ...21, 275
Mills, Isaac, Sr.
...18, 21, 27, 30, 40, 45, 78, 169, 182, 281
Mills, J. K. ...160
Mills, Mary Calderwood ...17, 177
Mills, Stephen ...21, 169
Mills, Dr. S. Roy ...241, 245, 248, 249
Mills, Dr. W. W. ...248
Minneapolis Tribune ...167
Mitchell, James E. ...92, 121, 124, 222
Mixer (Jones) ...111
Mohr, J. A. ...86
Molnar, Rev. C. V. ...181
Molyneaux, Dr. D. A. ...249
Molyneaux, Rev. P. ...181, 190, 206
Monongahela
 4, 7, 8, 9, 10, 16, 21, 31, 32, 33, 34, 36,
 37, 38, 175, 313, 314.
Monongahela Navigation Co. ...33
Monongahela Street Railway ...75
Monongahela Water Analysis....(note) 132
Monroe, William ...276
Montgomery, Thomas L. ...227
Moore, Abraham ...53
Moore, E. W. ...197
Moore, Frank ...94
Moore, George ...239, 242, 243
Moore, Mrs. ...295
Moorehead, J. K. ...50
Morgan, Jas. A. ...41
Morgan, Martha L. ...241
Morgan, Dr. W. T.
...230, 238, 239, 241, 242, 249, 295
Morgan, Mrs. W. T. ...292
Morris, John W. ...276
Morris, Robert ...100, 108
Morrison, R. G. ...91
Morrison, Thomas ...91, 95, 122, 197, 222
Morrison, William J. ...52
Morrell Institute ...202
Morrow, Dr. F. L. ...249
Morrow, Dr. H. W. ...241
Morrow, James ...275
Morrow, Robert ...275
Morrow, W. E. ...221, 222
Morrow, Mrs. W. E. ...231
Mosellin, Mrs. B. ...229
Mother Braddock ...94
Mount Rainier ...197

Mucklerat 30
Mud (Port Perry)....................................53
Muir, J. C...309
Mullett, R. T. 93
Mura, Emil 42
Murdough, Mrs. W................................285
Murphy, Rev. J.......................................190
Murphy, William 88
Murray, C. B..........................122, 125, 131
Murray, Dr. 245
Musselman, D. Z.............................276, 308
Mustin, J. G..88, 89
Myers, Mrs. Martha..........................58, 59

N.

Nageley, L. W...124
Nash, George 88, 89, 162, 216
Nash, James 278
Naturalization, Bureau of 156
Naylor, Chas. 62
Nease, Wm. 93
Negley, Gen. Felix 29
Nelson, John 88
Nemacolin 31
Nesbitt, C. E. 131
Neville, Rev. Thos. 61
Newman, Mrs. 294
Newman, Dorothy 241
Newman, Fannie 239, 241
Newman, Ferd 241
News Herald Pub. Co............................174
Newton, C. S. 279
Newton, Sheridan 43
New York City 10, 37
Nicholls, J. C., M. D..........241, 242, 249, 295
Nicholls, Winslow 174, 175
Nickel, A. C. 160, 162
Nill's Bakery 302
Nimon, George 56, 108, 117, 120
Noey, John....57, 100, 108, 117, 120, 122, 131
Nolan, Rev. J..190
Noland Furniture Co.............................306
Norris, Grant 198
North Braddock Vol. Fire Dep't.,..........
  organized 278
North Braddock Vol. Fire Dep't.,..........
  champion teams 279
Norton, Patrick 275
Nucci & Ferreri 309
Nugent, Ed. 3, 41, 307
Nugent, Mary 304
Nugent, Thos. W. 303
Nugent's Dept. Store....................303, 305
Nullmeyer, F. H. 88, 89

O.

Oakley, F. W...........................166, 178, 230
Oartel, J. A. ....(note) 139
O'Connell, P. J. 279
O'Connor, T. E. 3
Octagon House 217
Odd Fellow's Hall..................................188
Odeon Hall 171
O'Farrell, Father 189
Ohio Co. 31
Oliver, Dr. 53
Oliver, Mrs. Mary..................................201
Olson, P. 88
Olympia Restaurant 302
Opperman, Fred 276
Opperman Hotel 303
Oskin, Albert 276
Oskin, Daniel 278, 308
Oskin, Mrs. Daniel................................233
Oskin, Edward 19
Oskin, Edward, Jr..................................276
Oskin, George, Jr...................................275
Oskin, W. T...276
Oskin, Zachariah 78, 275
Owens, Samuel G...................................276

P.

Packer, W. S. 16, 40, 210
Packer, Wilson 276
Packer, Mrs. W. S., Sr...........................233
Page, George Stevens................(note) 102
Panama 10
Pancoast, Elisha 56
Parker, A. M.............................20, 217, 278
Parker, Miss S. 285
Parkman, Francis 7
Parsons, Rev. Morten 181
Patch, Sarah 200
Patterson, E. J...93
Patterson, E. M. 3, 206
Patterson, Frank, M. D.........................248
Patterson, N...58
Patterson, Robert R................................60
Patton Township 58
Peacock, A. R...91
Pears, Rev. T. C., Jr......................181, 185
Pendergrass, R. A. 93
Penfield, R. S. 205, 206
Penn, George W.................173, 178, 212
Pennsylvania & Ohio Ry........................67
Pennsylvania Canal 66, 67

Pennsylvania Railroad 67, 314
Penny, Frederick L.................................158
Penny, William, M. D..............................245
Peoples' Trust Co....................................215
Perry, David 78
Perry, Syd 98
Peters, H. W. 206
Peterson, Rev. Theodore..........................188
Petty, A. L..............................174, 176, 178
Petty, George 78
Petty, J. D...............................174, 176, 178
Petty, James 19, 40
Phelan, Rt. Rev. Richard........................190
Phillips, James 276
Phillips, John 43
Phillips, Mrs. O. H..................................233
Phillips, Rose 222
Phipps, Henry..................98, 104, 108, 110
Pierce, Byron 74
Pierce, Franklin, President....................158
Pierce, William R..............108, (note) 117
Pieries, Mr. 50
Pig machine 125
Pitt Township 58
Pittman, E. W..93
Pittsburgh & Connellsville Ry.....52, 66, 67
Pittsburgh & Lake Erie Ry......................70
Pittsburgh Base-ball Club......................107
Pittsburgh Christian Advocate..............172
Pittsburgh Incorporation..........................58
Pittsburgh Machine Tool Co....................93
Pittsburgh, McKeesport & Yough-
    iogheny R. R..................................52, 70
Pittsburgh Magazine Almanac................62
Pittsburgh Rys. 77
Pittsburgh, Virginia & Charleston Ry....70
Plowman Construction Co.....................163
Plum Township 58
Plymouth Rock 7
Politics, Local 46, 47
Polk, J. K., President................................51
Polk, O. I., M. D.....................................249
Poorman, Harry 308
Porter, J. L. 51
Porter, Sup't...88
Powell, William.......................................114
Power, F. A. 133, 222
Preusse, A. J. 108, 127a
Preusse, Mrs. Ada R. 54, 289
Price, Mr...19
Price, A. B..276
Price, B. F., M. D............................245, 249
Price, Mrs. B. F. 233

Price, Joseph 90
Price, Robert A.................................160, 162
Price & Alman..90
Proctor, W. M., M. D..............................249
Propheter, Adolph 191
Purcell, James 40, 56, 276
Purcell, Patrick 56
Pustinger, A. P..306
Pyle, W. T., M. D....................................241

Q.

Quinn, Jas. L........................3, 170, 174
Quinn, John 275
Quinn, M. A...93

R.

Railroads 65
Ramage, E. C............................(note) 137
Rankin, Mrs. J. H...................................233
Rankin, Thomas..24
Rankin Borough..........42, 154, 156, 157, 306
Rankin Vol. Fire Dep't., organized....278
Rankin Wire Mill......................................87
Rath, S. A...62
Reagle, Rev. W. G...................................184
Reagle, Mrs. W. G...................................233
Redman, Charles 16
Redman, Frank 276
Redman, "Grandma".....................16, 17, 18
Redman, Robert 276
Redman, William 16, 17, 18, 40, 78
Redstone, ...31, 32
Reese & Berger 20
Reid, A. T...42
Reid, R. G...60
Remington, P. D....................217, 306, 307
Remlinger, Benjamin 278
Revolutionary War 33
Reyneke, M. E..88
Reynolds, Mrs. S.....................................285
Rhinehart, Otto 117
Richardson, Daniel 84
Richardson, John 84, 131
Riedl, W. M..88
Riley, George M.......................................276
Riley, Mrs. J. T.......................................285
Riley, Mell F..276
Rinard, John 91, 100, 108, 127a
Ripper, Miss Sophie E...........................241
Riston, J. C..275

Riston, Joseph 276
Riston, Mrs. Virginia 237, 285, 294
Robin, Dr. M. H. 307
Robinson, Mrs. 184
Robinson, Mrs. E. 285
Robinson, J. R. 310
Robinson, John 14, 28
Robinson House 14, 18, 28
Robling, David T. 92
Roby, George P. 308
Roderus, A. P. 3, 41, 42, 46
Roderus, Phillip 276
Roderus, Phillip C. 160, 162
Roderus & Klaban 291
Rodgers, Professor W. A. 60
Roosevelt, Theodore, President 57
Rose, Charles 298, 307
Rose, Dr. Chas. E. 307
Rose, William 301
Rosenbloom, Jacob, M. D. 248
Roskovics, Rev. C. 181
Ross, L. F. 175
Ross Fruit Store 62
Rossiter, F. S., M. D. 248
Rothauff, Samuel 19
Rotthof, William 86
Routh, John 69
Rowletter, Peter 13
Rubenstein, L. G., M. D. ....
.... 238, 239, 241, 249, 295
Russell, Frank 79
Russell, James A. ....
  22, 40, 45, 51, 52, 79, 91, 163, 214, 216,
  305, 306.
Russell, John 51
Russell, Robert, M. 306
Ryan, Michael 86
Rykaczewski, Rev. J. A. 181, 191, 207
Rylander, A. J. 88

S.

Sacred Heart Polish School 207
Sadler, Robert S. 43
Sailor, A. L. 218
St. Brendin's Parish 206
St. Clair, Floyd 117
St. Joseph's Parish 206
St. Joseph's Young Men's Club 190
St. Michael's School 206
St. Paul Pioneer Press 167
St. Thomas' Parish 206
St. Vincent de Paul Society 206
Sandels, W. A., M. D. 247, 249
Saratoga 7

Sargent, Dr. H. H. 307
Sarver, William 20, 78
Saunders, J. T. 88
Sawhill, Rev. B. F. 183
Saylor, A. L. 75
Schaefer, E. B. 41
Schaeffer, Supt. N. C. 222
Schellenberg, F. F. 93
Schenley High School 204
Schilling, Conrad 276
Schmidt, A. 306
Schmidt, L. 231, 306
Schmidt, Rev. 186
Schoenberger, J. H. 102
School, St. Thomas 189
Schooley, A. W., M. D. ....
  ...3, 19, 222, 238, 241, 246, 247, 248, 249
Schooley, Mrs. A. W. ....
  .... 231, 237, 238, 239, 289, 294
Schooley, J. D., M. D. ....
  .... 19, 210, 246, 247, 249
Schooley, William C. 171
Schools 283
Schools, Turtle Creek 60
Schramm, Rev. S. 190
Schultz, Augustus 79
Schwab, C. M. ....
  54, 95, 108, 111, 113, 129, 189, 222, 226,
  227.
Schwab, Mrs. C. M. 186, 189, 233
Schweinberg Family 14
Scott, A. M. 3
Scott, Mrs. A. M. 289, 292
Scott, H. M. 216
Scott, John 98, 104, 110
Scott, M. B. 56
Scott, Margaret B. 294
Scott, Margaret M. 237
Scritchfield, Mrs. Elmira ....
  ....231, 237, 239, 242, 285, 288, 293, 294
Sechlar, J. L. 174, 178
Sechler, John 276
Sechler, John L. 276
Second Ave. Passenger Co. 74
Second Ward School, N. B. 203
Seddon, Miss A. 285
Seddon's Hall 184
Seewald, Peter 19, 40, 172, 275
Seewald Building 172
Seewald Motor Co. 308
Seewald's Hall 187, 188, 189
Seibert, J. G. 276

Seifers, George 43
Semmens, W. H. 59, 63
Shady Park School 203
Shallenberger, H. C. 3, 22, 40, 55, 217, 276
Shallenberger, Mrs. J. N. 233
Shallenberger, Jonathan 22
Sharah, E. M. 56, 201, 208
Sharah, Philip 22, 56
Sharah, W. H. 3, 56, 275, 279
Sharp, Miss B. 285
Sharp, T. W. 20, 40, 275
Shaw, M. M. 162
Shaw, Mrs. S. J. 233
Shaw, Samuel T. 170, 175, 176
Shearer, Samuel 276
Shearinger, Rev. J. L. 181
Sheekey, James 308
Sheekey, Owen 22, 86, 162
Sheets, C. H. 161, 162, 275
Shelby, David 229
Sherwin, Mrs. G. 285
Sherwin, John 19
Sherwin, William 40, 78
Shields, John 41, 56
Shields, Rev. J. P. 61
Shilling, Frank 276, 307
Shinn, William P. 98, 104, 108, 110
Shirley, General 9
Shoemaker, William 98
Shrewsburg 150
Shultz, Edwin F. .... (note) 116
Silvey, Alex. H. 170, 171
Silvey, T. M. 171
Simcox, F. E. 197
Simms, Dan 56
Simms, John 56
Simon, J. D. 308
Simpson Farm 52
Singer, Nimick & Co. 102
Sisters of Divine Providence 190, 191
Skelley, John K. 218
Skelton, J. M. 60
Slease, Rev. 61
Slick, E. E. 121, 122
Slick, F. F.
   3, 63 131, 132, (note) 133, 138, 139, 222
Slick, Mrs. Gail Hunter 63
Sloan, George A. 42, 307
Sloss, James 91
Smail, E. J. 222, 276, 307
Smelsz, Rev. Anthony 191
Smith, E. R. 60
Smith, George W. 79, 93
Smith, H. G. 93

Smith, J. B., M. D. 241, 249
Smith, W. J. 60
Smith, William 78
Swith & Worthington 308
Snodgrass, Dr. 53
Snodgrass, Colonel John 21
Snowden, W. J. .... (Packet) 61
Snowwhite, T. H., M. D. 241, 249
Soles, David 24
Soles, Hugh 19
Soles, John 19, 78
Soles, Mr. 84
Soles, Mrs. Ella 288
Soles, Mrs. Helen 85
Spangler, George C. 276
Spear, R. E. 276
Speedy, J. Alex. 45
Spear, A. H. 307
Speer, Rev. H. L. 181
Speer, Mrs. W. H. 159, 233
Speicher & Daniels 308
Speidel, Albert 276
Speidel, Conrad 19, 79
Speidel, George S. 226
Sperry, Helen 222
Spigelmire, A. J. 190, 216, 305
Spigelmire, Mrs. A. J. 289
Spitler, J. L. 203
Spitzer & Speidel 305
Stage Coaches 59
Stamets, George E. T. 74
Standard Chain Co. 92
Stanton, Dr. James N. 248
Stanwix, Fort 151
Stanyon, Henry 91
State Bank 19, 217
State College 203
Stebick, E. J. 307
Steczovich, Rev. Nicholas 191
Stein, Rev. C. H. 181, 185
Steiner, W. R. W. 278
Steinmetz, Dillie 11
Steinmetz Family 241
Steltz, Professor F. C. 3, 198
Stengel, Rev. A. C. 187
Stephens, Gilbert 54
Stephens, Miss R. 285
Stephens, Rich. 54
Stephens, Mrs. Richard 231
Stephens Furniture Co. 306
Sterling Steel Foundry 93
Stevens, Richard
   .... 108, 109, 111, 117, 120, 122, 131
Stevens, Mrs. Richard 289

Stevenson, A. B., Esq.............221, 222, 235
Stevenson, Mrs. A. B..............................289
Stevenson, John, Jr................................108
Stewart, Caroline M. (Mrs. R. E.) 237, 294
Stewart, David A.........................98, 104, 110
Stewart, James 23
Stewart, James V....................................131
Stewart, Major R. E...24, 210, 222, 237, 294
Stewart, S. E..306
Stewart, Dr. W. S....................................249
Stewart, Mrs. W. S..................................233
Stokes, C. A..............173, 174, 217, 222, 306
Stokes, Mrs. C. A....................................233
Stokes Hall 188
Stone, W. C..87
Strang, P. G. D...131
Strathern, James 78
Strathern, John 78
Strathern, Thomas 17
Street, Rev. George F............................185
Street-Cars 73
Striebich, E. C. 191, 214, 216
Striebich, E. H...242
Striebich, Mrs. Joseph 57
Stright, S. A...308
Stright Pharmacy 247
Striker, Christopher 58
Struble, Madge 53
Stucki, P. 51
Stumpf, Rev. Louis................................181
Sullivan, William 278
Sullivan, William H........................3, 310
Sullivan, Jones & Ryan........................305
Superintendent's Club, Edgar Thomson..
....127

Sweeney, Edward 14
Sweeney, James A..................................53
Swenson, Rev. William..........................188

T.

Taft, President Wm. H..........................214
Taggart, E. L. 94
Tallent, Agnes 203
Tannery, Braddock 86
Taylor, B. H...221
Taylor, John 28
Taylor, Joseph 28
Teachers—
  Braddock teachers alphabetically arranged 198
  North Braddock teachers 204
  Rankin teachers 206
Teeter, C. C. 100, 107, 108, 111, 112, 117, 121

Teeter, H. C....................................275, 276
Tegethoff, Fritz 276
Tell, Dr. George......................................249
Temple, Prof. Henry..................................9
Tener, R. W..91
Third Ward School, N. B.......................203
Thier, Christ 276
Thompson, Elizabeth 205
Thompson, E. D.......................................88
Thompson, Martin H..............................86
Thompson, R. E.....................................306
Thompson Run 58
Thomson, F. DuPeyster 121
Thomson, J. Edgar 69, 98, 99
Tierney, Theodore 278
Tillbroke, Steward 62
Tingle & Sugden 102
Tinstman, A. O..................................59, 63
Tinstman, C. P. M.............................59, 63
Todd, George A. 161, 212
Todd, Mrs. P. S............................231, 233
Tolman, C. M....................117, 120, 122
Tompos, John 88
Toner, Mrs. M. C.....................................51
Tonnaleuka.........................25, 195, 273
Torrance, H. C. 108
Torreyson, Thayer M................................3
Townsend, Rev. C. W............................61
Tracey, Rev. F..189
Tracey, Wm. J..308
Traynor, P. J..42
Treese, Mrs. Kate M................................
..........................231, 237, 285, 293, 294
Trent, Capt. 31
Trevaskis, A. L..63
Trevaskis, C. R. 60
Trevaskis, J. T...63
Trott, H. B. 88
Troutman, W. E......................................91
Tuigg, Bishop John 190
Tupper & McKowan..............................102
Turner, Dr. H. H....................................249
Turtle Creek 58, 151, 299
  moved 121
Twitmyer, E. D..................121, 197, 198

U.

Unangst, J. T..306
Unger, J. S...95
Union National Bank....................216, 217
Union Railroad 52
United States Bank........................21, 34

United States Post Office Department....
....158, 162, 163
United States Steel Corporation............
....9, 238, 240
Upton, Charles 275
Upton, L. T. 131
Urmson, R. M...307

V.

Valetta Commandery, K. of M.................241
Vance, W. J.......................127, 221, 222, 278
Vande Ventea, J. W..................................198
Vandervort, J. W......................................110
Vankirk, Mrs. 292
Vantine, A. M..198
Vanyo, Stephen 306
Verosky, Michael 41
Versailles 50
Vitale, Rev. N. J..61
Voltaire 7

W.

Wages (1875) 110
Wagner Family 18
Wagner, Henry 310
Wagner, John 305, 307
Wagner, Joseph 307
Wakeham, Elizabeth 203
Walden, Bishop 188
Walker, G. Roy.......................................308
Walker, John 35, 306, 308
Wall, Dr. A. A...249
Wallace, Col. 183
Wallace, Geo., Judge....8, 13, 14, 24, 58, 316
Wallace Mansion..........................15, 18, 316
Wallace, Rev. W. C........................184, 227
Walter, Lucas J.......................................191
Walters, Elmer 278
Walters Family 14
Walters, "Granny" 14
Walters, Jacob 276
Walters, P...308
Walton, Joseph 20
Ward, M. J...57
Ward, Thomas 276, 302
Ward's Cafe 302
Washington, George.................................
  7, 8, 9, 11, 12, 13, 25, 31, 59, 150, 281, 313, 314.
Washington & Jefferson College...............9
Water Works....................................45, 46
Watkins, Thomas 278

Watkins, W. C...42
Watt, Geo. C...3, 206, 209, 214, 215, 216, 227
Watt, Harry 86
Watt, W. H......................................214, 216
Watters, John 14
Watts, Dr. Anna.....................................249
Weakland, C. V......................................305
Weaver, W. C...61
Webb, D. B..93
Weber, Jacob 19
Weddel, Dr. J. W....................................249
Weeks, Joseph D....................................129
Wehaloosing 150
Weida, Dr. C. B......................................249
Weil, Geo. 41, 217, 307
Weil, Dr. Grover C.................................248
Weiler, Emanuel 218
Weimer, Elizabeth L. R...........................23
Weimer, Mrs. 23
Weir, Mary J..................................242, 296
Weiss, Bernath 241
Welham, Rev. F..............................181, 187
Wells, Henry 191
Welsh, L. B..198
Wentzel, Franklin 275, 301
Wentzel, Wash.......................................276
Wertenbach, Rev. A. A..........................190
Wertz, Rev. Jacob M..............................190
West, Mr. 189
Western Maryland R. R...........................70
Westinghouse Companies 62
Weyels, Charles 308
Weyels, John 308
Wheeler, I..76
Whiskey Insurrection..............8, 13, 49, 65
White, A. H..275
White, Mrs. A. H....................................231
White, E. B....................................122, 131
White, E. V..204
White, H. S..88, 89
White, Isabel 203
Whitehead, Cortlandt 186
Whitfield, Dr. Finley K............................
.............3, 40, 41, 227, 241, 242, 248, 249
Whitfield, Geo. B.....................................42
Whitfield, Geo. B., Jr.............................306
Wieder, Rev. R......................................190
Wilhelm, Fred R......................................77
Wilkins Township 58
Wilkinson, Sam. C............................56, 63
Willard, Frances 284
Williams, Jacob 14
Williams, L. H.......................................213
Williams, W. H..................................41, 45

Wills, James E. 41
Wills & Shelby 307
Wilson, D. Leet 213
Wilson, President Woodrow 163
Windt, J. 241
Winkenbaugh Family 14
Winter, Casper 187
Wolf, Joseph 74, 218
   property destroyed by fire 277
Wolff, A. F. T. 131
Woman 280
   Achievements 296
Woman Suffrage 286
Woman's Christian T. U. 241, 283, 286
Woman's Club 241, 288
Wood, Capt. B. L. 53, 54
Wood, C. W. 53, 54, 171
Wood, J. K. 51
Wood, Wm. P. 54, 171
Woodside, Margaret W. 241, 242
Woolworth's 5 & 10 cent 161, 308, 309
Worthman, Rev. D. 181, 188
Wright, E. S. .... 131, (note) 137
Wright, Rev. J. V. 180, 181, 206
Wrightman, Rev. 61

Wymard, Wm. 276
Wynne, J. A. 168

Y.

Yarlett, J. M. 276
Yarlett, William 276
Yellow Car Line 76
Yinger, Charles 275
Yinger, John 275
Young, C. S. 88
Young, Geo. M. 158, 159
Young, Rev. J. H. 187
Young, Jackson 51
Young, Mary 241
Young, William 275

Z.

Zeok, Dr. John 248, 249
Zimmerman, Mrs. Emma 231
Zischkau, R. G. 60
Zorn & Glasser 306
Zugsmith, Chas., Jr. 217, 218

www.ingramcontent.com/pod-product-compliance
Lightning Source LLC
Chambersburg PA
CBHW070719160426
43192CB00009B/1242